# Style and Narrative in Translations

*The Contribution of Futabatei Shimei*

by

**Hiroko Cockerill**

St. Jerome Publishing
Manchester, UK & & Kinderhook, USA

Published by

St. Jerome Publishing
2 Maple Road West, Brooklands
Manchester, M23 9HH, United Kingdom
Telephone +44 (0)161 973 9856
Fax +44 (0)161 905 3498
stjerome@compuserve.com
http://www.stjerome.co.uk

InTrans Publications
P. O. Box 467
Kinderhook, NY 12106, USA
Telephone (518) 758-1755
Fax (518 758-6702

ISBN 1-900650-91-6 (pbk)



Printed and bound in Great Britain by
T. J. International Ltd., Padstow, Cornwall, UK

Typeset by
Print-tech India (www.printtechindia.com)

*British Library Cataloguing in Publication Data*
A catalogue record of this book is available from the British Library

*Library of Congress Cataloguing in Publication Data*
Cockerill, Hiroko.
Style and narrative in translations : the contribution of Futabatei Shimei / Hiroko Cockerill.
p. cm.
Includes bibliographical references and index.
ISBN 1-900650-91-6 (pbk. : alk. paper)
1. Futabatei, Shimei, 1864-1909--Criticism and interpretation.
2. Literature--Translations into Japanese--History and criticism. I. Title.
PL806.T3Z56 2003
895.6'342--dc22

2006003981

文學嫌の文學者　（坪内逍遥）

"A literary master who disliked literature"

Tsubouchi Shōyō

Cover photograph of Futabatei Shimei is from *The Complete Works of Meiji Literature Vol.17, Selected Works of Futabatei Shimei and Saganoya Omuro*, and is reproduced here by kind permission of Chikuma Shobō Company, Japan.

# Table of Contents

# Table of Tables

# Acknowledgements

This book is the fruit of doctoral studies undertaken at the University of Queensland in Australia from 1998 to 2003. It was a great privilege to be able to spend so much time pursuing my interest in the literatures of Japan and Russia. This was facilitated by scholarships from the University of Queensland, which have enabled me to participate in full-time studies for part of my Ph.D. candidature, and to travel to Japan to collect material for this thesis. My supervisors during that time, Dr. Tomoko Aoyama and Dr. John McNair, were untiring in their help and this book owes much to them. My Head of Department, Associate Professor Nanette Gottlieb, was also most encouraging, finding time in her busy schedule to read my draft chapters, and encouraging me to develop a book from my research. I am grateful also to Associate Professor Kenneth Henshall and Dr. David Wells, who as examiners made valuable suggestions.

While I was in Japan to collect material for this study I received valuable assistance from the librarians at the Tokyo University of Foreign Studies, Hitotsubashi University, Waseda University, Nagoya University and Aichi Prefectural University. I am also grateful to my sister Professor Shimono Keiko, for sending me numerous books and articles, and to my friend at Tokyo University, Dr. Shimizu Michiko, who sent me valuable material and gave kind advice.

I would like to thank Alan Turney, who as referee carefully read my manuscript and suggested a number of improvements, and Mona and Ken Baker at St. Jerome for their invaluable help in editing my manuscript and guiding me through the process of producing this book.

Finally I would like to thank my husband, Alan, who has not only supported me emotionally through this challenging endeavour, but has also spent many hours over the past seven years assisting with the typing and proof reading.

# Introduction

Futabatei Shimei (1864-1909) is generally regarded as the founder of the modern Japanese novel, because of the significant innovation in content and style of his first *genbun itchi*[1] novel *Ukigumo [Floating Clouds]* (1887-1889). Despite his early success in writing *Floating Clouds*, it was nearly two decades before he produced his two other novels *Sono omokage [In His Image]* (1906) and *Heibon [Mediocrity]* (1907). While Futabatei may have been a reluctant writer, he was an enthusiastic and productive translator. During the long interval between his first and second novels Futabatei wrote numerous translations from Russian literature, becoming the first significant Japanese translator of Russian literature, and introducing Japanese readers to works by Turgenev (nine works), Gogol (three works), Tolstoy (one work), Garshin (two works), Gorky (five works) and Andreyev (one work). The influence of his translations rivalled, and at times exceeded that of his original works. A particularly strong impression was made by his first published translations, which were of two stories by Turgenev: *Svidanie [The Rendezvous]* and *Tri vstrechi [Three Encounters],* and appeared in 1888 under the titles *Aibiki [The Tryst]* and *Meguriai [A Chance Encounter].* These early translations were received with even greater acclaim than *Floating Clouds,* and had considerable influence upon young writers of the Japanese naturalist school such as Kunikida Doppo, Tayama Katai and Shimazaki Tōson. His first novel and first two translations together represent the first period of Futabatei's literary activity (1887-1889). A second period of literary activity (1896-1898) was devoted entirely to translations, and a third period (1904-1908) included a diverse selection of translations and two novels.[2]

Compared with the extensive critical literature devoted to Futabatei's three original novels, the number of books and articles about his translations is undeservedly small: a single monograph by Satō Seirō (1995) and several articles, almost all written by Japanese slavists and translators from Russian. Given the significant impact of *The Tryst* and *A Chance Encounter,* it is not surprising that many of these articles focus on Futabatei's translations from Turgenev. Jinzai Kiyoshi (1954), Kimura Shōichi (1956), Yonekawa Masao (1963) and Yanagi Tomiko (1971, 1973) all evaluate these translations very highly. Jinzai in particular determined the direction of research on Futabatei's translations by emphasizing his "faithfulness" in the translation of Turgenev's works. Jinzai points out that most of Futabatei's translations from Turgenev were made during his early years, and that the first versions of *The Tryst* and *A Chance Encounter* explicitly demonstrate Futabatei's faithfulness to the original. He concludes that "for Futabatei, Turgenev was the most congenial writer" and that "Turgenev was the writer whose style was most suited to Futabatei's own" (Cited in Futabatei Shimei 1965e: 176).

Interestingly, Futabatei made revised translations of *The Rendezvous* and *Three Encounters* in 1896, some eight years after his first translations had appeared. He retained the title *Aibiki* for *The Rendezvous,* but when translating *Three Encounters* adopted the new title of *Kigū [A Fortuitous Encounter].* He then went on to translate another five works by Turgenev: *Asya, Son [The Dream], Rudin, Zhid [The Jew]* and *Petushkov,* which were published under

[1] *Genbun itchi* refers to the use of a style derived from spoken language in a written narrative.

[2] See Appendix 1 for a list of the translations and original works written during each period.

the titles *Katakoi [One-sided Love], Yumekatari [Dream Talk], Ukikusa [Floating Weed], Yudaya-jin [The Jew]* and *Kusare-en [The Mismatch]* respectively. This persistence in translating works by Turgenev appears to support Jinzai's argument, but he may have been hasty in concluding that Turgenev was the most congenial writer for Futabatei. He also appears to have neglected a crucial question: why did Futabatei revise his first versions of *The Tryst* and *A Chance Encounter*?

The disproportionate attention paid to Futabatei's translations from Turgenev has meant a corresponding neglect or even negation of his other translations. His translations of works by Gogol and Gorky are often the target of strong criticism. Yonekawa Masao is at the forefront of those who, while admiring the translations of 1888, have criticized later translations, especially those from Gogol and Gorky, for an excessive use of words originating in Edo light literature and of Japanese dialect. These later translations are characterized as being coloured by "Futabatei's own tone".

Araya Keizaburō (1967), on the other hand, calls into question the importance of Futabatei's translations from Turgenev. He questions the influence of *The Tryst* on writers of the naturalist school. He points out that what so impressed them about *The Tryst* was not the rendezvous between an arrogant servant and a pitiable peasant girl, which forms the core of Turgenev's story, but the description of the beauty of the forest, which is a peripheral element of the original. He then notes that two of Turgenev's stories translated by Futabatei—*Three Encounters* and *Petushkov*—display features of Russian naturalism, of which Gogol was a major proponent, along with Dostoevsky. He hints that the most congenial Russian writer for Futabatei may not have been Turgenev, but Gogol.

Araya further notes that the very first translation Futabatei made was of a work by Gogol. This translation was not published, but only shown to his mentor Tsubouchi Shōyō. He also points out that Futabatei's three published translations from Gogol —*Shōzōga [The Portrait]* (1897), *Mukashi no hito [Olden Day People]* (1906) and *Kyōjin nikki [A Madman's Diary]* (1907)—appeared during the second and third periods of his literary activity. This shows that Futabatei's interest in Gogol's works was persistent. It is particularly significant that the last two translations from Gogol appeared just before the writing of his final two original works: *In His Image* and *Mediocrity*.

More recently Hatano Kazuhiro (1982) and Isahaya Yūichi (1982) have studied Futabatei's translations from Gogol, and have sought to demonstrate a stylistic resemblance between *Floating Clouds* and works by Gogol. Both these slavists independently noted that the opening of Gogol's *Nevsky Prospekt [Nevsky Avenue]* is almost identical in structure and style to that of *Floating Clouds.* Hatano (1994) continues to examine Futabatei's translations from Gogol in another article, but does not attempt to identify any direct links between them and Futabatei's original work.

Minamoto Takashi (1989a, 1989b) turned his attention to Futabatei's later translations, writing two articles with a focus on his final translation *Kesshōki [An Account of Bloodied Laughter]* (1908) and its relationship to his novel *Mediocrity. An Account of Bloodied Laughter* was translated from Andreyev's *Krasnyi smekh [Red Laughter]*. Minamoto concentrates on Futabatei's "serious" translations and for the most part neglects what he sees as the "frivolous" translations of works by Gogol and Gorky, though these were in fact more numerous than the "serious" war stories translated from Garshin, Tolstoy and Andreyev.

Futabatei's translations of works by Gorky—*Jū no ukiyo [The Hard Life of a Jew], Fusagi no mushi [The Depression Bug], Ni kyōjin [Two Madmen]* and *Kojiki [The Beggars]*—have been almost totally ignored by scholars. This may reflect the hostile reception given to these works when they first appeared. *The Depression Bug,* in particular, was harshly criticized soon after its publication for an excessive use of dialect and an air of frivolity created by Futabatei's distinctive choice of vocabulary. One critic (Masamune Hakuchō 1928) did respond positively to the work, but as an adaptation rather than as a translation. It would appear that the main reason for the neglect of Futabatei's translations from Gogol and Gorky lies in a critical attitude towards the vocabulary used by Futabatei and its origins in Edo light literature.

However, as Araya (1967: 66) suggests, Futabatei's vocabulary is akin to Gogol's, and, as Hatano (1994: 69-79) has pointed out, the "frivolity" in Futabatei's translations may be an appropriate expression of Gogol's humour. Komori Yōichi (1988: 85-124) has examined the role of the narrator in those of Gogol's works which were translated by Futabatei, and believes he has found in them the origins of *Floating Clouds*' narrator. Komori observes that in *Floating Clouds* the narrator's voice is polyphonic, and that the novel is created dynamically from the tension which arises between the narrator's voice and the voices of the characters.

This study will attempt a balanced and comprehensive examination of Futabatei's major translations made in the colloquial *genbun itchi* style, and of the influence they exerted upon his original work. Translations of fragments or translations whose source has not been identified will not be examined. Nor will translations made in a pseudo-classical style, which had no significant stylistic influence upon his novels. No attempt will be made, either, to examine translations of works by minor writers, as to do so would have made this study of unacceptable length. The need to prevent this study from becoming too long has also meant that we will not give detailed attention to *Dream Talk*, *The Hard Life of a Jew*, *The Beggars*, or *An Account of Bloodied Laughter*. Otherwise, Futabatei's major translations will be examined in chronological order, comparing them with the Russian originals so as to trace in detail the development of his translation style. Particular attention will be given to translations of works by Gogol and Gorky, which have suffered relative neglect. Evidence will be presented supporting Araya's suggestion that for Futabatei the most congenial Russian writer was not Turgenev, but Gogol. An attempt will be made to show direct connections between Futabatei's translations (particularly from Gogol and Gorky) and his original works.

Chapter One explains the historical significance of Futabatei's first published translation, *The Tryst.* A comparison will be made between the narrative of *The Tryst* and the narratives of earlier translations such as *Karyū shunwa [A Springtime Tale of Blossoms and Willows]* (1878) by Niwa Jun'ichirō and *Hachijū nichi kan sekai isshū [A Tour of the World in Eighty Days]* (1878) by Kawashima Chūnosuke. It is revealed that in *The Tryst* Futabatei achieved Kawashima's goal of faithfully translating past tense verb forms. Futabatei attempted to reproduce the original in every detail, and translated all past tense verbs using "-ta" form verbs. Together with the faithful rendition of the first-person pronoun "ya" as "jibun", the use of "-ta" forms created an original style with a firm retrospective narrative point of view. Part Two of *Floating Clouds* shows a corresponding increase in the use of "-ta" forms and a shift in the narrative point of view. This appears to show the clear influence of Futabatei's translation upon his novel.

Chapter Two will clarify how and why Futabatei revised his early translations *The*

*Tryst* and *A Chance Encounter.* Although the first versions are generally considered to be of higher quality (Nakayama Shōzaburō 1937: 72; Nakamura Mitsuo 1958: 214), many scholars have pointed out that both versions are faithful to the originals, and that in some respects the second versions are more accurate. While the style of the first versions was admired by the naturalist writers, other critics found the constant use of "-ta" forms at the end of sentences monotonous. Futabatei appears to have responded to their concerns when he made revised translations of *The Rendezvous* and *Three Encounters.* In Chapter Two the style of *A Fortuitous Encounter* will be examined through a comparison with the Russian original, and explanations will be sought for the changes that Futabatei made. The issue will be raised as to whether Futabatei was reverting from a "foreignizing" to a "domesticating" translation strategy. That is, to what extent did Futabatei continue to register the linguistic and cultural differences of the original in his translation? In some respects the style of the second versions resembles that of Part One of *Floating Clouds,* and is closer to a traditional Japanese literary style. A comparison of the verbs of the second versions with those of the originals reveals that Futabatei's choice of Japanese verb forms was still motivated by an attempt to convey the style of the original Russian, and that Futabatei was still adopting a foreignizing strategy, albeit a different one. It will be seen that whereas in the first versions Futabatei had been focusing on the tense of the original verbs, in the second versions he focused on their aspect (perfective or imperfective). In discussing Futabatei's choice of verb forms in the second versions, reference will be made to aspectual forms in Japanese, drawing on the theories of Kindaichi (1976, 1988) and Teramura (1984).

The appearance of the second version of *The Tryst* and of *A Fortuitous Encounter* marked the beginning of the second period of Futabatei's literary activity, during which he translated a further five works by Turgenev and one by Gogol. In all these works Futabatei adopted a style similar to the style developed in the second version of *The Tryst* and *A Fortuitous Encounter*. The translations of this second period are examined in the third, fourth and fifth chapters of this study. Chapter Three deals with the translations of Turgenev's first-person narratives: *One-sided Love,* and *The Jew*. Chapter Four focuses on the first of Futabatei's third-person narrative translations, *The Portrait,* translated from Gogol's work of the same name. This translation is of particular interest, as it appears to mark a high point in the development of Futabatei's translation style, with particularly effective use being made of a variety of Japanese verb forms. It is also interesting to note a striking resemblance with the style of Part One of *Floating Clouds,* suggesting that Futabatei had a particular affinity for Gogol and had already developed a style suitable for the translation of his works. Chapter Five examines the remaining third-person narratives translated during Futabatei's second period: *Floating Weed* and *The Mismatch.* In chapters three to five the narrator's position relative to the implied author and the protagonists is also examined, with reference to the theories of Genette (1980) and Booth (1961). In Chapter Six we make a comparison between the style developed in the translations of Futabatei's second period, and that of two writers contemporary to Futabatei, Ozaki Kōyō and Hirotsu Ryūrō, whose works have been argued to have exerted influence upon Futabatei's translation style (Mizuno Kiyoshi 1958). The stylistic comparison with Kōyō's works is of particular significance, as Kōyō is a controversial writer who appears to determine the direction of the literary *genbun itchi* movement.[3]

[3] The *genbun itchi* movement began as a stylistic revolution, a conscious departure from the classic style in which the spoken and written modes are completely separate.

Futabatei's third period of literary activity began in 1904, just after the outbreak of war between Russia and Japan, with the publication of two war stories: Tolstoy's *Rubka lesa [The Woodfelling]* (under the title *Tsutsu o makura [A Rifle for a Pillow]*) and Garshin's *Chetyre dnya [Four Days]* (under the title *Yokka-kan [Four Days]*). It closed with the publication of a third war story, a translation of Andreyev's *Red Laughter.* Interestingly, all these translations are first-person narratives. During this period Futabatei also translated two stories by Gogol and four by Gorky, which for the most part are third-person narratives (the exception being *A Madman's Diary*). In these translations, and particularly in those made from Gorky, Futabatei is generally considered to have adopted a domesticating strategy, because of his frequent use of idiomatic expressions from Edo light literature and of dialect. The third period also encompasses Futabatei's final two novels.

As well as looking at the translations of war stories by Tolstoy and Garshin, Chapter Seven examines two other translations made prior to the publication of Futabatei's second novel *In His Image,* and seeks to reveal any influence they exerted on that work. These stories have the same third-person narrative structure as *In His Image* and their verb forms are studied closely. They are *The Depression Bug* and *Olden Day People*, which were translated from works by Gogol and Gorky.

Chapter Eight completes the study with an examination of the final year of Futabatei's literary activity and seeks any connections between the first-person narrative translations of this period and his final novel *Mediocrity.* The principal works examined are the translations *Two Madmen* and *A Madman's Diary* and Futabatei's novel *Mediocrity*. Finally, a brief comparison is made between the narrative styles of Sōseki's *Kōfu [The Miner]* and Tōson's *Haru [Spring]*. These two novels appeared successively in the *Tokyo Asahi shinbun* immediately following the publication of *Mediocrity*.

It is hoped that this study will provide a more comprehensive and sympathetic account of the development of Futabatei's translation style than has been undertaken to date, and that it will provide some new insights into Futabatei's use of verb forms. The style developed during Futabatei's second period has been regarded as the reverse of the existing old-fashioned style, because of its seeming resemblance with the styles of Ozaki Kōyō and Hirotsu Ryūrō. However, Futabatei's choice of verb forms ("-(r)u" or "-ta") in these translations appears to have its own regularity and to have been conditioned by the verb forms of the originals.

In conducting this research I have been compelled to use three languages: English as the main language of discourse, Russian and Japanese for the material under study. All block quotations from Russian originals are given in Russian script, though the orthography has in some cases been modified in line with current usage. When Russian words appear in a body of English text, they are transliterated according to the system used in *Oxford Slavonic Papers*. All lengthy quotations from Japanese originals are cited in Japanese script, with the retention of the original *kana* syllabary and *kanji*. When Japanese words appear in a body of English text they are generally Romanized, with long vowels being written as "ā", "ī" etc.

In order to make the study accessible it has been necessary to give English translations of all the Russian and Japanese passages under examination. I have tried to make a virtue of necessity, and used these English translations to highlight subtle differences in meaning from one text to the next. I have frequently referred to existing translations, but have often modified these in order to more literally translate the verb forms. It is of particular significance to differentiate meanings of tense and aspect, and these will be explained in some detail in chapter two. The English translations do have the potential to confuse the issues, however, as the system of verb aspect in English differs significantly from that in Russian. The perfect tense in English and the perfective aspect in Russian, for instance, are quite different, and should not be confused.

I have used a system of underlining to indicate the tense and aspect of verbs, as explained in the following note:

### *System for Indicating Tense and Aspect of Verbs*

Throughout this study a system of underlining Russian verbs to indicate tense and aspect has been adopted. A single line under a verb indicates that it is of imperfective aspect, while a double line indicates that it is of perfective aspect. An unbroken line indicates past tense, a dotted line indicates present tense, and a wavy line indicates future tense. When a Russian passage is followed by an English translation, the verbs in the English translation are underlined in exactly the same way as the corresponding Russian verbs, as these translations are primarily intended for readers not able to follow the Russian, and serve to mark the tense and aspect of the original Russian verbs. The following passage illustrates how this system operates:

> Нигде не останавливалось столько народа, как перед картинною лавочкою на Щукином дворе. Эта лавочка представляла, точно, самое разнородное собрание диковинок: картины большею частью были писаны масляными красками, покрыты темнозеленым лаком, в темножелтых мишурных рамах. ... Всякой восхищается по-своему; мужики обыкновенно тыкают пальцами; кавалеры рассматривают серьёзно; лакеи-мальчики и мальчишки-мастеровые смеются и дразнят друг друга нарисованными карикатурами; старые лакеи во фризовых шинелях смотрят потому только, чтобы где-нибудь позевать; а торговки, молодые русские бабы, спешат по инстинкту, чтобы послушать, о чем калякает народ, и посмотреть, на что он смотрят. В это время невольно остановился перед лавкою проходивший мимо молодой художник Чартков.

> [Nowhere were so many people standing as in front of the picture shop in Shchukin Court. The shop, indeed, presented the most heterogeneous collection of marvels: the pictures were painted for the most part in oil colours, covered with dark-green varnish, in dark-yellow tinsel frames. ... Each one admires them in his own way: the peasants usually poke their fingers at them; the cavaliers examine them seriously; the footboys and apprentices laugh and tease each other over the painted caricatures; the old lackeys in frieze overcoats look at them simply to have something to gape at; and the market women, young Russian peasant women, hurry here by instinct, to hear what people are gossiping about, and to see what they are looking at. At this moment, a young artist, Chartkov, who was passing by, involuntarily stopped in front of the picture shop.]

A similar system has been adopted for indicating tense and aspect of Japanese verbs, as illustrated in the following passage. In this case "-(r)u" and "-te iru" form verbs are underlined with a dotted line, "-ta" and "-te ita" forms are underlined with a single line, and "-ta" forms carrying perfective aspectual rather than past tense meaning are underlined with a double line.

何處と云つて、シチウキン長屋の繪屋の前ほど、人の群聚る處は有るまい。それも其筈で、此處には種々珍らしい物がある。繪は大抵油繪で、青黒い漆を塗つて、濁黒い金縁を附けてある。（中略）さて覽方だが、これが人に由つて違ふ。百姓は兎角指を指したがる。兵士は眞面目な面をして見る。丁稚小僧は鳥羽繪を覽て高笑をして調戯ひあふ。フリーズ（織物の名）の外套を着た年老つた僕は何處かで閑を潰したいばかりで視てゐる。若い嚊衆は人が饒舌てゐる事なら、何でも聽きたい、視てゐるものなら、何でも視たい、といふ一心で嗅付けて急いで來る。

此時チャルトコフといふ通りすがりの若い畵家が何心なく店頭に立止つた。

[Nowhere are so many people crowding as in front of the picture shop in Shchukin tenement house. It is no wonder, as various marvels are presented here. The pictures are almost all oil paintings, covered with dark-green Japanese lacquer in murky gold frames. ... Now the way of looking at the pictures varies, depending on the person. The peasants tend to poke their fingers at them. The soldiers gaze at them seriously. The apprentices laugh and tease each other over the caricatures. The old servants in frieze (the name of the material) overcoats are looking at them simply to kill time. The young peasant women hurry here by instinct only to want to listen to what people are gossiping about and to see what people are looking at.

At this moment a young artist called Chartkov (who was) passing by, involuntarily stopped in front of the shop.]

Throughout the text certain words of significance to the discussion have been highlighted by the use of bold font.

# Chapter 1 — The Significance of *The Tryst* in Japanese Translation History

Hasegawa Tatsunosuke, better known by his pen name, Futabatei Shimei, was clearly one of the leading writers of his day, but appears to have been strangely uncomfortable in this role. Despite making a relatively smooth debut with *Ukigumo [Floating Clouds]* (1887-1889), generally acknowledged to be the first modern Japanese novel, this work was left incomplete. After publication of Part Three of the novel, Futabatei abandoned literary work to take up a position at the office of *Kanpō*, the official gazette of the Japanese government. Futabatei was so modest in his assessment of his own literary abilities, that he published the first two parts of *Floating Clouds* under the name of his mentor, Tsubouchi Shōyō, and even suggested that Shōyō should share the royalties.

While working on *Floating Clouds* Futabatei also published two very successful and extremely influential translations from short stories by Turgenev. The first of these, *Aibiki [The Tryst]* (1888), incorporated colloquial language to an unprecedented degree, and inspired a generation of naturalist writers in Japan. Yet Futabatei appears not to have been satisfied with these translations either, as he produced revised editions some eight years later (which were not, however, so well received). The publication of these revised translations marked the beginning of a second period of literary activity, during which he produced numerous translations (mainly from Turgenev), but no original work. Despite producing translations of a high quality, Futabatei once again left the literary scene, to take up a professorship at his former college, now the Tokyo University of Foreign Studies, in 1899.

Futabatei was apparently well-regarded as a teacher, but in 1902 he resigned his post and travelled to Harbin and Peking, to assess the pre-war situation in China. When war finally broke out between Russia and Japan, Futabatei became a Tokyo correspondent for the *Ōsaka Asahi shinbun*, a major newspaper. It appeared that Futabatei had finally found a job that matched his aspirations, but he failed as a war correspondent, and was instead requested by the chief editor of the newspaper's Tokyo branch to write another novel. Futabatei was thus impelled to produce another original work in order to retain his position with the newspaper. He wrote *Sono omokage [In His Image]* (1906) and *Heibon [Mediocrity]* (1907) rather reluctantly, but these novels were received well enough to make possible a complete return to literary work. Once again, however, Futabatei turned his back on literary success, departing for Russia in 1908 as a foreign correspondent for the *Asahi shinbun*. While in Moscow he contracted tuberculosis, and he died on the return voyage to Japan at the age of 46.

Futabatei's restless and apparently contradictory behaviour as a writer derived from his excessively self-critical nature. He was a man who drove himself mercilessly, whatever he undertook. The harder he worked, the more self-critically and even self-destructively his mind operated. One day he was so driven to despair that he cursed himself with the words "Kutabatte shimē! [Go to hell!]" His rather anachronistic pen name, reminiscent of Edo *gesaku* [light literature] writers, is said to have derived from this expression.

Futabatei's translation *The Tryst* appeared during what Donald Keene has called "the age of translation". During the early Meiji period, in the 1870s and 1880s, Japan had thrown its doors open, and encouraged its citizens to seek inspiration in the West. Translators acted as mediators of western culture. Keene (1984: 63-66) groups these early translators of western literature into three categories. The first consisted of those whose aim was to enlighten ignorant readers. Translators in the second group wished to transmit political ideas expressed in western novels. The third (and from our point of view most important) group was made up of those who were interested in foreign literature for its own sake. Futabatei most assuredly belonged to this third group.

In 1878 two representatives of this third group published translations. Niwa Jun'ichirō (who later changed his surname to Oda) published an abridged translation from English of two works by Bulwer-Lytton: *Ernest Maltravers* and *Alice*. This compilation appeared under the title *Ōshū kiji: Karyū shunwa [A Marvellous Affair in Europe: A Springtime Tale of Blossoms and Willows]*. Kawashima Chūnosuke published a translation from French of Jules Verne's *Around the World in Eighty Days* under the title *Shinsetsu: Hachijū nichi kan sekai isshū [A New Story: A Tour of the World in Eighty Days]*. (The titles of these two translations will henceforth be abbreviated to *A Springtime Tale* and *Eighty Days*.)

As is clear even from the titles, these two publications represent very different attitudes to the translation process. While *A Springtime Tale* is an abbreviated and highly domesticated version of Bulwer-Lytton's two long novels, *Eighty Days* is a faithful word-for-word translation of Jules Verne's original. They are also strikingly different in content. Whereas *A Springtime Tale* is a conventional story of love between a man of talent (*saishi*) and a beautiful young lady (*kajin*), and would have appealed to the sensitivities of most Japanese readers, *Eighty Days* is an adventure or expeditionary story of a type most Japanese readers would never have encountered. Although *Eighty Days* was not as popular as *A Springtime Tale*, these two works represent the two dominant trends in translation during the 1880s.

Marleigh Ryan, the author of a painstaking translation of Futabatei's *Floating Clouds*, noted the novelty of Futabatei's first published translation, *The Tryst*. In his view (1967: 121) "it differs categorically from the translations of his contemporaries". We shall now demonstrate this novelty by comparing an extract from *The Tryst* with extracts from *A Springtime Tale* and *Eighty Days*, which were published ten years earlier. Let us begin with *A Springtime Tale*. (Generally we shall give the original first, followed by the translation.)

<u>Ernest Maltravers</u>

It <u>was</u> a lovely evening in April, the weather <u>was</u> unusually mild and serene for that time of year, in the northern districts of our isle, and the bright drops of a recent shower <u>sparkled</u> upon the buds of the lilac and laburnum that clustered round the cottage of Maltravers. The little fountain that played in the centre of a circular basin, on whose clear surface the broadleaved water-lily cast its fairy shadow—<u>added</u> to the fresh green of the lawn;—

"And softé as velvét the yongé grass,"

on which the rare and early flowers <u>were closing</u> their heavy lids. That twilight shower <u>had given</u> a racy and vigorous sweetness to the air which stole over many a bank of violets, and slightly <u>stirred</u> the golden ringlets of Alice, as she <u>sate</u> by the side of her entranced and silent lover. They <u>were seated</u> on a rustic bench just without the cottage—and the open windows behind them <u>admitted</u> the view of that happy room—with its litter of books and musical instruments—eloquent of the POETRY of HOME.

Maltravers <u>was</u> silent,... (Bulwer-Lytton 1839: 34-35)

*A Springtime Tale*

杜鵑血ニ叫ンデ緑樹陰ヲ成シ晩鶯口ヲ箝ンデ牡丹花(ハナ)ヲ着ントシ恰モ是レ春末夏初ノ天ナリ時ニ見ル繍幕半ハ開ヒテ窓下ニ萬巻ノ書ヲ積ミ瓶花盛ンニ綻ビテ牀上ニ一張ノ琴ヲ置キ中ニ佳麗ナル一少女(アリス)アリ頭ニハ緑ノ美髪ヲ結ンデ身ニハ淺紺ノ美衣ヲ着ケ坐シテ籠中ノ鸚鵡ニ新詩ヲ教ユ傍ラニ一少年アリ机ニ凭テ頻リニ書ヲ讀ミ**一室ノ景況活畫ニ異ナラズ誰カ此兩人ヲ羨マザルモノアランヤ**
(Yanagida 1935: 18-19) (Hereafter we shall use bold font to highlight some words of significance.)

[Little cuckoos sound loudly, trees cast their shadows over, bush warblers have stopped singing their songs and peonies are just coming into blossom. It is, indeed, late spring time or early summer time. A curtain with some patterns is seen half opened, books are piled up near the window, flowers in the vase are in full bloom, and a *koto* is set on the floor. There is a beautiful girl in the room (Alice). She ties her glossy black hair back and wears a fine light blue coloured dress. Sitting on the floor, she teaches a new-style poem to the parrot. There is also a boy sitting near the girl. He is absorbed in reading, leaning against the desk. **The scene in the room resembles a fine painting. (I wonder) who would not envy this couple!**]

In the original a detailed description of Maltravers' mental state continues, but this is not included in the translation. Niwa not only abbreviated the original, but also modified its content. He solicitously transforms the unfamiliar western setting of the original into a more familiar Japanese setting to make the work more palatable for his readers. "Little cuckoos" are singing in a garden of "peonies". Alice, whose hair has been transformed from "golden ringlets" to "glossy black", teaches a "new-style poem" to her "parrot". Her musical instrument is a "Japanese *koto*". We may further note that the verb forms of the original are past tense, while in Niwa's version the predominant verb form is the present (or non-past) tense. Attention should also be drawn to the final sentence of the translation: "Tare ka kono ryōnin o urayama zaru mono ara n ya [I wonder who would not envy this couple!]" In *A Springtime Tale* there is a narrator who apparently witnesses each scene and at times comments directly on what he sees.

The style employed in *A Springtime Tale* is known as the *kanbun kundoku* or Sinified Japanese style, which evolved during earlier 'translation' of classical Chinese texts. While nouns, verb stems, adjectives and adverbs are shown in Chinese characters, particles, verb conjugations, adjectival and adverbial endings and auxiliary verbs are written using *katakana* (one of the two phonetic syllabaries used in modern Japanese, the other being *hiragana*). This *kanbun kundoku* style is also known as the men's writing style. Official documents and many scientific and technical texts were written or translated using this style during the early Meiji period. The staccato, yet soul-stirring rhythm which characterized this style was well-suited to recitation aloud. Many Chinese poems were recited aloud, and it is likely that *A Springtime Tale* would have been as well. The solemn declarative style of this translation gave prominence to the narrator, and the reader would have felt at one with the narrator in reciting the text.

The palatable content, and rhythmical tone of *A Springtime Tale* thus made it a best seller.

It became so popular that it was said a book would not sell unless "shun [springtime]" or "wa [tale]" appeared in the title (Yanagida 1935: 18).

Let us now turn to Kawashima's *Eighty Days*, which was also translated in the *kanbun kundoku* style. The following extracts are taken from the beginning and ending of Chapter One.

*Le Tour du Monde en Quatre-vingts jours*

En l'année 1872, la maison portant le numéro 7 de Saville-row, Burlington Gardens—maison dans laquelle Sheridan mourut en 1814—, était habitée par Phileas Fogg, esq., l'un des membres les plus singuliers et les plus remarqués du Reform-Club de Londres, bien qu'il semblât prendre à tâche de ne rien faire qui pût attirer l'attention. ...

Cela dit, Phileas Fogg se leva, prit son chapeau de la main gauche, le plaça sur sa tête avec un mouvement d'automate et disparut sans ajouter une parole.

Passepartout entendit la porte de la rue se fermer une première fois: c'était son nouveau maître qui sortait; puis une seconde fois: c'était son prédécesseur, James Forster, qui s'en allait à son tour.

Passepartout demeura seul dans la maison de Saville-row. (Verne 1977: 9, 15)

[Mr. Phileas Fogg lived, in 1872, at No. 7, Saville Row, Burlington Gardens, the house in which Sheridan died in 1814. He was one of the most prominent members of the London Reform Club, though he never did anything to attract attention; an enigmatic character about whom little was known except that he was a polished man of the world. ...

Phileas Fogg got up, took his hat in his left hand, put it on his head with an automatic motion, and went off without a word.

Passepartout heard the street door shut once; it was his new master going out. He heard it shut again; it was his predecessor, James Foster, departing in his turn. Passepartout remained alone in the house in Saville Row.] (Verne 1991: 9, 13)

*Eighty Days*

千八百七十二年中ニ龍動ボルリントン公園傍サヴヒルロー街第七番ニ於テ千八百十四年中シエリダンガ物故セシ家ニ同府改進舎ノ社員ニテ自身ハ勉メテ行状ノ人ノ目ニ立タヌ様注意シアリシモ何時トナク奇癖家ノ名聞轟キケルフアイリース、フヲツグ氏ト称スル一紳士ゾ住ヒ**ケル**（中略）
フヲツグハ立テ帽ヲ右手ニ持シ彼ノ自動ノ木偶ト一般ナル動作ニテ其帽ヲ頭上ニ戴キ又他ノ壱語ヲ交ヘズシテ出デ去リ**ケル**パスパルツーハ頓テ門戸ヲ開閉スル響ヲ聞クコト両次是レ則チ先ヅ主人ノ立出デシト次ニ旧僕フヲスタルガ爰ヲ辞シテ去ルナリ斯クテ終ニサビルロー街ノ家ニ留リシハパスパルツー一人トナリタリ**ケリ** (Verne 2002: 3, 9)

(Note: In this text underlining occurs in the original. Double lines indicate place names and single lines indicate personal names.)

[In 1872 at No. 7, Saville row, Burlington Gardens, the house in which Sheridan died

> in 1814, lived a gentleman called Phileas Fogg, who was a member of the London Reform Club, though he tried not to attract any attention to his conduct, his eccentric character somehow became widely known. ...
>
> Fogg got up, took his hat in his right hand, put it on his head with a motion like an automatic puppet and went off without saying another word. Passepartout soon heard the door open and shut twice; the first was his master going out, then the second was the old servant Foster departing the house. Thus the only person left in the house in Saville Row was Passepartout alone.]

Although the *kanbun kundoku* style employed here is similar to that found in *A Springtime Tale*, it is clear from the lengthy opening sentence of *Eighty Days* that Kawashima is intent on making a much more faithful and literal translation. He has not omitted a single word or detail from Jules Verne's opening sentence.

His faithfulness to the original is most strikingly shown in his use of the classical auxiliary verb "-keri" when translating the verb "était habitée [was lived in]". In his commentary on this translation, Nakamura Nobuaki (2002: 505-506) points out that the *kanbun kundoku* style employed by Kawashima contains many irregular or solecistic adaptations of this classical style. One such adaptation is the use of classical auxiliary verbs such as "keri", "-tsu" and "-nu" to express past tense or complete aspect. Nakamura notes that around the time Kawashima made this translation, many young Japanese people were eagerly studying *kanbun* (Chinese writing), as many textbooks on western science and technology were translated using the *kanbun kundoku* style. This style became extremely fashionable amongst young people such as Kawashima, and because they were unfamiliar with its more conventional usage, they freely violated its grammar and created new compounds of Chinese characters. In this context, Kawashima would have felt relatively unconstrained in his innovative use of the auxiliary verb "-keri" as a past tense marker.

Kawashima's use of "-keri", and the length of his sentences, violate the intense, staccato and masculine rhythm of the traditional *kanbun kundoku* style, which had been so evident in *A Springtime Tale*. The use of "-keri" also shifts the point of view of the narrator. There are two classical auxiliary verbs expressing the past tense: "-ki" and "-keri". Whereas "-ki" expresses the past when it is recollected as part of one's own experience, "-keri" is used to report on the experience of others. In the conventional *kanbun kundoku* style, "-ki" is invariably chosen to express the past tense, while in *wabun* (Japanese writing) both "-ki" and "-keri" are employed. The authors of traditional Japanese stories often used "-keri" in the introduction of their narratives[1], and this had the effect of distancing the narrator from the story. The use of "-keri" by the narrator of *Eighty Days* has just this effect, in contrast to the narrator of *A Springtime Tale*, who appears to position himself within the story.

However, the use of "-keri" in *Eighty Days* is neither consistent, nor all that prominent. It appears at the beginning or end of each chapter and its effect remains minor. In any case, *A Springtime Tale*, with its authentic *kanbun kundoku* style and its domestication of the content, enjoyed much greater popularity than the more faithful *Eighty Days*.

In comparison with both the works cited so far, Futabatei's *The Tryst* was unprecedented in attempting a rigorously faithful translation in a highly colloquial style. The following,

---

[1] The renowned Japanese story *Genji monogatari [The Tale of Genji]* opens with the following sentence, ending in "-keri": "...ito yangotonaki kiwa ni wa ara nu ga, sugurete tokimeki tamau ari keri. [...there was a lady in the Emperor's favour, though she was not from the high aristocracy.]"

oft-cited extract from Futabatei's first published translation represents a sudden leap into the modern Japanese literary idiom. The Russian original is presented first:

<u>*Svidanie [The Rendezvous]*</u>

**Я** <u>сидел</u> в березовой роще осенью, около половины сентября. С самого утра <u>передавал</u> мелкий дождик, сменяемый по временам теплым солнечным сиянием; <u>была</u> непостоянная погода. Небо то всё <u>заволакивалось</u> рыхлыми белыми облаками, то вдруг местами <u>расчищалось</u> на мгновенье, и тогда из-за раздвинутых туч <u>показывалась</u> лазурь, ясная и ласковая, как прекрасный, умный глаз. **Я** <u>сидел</u> и <u>глядел</u> кругом, и <u>слушал</u>. Листья чуть шумели над моей головой; по одному их шуму <u>можно было узнать</u>, какое тогда стояло время года. (Turgenev 1865: 12)[2]

[**I** <u>was sitting</u> in a birch grove in autumn, around the middle of September. From the morning a fine rain <u>had been falling</u>, replaced from time to time by warm sunshine. The weather <u>was</u> unsettled. One moment the sky <u>was covered over</u> with fluffy white clouds, the next it suddenly <u>cleared</u> in patches, and from behind the parting clouds a patch of azure sky <u>showed</u>, clear and tender, like an intelligent eye. **I** <u>sat</u> and <u>looked</u> around, and <u>listened</u>. The leaves were rustling slightly above my head; from that rustling alone one <u>could tell</u> the season of the year.][3]

<u>*The Tryst*</u>

秋九月中旬といふころ、一日**自分が**さる樺の林の中に座してゐたことが<u>有ツた</u>。今朝から小雨が降りそゝぎ、その晴れ間にはおりおり生ま煖かな日かげも射して、まことに氣まぐれな空ら合ひ。あわあわしい白ら雲が空ら一面に棚引くかと思ふと、フトまたあちこち瞬く間雲切れがして、無理に押し分けたやうな雲間から澄みて怜悧(さか)し氣に見える人の眼の如くに朗かに晴れた蒼空(あをそら)が<u>のぞかれた</u>。**自分は**座して、四顧して、そして耳を<u>傾けてゐた</u>。木の葉が頭上(づじやう)で幽かに戰いだが、その音を聞たばかりでも季節は<u>知られた</u>。(Futabatei Shimei 1964a: 158)

[In autumn, around the middle of September, there was a day when **I** <u>sat</u> in a birch grove. From morning a fine rain had been falling, but from time to time there were intervals of warm sunshine; it was very unsettled weather. One moment fluffy white clouds trailed all over the sky, and the next the sky suddenly cleared in parts, and from behind the clouds which were forced to move, a bright and cheerful azure patch, like a beautiful and intelligent eye, <u>was seen</u>. **I** sat, looked around and <u>listened</u>. The leaves rustled slightly above my head, and I <u>knew</u> the season just by listening.]

---

[2] Kimura Takashi (1997: 120-128) has identified the versions of Turgenev's *Svidanie* and *Tri vstrechi* which were used by Futabatei in making his translations. They were contained in an edition published by the Salaev brothers.

[3] In making this translation I consulted the translation by Constance Garnett. (Turgenev 1895: 92)

Futabatei's *The Tryst* stands out from other contemporary translations in many ways. The brief, simple title, written in *hiragana*, contrasts markedly with the complicated and decorative titles which commonly graced other translations. These commonly consisted of a main title of four Chinese characters, followed by a subtitle of a further four Chinese characters. We have already cited the full title of *A Springtime Tale*, which consists of eight characters and translates as "A Marvellous Affair in Europe: A Springtime Tale of Blossoms and Willows". Boccaccio's *Decameron* was translated under the title *Ikoku jōshi: En'ō kikan [A Romantic Tale from Italy: A Strange View of Lovebirds]*. Most translations, much abridged and altered, bore these decorative and eye-catching titles. *Hachijū nichi kan sekai isshū [Eighty Days Around the World]* had been something of an exception in its faithfulness and simplicity, and its subtitle was also simple: *Shinsetsu [A New Novel]*.

Another striking feature of *The Tryst* was its use of *hiragana* throughout the narrative. Whereas texts written with *katakana*, such as *A Springtime Tale* or *Eighty Days*, demand more patience and effort of today's readers (and even of readers of the time), *The Tryst*'s text is far more accessible. We must note, though, that Futabatei cannot take the credit for this particular innovation. By the time *The Tryst* was published, *hiragana* had already become more commonly used than *katakana* in literary works. One of Futabatei's contemporaries, Morita Shiken, who published his first translations in 1886, and used what he called *shūmitsu buntai* [a meticulous translation style], also used *hiragana*. While Morita's translations were exceptionally loyal to the original, his *shūmitsu buntai* was still only a variant of the *kanbun kundoku* style. He worked for a newspaper, and his use of *hiragana* was mainly aimed at attracting a broad readership.

A third feature of *The Tryst* which captures our attention is the use of western punctuation marks, including commas, full stops, exclamation marks and dashes. This was unprecedented. The following recollection from Tayama Katai, a leading writer of the naturalist school, is indicative of the impression made by this innovation:

> How mysterious the *genbun itchi* style found in that translation was to young literary enthusiasts. How extraordinary and marvellous was the impression *The Tryst* made on intellectuals at that time. In fact, I was also one of those who marvelled at the style. "Yes, we could write this kind of sentence, if we tried. We can write fully, meticulously and accurately as Futabatei did in his translation". I could not help thinking like this. It is easy to imagine my excitement. Futabatei's new style, containing punctuation marks such as '?', '!' and '—', stood out amongst conventional styles such as para *kanbun kundoku*, Chikamatsu-like or Kōson-like styles. None of these styles had punctuation marks and their sentences meandered endlessly. (Cited in Hasegawa Izumi and Isogai Hideo (eds) 1979: 18)

Perhaps Katai should have also mentioned more basic punctuation marks such as commas, full stops and semi-colons, as even these were absent from traditional styles and from translations such as *Eighty Days*, however faithful it might be in other respects. To write "fully, meticulously and accurately as Futabatei did", punctuation marks are indispensable. Futabatei, who was always set the highest standards of exactness in his work, attempted to reproduce punctuation marks in every detail. The following is his own account of his views on punctuation and formal aspects of style, taken from an oft-cited lecture he gave in 1906:

> If you think solely of meaning when translating a foreign language, and attach excessive importance to it, you take the risk of violating the original. I have always believed that you must saturate yourself with the rhythm of the original for some time, then transfer it to your own work. In my attempt to reproduce Russian rhythms in my translations, I did not omit a single comma or full stop. <u>If the original contained three commas and one full stop, the translation also had three commas and one full stop</u>. (Futabatei Shimei 1965a: 174. Underlining added.)[4]

We should note here that in attempting to adhere to the original punctuation, Futabatei was concerned first and foremost not with meaning, but with the rhythm of the original. It is ironic that despite this overriding concern, the resulting translations appeared to Futabatei himself to be rather stiff and rigid, lacking the rhythm he had sought. When we compare *The Tryst* with *A Springtime Tale*, the latter appears far more rhythmical, as it is written in the stirring *kanbun kundoku* style. Momiuchi (1999: 99) suggests that some rhythms from the Russian original may have been reproduced through repetition of sounds, as in "<u>awa</u>'<u>awa</u>shī shi<u>ra</u> kumo ga so<u>ra</u> ichimen ni [fluffy white clouds [trailed] all over the sky]", rather than through duplicating the punctuation. The actual result of attempting to duplicate all punctuation marks was to make the text meticulous and accurate, as noted by Katai.

In *The Tryst* Futabatei did not in fact adhere to the punctuation quite as rigorously as is suggested by his lecture. While the number of full stops is almost identical to that of the original, commas and semi-colons are used rather freely. His second translation, *A Chance Encounter*, is far more rigorous in this respect. What is more significant, however, is not how faithfully he reproduced punctuation, but the fact that he used punctuation at all. Futabatei's use of punctuation in *The Tryst* set a precedent which has been largely adhered to in literary works to the present day.

The fourth, and most significant feature of *The Tryst*, is the use of a colloquial idiom which is remarkably close in its syntax and lexicon to that found in literature today. Even for today's readers, the colloquial style of *The Tryst* is so fresh that we can only wonder how he could produce it in 1888.

Japan's leading symbolist poet, Kanbara Ariake, recalled his experience of reading *The Tryst* as follows:

> I first came to know Futabatei's name through *The Tryst*, which appeared in *Kokumin no tomo [Friend of the Nation]*. I was then in my first year of middle school, and my ability to appreciate literature was, of course, undeveloped. I was still at a stage where I enjoyed reciting *Kajin no kigū [Strange Encounters with Beautiful Women]*. A translation from the work of the Russian novelist Turgenev sounded very exotic. I thought I would have a look at it. Futabatei's *genbun itchi* style, with its masterly use of colloquial language—that unique style—sounded so fresh, its echoes seemed to go on whispering endlessly in my ears. A nameless joy filled me. At the same time I was so moved that something deep within me almost wanted to shut it out. I just did not want to be spoken to so intimately. (Cited in Futabatei Shimei 1964a: 413)[5]

---

[4] In making this translation I consulted the translation by M.G. Ryan (Ryan 1967: 120)

[5] In making this translation I consulted the translation by M.G. Ryan (Ryan 1967: 117-118)

Ariake's experience was at once joyful and painful. For him the act of reading had been changed by the degree of intimacy expressed in Futabatei's style. *Strange Encounters with Beautiful women* (1885-1897) is "an episodic account of the adventures of a patriotic young Japanese man, who had opposed the Imperial forces at the time of the Restoration, and is living in exile abroad" (Ryan 1967: 117). It was an extremely popular political novel, and is written in the same *kanbun kundoku* style as that found in *A Springtime Tale*. Texts written in this style generally appear to be narrated extemporaneously by the implied author, and lend themselves to being recited aloud. *The Tryst* provided a stark contrast for Ariake, as the narrator no longer appeared to be declaiming to an audience, but rather to be "whispering" in his ear. This is more akin to the experience of the modern reader, who reads quietly in his own personal space.

*The Tryst* is in itself a very personal narrative. For the young naturalist writers of Futabatei's time, *The Tryst* appeared as a revelation. One of them, Kunikida Doppo, wrote his famous essay *Musashino*[6] in response to *The Tryst*, and in it the following sentence appears:

> 林の奥に座して四顧し、傾聴し、睇視し、黙想す。 (Kunikida Doppo 1974: 4)
>
> [I sit in the grove, look around, listen, cast my eyes down and contemplate.]

This sentence from *Musashino* is copied from a sentence in *The Tryst*:

> **自分は**座して、四顧して、そして耳を傾けてゐた。 (Futabatei Shimei 1964a: 158)
>
> [**I** sat, looked around and listened.]

What had struck Doppo was the way in which the narrator-protagonist positioned himself in nature. Sugiyama Yasuhiko cites a similar sentence from the very beginning of *The Tryst*:

> 秋九月中旬といふころ、一日**自分が**さる樺の林の中に座してゐたことが有ツた。 (Futabatei Shimei 1964a: 158)
>
> [In autumn, around the middle of September, there was a day when **I** sat in a birch grove.]

Sugiyama (1968: 36-38) suggests that the novelty of *The Tryst* lies in its clear narrative point of view. The narrator views himself in the midst of nature, neither disappearing into it, nor observing it totally objectively. In fact, what is common to both the opening sentence cited by Sugiyama, and the sentence which so impressed Doppo, is the clear rendition of the first person singular pronoun as "jibun [I]", and the translation of the Russian past tense verbs using the colloquial auxiliary verb "-ta".

[6] *Musashino* is the name of a district of Tokyo.

We must remember that in *The Tryst* Futabatei was meticulous in his efforts to translate every word accurately. All past tense verbs are translated with the aid of the auxiliary verb "-ta". In *Eighty Days*, which was a pioneering attempt at accurate literary translation, the classical auxiliary verb "-keri" had been used. Its use, however, had not been consistent. In *The Tryst* the use of "-ta" is consistent, and predominant. In association with the first-person pronoun "jibun", "-ta" endings establish a clear, retrospective narrative point of view.

Turgenev's original, *Svidanie [The Rendezvous]*, is a brief episode from *Zapiski okhotnika [A Sportsman's Sketches]*, a work which brought him fame in Russia and abroad. The sportsman-narrator by chance witnesses a rendezvous between an arrogant male servant and a peasant girl in a birch grove. The girl's feelings are very sincere, but the servant regards their liaison as only a casual affair, and abandons her quite callously. The narrator openly sympathizes with the girl's plight.

What impressed the young writers of the naturalist school, however, was not the overt content, the rendezvous, but the fresh description of nature from a retrospective first-person narrative point of view. This in turn was facilitated by the use of the auxiliary verb "-ta", whose origin we shall now examine.

There were six classical auxiliary verbs that expressed the meaning of the past tense or complete aspect: "-ki", "-keri", "-tsu", "-nu", "-tari" and "-ri". Of these, only "-tari" survives, in its abbreviated form "-ta". In its classical form, "-tari" expressed the state of being which results from the successful completion of an action. It might thus be more accurate to say it expressed complete aspect, rather than past tense, and it was often used in isolation, following a string of non-past verbs. The following passage, from the opening of Futabatei's first novel, *Floating Clouds*, illustrates the original use of the "-ta" form:

> **千早振る神無月**も最早跡二日の餘波となツた廿八日の午後三時頃に神田見附の内より塗渡る蟻散る蜘蛛の子とうようよぞよぞよ沸出でゝ來るのは孰れも頤を氣にし給ふ方々**しかし熟々見て篤と點撿すると**是れにも種々種類のあるものでまづ髭から書立てれば口髭頬髯顋の鬚暴に興起した拿破崙髭に狆の口めいた比斯馬克髭そのほか矮鷄髭貉髭ありやなしやの幻の髭と濃くも淡くもいろいろに生分る髭に續いて差ひのあるのは服装白木屋仕込みの黒物づくめには佛蘭西皮の靴の配偶はありうち之を召す方様の鼻毛は延びて蜻蛉をも釣るべしといふ是れより降つては背皺よると枕詞の付く「スコツチ」の背廣にゴリゴリするほどの牛の毛皮靴そこで踵にお飾を絶さぬ所から泥に尾を曳く龜甲洋袴いづれも釣しんぼうの苦患を今に脱せぬ貌付デモ持主は得意なもので髭あり服あり我また奚をか覓めんと濟した顔色で火をくれた木頭と反身ツてお歸り遊ばす**イヤお羨しいことだ**其後より續いて出てお出でなさるは孰れも胡麻鹽頭弓と曲げても張の弱い腰に無殘や空辨當を振垂げてヨタヨタものでお歸りなさるさては老朽しても流石はまだ職に堪へるものかしかし日本服でも勤められるお手輕なお身の上**さりとはまたお氣の毒な**

途上人影の稀れに成つた頃同じ見附の内より兩人の少年が話しながら出て參つた (Futabatei Shimei 1964a: 4-5 - Punctuation deleted to mimic original.)

[It is three o'clock in the afternoon of a late **October** day. A swirling mass of men stream out of the Kanda gate, marching first in antlike formation, then scuttling busily off in every direction. Each and every one of these fine gentlemen is primarily interested in getting enough to eat.

**Look carefully and you will see** what an enormous variety of individual types are represented in the huge crowd. Start by examining the hair bristling on their faces: moustaches, side whiskers, Vandykes, and even extravagant imperial beards, Bismarck beards, reminiscent of a Pekinese, bantam beards, badger's beards, meagre beards that are barely visible, thick and thin they sprout in every conceivable way.

Now see how differently they are dressed. Here is a dandy in a fashionable black suit, purchased at Shirokiya set off by shoes of French calfskin. And now confident men oblivious of the ill-fit of their tweeds worn with stiff leather shoes — trousers that trail in the mud like the tail of a tortoise; suits bearing the indelible stamp of the ready-made clothes rack. "I have a beard, fine clothing, what more do I need?" they seem to say. Glowing like embers on the fire, these **enviable** creatures swagger home, heads erect.

Now behind them come the less fortunate. **Pitifully** stooped, their hair grey, they stagger along with empty lunch boxes dangling from their waists. Despite their advanced years they still manage to hold a job, but their duties are so negligible they can easily work in old-fashioned Japanese clothes.

The crowd had thinned out by the time two young men engrossed in conversation came through the gate. ] (Ryan 1967: 197-198)

In fact, the verb "dete maitta", which appears at the end of this passage, is the only "-ta" form verb to appear in the whole chapter. Moreover, the verb "mairu" to which the "-ta" form is attached, normally refers in humble form to the speaker's own actions. Here, when used to describe the actions of two young protagonists, it should be understood to express "humbleness to the listener, when the speaker is describing the action of a third person on the speaker's side" (*Nihon kokugo daijiten*. Vol. 18, 1975: 284-285). The last sentence might literally be translated: "**I** notice two of **our** young men, engrossed in conversation, have come through the gate now that the crowd has thinned out". It is apparent here that the colloquial auxiliary verb "-ta", employed in this isolated instance in *Floating Clouds*, carries the meaning of complete aspect rather than past tense. It is also apparent that the narrator of *Floating Clouds* is present at the scene, in a way that permits him to comment on the action as it unfolds. This narrator often uses ornate expressions, such as "hi o kureta mokuzu to sokkurikaette okaeri asobasu [glowing like embers on the fire [these creatures] swagger home]" (phraseology typical of Sanba, a popular Edo comic story writer) or the *makurakotoba*[7] "chihayaburu". More significantly, the narrator directly expresses his feelings

---

[7] *Makurakotoba* [literally "pillow word"] is a set epithet, which ornates and modifies the word it qualifies. Here "chihayaburu [originally: almighty]" modifies "kami [god]" in "kan'nazuki [October (literally godless month)]", resulting in an expression which resembles "Almighty godless month". *Makurakotoba* are thus virtually untranslatable.

towards the characters during his narration: "iya ourayamashī koto da [My, how jealous I am!]" or "sari to wa mata okinodokuna [I am truly sorry to see that]. This loquacious narrator closely resembles that found in *A Springtime Tale*. Moreover, although the first part of *Floating Clouds* is written using *hiragana*, it contains only a few commas, with no spaces following them. Thus, the colloquial style employed in Part One of *Floating Clouds* possesses features which make it more similar to the *kanbun kundoku* style than to the innovative colloquial style of *The Tryst*.

Nonetheless, *Floating Clouds* is commonly acknowledged to be "the first modern Japanese novel" because of its psychological and social realism (its unprecedented negative hero, Bunzō, loses his job in the civil service and is shunned by the woman he loves), and also because it is written in the colloquial *genbun itchi* style, which brought together spoken and written styles (Keene 1984: 111-113; Ryan 1967: xiv-xv). In a departure from previous convention, Futabatei employed this colloquial style even in the narrative of his novel.

Futabatei's theoretical essay "Shōsetsu sōron [A General Discussion of the Novel]" throws some light on the creation of the negative hero Bunzō. The essay appeared in 1886, one year before Futabatei commenced writing *Floating Clouds*, and was based on the views of the Russian critic Vissarion Belinsky, and on the logic of Vladimir Stoyunin (Kitaoka Seiji 1965: 12-30 and 1967: 292-307). On this platform Futabatei constructed his own understanding of the novel, suggesting that it should reveal the natural essence [idea] hidden behind various phenomena [form]. In the modern novel an author often creates a type from numerous individuals. Futabatei apparently applied this understanding of the novel in the creation of his own negative hero, Bunzō, a "type" never before encountered in Japanese literature. Surprisingly, however, Futabatei made no reference to style in his essay.

Futabatei did not comment on the genesis of *Floating Clouds'* colloquial style until many years later, when he referred to the influence of Russian literature on his style. In essays written in 1897 ("Sakka kushin dan [A Talk on a Writer's Labours]"), 1906 ("Roshia bungaku dan [A Talk on Russian Literature]") and 1908 ("Yo ga hansei no zange [Confessions about My Life]"), he repeatedly acknowledged the influence of Dostoevsky and Goncharov on his work. His clearest statement about *Floating Clouds* is contained in the essay of 1908:

> As far as the style is concerned, Part One is a mixture of Sanba's, Fūrai's, Zenkō's and Aeba's styles. As for Part Two, I adopted a western style, abandoning Japanese style. In short, I intended to import a western style. First I had studied Dostoevsky's style, then Goncharov's, and I was inclined to copy mainly Dostoevsky's. As for Part Three, the influence of these two writers was still strong, but what I copied most was Goncharov's style. (Futabatei Shimei, 1965a, 268)

In 1897 Futabatei had been more inclined to acknowledge the influence of Dostoevsky in Part Three of the novel. In spite of this discrepancy, one thing is clear. While Part One is written in a distinctly Japanese style, Futabatei adopted a western (Russian) style when working on Parts Two and Three. We also know that Futabatei's first translations (*The Tryst* and *A Chance Encounter*) appeared between the publication of Parts Two and Three, in the summer and autumn of 1888. It seems reasonable to suppose that work on the translations commenced before he wrote Part Two, given the marked difference in style which is evident in Part Two of the novel. Indeed, it has been reported (Uchida Roan cited in Usui Yoshimi (ed) 1980: 314) that Futabatei first wrote Part Two in Russian, and then translated it into Japanese. The following passage is taken from Part Two of *Floating Clouds*, and illustrates the changes in Futabatei's style:

> 漸くの事で笑ひを留めてお勢がまだ莞爾々々と微笑のこびり付てゐる貌を擡げて傍を視ると昇は居ない「ヲヤ」ト云ツてキヨロキヨロと四邊を環視はしてお勢は忽ち眞面目な貌をした
> 只見れば後の小舎の前で昇が磬切といふ風に腰を屈めて其處に鵠立でゐた洋装紳士の背に向ツて荐りに禮拝してゐた（中略）昇は忽ち平身低頭何事をか喃々と言ひながら續けさまに二ツ三ツ禮拝した
> （中略）お勢は紳士にも貴婦人にも眼を注めぬ代り束髪の令嬢を穴の開く程目守めて一心不亂傍目を觸らなかつた呼吸をも吻かなかツた母親が物を言懸けても返答をもしなかつた (Futabatei Shimei 1964a: 60-61. Punctuation deleted.)

> [Osei's laughter finally subsided and she looked up, her face still wreathed in smiles. Noboru is [H.C.] not at her side. Her smile vanished as she glanced about. There was Noboru eagerly bowing to the back of a gentleman in western clothes. — He bowed down over and over, babbling obsequiously all the while. ...
>
> Osei did not pay much attention to the gentleman or the older lady. Instead she stared with the utmost concentration at the girl, until it seemed she would stare a hole right through her. She never looked away or drew a breath. She even failed to answer her mother when she spoke to her.] (Ryan 1967: 264-265. Modified translation. )

This passage is taken from chapter seven, in which Noboru, Bunzō's rival for Osei's affections, takes Osei and her mother on an excursion to see chrysanthemums. They meet Noboru's supervisor by chance. The interesting thing in this scene, when Noboru is flattering to his supervisor and his family, is that it is depicted not only from the narrator's viewpoint, but from Osei's. This shift in viewpoint is facilitated by the repeated use of the auxiliary verb "-ta". In Part Two there is a marked increase in the frequency of this auxiliary verb, as a result of which, the loquacious narrator, who has reported and commented on the development of the story throughout Part One, retreats into the background. The consistent use of "-ta" in Part Two of *Floating Clouds* is most probably directly transferred from the innovative colloquial style developed during work on *The Tryst*. While working on Part Two of *Floating Clouds*, Futabatei may not have been as conscious of using the past tense as he was while writing his translations, but in some scenes we find the same consistent use of "-ta" sentence endings. The following verbs from the passage just cited are clearly past tense verbs: "reihaishite ita [bowed down]", "wakime o furanakatta [never looked away]", "iki o mo tsukanakatta [did not even draw breath]" and "hentō o mo shinakatta [even failed to answer]".

Part One of *Floating Clouds* might be characterized as "semi-modern", due to the conventional colloquial narrative style, which appears to have been borrowed from Edo *gesaku* literature, or, as suggested by Togawa Shinsuke (1971: 105-109), from the style of the renowned raconteur San'yūtei Enchō. In Part One the narrator directly intrudes into the story and comments on the action. He even addresses the reader directly during the transition between chapters, and frequently interjects words requesting the reader's empathy. In traditional works the narrator was often identified with the author. As Futabatei worked concurrently on translating Turgenev's first-person narrative in *The Rendezvous*, and on Parts Two and Three of his own work, he must have been become conscious of two ways in which he could transform *Floating Clouds* into a genuinely modern novel. One option was to make his narrator one of the characters in the story, transforming the narrative from third-person to first-person. The other was to remove the narrator's direct utterances from the novel, to employ the auxiliary verb "-ta" consistently, and to create a third-person narrative in which the story is independent of the narrator, who is then identified with the implied author. Futabatei apparently chose the latter path, and in Part Two he began to eliminate the narrator, a relic of past literary practices, by employing "-ta" more frequently and consistently, under the strong influence of the style developed while working on *The Tryst*.

Considering the remarkable achievement of Futabatei's first two translations, it seems strange that he felt compelled to make revised versions some eight years later. In the next chapter we shall look at these revised versions, in which Futabatei developed a significantly different translation style.

# Chapter 2 — The Development of Futabatei's Translation Style

In this chapter we shall examine in depth Futabatei's revised translations of Turgenev's *Svidanie [The Rendezvous]* and *Tri vstrechi [Three Encounters],* focusing particularly on the two translations of *Three Encounters: Meguriai [A Chance Encounter]* and the later version *Kigū [A Fortuitous Encounter].* A close comparison of the two versions will reveal that the key difference between them lies in the approach to translating past tense Russian verbs of perfective and imperfective aspect, and in the consequent elimination in the second version of the repetitive use of "-ta" auxiliary verbs.

In 1896, almost eight years after the publication of his first translations of Turgenev's stories *The Rendezvous* and *Three Encounters,* Futabatei broke his long silence with the publication of his translation of Turgenev's *Asya,* under the title *Katakoi [One-sided Love].* At the same time he published revised translations of *The Rendezvous* and *Three Encounters,* changing the title of the latter work from *A Chance Encounter* to *A Fortuitous Encounter.* In the following year, 1897, he published translations of Gogol's story *Portret [The Portrait],* and of two more works by Turgenev: *Son [The Dream]* (under the title *Yumekatari [Dream Talk]*) and the novel *Rudin* (under the title *Ukikusa [Floating Weed]*). In December that year, Futabatei resigned from his position at the official gazette bureau, where he had been working for eight years and which had assured him of a steady income. During 1898 he continued to translate Turgenev's stories. Translations of *Zhid [The Jew]* and *Petushkov* were published under the titles of *Yudaya-jin [The Jew]* and *Kusare-en [The Mismatch].* The following year Futabatei took up a professorship at the Tokyo University of Foreign Studies and again stopped translating for almost four years.

Jinzai notes that the four-year period from 1896 to 1899 was Futabatei's second most productive as a translator, and points out that he translated mainly stories by Turgenev during this period. Jinzai, himself a prominent translator of Russian, makes the following comment on these translations:

> In his translations of Turgenev's stories we may see Futabatei's burning enthusiasm revealing itself. Turgenev's elegant poetic realism suits Futabatei and allows him to demonstrate his enthusiasm.
>
> Indeed, for Futabatei, Turgenev was the most congenial Russian writer. From a stylistic point of view, Turgenev was the writer whose style was most suited to Futabatei's own, at least during the first and second periods of his literary activity, and the translation of Turgenev's works must have been Futabatei's favourite field of work. (Cited in Futabatei Shimei 1965e: 176)

Comparing the first translation of *Tri vstrechi (A Chance Encounter)* with the second version *(A Fortuitous Encounter),* Jinzai gives unstinting praise to the earlier version, on the grounds that Futabatei made such a sincere effort to reproduce the structure of the original Russian sentences. Although *A Chance Encounter* is a rather stiff word-for-word translation, with only minimal syntactic adjustment to conform to the requirements of the Japanese language, it is a remarkable attempt at reproducing the tone of the original.

Making reference to Jinzai's article, the Japanese Slavist and translator of Russian Kimura Shōichi (1956: 41-49) suggests that *A Chance Encounter* is the most literal and faithful translation he has ever seen. Citing a passage in *A Chance Encounter,* Kimura points out that even the number of full stops in Futabatei's translation is the same as in the Russian original, and that past tense verbs are frequently used in *A Chance Encounter,* corresponding to the usage in the Russian original, even though this creates a certain monotony in Japanese, where all verbs come at the end of the sentence and all past tense verbs end in "-ta". Futabatei attempts to reproduce the word order of the original as far as Japanese syntax permits.

The first version of *The Tryst,* on the other hand, is a comparatively free translation, with the number of punctuation marks and the sentence structure varying from those of the original. Kimura concludes that *The Tryst* was thus a more natural Japanese translation, and that this may be why its impact on contemporary writers was much greater than that of *A Chance Encounter.* Kimura does, however, praise *A Chance Encounter,* and suggests that it occupies a place in the history of Japanese literary translation as a unique achievement by the young and enthusiastic Futabatei.

Kimura further suggests that Futabatei's translation style developed remarkably while working on the second versions of *The Rendezvous* and *Three Encounters,* and while translating *Asya* and *Rudin.* He considers that Futabatei's translation style was established by the time these translations were completed, and that it did not essentially change further during the third and final period of his translation activity.

Finally Kimura makes reference to Nogami's concept of a "monochromatic" approach to translation (Nogami 1938: 94-111). He cites Nogami as follows:

> It is ideal to reproduce the tone and style of the original. However, if one cannot expect such a translation, it is preferable to have a monochromatic translation, rather than one which demonstrates the translator's own tone and style. (Kimura Shōichi 1956: 49)

Nogami considers Ōgai's translations to be an example of the monochromatic approach, and Futabatei's translations to be an example of one which demonstrates the translator's own tone and style. Kimura, on the other hand, argues that both Ōgai's and Futabatei's translations have their own style, and asserts that a translator should be ashamed if he lacks any particular translation style of his own. Although Futabatei established his own translation style, which might have differed from the style of the original, Kimura concludes that he did so on the basis of a literal and faithful translation. Indeed, although Futabatei's translation has its own noticeable tone, which is at times similar to the tone of *gesaku* (Edo light literature)[1], he always follows the original faithfully. Kimura's argument lacks any detailed discussion of how Futabatei changed the earlier version of *The Tryst* and *A Chance Encounter*, or of the most significant differences between the earlier and later versions.

Nogami's concept of a "monochromatic" approach to translation has attracted attention from other scholars. Kondō and Wakabayashi have written:

---

[1] *Gesaku* is a form of popular prose literature which developed during the late Edo period (1770-1870). It literally means "playful composition", a term originally intended to indicate that the author disclaimed responsibility for a frivolous work. (Keene 1978: 573).

> Nogami Toyoichirō (1883–1950) advocated a 'monochromatic' approach whereby no particular attempt is made to reproduce the tone and style of the original. He suggested that translations should sound foreign so as to introduce fresh expressions and forms into the language. (Kondō and Wakabayashi 1998: 492)

In a word, Nogami aimed at "foreignizing" translations. Laurence Venuti has explained what is meant by a foreignizing strategy in translation:

> A foreignizing strategy in translation was first formulated in German culture during the Classical and Romantic periods, perhaps most decisively by the philosopher and theologian Friedrich Schleiermacher. — Schleiermacher acknowledged that most translation was domesticating, an ethnocentric reduction of the foreign text to target-language values, bringing the author back home. But he much preferred a foreignizing strategy, an ethnodeviant pressure on those values to register the linguistic and cultural difference of the foreign text, sending the reader abroad. (Venuti 1998: 241-242)

Futabatei Shimei is considered by Kondō and Wakabayashi to be a writer who resisted this "foreignizing" strategy and adopted a "domesticating" strategy. They continue:

> Inevitably, however, translations that were 'faithful' to the original in an attempt to create a new style met with resistance from people who regarded this approach as detrimental to the Japanese language. Such writer-translators as Uchida Roan, Tsubouchi Shōyō, Hasegawa Futabatei and Mori Ōgai advocated rewriting foreign works into natural Japanese. (Kondō and Wakabayashi 1998: 492)

Kimura also suggests that Futabatei and Ōgai adopted a domesticating strategy. However, he emphasizes the faithfulness to the original of Futabatei's translations. The key issue here is whether this faithfulness to the original functions as an instrument of innovation for the language into which the foreign works are translated.

Let us examine more closely the style which emerged while retranslating *The Rendezvous* and *Three Encounters*. When we compare the earlier and later versions of these two stories, we soon notice that the sentence endings have been changed in the later versions. As Kimura points out in his article, in the earlier versions Futabatei faithfully translates the past tense verbs of the original employing the Japanese auxiliary verb "-ta". This had a direct impact on the use of the past tense in Part Two of *Floating Clouds,* where it served to eliminate the physical presence of the narrator. However, since verbs normally appear at the end of a Japanese sentence, the continual use of past tense forms became monotonous, with nearly every sentence ending in "-ta". In the later versions, Futabatei attempted to reduce the repetitive use of the auxiliary verb "-ta" by changing some "-ta" forms to the "-(r)u" form. (Hereafter the term ""-(r)u" form" will be taken to mean "non-ta" (non-past) form", while ""-ta" form" refers to the placement of the auxiliary "-ta" after the verb.)

From the point of view of the translation strategy, we might say that in the earlier versions Futabatei opted for a literal translation. He tried hard to reproduce the original text as exactly as possible, even down to the number of punctuation marks. As a result, he found a narrative style which, in its use of past tense forms, was new to Japanese literature, and he went on to adopt this innovative narrative style in his own novel *Floating Clouds.* Using the terminology discussed above, we may say that Futabatei adopted a "foreignizing" strategy in his earlier versions of Turgenev's stories, which worked as "an instrument of cultural innovation".

So when Futabatei retranslated Turgenev's stories and eliminated some of the "-ta" auxiliary verbs, did he change his strategy from a foreignizing one to a domesticating one? Did he merely rewrite the narrative to be more easily read by Japanese readers, or was he led to change his translation of selected verbs in the Russian original, in order to convey some nuances of meaning in the Russian which had been missed in his earlier translation?

Before we address these questions, we will examine the use of the auxiliary verb "-ta" in *Floating Clouds* and the way in which its use influences the narrative point of view.

Noguchi points out that the auxiliary verb "-ta" in the modern Japanese novel functions not so much to indicate the past relative to the narrator's present time, as to indicate that the novel is fiction. Referring to linguist Ōno Susumu's *Nihongo no bunpō o kangaeru [An Examination of Japanese Grammar],* Noguchi defines the meaning of the auxiliary verb "-ta" as follows:

> The modern Japanese auxiliary verb "-ta" is nowadays used to express the meanings of both the past and the perfective, though it originally derived from the classic auxiliary verb "-tari", which was used to express the perfective. According to Ōno, this classic auxiliary verb "-tari" took the place of the other two auxiliary verbs "-ki" and "-keri", and it has included their meanings. Whereas "-ki" was used when one had a clear memory of the past, "-keri" was used when one became aware of things which had belonged to the unknown past. Thus "-keri" was often used in folklore as a marker for fiction. (Noguchi Takehiko 1980: 39-40)

Thus the auxiliary verb "-ta", insofar as it carried the meaning "-keri", functioned as a marker of fiction. Noguchi goes on to cite the final paragraph of Part Three of *Floating Clouds* as an illustration of the new narrative point of view ushered in by Futabatei's use of the auxiliary verb "-ta". In this passage the ever-present narrator of earlier parts of the novel, whom Futabatei had borrowed from Edo light literature, and whose colloquial narrative was the hallmark of the *genbun itchi* style, has shifted to the background. Futabatei has found a new narrative style set in the main character's inner thoughts:

> 出て行くお勢の後姿を見送つて、文三は莞爾した。如何してかう様子が渝つたのか、其を疑つて居るに遑なく、たゞ何となく心嬉しくなつて、莞爾した。それからは例の妄想が勃然と首を擡げて抑へても抑へ切れぬやうになり、種々の取留も無い事が續々胸に浮んで、遂には總て此頃の事は皆**文三の**疑心から出た暗鬼で、實際はさして心配する程の事でも無かつたかとまで思ひ込んだ。が、また心を取直して考へてみれば、故無くして**文三を**辱めたといひ、母親に忤ひながら、何時しか其いふなりに成つたといひ、それほどまで親かつた昇と俄に疏々敷なつたといひ、—どうも常事でなくも思はれる。と思へば、喜んで宜いものか、悲んで宜いものか、

> 殆ど**我にも**胡亂になつて來たので、**宛も遠方から擦る眞似をされたやうに、思ひ切つては笑ふ事も出來ず、泣く事も出來ず、**快と不快との間に心を迷せながら、暫く縁側を往きつ戻りつしてゐた。が、兎に角物を云つたら、聞いてゐさうゆゑ、今にも歸ツて來たら、今一度運を試して聽かれたら其通り、若し聽かれん時には其時こそ斷然叔父の家を辭し去らうと、遂にかう決心して、そして一と先二階へ戻つた。 (Futabatei Shimei 1964a: 152-153)

> [Bunzō smiled as he watched them go, accepting his happiness without question for the moment. His favourite fantasies came to the fore again. Perhaps there was nothing to worry about after all. Perhaps it had all been a product of **Bunzō's** [H.C.] suspicious mind. But no, something certainly was wrong. He could not overlook her vicious, senseless attack on **Bunzō** [H.C.]; her initial defiance of her mother followed by her new submissiveness; her gradual estrangement from Noboru, with whom she had been on such intimate terms. "There are [H.C.] tangible contradictions to **my** [H.C.] fantasy. Something is [H.C.] wrong", he thought [H.C.] and he did not know how to reach a greater understanding of the problem. **He did not even know if he should feel happy or sad.** Restlessly he wandered about the house. Eventually he reached a decision. He would try to talk to her when she came back. He would gamble everything on her response. If she would not listen, he would leave that house once and for all. He went back upstairs to wait.] (Ryan 1967: 356. Some pronouns and verbs have been modified.)

Noguchi points out that the underlined words "Bunzō no (gishin) [Bunzō's (suspicious mind)]", "Bunzō o (hazukashimeta) [(shamed) Bunzō]" and "ware ni mo [even myself]" may be replaced with "jibun no [my]", "jibun o [me]" and "Bunzō ni mo [even Bunzō himself]", and suggests that this whole paragraph is half monologue. He seems to believe that Futabatei finally created a "modern" novel by using the "-ta" auxiliary verb to distance the narrator. However, in my view Futabatei could not remove the narrator completely. In Part Three the narrator still exists and describes Bunzō somewhat comically. Ryan appears to have felt uncomfortable with this prominent narrator and has omitted some of the above passage from his translation. The paragraph just cited contains the following:

> **宛も遠方から擦る眞似をされたやうに、思ひ切つては笑ふ事も出來ず、泣く事も出來ず、**快と不快との間に心を迷せながら、暫く縁側を往きつ戻りつしてゐた。

> [Now he did not know whether he should be happy or sad. **He could not decide whether to laugh or cry, as if he saw somebody pretending to tickle him from a distance.** For a while he was wandering about the open corridor with mixed feelings.]

Referring to the paragraph cited by Noguchi, Karatani also stresses that almost all the sentences end with the auxiliary verb "-ta":

> It was Futabatei Shimei who first used and fixed the auxiliary verb "-ta" in the narrative of Japanese novels. ..... Sentences ending with "-ta" do not necessarily denote only the past tense, but also identify the narrator with the main character's inner thoughts in a reflective narrative. The auxiliary verb "-ta" is essential to neutralize [the role of] the narrator. ..... "-Ta" eliminates the narrator who directly tells the story. It gives [a sense of] reality to novels. It also guarantees the flow of time in novels; incidents are seen retrospectively from a certain point in time. (Karatani 1992: 241-242)

Karatani's observations support the conclusion advanced in chapter one, that the novelty in Futabatei's translations of *The Rendezvous* and *Three Encounters* was the use of the auxiliary verb "-ta" to render the past tense of the Russian original, which led in turn to the use of "-ta" in *Floating Clouds* to eliminate the physical presence of the narrator.

Close examination of the use of the auxiliary verb "-ta" in *Floating Clouds* reveals that Futabatei started using it at a noticeably higher rate in Part Two (though not in Part Three). In Part One the auxiliary verb "-ta" is hardly used, and those few sentences in which it is used exemplify the colloquial style of the specific narrator employed in *Floating Clouds*. The following are examples of its use in Part One:

1. 一、誰れの望みも彼れの望みも一ツにからげて背負ツて立つ文三が（話を第一回に戻して）今日思懸けなくも……論旨免職となつた。(Futabatei Shimei 1964a: 24-25)

[And yet today (to return to the events related in the first chapter) Bunzō, upon whom everyone's expectations rested, has been asked to leave his post.] (Ryan 1967: 222 - modified[2])

2. 「エーくやしい。」
ト歯を喰切ツて口惜しがる。その顔を横眼でジロリと見たばかりで、お勢はすまアし切ツて座舗を立出でゝ仕舞ツた。(Futabatei Shimei 1964a: 45)

[She flings the long bamboo pipe she has been holding to the floor and grits her teeth in a paroxysm of fury. Osei gives her a sharp, sidelong glance and [the next instant] has calmly left the room.] (Ryan 1967: 243 - modified)

3. 一、氣に入り過ぎはしないかと岡焼をする者も有るが、正可四十面をさげて……お勢には……シツ跫音がする、昇ではないか……當ツた。(Futabatei Shimei 1964a: 49)

---

[2] Verb forms in this and later citations from Ryan have been modified to more closely reflect the forms of the original.

> [There are even some who, out of jealousy, think her perhaps too fond of him. But for a woman in her forties... For her lovely daughter Osei... hush, I can hear footsteps. Is that Noboru coming down? I have guessed correctly.] (Ryan 1967: 249 - modified)

These instances of the auxiliary verb "-ta" in the narrative of Part One seem to express the perfective aspect rather than the past tense. As Noguchi points out, the auxiliary verb "-ta", in its origin, has both perfective and past meanings. Neither Noguchi nor Karatani pay much attention to whether the auxiliary verb "-ta" expresses the perfective aspect or the past tense. However, this is a crucial issue, since the "-ta" which expresses the perfective aspect shows the narrator's presence in the story more clearly than that which expresses the past tense. It was the use of the auxiliary verb "-ta" to express the past tense in Part Two of *Floating Clouds* which allowed the hitherto prominent narrator to shift to the background:

> 跡で文三は暫らくの間また腕を拱んで黙想してゐたが、フト何歟憶出したやうな面相をして、起上ツて羽織だけを着替へて、帽子を片手に二階を降りた。
>
> 奥の間の障子を開けて見ると、果して昇が遊に來てゐた。加之も傲然と火鉢の側に大胡座をかいてゐた。その傍にお勢がベツタリ坐ツて、何かツベコベと端手なく囀ツてゐた。少年の議論家は素肌の上に上衣を羽織ツて、仔細らしく首を傾げて、ふかし甘薯の皮を剥いて居、お政は囂々敷針箱を前に控へて、覺束ない手振りでシヤツの綻を縫合はせてゐた。
>
> (Futabatei Shimei 1964a: 80)

> [For a few minutes Bunzō continued to sit in the same position, his arms folded. Suddenly struck with an idea, he rose, changed his *haori* [a short outer garment], and went down holding his hat in his hand.
>
> He slid open the door of the sitting room. There was Noboru, sitting cross-legged beside the *hibachi* [a charcoal heater]. Osei was sprawled beside him, chattering foolishly away. Our young dialectician was concentrating on peeling the skin from a steamed sweet potato, his head cocked to one side. He wore a coat with nothing underneath. Omasa was awkwardly stitching the torn shirt, the sewing box before her.] (Ryan 1967: 284)

The description made using the same auxiliary verb "-ta" in Part Two is very different from the above-mentioned examples from Part One and even from Part Three. This difference derives partly from the constant use of "-ta" in Part Two, and partly from the specific form "-te ita" in which "-ta" is used. This "-te ita" form is the past tense of the "-te iru" form, which was first clearly defined as an aspectual expression by the Japanese linguist Kindaichi Haruhiko.

## Recognition of Aspect in the Japanese Language

While aspectual expression in Japanese was first recognized in the "-te iru" form, it took a while for the "-ta" form to be recognized as an aspectual expression. Kindaichi Haruhiko (1950: 48-63) initially grouped Japanese verbs into four categories on the basis of whether they can be marked by "-te iru". The first group is named "stative", since this group of verbs cannot be used in "-te iru" form, and they describe a state independently. Verbs such as "aru [to be]", "dekiru [to be able to]", "wakaru [to understand]"[3], "yōsuru [to need]" and "ataisuru [to be worth]" belong to this group. The second group is made up of "durative" verbs which can be used in the "-te iru" form. When used in this form they indicate that the denoted action continues and has not yet finished. Almost all verbs which indicate human actions such as "yomu [to read]", "warau [to laugh]", "hataraku [to work]" and "kangaeru [to think]" fall into this group. Verbs which describe natural phenomena such as "chiru [to fall]", and "moeru [to burn]" also fall into this category. The third group is made up of "instantaneous" verbs. This group can combine with "-te iru" forms. They denote human actions or natural movements and are characterized by the fact that the action finishes instantly. The "-te iru" forms of these verbs show that the denoted events or actions have finished, but the state brought on by the action remains. Verbs such as "shinu [to die]", "kekkon-suru [to marry]", "sotsugyō-suru [to graduate]", and "shiru [to know]" belong to this group, as do verbs such as "(dentō ga) tsuku [(a light) turns on]", "sawaru [to touch]", and "todoku [to arrive]". The fourth and final category of verbs are those which are always used in "-te iru" forms unless placed in a subordinate clause, and they describe a state. Examples are "sobie-te iru [to tower]", "sugure-te iru [to excel]", and "ni-te iru [to be similar]". Kindaichi called this group simply the fourth category of verbs. In this system of classification he thus acknowledged "-te iru" as an aspectual expression, but not "-ta".

Kindaichi subsequently (1976) discussed the functions of the auxiliary verb "-ta" in his article "Nihongo dōshi no tensu to asupekuto [Tense and Aspect of Japanese Verbs]". He drew attention to Kazama's analysis of the following three aspectual forms:

1. The "-ta" form in the following sentence:
Kyō wa yuki ga fut-ta. [Today it snowed.]

2. The "-te iru" form in the following sentence:
Soto ni wa yuki ga tsumot-te iru. [The snow lies outside.]

3. The "-te shimau" form in the following sentence:
Yuki ga sukkari kie-te shimau. [The snow will melt completely.] (Kindaichi 1976: 29)

Kindaichi distinguished two functions of the auxiliary verb "-ta". One is to express the past tense, when "-ta" follows stative verbs, adjectives or the auxiliary verb "-da". The other is to express the perfect tense, when "-ta" follows action verbs such as "durative" and "instantaneous" verbs. "Durative" verbs such as "kaku [to write]" and "yomu [to read]", are temporarily used as "instantaneous" verbs when these verbs are followed by the auxiliary

[3] However, "wakaru" can be used with the "-te iru" form to describe the state of being clarified. Thus, Kindaichi's definition should be modified, to indicate that this first group of verbs may describe a state independently of the use of the "-te iru" form.

verb "-ta" to express the perfect tense. Interestingly, Kindaichi defined the two functions of "-ta" as those of the past and perfect tense, not as those of the past tense and perfective aspect. Thus Kindaichi did not yet see "-ta" as an aspectual form, suggesting that only "-te iru" and "-te shimau" are aspectual expressions.

Kindaichi defined the "-te shimau" form as an aspectual expression for describing actions. He distinguished the "-te shimau" form from the "-ta" form, which expresses the past and perfect tenses, and suggests that the "-te shimau" form expresses the completion of the action. It is an interesting notion that the "-te shimau" form has only perfective and imperfective forms, rather than past and non-past forms. According to Kindaichi's theory, the "-te shimau" form expresses the imperfective aspect, while the "-te shimatta" form expresses the perfective aspect. Apart from the "-te shimau" form, Kindaichi lists "-hajimeru [to start]" and "-tsuzukeru [to continue]", when used to form compound verbs such as "yomi-hajimeru [to start reading]" or "kaki-tsuzukeru [to continue writing]", as aspectual expressions in action.

In conclusion, Kindaichi defined tense and aspect as follows:

> Tense is a variation of forms which indicates that a state or an action expressed by a particular verb occurs before, at the same time or after a certain point in time. Each form of tense has a special meaning which is irreplaceable by other verbs.
>
> Aspect is a variation of forms which indicates different states in the process of the action expressed by a particular verb. Each form of aspect has a meaning which is replaceable by other verbs. (Kindaichi Haruhiko 1976: 60)

If we apply Kindaichi's theory to the passage cited from Part Two, we observe that it is written in past tense forms, since almost all the sentences are written in "-te ita" forms, which indicate a past state or past continuous actions, depending on whether they follow "instantaneous" or "durative" verbs. According to Kindaichi's theory the auxiliary verb "-ta" is defined as a past or perfect tense marker. Thus the "-ta" auxiliary verbs in the sentences cited from Part One of *Floating Clouds* and those in the passage cited from Part Two differ not in aspect but in tense. In the sentences cited from Part One the auxiliary verb "-ta" is seen to be a perfect tense marker, while in the passage cited from Part Two it is seen to be a past tense marker.

However, Kindaichi subsequently changed his position and acknowledged that the auxiliary verb "-ta" could carry the meaning of the perfective aspect. Referring to Teramura Hideo's description of the auxiliary verb "-ta" as a perfective aspectual marker, Kindaichi concedes that each "-ta" in the following two interrogative sentences expresses a different meaning:

1. Mō hirumeshi o tabeta ka? [Have you had lunch yet?]
2. Kinō hirumeshi o tabeta ka? [Did you have lunch yesterday?]

While the affirmative answers to these questions are the same—"tabeta [I have had/I did have]"—the negative answers are different:

1. Iya, (mada) tabe-te inai/tabe nai. [No, I have not had it yet.]
2. Iya, tabe nakatta. [No, I didn't have lunch.]

(Kindaichi Haruhiko 1988: 114-115)

According to Teramura, "-ta" in the first interrogative sentence expresses the perfective aspect, since the negative answer is marked by the "-te iru" form, and "-ta" in the second interrogative sentence expresses the past tense, since the negative answer is marked by "-ta". Teramura (1984:322) concludes that "the difference in "-ta" meanings is not only recognized by a grammarian, but is also understood between speaker and listener".

Teramura classifies predicates into three categories: verb, adjective and noun predicates. Verb predicates are further sub-divided into two: action and stative verb predicates. If the auxiliary verb "-ta" is used in action verb predicates such as "taberu [to eat]", "hajimaru [to start]" or " kuru [to come]", "-ta" expresses either the past tense or the perfective aspect. If "-ta" is used in stative verb predicates such as "iru [to be]" or "dekiru [to be able to]", or in adjective or noun predicates, it always expresses the past tense.

Teramura defines tense and aspect as follows:

> In the case of tense, the events are recognized as occurring at points in time, a judgement being made as to whether the events occur before or after the time of utterance.
>
> In the case of aspect, the events are recognized as a process in time and a judgement is made as to how the events are positioned in a certain time span. The perfective aspect is to express a certain point in the process. On the other hand, the imperfective aspect is to describe the event as a whole process. (Teramura 1984: 117-118)

Teramura then classifies aspectual expressions of Japanese into three groups. The first group is defined by the aspectual opposition "suru" [mizen/imperfective] versus "shita" [kinzen/ perfective]. The second aspectual group is made up of auxiliary verbs following after "-te" form verbs such as "-te iru", "-te shimau", "-te aru", "-te kuru" and so on. The third group is indicated by parts of compound verbs such as "yomi-hajimeru [to start reading]", "kaki-tsuzukeru [to continue writing]", and "tabe-oeru [to finish eating]".

It is interesting to note that those examples of "-ta" which Teramura indicates to be perfective aspect are all chosen from dialogue and that they were used in isolation:

1. Rōjin wa chikayotte kite, watashi no atama e te o yari, "Ōkiku natta" to itta.
   [The old man came up to me and said: "Gee you have grown."]

2. "Mō wakatta yo. Nanben kurikaeshitatte onaji koto da."
   ["I have understood it. It's the same thing even if you repeat it again and again."]

Commenting on dialogue cited from Shiga Naoya's novel *An'ya kōro [A Dark Night's Passing]*, Teramura asserts (1984: 119-120) that "-ta" in these sentences expresses the speaker's recognition of a current state or of the completion of an action.

Comrie (1976: 1-3) is another scholar to have offered an explanation of the difference between tense and aspect. He suggests that while tense indicates the time of a situation or event with reference to some other time, usually the moment of utterance, aspectual expressions indicate different ways of viewing the internal temporal constituency of a situation.

## Futabatei's Use of "-ta" Form Verbs

If we now apply Teramura's theory to the sentences cited from Part One of *Floating Clouds*, "-ta" in "ronshimenshoku to natta [has been asked to leave his post]", "tachi'idete shimatta [has left]" and "atatta [I have guessed correctly]", expresses the completion of the action. They are aspectual expressions, as they clearly show that they are the utterances of a specific narrator and they are employed in isolation amongst sentences ending in "-(r)u" form verbs. On the other hand, the passage cited from Part Two is mainly written in the "-te ita" form, which also expresses a state or the continuity of action (aspect), though the "-ta" within the "-te ita" form expresses not aspect, but the past tense. It may also be observed that the "-te ita" forms are used consistently. Thus, while Futabatei was writing Part Two of *Floating Clouds*, the meaning of the auxiliary verb "-ta" had shifted from an aspectual expression to a tense expression. As a result the specific narrator borrowed from the *gesaku* gradually shifted to the background of the novel.

It is here that we can see the impact of Futabatei's translation of Turgenev's two stories *The Rendezvous* and *Three Encounters,* generally supposed to have been carried out while Part Two of *Floating Clouds* was in progress. This impression is greatly reinforced by information supplied by Karatani Kōjin (1988: 60), who writes that Futabatei, dissatisfied with Part One of *Floating Clouds,* attempted to write Part Two in Russian, then translated it into Japanese. Karatani bases his assertion on the memoirs of Futabatei's best friend, Uchida Roan, entitled *Omoidasu hitobito [Those whom I Remember].* Roan, who with Futabatei's help translated Dostoevsky's *Crime and Punishment* from English, wrote:

> Aside from Part One of *Floating Clouds,* which was modified by Harunoya (Tsubouchi Shōyō), Futabatei in Part Two created a new style which is totally different from existing older styles. According to Futabatei's personal account, when Futabatei was stuck in writing chapters in Part Two, he first wrote them in Russian, then translated them into Japanese. ... Futabatei often told people that he copied Goncharov's style, but had failed to create a new style. This was his humble and at the same time complacent statement. (Cited in Usui Yoshimi (ed) 1980: 314)

So it seems reasonable to conclude that Futabatei developed a new narrative style by writing some chapters of Part Two in Russian, and that under the influence of his translation of Turgenev's stories, a new style emerged in which past tense forms dominated. We return, then, to the following question. When Futabatei retranslated the same two Turgenev stories, eliminating some of the "-ta" auxiliary verbs, what change was induced by this operation? Did the auxiliary verb "-ta" change its meaning in the second versions of the translations? Focusing on the meaning of the auxiliary verb "-ta", examining whether it expresses only the past tense or both past tense and perfective aspect, considering the use of other aspectual forms such as "-te iru" and "-te shimau", I shall compare the Russian originals with the two versions of Futabatei's translations of *Three Encounters.*

Russian has its own predominant system of verb aspect. Most Russian verbs have two aspects, imperfective and perfective. The imperfective focuses on an action in progress or denotes frequency of occurrence, whereas the perfective emphasizes successful completion and result. I shall trace how different aspectual forms were translated in each version of

Futabatei's translations. Then it will become clear what Futabatei was aiming for in each version. This approach will also contribute to a better understanding of the development of the so-called "Futabatei tone" or "Futabatei style", which many researchers have identified, though without clear definition or systematic analysis.

In comparing *A Chance Encounter* and *A Fortuitous Encounter* with Turgenev's original (*Three Encounters*), the first thing one notices is the different use of tenses in the three texts. The first paragraph of the Russian original is written using mixed tense forms, since this paragraph is a kind of prologue, in which the narrator (a sportsman) recalls the house where he met by chance a beautiful "stranger" (*neznakomka*) whom he had earlier encountered in Italy. The description of the house is followed by a description of an old emancipated serf, Luk'yanych, who is symbolically linked with the house, and with whom the narrator will have incoherent conversations twice during the story. Four sentences in the original text are written in the present tense, the other seven sentences in the past tense. However, in his first version, Futabatei employs the auxiliary verb "-ta" to convey the sense of the past tense all through the paragraph. In contrast, in the second version Futabatei employs mainly "-(r)u" forms, which are normally considered to express the present tense. Consider the following passage from the first paragraph, presented here in the three versions.

> От болота до Глинного не более двух верст; дорога идет всё лощиной, и только на половине пути приходится перебраться через небольшой холм. На вершине этого холма лежит усадьба, состоящая из одного необитаемого господского домика и сада. Мне почти всегда случалось проходить мимо нее в самый разгар вечерней зари, и, помнится, всякий раз этот дом, со своими наглухо заколоченными окнами, представлялся мне слепым стариком, вышедшим погреться на солнце. Сидит он, сердечный, близ дороги; солнечный блеск давно сменился для него вечной мглою; но он чувствует его, по крайней мере на приподнятом и вытянутом лице, на согретых щеках. (Turgenev 1963b: 233-234)
>
> [From the swamp to Glinnoe is not more than two versts; the road follows a hollow all the way, and only at the half way point is it necessary to climb over a small hill. On the crest of this hill lies a country estate, consisting of one uninhabited manor-house and a garden. I nearly always happened to pass it at the glorious climax of the sunset, and, I remember, each time this house, with its tightly nailed-up windows, reminded me of a blind old man who has come out to warm himself in the sun. He sits, a warm-hearted old fellow, near the road; for him the sunshine has long since given way to eternal darkness; but he feels it at least on his uplifted and outstretched face, on his warmed cheeks.]
>
> First version (*A Chance Encounter*)
>
> 沼から「グリンノエ」までは道程(みちのり)凡そ二露里計り總て中凹(なかくぼ)の道で、只中ごろで大きくも無いが丘を一ツ踰(こ)さなければならなかツた。此丘の頂に一構(ひとかまへ)の莊館(やしき)、と云ツた所が住み棄てた母屋(おもや)一棟と園一區の他何も無かツたが、それが有ツた。自分が此莊館の側(わき)を通るは大抵ゆふやけの眞熾(まつさか)りの

頃で有ツたが、今でも憶ひ出す、いつも此家の窓をぴツたり釘付けにした所が日向ぼこりに出た盲目の老人のやうに思はれた、老人むツと面して路傍に坐つてゐた。此人の爲めには常闇の日の光に代ツてから（久敷窓を閉ぢてゐたからで）もウ餘程になるが、それでもまだ少くも（at least）擡げて延伸ばしてゐた面と温めてゐた頰とだけには日光を受けてゐた。(Futabatei Shimei 1964a: 172-173)

[From the swamp to 'Glinnoe' was about two versts; the road followed a hollow, and only at the half way point did I have to climb over a hill—and not a big one. On top of this hill there was a country estate, which consisted of nothing more than one uninhabited manor-house and a garden. I almost always passed by this estate at the height of the evening glow, and, as I remember, each time this house, with its tightly nailed-up windows reminded me of a blind old man who had gone out to warm himself in the sun; he sat angrily near the road. For him the sunshine had long since given way to eternal darkness (as the windows had been shut for a long time), but he received the sunshine at least on his uplifted and outstretched face and on his warmed cheeks.]

Second version (*A Fortuitous Encounter*)

沼からグリンノエまでは半里計もあらうか、總て中凹の道だが、唯中ごろで小さな丘を一つ踰さなければならぬ。此丘の上に一構の邸、といつた所が、住棄てた母屋一棟と園の外何もないが、邸がある。その側を通るのは大抵夕榮の熾の頃であつたが、今でも憶出す、いつも此家の窓をぴつたり釘附にした所は盲目の老人が日向ぼこりでもしてゐるやうに見える。老人さも信切さうな面をして路傍に蹲踞むでゐる、此人のためには日の光が常闇に代つてから最う久しくなるが、流石に未だぐいと擡げた面と暖かさうな頰とだけには日光を受けてゐる。(Futabatei Shimei 1964a: 270)

[From the swamp to Glinnoe would be about half a *ri*[4], the road follows a hollow, and only at the half way point is it necessary to climb over a small hill. There is a country estate, which consists of nothing more than one uninhabited manor-house and a garden. I almost always passed by this estate at the height of the evening glow, and, I remember, this house, with its tightly nailed-up windows, always looks like a blind old man who is warming himself in the sun. He squats cordially near the road; for him the sunshine has long given way to eternal darkness; he still receives the sunshine at least on his uplifted face and his seemingly warm cheeks.]

Both versions demonstrate Futabatei's "faithfulness" to the original. Especially in the first

[4] The *ri* is an old Japanese unit of distance, equivalent to 3.9273 kilometres.

version, Futabatei makes every effort to be precise by providing commentaries or sometimes English translations. In consequence both versions are quite similar, except for the verb forms.

In the first version, Futabatei employs the auxiliary verb "-ta" for almost all predicates in the text, regardless of their tense form in the Russian original. Presumably Futabatei did this to maintain consistency with the rest of the passage, where he constantly used the auxiliary verb "-ta" to translate the past tense verbs of the original. In the second version, however, Futabatei employs mainly "-(r)u" forms. He initially uses these to translate the present tense verbs of the original, then continues to use "-(r)u" forms to the end of the paragraph, regardless of the tense form of the verbs in the original.

From the aspectual point of view, attention must be drawn to the "-te iru" forms which appear in the second version. "Shagande iru [(he) squats]" and "hikari o ukete iru [(he) receives the sunshine]" are the translations for "sidit (on) [he sits]" and "on chuvstvuet ego [he feels it]" in the original. Here both Russian verbs are imperfective (present tense). These two imperfective Russian verbs are used to express the idea of continuity. The old house is personified and its state is likened to an old man's quiet actions. This description straight away merges with that of the old emancipated serf Luk'yanych. Using the Japanese aspectual expression "-te iru", Futabatei precisely renders the aspectual expressions in the Russian original. The Japanese verbs "shagamu [to squat]" and "ukeru [to receive]" are "instantaneous" verbs, so the "-te iru" forms of these verbs express a state.

Interestingly, in the first version Futabatei translated these two verbs into "-te ita" forms, that is, the past tense of the "-te iru" form, in spite of the present tense forms of the original. What is more, when Futabatei retranslated, he changed the verb forms from "-te ita" to "-te iru" throughout the remainder of the first paragraph (which extends beyond the passage cited above). "Sumatte ita [lived]" and "to yū koto dake de atta [All I heard from him was that]" in the first version, are changed to "sumatte iru [lives]" and "to itte iru [is saying]" in the second version. The equivalent Russian words in the original are "pomeshchalsya [was located]" and "ya tol'ko uznal ot nego, chto [all I learnt from him was that]". While "pomeshchat'sya [to be located]" is imperfective, "uznat' [to find out]" is a perfective verb. Both verbs are used by Turgenev in the past tense. In the second version Futabatei translates "ya tol'ko uznal ot nego, chto" freely, and uses the aspectual expression "itte iru" to describe the old man's action graphically. In so doing, Futabatei aimed to make the whole first paragraph, which describes the old house where the sportsman narrator is to meet the beautiful stranger, more vivid.

It may also be observed that the auxiliary verb "-ta", used throughout the first paragraph of the first version, expresses the past tense rather than the perfective aspect, as there are no instances of it following an action verb. In the second version too, the only instance of the auxiliary verb "-ta", which occurs in the opening sentence of the first paragraph, expresses past tense rather than perfective aspect. It is used to express past habit:

> Никуда я, бывало, не ездил так часто на охоту в течение лета, как в село Глинное, лежащее в двадцати верстах от моей деревни. (Turgenev 1963b: 233)
>
> [There was nowhere I would go so often to hunt during the summer as the village of Glinnoe, which was some twenty kilometres from my own estate.]

First version (*A Chance Encounter*)

何處へと云ツて夏の中は「グリンノエ」村へほどよく遊獵に往ツた所はなかツた、自分の荘園(しやうゑん)から二十露里計(ばかり)の所に有る（「グリンノエ」村へほど）。(Futabatei Shimei 1964a: 172)

[There was nowhere I would go so often to hunt during the summer as the village of Glinnoe. (Glinnoe) was some twenty kilometres from my own estate.]

Second version (*A Fortuitous Encounter*)

自分の持村(もちむら)から五里ばかりの處にグリンノエといふ村が有つたが、夏の中は屡(よ)く此村へ遊獵に往(い)つた。(Futabatei Shimei 1964a: 270)

[There was a village called Glinnoe, which was twenty kilometres away from my own estate. I often went there to hunt during the summer time.]

The first version demonstrates the rigorous faithfulness Futabatei applied in his translations. Although Futabatei significantly changes the sentence structure in the second version, he retains the auxiliary verb "-ta", which expresses the past tense. In the second version, once the paragraph has opened, Futabatei shifts the verb form from "-ta" to "-(r)u", describing the old house and the old man by employing the aspectual form "-te iru", which at first precisely renders the imperfective aspect of the original. He then keeps using the present aspectual form "-te iru" regardless of the tense form of the original, in order to make the description vivid and immediate. This turned out to be the most effective way to eliminate the awkward repetition of "-ta" auxiliary verbs found in the first version. In the first paragraph of *A Fortuitous Encounter*, then, Futabatei eliminated many instances of "-ta" as a past tense marker, but retained and extended the use of the aspectual expression "-te iru".

## Futabatei's Translation of Past Imperfective and Past Perfective Verbs

Did Futabatei sustain this pattern of use in the remainder of *A Fortuitous Encounter*? Let us now examine the passage where the narrator recalls his first encounter with the beautiful stranger:

Я нагнулся через плетень: передо мной красный полевой мак поднимал из заглохшей травы свой прямой стебелек; большая круглая капля ночной росы блестела темным блеском на дне раскрытого цветка. Всё дремало, всё нежилось вокруг; всё как будто глядело вверх, вытянувшись, не шевелясь и выжидая... Чего ждала эта теплая, **эта незаснувшая ночь**?

Звука ждала она; живого голоса ждала эта чуткая тишина—но всё молчало. (Turgenev 1963b: 235)

[I bent over the wattle fence; in front of me a red field poppy lifted up its straight stem from the wild grass; a big round drop of evening dew glittered with a dark lustre at the bottom of the open flower. Everything was slumbering, everything nearby lay luxuriously; and it seemed as if everything was gazing upwards, stretching out motionless and waiting expectantly ... For what was **this warm and sleepless night** waiting?

It was waiting for a sound; a living voice was what this sensitive quietness was waiting for—but everything was silent.]

First version (*A Chance Encounter*)

および腰になつて垣の内を窺いて見ると、つひ鼻の端に眞紅な野罌粟がこんもり生え茂ツてゐたが、そのぱツと開いた花の底に夜露の圓い大きな玉が薄暗く光ツてゐた。何も角もうつらうつらとしてゐた、何も角も四邊の物はだらりとして鎔けてゐた（注、省略）何も角も宛然虚空を視詰めてゐるやうで有ツた、延び上ツて、身動きもせずに、何をか待ちながら……何を待ちわびてゐた**この煖かなこの眠入りもせぬ夜は？**

響きを待てゐた、生物の聲をこの耳敏い靜かさは（トいふは余り靜かなのでチョイと物音がしても耳立ツて聞えるからで）待ツてゐた—何も角も皆黙然としてゐた。(Futabatei Shimei 1964a: 174-175)

[With my back bent I peeped through the fence; under my very nose pure red field poppies were growing thickly, at the bottom of a fully open flower a big round drop of evening dew was shining darkly. Everything was slumbering, everything nearby was melting languidly [long commentary]. It looked as if everything was gazing at the sky, stretched out, not moving, and waiting for something. What was **this warm and awake night** longing for?

It was waiting for a sound, a living voice was what this keen silence (for it is so quiet that even a small sound becomes a big noise) was waiting for—everything remained silent.]

Second version (*A Fortuitous Encounter*)

垣の内を覗いて見ると、つい鼻の頭に眞紅な野罌粟の莖が草叢の中からすつと出てゐて、そのぱつと咲いた花の底には大粒の圓い夜露が薄光りに光つてゐる。何も彼も恍惚としてだらけて、宛然延上つて、身動をもせずに、何をか待ちながら、空を向上げてゐるやうである……**此生暖な夜に眠入もせず**何を待つてゐるのであらう？

物音を待つてゐるのである、靜まり返つて耳を澄まして生物の聲のするのを待つてゐるのである—けれども、ごそとも云はない。(Futabatei Shimei 1964a: 272)

[I peep through the fence; under my very nose there is a pure red field poppy, its stem protruding from the grass; at the bottom of its fully open flower a big round drop of evening dew is shining darkly. Everything is enraptured and lies languidly. It seems as if everything is stretched out, not moving, but waiting for something, and gazing at the sky. **On this warm night, being awake**, what is [everything] waiting for?

It is waiting for a sound. Being still and alert it is waiting for a living voice—but no sound is heard.]

This passage is part of a description of a garden into which the narrator has strayed, and from which he watches the window where he will see his beautiful stranger. In the first version Futabatei clearly adopted a foreignizing strategy. The number, kind and position of the punctuation marks are all reproduced faithfully. Even the word order is reproduced to the extent that Japanese syntax will allow. As a result, Futabatei employs an inanimate subject in the first version. He also adds lengthy commentaries to explain words which would be hard for his readers to understand.

As for the verb forms, we notice that Futabatei employs the "-te ita" form for almost all verbs in the first version, whereas in the second version the "-te iru" form is used for almost all verbs. When we refer back to the Russian original, we notice that all verbs except for the first one are imperfective verbs used in the past tense. Table 1 shows all the verbs in the original and Futabatei's translations for these verbs:

***Table 1 : A comparison of Futabatei's translations of past imperfective verbs***

| *Three Encounters* | *A Chance Encounter* | *A Fortuitous Encounter* |
|---|---|---|
| nagnulsya (perf)<br>[bent over] | nozoite miru to, | nozoite miru to, |
| podnimal (imp)<br>[lifted up] | haeshigette ita ga, | sutto dete ite, |
| blestela (imp)<br>[glittered] | hikatte ita. | hikatte iru. |
| dremalo (imp)<br>[was slumbering] | utsurautsurato shite ita, | }<br>}uttorito shite darakete,<br>}<br>} |
| nezhilos' (imp)<br>[lay luxuriously] | dararito shite tokete ita | |
| glyadelo (imp)<br>[gazed] | mitsumete iru yō de atta, | miagete iru yō de aru.... |
| zhdala (imp)<br>[was waiting] | machiwabite ita<br>mate ita,<br>matte ita— | matte iru no de arō?<br>matte iru no de aru;<br>matte iru no de aru— |
| molchalo (imp)<br>[remained silent] | mokuzento shite ita. | goso to mo iwanai. |

All imperfective verbs in the past tense form are meticulously rendered in the first version by employing the "-te ita" form, which expresses either a continuous action or a state. In the second version Futabatei changed the tense form from past to present in order to eliminate "-ta", but kept the aspectual expression to render the idea of continuity. Because of the new sentence ending "-no de aru", the second version is more explanatory, while at the same time more visual and distinct. The descriptions employing the aspectual expressions "-te ita" (in the first version) and "-te iru" (in the second version) are the most distinctive characteristics in this scene where the narrator is about to encounter the beautiful stranger.

Sugiyama Yasuhiko (1968: 39-42) points out that in Futabatei's translations (especially in the first version, *A Chance Encounter*) nature is personified and becomes independent from human beings, even at times hostile to them. Unlike earlier descriptions of nature in Japanese literature, in Futabatei's translations there was a tension between nature and the narrator-protagonist. This personification is effected by employing the aspectual forms "-te ita" or "-te iru", which render the imperfective verbs of the original. The following are more examples of the use of the "-te ita/-te iru" forms from the description of the garden in Futabatei's first and second versions:

1. ...разбитый по-старинному, он состоял из одной продолговатой поляны. (Turgenev 1963b: 234)

[...laid out in the old-fashioned style, it consisted of a rather long clearing.]

園は古風な作りざまで細長い一區(ひとしきり)の地（field)が出來てゐた。／園の作様(つくりざま)は昔風で、細長い芝生一區(ひとしきり)で出來てゐる。(Futabatei Shimei 1964a: 173-174/271)

[The garden was made in the old fashioned style and it consisted of a long and narrow green sward./The garden is made in the old fashioned style and it consists of a long and narrow green sward.]

2. ...высокие липы окружали ее ровной каймой. (Turgenev 1963b: 234)

[...tall lime trees surrounded it in an even border.]

それを菩醍樹が高低なしに縁(へり)めかして取巻いてゐた。／周圍(ぐるり)は高い菩醍樹が並び善く縁を取つてゐる。(Futabatei Shimei 1964a: 174/271)

[Lime trees surrounded it evenly like a border./ Tall lime trees rim its border evenly.]

3. ...и сквозь отверстие виднелась часть низенького дома с двумя, к удивлению моему, освещенными окнами. (Turgenev 1963b: 234)

[...and through an opening could be seen part of a low house with, to my surprise, two illuminated windows.]

其の隙間から低い家居の一部分が見えたが、不思議や今宵は窓二つとも燈(あか)

> 火が射してゐて。／その間隙から低い棟の家が僅か見透されたが、不思議な事も有れば有るもので、今夜は窓二ツとも燈火が射してゐる。(Futabatei Shimei 1964a: 174/271)
>
> [...through the opening, part of a low house was seen. To my surprise, tonight both windows were shining with light. /...through the opening, part of a low house is seen. To my surprise, tonight both windows are shining with light.]
>
> 4. ...перед каждой яблоней лежала на белеющей траве ее слабая пестрая тень. (Turgenev 1963b: 235)
>
> [...before each apple tree its faint motley shadow lay on the whitish grass.]
>
> 林檎の木の前にはその薄い影が白むだ（露に濡れ又日に照されて）草の上をまだらに這ツてゐた。／樹の根方には其影が白ぽい草を薄く斑に染めてゐる。(Futabatei Shimei 1964a: 174/271)
>
> [...before the apple trees their faint shadows were creeping variegatedly on the whitish (wet with dew and illuminated by the sun) grass. / ...near the tree roots their shadows dye the whitish grass slightly and variegatedly.]

What we can observe from these examples is that Futabatei rendered Russian imperfective verbs as "-te ita" forms in the first version, whereas they were rendered as "-te iru" forms in the second version. Moreover, in the first version "-te ita" forms at first describe a state ("dekite ita [consisted]"), then gradually are used to depict actions ("torimaite ita [surrounded]" and "hatte ita [were creeping]"). Applying Kindaichi's classification of verbs "dekiru [to be made]" is an "instantaneous" verb, whereas "hau [to creep]" is "durative". "Torimaku [to surround]" can be classified as either instantaneous or durative. Thus when Futabatei first translated *Three Encounters* he was aware of both the tense and aspect of verbs. Futabatei also sensed the personification of nature in the original and he even accentuated it by choosing the words "hatte ita [were creeping]" for "lezhala [lay]". However, in the second version "dekite iru [consists]", "fuchi o totte iru [rim its border]" and "madara ni somete iru [dye variegatedly]" all describe a state, as all the verbs are instantaneous, and the personification is less noticeable. However, Futabatei was acutely aware of the effect created by the aspectual expression "-te iru", as shown clearly by example three. Here Futabatei even translated a modifier "s dvumya osveshchennymi oknami [with two illuminated windows]" as a sentence, "Kon'ya wa mado futatsu to mo akari ga sashite iru. [Tonight both windows are shining with light.]", employing the aspectual expression "-te iru".

When the garden description comes to an end, the personification becomes more obvious. Russian verbs employed to depict nature such as "dremalo [was slumbering]", "glyadelo [was gazing]", "zhdala [was waiting]", and "molchalo [remained silent]" are all imperfective verbs in the past tense form, used to personify nature in the original. In the first version Futabatei translated these verbs as "utsurautsurato shite ita [was slumbering]", "mitsume te iru (yō de atta) [(It seemed as if it) was gazing]", "machiwabite ita/matte ita [was longing for/was waiting for]" and "mokuzento shite ita [remained silent]", to depict continuous actions. All these verbs, with the exception of the last one, are the "-te ita" forms of durative verbs. In the second version Futabatei translated "dremalo" as "kōkotsuto shite (darakete) [is enraptured (and lies languidly)]". Although this translation does not show the aspectual expression clearly, the aspectual expression of the other two Russian verbs, "glyadelo [was looking]" and "zhidala [was waiting]" are rendered clearly as "miagete iru yō de aru [(It seems as if it) is gazing at]" and "matte iru no de aru [is waiting for]". The only difference between the two versions is in the tense form.

So, in the second version, Futabatei translated the description where the garden is personified by employing a present tense aspectual expression—the "-te iru" form. Did Futabatei make this change simply in order that the scene would be more clearly visualized? To answer this question, let us examine the following passage from the second version, which concludes the description of the garden:

Second version (*A Fortuitous Encounter*)

幸福を待つのでもなく、憶出したのでもなく、何とも口には言はれぬ心地に萎されて、身動きをもせずに、この月に照され、露に濡れて、寂寞としてゐる園の前に佇立むだまま、黯淡い中にうす赤く見える二ツの窓を、如何いふ積りか、傍眼も觸らず諦視めてゐると、ふと家の内で鳴物の調子を諧せる音がした一音がして、浪のやうにうねりを打つて響き渡ると……空氣は焦心て響き反へす……自分は我知らず慄然とした。
鳴物の音に續いて女の聲で歌を唱ひだした。一心に聽入ると……や、驚くまい事か……二年前に伊太利のソルレントで此歌も此聲も聞いた事がある……それそれ…… (Futabatei Shimei 1964a: 272-273)

[Neither waiting for happiness, nor remembering it, but tearing my heart with inexplicable feelings, I am standing, without moving, in front of the garden, which is lit by the moonlight, wet with dew, and still. Without knowing why, I keep my eyes riveted on the two windows silhouetted pale red in the darkness, when suddenly a chord is [has been] heard in the house,—it sounds and resounds like a wave. The air resounds as if it is irritated... I have shivered involuntarily.

Following the chord a song has begun in a woman's voice. When I listen to it with all my heart ... To my surprise... [I realize that] Two years ago in Italy, in Sorrento, I have heard this same song and this same voice... Yes, yes...]

The narrator's attention turns from the garden which he was describing to himself, as he observes it. The description of the narrator himself is still made by employing the "-te iru" form, and soon afterwards three "-ta" auxiliary verbs are used: "narimono no chōshi o awaseru oto ga shita [a chord is heard]", "jibun wa wareshira zu buruburuto shita [I have shivered involuntarily]" and "onna no koe de uta o utai dashita [a song has begun in a woman's voice]". Do these "-ta" auxiliary verbs convey the meaning of the past tense or the perfective aspect? Compare them with the "-ta" auxiliary verbs used in the first version:

First version (*A Chance Encounter*)

待ちわびるでもなく、又昔しの仕合を憶ひ出すでもなく、何とも言へぬ感情に胸を悩まされて、自分は肯て身動をもせず、此月の光と露とを浴びた寂然な（直譯は動かぬ）園の前に立在んで、どういふ積りか、只管やさしい(soft)うすくらがり (half-shade)の中にほの赤く見える夫の二ツの窓を視詰めてゐるとふと家内にaccord(調子を諧はせる音）が響いた……
焦心ツたやうに鳴り渡ツて空氣は反響を響きかへした……自分は我知らずぶるぶるとした。
Accordに續いて婦人の聲が響いた……自分は一心に聞入ツ—て……びツくりした（直譯は驚きは口で云はれやうか　といふのだが是れでは原文の語氣がでませんから余義なく意譯しました）……二年前伊太利で「ソルレント」でこの歌を聞いた、この聲を……さうさう…… (Futabatei Shimei 1964a: 175)

[Neither waiting for something, nor remembering past happiness, but tearing my heart with inexplicable feelings, I was standing, without moving, in front of the still garden drenched with the moonlight and the dew, and, without knowing why, I was staring at the two windows, silhouetted pale red in the soft half darkness, when suddenly in the house a chord resounded. ... It resounded as if with irritation, and the air echoed to it. I shivered involuntarily.

Following the chord, a woman's voice was heard.... When I listened to it with all my heart ... I was surprised (although the literal translation is 'how can I express my amazement' I had to translate freely to convey the sense of the Russian original)... Two years ago in Italy, in Sorrento, I had heard that same song and that same voice ... Yes, yes...]

In the second version Futabatei eliminated most of the "-ta" auxiliary verbs and most of the description of the garden was made employing "-te iru" form verbs. Consequently, those "-ta" auxiliary verbs which remain— "oto ga shita", "buruburuto shita" and "utai dashita" (following the description of the garden)—seem to express not the past tense but the perfective aspect. Notably all these verbs are "instantaneous" verbs, which in combination with the auxiliary verb "-ta" express the perfective aspect. According to Teramura, "-dasu" in "utai dashita" is also an aspectual expression used to depict the beginning of an action. So these three verb forms convey a sense of aspect very clearly. However, in the first version, although the corresponding translations are very similar— "*accord* ga hibīta", "buruburuto shita" and "fujin no koe ga hibīta"—the aspectual sense is less noticeable, since all the preceding description of the garden is made employing "-te ita" forms.

We may therefore conclude that Futabatei changed the tense form from past to present in the case of imperfective verbs in order to create a contrast which emphasized the aspectual function of the auxiliary verb "-ta". This conclusion is supported by an examination of the Russian original:

> Сердце во мне томилось неизъяснимым чувством, похожим не то на ожиданье, не то на воспоминание счастия; я не смел шевельнуться, я стоял неподвижно пред этим неподвижным садом, облитым и лунным светом и росой, и, не знаю сам почему, неотступно глядел на те два окна, тускло красневшие в мягкой полутени, как вдруг раздался в доме аккорд,— раздался и прокатился волною... Раздражительно звонкий воздух отгрянул эхом... я невольно вздрогнул.
>
> Вслед за аккордом раздался женский голос... Я жадно стал вслушиваться— и ... могу ли выразить мое изумление?.. два года тому назад, в Италии, в Сорренто, слышал я ту же самую песню, тот же самый голос... Да, да... (Turgenev 1963b: 235-236)

> [My heart languished with an inexplicable feeling something like an expectation, something like a recollection of happiness; I dared not move, I stood motionless in front of this motionless garden, drenched in moonlight and by the dew, and, I know not why, gazed persistently at those two windows, showing dimly red in the soft half-light, when suddenly in the house a chord resounded,— resounded and rolled past like a wave... In agitation the resonant air echoed back... I shuddered involuntarily.
>
> After the chord a woman's voice resounded... I avidly began to listen to it—and... Can I express my amazement?.. Two years earlier in Italy, in Sorrento, I had heard the same song, and the very same voice... Yes, yes...]

The verbs in the Russian original which correspond to the three predicates in the second version with the auxiliary verb "-ta" ("oto ga shita", "buruburuto shita" and "utai dashita") are "razdalsya (akkord)", "vzdrognul" and "razdalsya (golos)", which are all perfective verbs. While imperfective verbs in Russian tend to describe actions in their progress and continuity, perfective verbs tend to emphasize result, and to advance the action in a narrative step by step. If we assume that Futabatei was more conscious of the aspect of the verbs he was translating than of their tense, then we can explain the existence of "-ta" auxiliary verbs in the above passage very well. It would be interesting to find more evidence in the second version of a correspondence between "-ta" auxiliary verbs and perfective aspect. It seems to suggest a form of influence or pressure being exerted by the Russian language upon Futabatei's Japanese style. If we can find more evidence of a correspondence between the use of the auxiliary verb "-ta" and the perfective aspect, and also between the "-te iru" form and the imperfective aspect, then we may conclude that even in the second version Futabatei can be said to have adopted a foreignizing strategy, where the tension between the Russian original and the Japanese language led to the creation of a new narrative style.

For now we may simply observe that at the end of the garden description Futabatei appears to use "-ta" forms to convey the sense of the perfective aspect of Russian verbs. In the personified description of the garden the form "-te iru" is used to convey the sense of the imperfective aspect. To see how consistently Futabatei adopts this practice we need to examine more text, and especially those passages where Turgenev employs perfective verbs.

Wade (1992: 286) refers to an interesting instance of perfective usage in Russian called the "pure-perfect", which describes a present state resulting from past action. Examples of the pure perfect are "On opozdal [He is late = He has arrived late]" and "Ya privyk k etomu [I am accustomed to this = I have become used to this]". Futabatei's use of "-ta" forms in a text dominated by "-(r)u" forms may be interpreted as a manifestation of pure perfect in

Japanese, as an attempt to describe a present state by reference to immediate past action.

Let us now turn to a second passage, where Turgenev uses many perfective verbs to advance the action of the story step by step. Let us see which verb forms Futabatei uses in his translation:

> Наконец, раздались в отдалении шаги... они приблизились; мужчина такого же почти роста, как я, показался на конце улицы, быстро подошел к калитке подле самого павильона, которой я прежде не заметил, стукнул, не оглядываясь, два раза железным ее кольцом, подождал, стукнул опять и запел вполголоса: «Ecco ridente...» Калитка отворилась... он без шуму скользнул в нее. (Turgenev 1963b: 237-238)
>
> [At last, footsteps sounded out at a distance... they came closer; a man almost the same height as me appeared at the end of the street, quickly came up to a gate that I had not noticed before, beside that very pavilion, and without looking around, knocked twice with its iron ring, waited, knocked again and started singing in an undertone "Ecco ridente..." The gate opened... he slipped through it without a sound.]
>
> First version (*A Chance Encounter*)
>
> 彼是する内に遠方で人の足音が響いた……近いた、殆ど自分程の背恰好の男が町盡頭に現はれて、以前自分の認めて置いた觀樓の傍の角門まで足疾やに來て、いきなり（直譯すれば四邊を視まはしもせずに）その鐵輪（おそらくは引手の）を二度突き鳴らして、待ツて見て、また鳴らして、そして小聲で"Ecco ridente……"と唱ひだした。角門が開いた……男は音をもさせずに内へ滑り入ツてしまツた。(Futabatei Shimei 1964a: 177)
>
> [In the meantime, footsteps were heard at a distance.... they came close; a man almost the same height as me appeared at the end of the street, he quickly came up to a gate beside the pavilion that I had noticed before, abruptly (literally, without looking around) he twice pushed and made a sound with a metal ring (probably a handle), waited, and rang it again, then started singing in an undertone "Ecco ridente...". The gate opened... the man slipped through it without making a noise.]
>
> Second version (*A Fortuitous Encounter*)
>
> 彼此する中に、遠方に人の足音がして……段々近寄る。只見れば、自分と殆ど同じ程の背格好の男が町盡頭に顯はれて、全然氣が付かなかつたが、觀樓の側に耳門があつた、その耳門まで急足に來て、卒然その鐵輪を二度程突鳴らして、待つてゐながら、小聲で"Ecco ridente"と唱ひ出すと、耳門が開く……男はすつと門内へ入つて了つた。(Futabatei Shimei 1964a: 274)

[In the meantime, footsteps are heard at a distance.... they gradually come close. I glance over, a man almost the same height as me has appeared, he quickly comes up to a gate, there was a gate beside the pavilion which I hadn't noticed at all, he abruptly pushes and makes a sound twice with its metal ring, while he is waiting he starts singing "Ecco ridente...", the gate opens... the man has slipped through it quietly.]

This is the scene where the narrator, after seeing the beautiful stranger, witnesses her meeting with her lover and experiences inexplicable anger. In the second version Futabatei changes two things. Firstly he eliminates some "-ta" auxiliary verbs by changing two verbs from the "-ta" form to the "-(r)u" form, though he leaves the final verb in the "-ta" form. Secondly he avoids the repetitive use of the "-te" form. In the Russian original, Turgenev describes the actions of a man supposed to be a lover of this mysterious and beautiful woman, advancing the action step by step with the use of perfective verbs of the past tense. As a result, the reader is able to visualize the sudden appearance of the man and his successive movements. In order to reproduce the rhythm of the original, in the first version Futabatei employs repetitive use of "-ta" forms and "-te" forms. Kindaichi Haruhiko (1988: 122) comments on this "-te" form. There is no suspensive form for the "-ta" auxiliary verb which expresses the past tense, but there used to be a suspensive form for that "-ta" auxiliary verb which expressed the perfective aspect and it was the "-te" form. Although Kindaichi notes that the "-te" form has lost the function of expressing the perfective aspect, Futabatei apparently employed it to translate some past perfective verbs. In the second version the particular, rather monotonous rhythm, which is created by the alternating sounds of the "-ta" and "-te" endings, is intentionally eliminated by substituting "-(r)u" forms and the particle "to [then]" for "-ta" forms, and the particle "nagara" [while] for "-te" forms.

The following passage from *The Rendezvous* has a similar staccato rhythm to that of the passage just cited:

Начал он ломаться, как только увидал молодую крестьянку, его ожидавшую; медленно, развалистым шагом подошел он к ней, постоял, подернул плечами, засунул обе руки в карманы пальто и, едва удостоив бедную девушку беглым и равнодушным взглядом, опустился на землю. (Turgenev 1963a: 263-264)

[He started putting on airs as soon as he saw the young peasant girl who had been waiting for him; he slowly walked up to her with big strides, stood for a while, stretched his shoulders, thrust both hands into the pockets of his coat and, scarcely favouring the poor girl with a fleeting and indifferent glance, sat down on the ground.]

Now consider Futabatei's translations in the two versions of *The Tryst*:

First version

待合せてゐた例の少女の姿を見た時から、モウ様子を賣り出して、ノソリノソリと大股にあるいて傍へ寄りて、立ち止ツて、肩をゆすツて、兩手を外套のかくしへ押し入れて、氣の無さゝうな眼を走らしてヂロリと少女の顏を見流して、そして下に居た。(Futabatei Shimei 1964a: 162)

> [As soon as he saw the girl who had been waiting for him, he started putting on airs, he slowly walked up to her with big strides, stopped, shook his shoulders, thrust both hands into the pockets of his coat, cast over the girl a fleeting and indifferent glance, and sat down.]

Second version

> 待合せてゐた少女を見るから、最う氣取り出して、のそりのそり大股に歩いて傍へ來て、立止ると、一寸肩を揺つて、兩手を外套の隱袋へ入れたが、氣の無さゝうにジロリと少女の面を視て、其處へ坐つた。(Futabatei Shimei 1964a: 307)

> [As soon as he sees the girl who has been waiting for him, he starts putting on airs, he slowly walks up to her with big strides, stops and slightly shakes his shoulders, thrusts both hands into the pockets of his coat and, giving the girl an indifferent glance, he has sat down there.]

In both *Three Encounters* and *The Rendezvous* Turgenev often employs a sequence of perfective verbs to describe the successive actions of the main characters. To reproduce the rhythm of the original, in the first version Futabatei uses "-te" forms. In the second version he again breaks the monotony of these verb forms by substituting the particles "ga" and "to" for some of the "-te" forms.

Ōta Hiroko reveals that the most frequently used *hiragana* in the first version of *The Tryst* is "ta" (308 instances), followed by "te" (282), then (in order of decreasing frequency) "no", "ni", "shi", "wo", "na", "ka", "ha" and "i". Ōta suggests (1997: 33-39) that the comparatively higher frequency of "ta" is easily explained by the common use of the past tense in story narrative, and that the most striking characteristic of the first version of *The Tryst* is the unusually high use of "te". From our observations it is clear that this high frequency of "te" results from repeated use of "-te" forms which are used to express the perfective aspect.

In relation to these "-te" forms, Yamamoto Masahide (1965: 500-501) points out the staccato rhythm created by the repetitive use of "-te" forms in Part Two of *Floating Clouds*. He cites the following passage from *Floating Clouds* Part Two as an example:

> お政は菊細工には甚だ冷淡なもので、唯「綺麗だことネー。」ト云ツてツラリと見亘すのみ、さして眼を注める様子もないが、その代り、お勢と同年配頃の娘に逢へば、叮嚀にその顏貌風姿を研窮する。まづ最初に容貌を視て、次に衣服を視て、帯を視て爪端を視て、行過ぎてからズーと後姿を一瞥して、また帯を視て髪を視て、其跡でチヨイとお勢を横目で視て、そして澄まして仕舞ふ。妙な癖も有れば有るもので。 (Futabatei Shimei 1964a: 60)

> [Omasa shows little interest in the displays they see. She looks them over casually, remarking occasionally on how nice they are, but actually pays little attention to them.

> On the other hand, she is very interested in making a careful examination of any girl Osei's age who comes by. She normally looks first at the girl's face, then looks at her clothes, looks at her *obi* [a belt], and looks on down to the tips of her toes. After the young lady has passed, Omasa turns her head and looks at the back of her *obi* and looks at her hair. Then she darts a quick sidelong glance at Osei, makes a rapid comparison, and concludes in her daughter's favour. A curious habit.] (Ryan 1967: 264 - modified)

Yamamoto comments that in Part Two of *Floating Clouds* Futabatei followed Goncharov's and Dostoevsky's models, and created an original *genbun itchi* style, raising it to a new level of literary respectability. He further suggests that what is transferred from Russian writing into Futabatei's writing is a characteristic rhythm, rather than any individual writer's style.

It would seem, from the observations made thus far in this chapter, that there is rather a close link between Futabatei's translations of Turgenev's stories and Part Two of *Floating Clouds*. We can see a clear resemblance between the passages from *Floating Clouds* cited by Yamamoto, and the passages that have been cited from Futabatei's earlier translations of *Three Encounters* and *The Rendezvous*. Saitō Ryoku'u, one of Futabatei's contemporaries, wrote the following parody of Futabatei's style:

> 「煙管を持つた煙草を丸めた鴈首へ入れた火をつけた吸つた煙を吹いた」
> (Saitō Ryoku'u 1990: 5)

> [He held a pipe. (He) rolled some tobacco. (He) filled his pipe with it. (He) lit it. He drew on it. (He) blew out some smoke.]

This could be rewritten as follows, placing emphasis in the use of "-te" forms:

> 「煙管を持つて、煙草を丸めて、鴈首へ入れて、火をつけて、吸つて、煙を吹いた。」

> [He held a pipe, rolled some tobacco, filled his pipe with it, lit it, drew on it, and blew out some smoke.]

or more precisely, by employing a more equal number of "-te" and "-ta" forms:

> 「煙管を持つた。煙草を丸めて、鴈首へ入れて、火をつけて、吸つた。煙を吹いた。」

> [He held a pipe. He rolled some tobacco, filled his pipe with it, lit it, drew on it. He blew out some smoke.]

Indeed, when we examine the text of *Floating Clouds* Part Two, we find this repetitive use of "-te" forms in every chapter (chapters 7 to 12), whereas in parts one and three it is hardly found at all. This is further evidence in support of my hypothesis that Futabatei worked on *A Chance Encounter* and *The Tryst* between working on Part One and Part Two of *Floating Clouds,* although Part Two was published earlier than these translations.

Let us now return to the issue of "-ta" auxiliary verbs and how Futabatei changed the verb forms which appear at the end of sentences in his second version of *Three Encounters (A Fortuitous Encounter).* Table 2 compares sentence endings and punctuation marks in the original and the two translations:

***Table 2 : A comparison of Futabatei's translations of past perfective verbs I***

| ***Three Encounters*** | ***A Chance Encounter*** | ***A Fortuitous Encounter*** |
|---|---|---|
| razdalis'...<br>[were heard] | hibīta... | ashioto ga shite... |
| priblizilis';<br>[came nearer] | chikazuita; | dandan chikayoru. |
| zapel.<br>[started singing] | utai dashita. | utai dasu to, |
| otvorilas' ...<br>[opened] | kuguri ga aita... | kuguri ga hiraku... |
| skol'znul.<br>[slipped] | suberi'itte shimatta. | haitte shimatta. |

In the first version Futabatei adopted a foreignizing strategy and rendered all five perfective Russian verbs (used before ellipses, semi-colons or full stops) as "-ta" forms. In the second version he substituted two "-(r)u" forms, one "-te" form (the suspensive form of "-ta") and one conjunction ("-to") for four of these "-ta" forms. For the final perfective Russian verb "skol'znul [slipped]" he employed the aspectual expression "-te shimatta" in both versions.

This "-te shimatta" form is a distinctive aspectual expression often encountered in Futabatei's translations. Kindaichi names this form "shūketsu tai [the completive form]" and defines it as depicting the completion of an action. He also points out that the "-te shimau" form has two different meanings depending on whether it follows after "durative" or "instantaneous" verbs. If it follows after "durative" verbs it expresses the completion of an action, as in "kaite shimau [to finish writing]" and "yonde shimau [to finish reading]". If the "-te shimau" form follows after "instantaneous" verbs it indicates that events and actions have truly occurred and often suggests a feeling of regret or disappointment. For example "shinde shimau" suggests feelings of sorrow that someone has died and we cannot have them back. Takahashi Tarō (1976: 131-132) points out that the "-te shimau" form is mainly used to express the realization of an action which is completed at the end of a process. When verbs of motion are used in this form, they generally express the realization of disappearance. Teramura suggests (1984: 152-156) that it is enough to understand this form to express or emphasize the completion of an action. However, we need to distinguish whether the "-te shimau" form is used to express a mental reaction to an action or merely the objective observation of it. If the "-te shimau" form is used to express a mental reaction to an action or event, it is normally associated with feelings of sorrow or regret. Thus the two translations of the final Russian verb in this passage, "suberi'itte shimatta" (*A Chance Encounter*) and "haitte shimatta" (*A Fortuitous Encounter*), can be understood either simply to express the completion or realization of the action of the man who is supposed to be the mysterious lady's lover, or to express the regret of the narrator who witnesses the "rendezvous".

Whereas in the description of the garden Futabatei consistently changes from "-te ita" forms to "-te iru" forms in order to render the aspectual sense of the Russian imperfective verbs, in the scene where the main characters' actions are recounted he substitutes a variety of forms. Some "-ta" forms are changed to "-(r)u" form, others to "-te" form, some are replaced with the particle "to" while the final verb is left in the "-te shimatta" form which depicts the completion of an action. It seems that in the second version Futabatei emphasized the aspectual meaning of the final verb. Teramura points out that we cannot judge whether a "-ta" form expresses the past tense or the perfective aspect without knowing the context. He gives an interesting example from conversational Japanese:

> Otaku no kaki no ki wa ōkiku nari mashita ka?
>
> [a. Did your persimmon tree grow tall?
> b. Has your persimmon tree grown tall?]
>
> a. Iya, ōkiku nari masendeshita.
>
> [No, it didn't grow tall.]
>
> b. Iya, mada amari ōkiku natte imasen.
>
> [No, it hasn't grown tall yet.] (Teramura 1984: 121)

Teramura suggests that the auxiliary verb "-ta" which appears in the interrogative sentence can be understood either to carry the meaning of the past tense or that of the perfective aspect. It depends on the present situation; whether the persimmon tree has stopped growing or not.

When we study the passages from *A Chance Encounter* and *A Fortuitous Encounter* cited above, we notice that all "-ta" auxiliary verbs in the first version carry the meaning of the 'past perfect tense' (according to Kindaichi's original theory) since all "-ta" auxiliary verbs follow "instantaneous" verbs. However, whether these "-ta" auxiliary verbs carry the meaning of perfective aspect or past tense is hard to judge, since the present situation is not given in the first version. In the second version, however, the meaning of the perfective aspect of the auxiliary verb "-ta" in the final verb "haitte shimatta [slipped]" is clearly shown. This is partly because the "-ta" appears in the "-te shimatta" form. It is also explained that the "-ta" auxiliary verb is employed only in the last sentence, and the two preceding sentences are written with "-(r)u" forms, which are generally considered to carry the meaning of the present tense ("dandan chikayoru" "kuguri ga hiraku"). This "-(r)u" form is defined as being in aspectual opposition to the "-ta" form by Teramura. Although Teramura calls the "-(r)u" form "mizen", which carries almost the same meaning as "imperfective", when we trace the change of verb forms in the second version Futabatei seems to use the "-(r)u" form as if to render the "future tense" of the perfective Russian verbs. Thus by changing some verb forms from the "-ta" form to the "-(r)u" form and by leaving the last verb in the "-te shimatta" form, Futabatei seems to emphasize the meaning of the perfective aspect, that is of the completion of the action. As a result the scene described in the second version becomes more vivid. The reader feels the presence of the on-the-scene commentator more intimately. The narrative style in the second version is noticeably similar to that of *Floating Clouds*. The differences between them are firstly, that the narrator in *A Fortuitous Encounter* is given a specific identity—he is a sportsman—and secondly that "-ta" auxiliary verbs are used consciously to convey the meaning of the perfective aspect. By eliminating some of the "-ta" auxiliary verbs, Futabatei emphasizes the perfective aspectual meaning of those which are left in the text.

There were two ways to eliminate some of the "-ta" auxiliary verbs used in *A Chance Encounter* to render Russian perfective verbs. One was to change the "-ta" form to the "-(r)u" form. The other was to change the punctuation. Although there are two sentences in each version of this passage, only the first version follows the sentence structure of the original faithfully. In the second version the symbol "、", which equates to a semi-colon, is changed to a full stop, and the full stop to a comma. How often and where does Futabatei change full stops to commas? Does he change full stops to commas where the main characters' actions are described, as we observed in the second passage? To clarify regularities in Futabatei's use of "-ta" auxiliary verbs and commas, Table 3 compares these features in the original and in the two translations of *Three Encounters*. The story is divided into ten sections, so that each section has a unity of context, and so that it may be easier to trace stylistic characteristics.

In Table 3 the total shows the number of full stops, that is, the number of sentences. The table also shows the number of "node" or "de" endings and noun endings, these being commonly found in the texts of *A Chance Encounter, A Fortuitous Encounter* and *Floating Clouds*. However, when "node" or "de" endings are used, it is still possible to judge whether the sentence is written with the auxiliary verb "-ta" or not. For example:

主人は村の差配人親切な男で有ツたので。

[as the master was the leader of the village and he was kind.]

と返答をした、のろのろと沈んだ調子で。

[he answered slowly and gloomily].

Therefore this number does not affect the number of "-ta" auxiliary verbs.

Finally, if the sentence is written with mixed tense forms, only the verb form which appears in the main clause is counted.

***Table 3 : A comparison of verb forms and sentence endings in Three Encounters, A Chance Encounter and A Fortuitous Encounter***

| **a) Prologue (p. 233, line 7 - p. 234, line 18)** | | | |
|---|---|---|---|
| | ***3 Encounters*** | ***Chance Encounter*** | ***Fortuitous Encounter*** |
| Present tense (Russian) /non "-ta" auxiliary verb (Japanese) | 4 | — | 10 |
| Past tense (Russian) / "-ta" auxiliary verbs (Japanese) | 7 | 11 | 1<br>(0 from past perfective) |
| Comma | — | — | — |
| Others | — | node (2)<br>de (1) | node (0)<br>de (2) |
| **Total** | **11** | **11** | **12** |
| **b) First and second meetings (p. 234, line 19 - p. 239, line 28)** | | | |
| | ***3 Encounters*** | ***Chance Encounter*** | ***Fortuitous Encounter*** |
| Present / non "-ta" | 2 | 5 | 42 |
| Past / "-ta" | 80 | 76 | 21<br>(16 from past perfective) |
| Comma | — | 1 | 17 |
| Others | — | node (1)<br>de (5) | node (1)<br>de (2) |
| **Total** | **82** | **82** | **64** |
| **c) Narrator's conversation with innkeeper; village head (p. 239, line 28 — p. 241, line 6)** | | | |
| | ***3 Encounters*** | ***Chance Encounter*** | ***Fortuitous Encounter*** |
| Present / non "-ta" | — | — | 3 |
| Past / "-ta" | 11 | 11 | 5<br>(5 from past perfective) |

| Comma | — | — | 3 |
|---|---|---|---|
| Others | — | — | — |
| **Total** | **11** | **11** | **7** |
| **d) Narrator's dream (p. 241, line 7 — p. 242, line 33)[5]** | | | |
| | ***3 Encounters*** | ***Chance Encounter*** | ***Fortuitous Encounter*** |
| Present / non "-ta" | 21 | 21 | 22 |
| Past / "-ta" | 4 | 4 | 4<br>(0 from past perfective) |
| Comma | — | — | 4 |
| Others | — | nomi (1) | — |
| **Total** | **25** | **25** | **26** |
| **e) Narrator's first conversation with Luk'yanych (p. 242, line 34 — p. 244, line 12)** | | | |
| | ***3 Encounters*** | ***Chance Encounter*** | ***Fortuitous Encounter*** |
| Present / non "-ta" | — | — | 4 |
| Past / "-ta" | 19 | 18 | 8<br>(7 from past perfective) |
| Comma | — | — | 6 |
| Others | — | de (2) | — |
| **Total** | **19** | **18** | **12** |
| **f) Narrator's encounter with the couple in the forest (p. 244, line 13 — p. 248, line 8)** | | | |

[5] Note: In this passage it is hard to distinguish narrative from the monologue, from the narrator's inner thoughts.

| | *3 Encounters* | *Chance Encounter* | *Fortuitous Encounter* |
|---|---|---|---|
| Present / non "-ta" | 8 | 9 | 29 |
| Past / "-ta" | 47 | 46 | 20<br>(17 from past perfective) |
| Comma | — | — | 6 |
| Others | — | node (4)<br>de (4) | de (2) |
| **Total** | **55** | **55** | **49** |
| **g) Narrator's second conversation with Luk'yanych (p. 248, line 9 — p. 252, line 10)** | | | |
| | *3 Encounters* | *Chance Encounter* | *Fortuitous Encounter* |
| Present / non "-ta" | — | — | 21 |
| Past / "-ta" | 63 | 60 | 18<br>(13 from past perfective) |
| Comma | — | 3 (、) | 24 |
| Others | | de (2) | de (3) |
| **Total** | **63** | **63** | **39** |
| **h) Narrator's conversation with Luk'yanych's nephew (p. 252, line 11 — p. 255, line 21)** | | | |
| | *3 Encounters* | *Chance Encounter* | *Fortuitous Encounter* |
| Present / non "-ta" | 1 | 1 | 7 |
| Past / "-ta" | 17 | 16 | 8<br>(6 from past perfective) |
| Comma | — | 1 (、) | 3 |
| Others | — | — | noun (1) |

| **Total** | **18** | **18** | **15** |
|---|---|---|---|
| **i) Narrator's conversation with Shlykova and her sister Pelageya Badaeva (p. 255, line 23 — p. 257, line 28)** | | | |
| | ***3 Encounters*** | ***Chance Encounter*** | ***Fortuitous Encounter*** |
| Present / non "-ta" | — | — | 8 |
| Past / "-ta" | 29 | 27 | 10 (8 from past perfective) |
| Comma | — | 1 (、) | 10 |
| Others | — | node (1) | — |
| **Total** | **29** | **28** | **18** |
| **j) Final meeting with mysterious woman and her encounter with her former lover (p. 257, line 29 — p. 263, line 40)** | | | |
| | ***3 Encounters*** | ***Chance Encounter*** | ***Fortuitous Encounter*** |
| Present / non "-ta" | 4 | 5 | 22 |
| Past / "-ta" | 80 | 77 | 28 (19 from past perfective) |
| Comma | — | 1 | 32 |
| Others | — | — | — |
| **Total** | **84** | **83** | **50** |

Studying these figures, we realize yet again how literal and faithful Futabatei was in the earlier version of his translation. If all "-ta" auxiliary verbs are taken to express the past tense, the verb tense and number of full stops in *A Chance Encounter* correspond very closely to those of the Russian original, except in the prologue. The exceptions are very few: six commas are substituted for full stops in the narrative of the conversation section, five of these commas being the open commas which were used to stand for semi-colons. Interestingly, the clauses where Futabatei employs these open commas all correspond to perfective verb clauses in the original.

In the second version Futabatei substitutes commas for full stops much more frequently than he does in the first version, not only before quoting the direct speech of the main characters (as he does in the first version), but also during the narrative when describing their actions. This is especially noticeable in the narrator's first and second meetings with the mysterious lady, in his second conversation with Luk'yanych, in his conversation with Shlykova and her sister Pelageya Badaeva, and in his last meeting with the mysterious lady (which consists mainly of dialogue). In these sections Futabatei often combines more than two sentences. In the following passage from the narrator's second conversation with Luk'yanych he combines four sentences:

—Извольте,— произнес он наконец.— Пожалуйте...
И он, нагнувшись, шагнул через порог калитки. Я отправился вслед за ним. Перейдя через небольшой дворик, мы взобрались на шаткие ступеньки крыльца. Старик толкнул дверь; в ней и замка не было: веревочка с узлом торчала из ключевой скважины... Мы вошли в дом. (Turgenev 1963b: 250)

[ "If you wish," he finally said. "Please…"
And, bending over, he stepped across the threshold of the gate. I set off after him. Passing through a small courtyard, we went up the shaky steps of the porch. The old man pushed the door; there was no lock for it: a string with a knot was sticking out from the key-hole ...We went into the house.]

First version (*A Chance Encounter*)

「よろしう御座りまする」と遂に云ツた。—かう來さツしやりませ。
といつて、屈んで、角門の閾を跨いだ。自分も續いて這入ツた。餘り廣くも無い庭を通過ぎて、共に露階のゆらゆらする（壞れかかツて）段を昇ツた。老人は戸を突き開けた、ガ戸には關鎖といふ物がなくて、唯圈に結んだ繩が鍵の孔から出てゐた……打連れて家の内へ這入ツた。(Futabatei Shimei 1964a: 191)

["All right," he finally said. "Please come in," he said, and, bending over, he stepped across the threshold of the gate. I went in after him. Passing through a rather small courtyard, we went up the shaky (half-broken) steps of the porch. The old man pushed the door open, there was no lock for it, a rope with a knot was sticking out from the key-hole... We went into the house together.]

Second version (*A Fortuitous Encounter*)

「よろしう御座りまする。入らつしやりませ。」
老爺が屈むで耳門の閾を跨いだから、跟に隋いて入つて、餘り廣くも無い玄關先を通つて、ゆらつく階を昇ると、老爺が戸を突開けたが、戸には錠前もなくて、唯繩を圈に結んだ奴が鍵の穴から出てゐる……そこで一所に内へ入つた。(Futabatei Shimei 1964a: 287-288)

["All right. Please come in."

The old man bends over and steps across the threshold of the gate, I follow him, and go through a small courtyard, then go up the wobbly stairs, the old man pushes the door open, there is no lock on the door, only a rope tied round is sticking out from the key-hole... The next moment we have gone through the door with him.]

Compared with the first version, in which Futabatei uses the same number of the punctuation marks and the same past tense (expressed by "-ta" auxiliary verbs) as in the original, the second version differs markedly from the original. Futabatei changes the number and the variety of punctuation marks, as well as the form of the verbs. In the first version the rhythm of the original, induced by the succession of perfective verbs, is reproduced by employing the repetitive use of "-ta" forms, which can be understood to express both past tense and perfective aspect. In the second version, Futabatei changed one of the "-ta" forms to the "-(r)u" form (significantly from the "-te ita" form to the "-te iru", the corresponding verb in the Russian original being of the imperfective aspect:

[tada wa ni musunda nawa ga kagi no ana kara dete ita.../ tada nawa o wa ni musunda yatsu ga kagi no ana kara dete iru.../ verevochka s uzlom torchala iz klyuchevoi skvazhiny.../ a rope with a knot was sticking out from the key-hole...]

The other six "-ta" forms which render Russian perfective verbs in the first version are modified in various ways in the second version. (See Table 4)

***Table 4 : A comparison of Futabatei's translations of past perfective verbs II***

| ***Three Encounters*** | ***A Chance Encounter*** | ***A Fortuitous Encounter*** |
|---|---|---|
| proiznes. [said] | to tsuini itta. | — |
| shagnul. [stepped] | (shiki'i o) mataida. | (shiki'i o) mataida kara, |
| otpravilsya. [set off] | (jibun mo tsuzuite) haitta. | (ato ni tsuite) haitte, |
| vzobralis'. [climbed] | (kizahashi o) nobotta. | (kizahashi o) noboru to, |
| tolknul; [pushed] | (to o) tsukiaketa, ga | (to o) tsukiateta ga, |
| voshli. [entered] | haitta. | haitta. |

The passage in the second version where we find four sentences are combined by the particles "kara", "te", "to" and "ga" is similar textually to the one of the passages cited earlier, which describes the advancing actions of the mysterious lady's lover. It seems that Futabatei tends to delete "-ta" auxiliary verbs by substituting commas for full stops in those passages where the actions of the main characters are described. However, here, as in the second passage, the last verb in the sequence is left in the "-ta" form. Thus the effect created by the alterations is similar to that in the second passage. The use of the "-te iru" form to describe action unfolding in the present accentuates the perfective aspectual meaning of the final "-ta" auxiliary verb "haitta" [entered]. As a result the scene is clearly visualized by the reader.

We may thus conclude that Futabatei's substitution of commas for full stops may be observed mainly where the advancing actions of the main characters are described, corresponding to the use of perfective verbs in the original. This substitution of commas for full stops is another way of eliminating the repetitiveness of the "-ta" auxiliary verbs, which can be understood to express either the past tense or the perfective aspect, and a variation on changing "-ta" forms directly into "-(r)u" forms.

If we examine the tables we notice that in the sections containing dialogue (c, e, g, h, i and j), non "-ta" endings (sixty-five instances), "-ta" endings (seventy-seven instances) and commas (seventy-eight instances) appear comparatively evenly in the second version. On the other hand, in those sections where the narrator's first and second meetings with the mysterious lady and his encounter with the couple in the forest are described (b and f), non "-ta" endings (seventy-one instances) appear much more frequently than "-ta" endings (forty-one instances) or commas (only twenty-three instances). This can be explained as follows. In the sections containing dialogue, in the Russian original the narrative is written mainly in the perfective aspect, since the narrative is devoted to describing the main characters' actions. In these sections Futabatei eliminates the repetitive use of "-ta" auxiliary verbs found in the first version mainly by substituting commas for full stops. In those sections where the narrator's meetings with the mysterious lady and her lover are described, the narrative is written mainly in the imperfective aspect in the Russian original, since much of the narrative is devoted to describing the scenery which forms a background for the action. Employing imperfective verbs, Turgenev describes first the garden, then the street in Italy, and finally the forest. Then he describes the mysterious lady in the garden, the same lady in the pavilion, and the couple riding together on horseback in the forest. In these descriptions of nature from the narrator's point of view Futabatei eliminates the repetitive use of "-ta" auxiliary verbs by changing them into "-(r)u" forms. More precisely, he changes "-te ita" forms into "-te iru" forms. Moreover, those "-ta" forms which remain in the second version closely correspond to the perfective verbs in the Russian original and seem to carry the sense of the perfective aspect rather than of the past tense.

When we examine all the "-ta" auxiliary verbs which remain in the second version we notice another interesting feature of their use. Amongst the "-ta" forms there are quite a few instances of the specific aspectual form "-te shimatta", which emphasizes the completion of an action. As mentioned before, this "-te shimatta" form is the past tense of the "-te shimau" form, which expresses either the completion or realization of an action, and if it expresses a mental reaction to an action or event, normally expresses feelings of sorrow or regret. Futabatei employs this form to finish each scene or episode in the story. For example, the scene of the narrator's first encounter with the mysterious woman ends with the phrase "Otoko wa sutto naka e haitte shimatta [The man has slipped through the gate without a sound/on bezshumu skol'znul v nee]". Then the narrator, who has witnessed the woman's lover going through the gate, leaves Sorrento angrily: "Sono ban...Sorurento o tatte shimatta [By evening I had left Sorrento/v tot zhe vecher uekhal iz Sorrento]". The scene of the second chance meeting with the woman finishes with the following words: "Uchi no akari wa hodonaku kiete shimatta [A few moments later the light in the house has been put out/i cherez neskol'ko mgnovenii ogon' pogas v dome]", and the narrator, who has been left alone, again witnesses the woman's lover, leaving the estate on horseback: "(otoko wa) sugu mori ni kakurete shimatta [in a moment he has disappeared beyond the forest/totchas zhe ischez za lesom]".

We may also note that each section with dialogue finishes with the same "-te shimatta" form:

*A Chance Encounter/ A Fortuitous Encounter/ Three Encounters*

koya e kaetta [I went back to the shed] / koya e kaette shimatta [I have gone back to the shed] / poshel v sarai [I went to the shed] (The conversation with the innkeeper)

(ginka wa) jibun no ashimoto ni fusatta [(the silver coin) fell near my feet] / (ginka wa) jibun no ashimoto de fusatte shimatta [(the silver coin) has fallen near my feet] / (serebryanaya) legla u moikh nog [(the silver coin) stopped at my feet] (The first conversation with Luk'yanych)

to o shimekitte shimatta [(he) has banged the door] / to o shimekitte shimatta [(he) has banged the door] / khlopnul dver'yu [(he) banged the door] (The second conversation with Luk'yanych)

tsuini jibun wa sono ba o satta [I finally left] / wakamono to wa tsuini wakarete shimatta ga [I finally have parted with the young man] / i ushel nakonets [and (I) finally left] (The conversation with Luk'yanych's nephew)

mamonaku jishite kaetta [in a few minutes (they) left] / mamonaku kaette shimatta [in a few minutes (they) have left] / cherez neskol'ko minut uekhali [after a few minutes they left] (The conversation with Shlykova and her sister)

hikuku kashira o sagete soko ni tachidomatte shimatta [I have bowed deeply and remained on the spot] / hikuku kashira o sagete, soko ni tachidomatte shimatta [I have bowed deeply and remained on the spot] /ya gluboko ei poklonilsya i ostalsya na meste [I bowed deeply to her and remained on the spot] (The last meeting with the mysterious woman)

In the first version, Futabatei translates these phrases by employing either the "-te shimatta" form or simply the "-ta" form. The first version lacks consistency in this regard. In the second version he consistently uses the "-te shimatta" form, and in each case this corresponds to a perfective verb in the Russian original. We gain the distinct impression that Futabatei was acutely aware of the aspect of these verbs and tried to convey the perfective aspect rather than the tense, indicating the completion of actions.

This "-te shimatta" form is often used to express the narrator's mental reaction to events. Unlike the narrator of *The Rendezvous,* in *Three Encounters* the narrator is deeply involved in the events, and he even feels inexplicable jealousy towards the mysterious lady's lover. Here, particularly in the second version, the "-te shimatta" form often expresses the narrator's regret or embarrassment, as by chance he witnesses secret meetings and becomes an investigator of baffling situations.

Let us finally turn to the scene of the narrator's encounter with the couple in the forest.

This scene opens with the following sentence:

> Я поднял его [черныша], положил в ягдташ, оглянулся—и, как пригвожденный, остался на месте... (Turgenev 1963b: 245)
>
> [I picked it up [the chernysh—a bird] and put it into my game bag, then looked around—and, spellbound, was riveted to the spot... ]

In both versions Futabatei translates this sentence employing the "-te shimatta" form, expressing the narrator's astonishment.

> First version (*A Chance Encounter*)
>
> 自分はそれを拾ひ上げて、鳥嚢（とりぶくろ）に納（い）れて、振反ツて顧（み）て—その儘、釘付けにされた者のやうに、其場に立縮（たちすく）むで仕舞ツた…… (Futabatei Shimei 1964a: 186)
>
> [I picked it up and put it into my game bag, then turned back—and was rooted to the spot, as if I had been riveted.]
>
> Second version (*A Fortuitous Encounter*)
>
> さてそのチョールヌイシを拾上げて、嚢（ふくろ）に納（い）れて、何心なく振返つて見ると其儘—釘付にされたといふ身で、其場に立ずくむで了つた…… (Futabatei Shimei 1964a: 283)
>
> [I picked up the chernysh and put it into my game bag, then turned back unintentionally—and was rooted to the spot, as if I had been riveted...]

As might be expected, the description of the couple is made employing "-(r)u" forms in the second version. More interestingly, this form is employed in the first version as well:

> Лес, в который я вошел, был очень част и глух, так что я с трудом добрался до места, где упала птица; но в недальнем расстоянии от меня извивалась тележная дорога, и по этой дороге ехали верхом, шагом и рядом, моя красавица и тот мужчина, который обогнал меня накануне; я его узнал по усам. Они ехали тихо, молча, держа друг друга за руку; их лошади чуть выступали, лениво покачиваясь с боку на бок и красиво вытянув длинные шеи. (Turgenev 1963b: 245-246)
>
> [The forest into which I entered, was very thick and dense, so that it was with difficulty that I reached the place where the bird had fallen; but a short distance from me there wound a cart track, and along this track there rode, in step and side by side, my beautiful lady and the man who had overtaken me the day before; I recognized him by his moustache. They were riding quietly, silently, holding each other by the hand; their horses were stepping out slightly, lazily rocking from side to side, their

long necks stretched out beautifully.]

First version (*A Chance Encounter*)

自分の駈入ツた林といふは極めて樹深くて寂然としてゐた、それゆゑ鳥の墜ちた處まで行着くすら容易な事では無かツた、が其所から些し離れて、車路がうねツてゐて、今其所を例の美婦人と前夜自分を乗越したアノ男が騎馬で、靜に、打連れて通ツてゆく、アノ男といふは髯で解ツた。兩人共靜に、嘿黙ツて手を取かはしながら行く、其乗てゐた馬は二頭とも長い領を麗はしく延ばして、だるさうにヨタヨタと歩いて行く。(Futabatei Shimei 1964a: 186-187)

[The forest into which I ran was so thick and quiet that it was not easy even to reach the place where the bird had fallen; but a short distance from it there was a cart-road winding out, and on this road that beautiful lady and the man who overtook me last night on horseback are riding quietly together on horseback; I recognized him by his moustache. They are riding quietly, silently holding each other's hand; and both of the horses on which they are riding are walking lazily, beautifully straightening their long necks.]

Second version (*A Fortuitous Encounter*)

自分の駈込んだのは極く樹深い蓊欝とした森であつたから、鳥の落た處まで行着くすら容易な事ではなかつたが、其所を少し離れて車路が曲折つてゐて、その路を今例の美人と昨夜自分を乗越したあの男とが馬で靜に連立つて行く、あの男といふのは髭で判つた。二人とも黙つて、靜に手を取交して、乗つてゐた馬も二頭とも長い頸を美しく伸して、だるさうにぽくぽく行く。(Futabatei Shimei 1964a: 283)

[The forest into which I ran is so thick and dense that it was not easy even to reach the place where the bird had fallen, a short distance from it there is a cart-road winding out, and on this road that beautiful woman and the man who overtook me on horseback last night are riding quietly together on horseback; I recognized him by his moustache. They are riding quietly, silently, holding each other's hand, and both of the horses on which they are riding are pacing lazily, beautifully straightening their long necks.]

While in the original Russian text the description of the couple riding together is in the past tense, in both of Futabatei's versions "-(r)u" forms are used. In both versions cited above "-ta" forms also appear, and correspond precisely to the perfective verbs in the original. The "-(r)u" forms, on the other hand, correspond to the Russian imperfective verbs. However, when we consider each Japanese passage in its context, their effects differ. In the first version, the "-(r)u" forms—"(kiba de) tōtte yuku [are riding on horseback]", "te o torikawashi nagara iku [are riding holding each other's hand]", "yotayotato aruite iku [are walking lazily]"—serve to emphasize the climax of the story. Futabatei repeats this device in the denouement at the masquerade:

> По коридору, образуемому рядом колонн и стеной, шел он, тот мужчина, которого я встретил с нею в лесу. (Turgenev 1963b: 263)
>
> [Along the corridor, formed by the row of columns and the wall, was walking the man whom I had met with her in the forest.]
>
> First version (*A Chance Encounter*)
>
> 圓柱の列と壁とで出來た廊下をつたツて、林で婦人と打連れて往くを見かけた、ソレ、その男が通ツて行く。(Futabatei Shimei 1964a: 206)
>
> [Along the corridor, formed by the row of round columns and the wall, a man is walking, the very man whom I witnessed together with the lady in the forest.]

These two scenes, echoing each other, set the mood of the denouement. In the first version Futabatei consciously employs "-(r)u" forms to vividly convey the poetry of the scene. We are reminded of that striking phrase in *The Tryst:* "A aki da! " [Yes it's autumn!]

In the second version, however, the corresponding "-(r)u" forms, "shizukani tsuredatte iku [they are riding on horseback together quietly]", "darusōni pokupoku iku [are pacing lazily]", are less noticeable among the other "-te iru" forms employed to describe the woman's face and figure. Again Futabatei employs "-te iru" forms to translate the imperfective Russian verbs of the original:

> ...улыбка глубокой радости блуждала на ее губах;..
> ... обе руки ее бессильно лежали: одна—в руке ехавшего с ней мужчины, другая—на холке лошади. (Turgenev 1963b: 246)
>
> [...a smile of deep joy was playing on her lips...
> ... both her hands lay powerlessly: one in the hand of the man riding with her, the other on the horse's withers.]
>
> Second version (*A Fortuitous Encounter*)
>
> 深い喜から出た微笑が口元にほのめいてゐる、
> 手も力無さゝうに、片々は並んで行く男の手の中(うち)に、片々は馬の領髪(えりがみ)の上に落してゐる。(Futabatei Shimei 1964a: 283-284)
>
> [A smile of deep joy is playing on her lips...
> She drops her hands powerlessly; one hand is in the hand of the man who is riding with her, and the other is on the withers of her horse.]

Teramura Hideo (1984: 162-163) classifies this "-te iku" form (found in "shizukani tsuredatte iku") in the second aspectual group together with "-te iru" or "-te shimau". Although he hesitates to include "aruite iku" or "tsuredatte iku", he does recognize "(hi ga) kiete iku [(a fire) is going out]" or "(ki ga) karete iku [(a tree) is dying]" as aspectual expressions. Teramura defines the aspectual meaning of the "-te iku" form as the gradual disappearance of phenomena from the speaker's view. In this sense Futabatei may as well have translated not "tsuredatte iku" but "tsuredatte kuru", since "-te kuru" is the aspectual expression which depicts the gradual appearance of phenomena to the speaker. Interestingly, in the second version the echoing scene where the mysterious woman witnesses the former lover coming together with another woman, Futabatei switches from the "-te iku" form to the "-te kuru" form to emphasize the aspectual meaning:

> Second version (*A Fortuitous Encounter*)
>
> 圓柱の列と壁とで廊下のやうになつた所を、森で女と連立つて行くのを見掛けた、あの男が通つて來る。(Futabatei Shimei 1964a: 301)
>
> [Along the corridor-like space formed by the row of round columns and the wall, a man is coming, the very man whom I witnessed together with the lady in the forest.]

We thus see that in the second version each scene opens with sentences containing "-ta" auxiliary verbs, indicating the past tense. Then, if a description follows which in the original employs imperfective verbs, Futabatei employs mainly "-te iru" forms, indicating aspectual meaning, such as a continuous action or state of being. This aspectual meaning, especially that denoting continuous action, contributes to the personification of the garden in the original. As far as the "-ta" auxiliary verbs are concerned, in the second version, where he is describing the setting, Futabatei without exception changes the verb form from "-te ita" to "-te iru". As a result, the "-ta" auxiliary verbs which remain in the text are those which render the perfective verbs of the original. Thus, in the scenes where the narrator's first and second chance meetings with the mysterious lady are described, "-ta" auxiliary verbs mainly carry the meaning of the perfective aspect.

On the other hand, if a description of a characters' actions follows, which in the original makes use of perfective verbs, "-(r)u" and "-ta" forms are used together, and the "-ta" auxiliary verbs are noticeably fewer than in the first version. This reduction in the number of "-ta" auxiliary verbs is facilitated by the substitution of commas for full stops. Importantly, the "-ta" forms used here among the "-(r)u" forms carry a strong sense of the perfective aspect rather than of the past tense. Some of those "-ta" auxiliary verbs in the first version which render the past perfective verbs of the original (and which consequently can be understood to express both the past tense and the perfective aspect) are eliminated in the second version through combining sentences. Consequently, those "-ta" auxiliary verbs which remain in the second version are more prominent, and more significant in carrying the meaning of the perfective aspect.

Here we notice that the narrative of *Floating Clouds* Part One and that of the second version, *A Fortuitous Encounter*, are stylistically similar. In both narratives "-ta" auxiliary verbs are employed in isolation, in a colloquial sense, amongst the "-(r)u" forms, expressing the perfective aspect rather than the past tense. The main difference between the two narratives is that in *A Fortuitous Encounter* "-ta" auxiliary verbs are used more consciously to denote the perfective aspect, especially the completion of the action. Each scene in *A Fortuitous Encounter* almost invariably ends with the specific form "-te shimatta", which indicates the completion of the action, accompanied by the narrator's regret or embarrassment. Unlike the narrator in *Floating Clouds*, the narrator in *A Fortuitous Encounter* gets deeply involved in the events which he is describing, often expressing his feelings by the use of these "-te shimatta" forms.

In short, the second version was retranslated with the clear intention of emphasizing verbal aspect rather than tense. The "-ta" auxiliary verbs which remain in *A Fortuitous Encounter* mostly convey perfective aspect rather than past tense. Table 5 shows how Futabatei changed verb forms in the second version:

***Table 5: Regularities in Futabatei's translation of verb forms in his revised versions***

| | Past | Present | Future |
|---|---|---|---|
| Imperfective: | (on) pisal | (on) pishet | (on) budet pisat' |
| | 1) kai-ta<br>[wrote/has written] | kaku<br>[writes] | kaku (-darō)<br>[will write] |
| | 2) **kaite-ita** → | **kaite-iru** | kaite-iru (-darō) |
| | [was writing] | [is writing] | [will be writing] |
| | 3) kaki-tsuzuketa | kaki-tsuzukeru | kaki-tsuzukeru (-darō) |
| | [continued writing] | [continues writing] | [will continue writing] |
| Perfective: | (on) napisal | | (on) napishet |
| | 1) **kai-ta** → | | **kaku (-darō)** |
| | [wrote] ↓ | | [will write] |
| | 2) **kaite-shimatta** | | kaite-shimau |
| | [has/had written] | | [will have written] |
| | 3) kaki-oeta | | kaki-oeru |
| | [finished writing] | | [will finish writing] |

***The first, second and third aspectual groups as classified by Teramura are shown in the table by the numbers 1), 2) and 3).***

So those "-ta" auxiliary verbs which remain in the second versions are mostly used to render the perfective aspect of the original Russian verbs, and some of these auxiliary verbs are further emphasized and appear in the "-te shimatta" form, which clearly renders the perfective aspect of the original Russian verbs.

It may also be observed that the present tense verbs in the second versions are used together with verbs in the "-te iru" form. When translating verbs which are imperfective in the Russian original, Futabatei regularly changes the "-te ita" form of the first version to "-te iru" in the second version. We may conclude that in the second version Futabatei changed tense forms, but tried to be faithful to the aspect of the original verbs, accentuating aspectual connotations of the Japanese verb forms in the process.

So even here, the effect is innovative, using Japanese grammatical forms to convey the strong sense of aspect in the Russian. The tension between the Russian original and the target language is handled in a foreignizing way by Futabatei, as he strives to convey the aspectual nuances of the original. Once again, as in the first version, Futabatei creates a new narrative style.

Thus, in the second version, the impact of the final scene, which contains an echo of the forest scene, is heightened by the use of the "-te kuru" form, though the effect produced by this aspectual expression is then softened by the use of the "-te iru" form, which is used to describe the man's face and figure:

> Так же красиво вился его русый ус, такой же спокойной и самоуверенной веселостью светились его карие глаза. (Turgenev 1963b: 263)
>
> [His light brown moustache curled just as handsomely, his brown eyes gleamed with the same calm and self-assured good humour.]

Second version (*A Fortuitous Encounter*)

矢張り美しい茶褐色の、髭を捻上(ねぢあ)げて、沈着(おちつ)いた自信の厚さうな鳶色の眼を面白さうに光らせてゐる。(Futabatei Shimei 1964a: 301)

> [He has the same handsome, brown, curled moustache, and his calm and self-confident brown eyes are gleaming cheerfully.]

In its treatment of the denouement, the first version (*A Chance Encounter*) paints a more vivid image for the reader than the second (*A Fortuitous Encounter*). A similarly striking image is found in the denouement of the first version of *The Tryst*. The denouements in the second versions are less effective than those of the first versions, due to the experimental narrative style, which now emphasizes aspectual meaning. Futabatei needed to further explore and refine this new narrative style in both first- and third-person narratives. This exploration and refinement will be examined in the following chapters.

# Chapter 3 — Exploring the First-Person Narrative

Around the time that Futabatei published the second versions of *The Rendezvous* and *Three Encounters,* he translated another five works by Turgenev: *Asya* (under the title *Katakoi [One-sided Love]* in November 1896), *Son [The Dream]* (as *Yumekatari [Dream Talk],* April 1897), the novel *Rudin* (as *Ukikusa [Floating Weed],* April-October 1897), *Zhid [The Jew]* (as *Yudaya-jin [The Jew],* January 1898) and *Petushkov* (as *Kusare-en [The Mismatch],* November 1898). He also translated Gogol's story *Portret [The Portrait]* (as *Shōzōga [The portrait]*), which appeared in 1897 between *One-sided Love* and *Dream Talk.* Together, these works comprise the fruit of Futabatei's second period of translation activity.

What we observe here is that Futabatei chose to translate first-person narratives (*Asya, The Dream* and *The Jew*) and third-person narratives (*The Portrait, Rudin* and *Petushkov*) alternately. It is also worth noting that the second work Futabatei translated during this period was Gogol's story *The Portrait,* in which the narrative shifts from the third to the first person towards the end. Moreover, two of Turgenev's stories translated during this period—*The Jew* and *Petushkov*—are regarded as "Gogolian" stories because of their setting and their comic vein. In *Petushkov* especially, "the urban lower-middle-class setting is distinctly Gogolian" (Seely 1991: 96). Futabatei seems to seek inspiration for his *genbun itchi* style not only in Turgenev's works, but also in Gogol's.

This chapter will examine two of Futabatei's translations from first-person narrative stories by Turgenev: *One-sided Love* and *The Jew.* Attention will again be given to the verb forms which Futabatei employs. While *Dream Talk* is an interesting translation, the method employed in it is very similar to that employed in *One-sided Love*, and its analysis yields few additional insights. It also contains a fantastic element, the boundaries between dream and reality being confused, and this makes the narrative point of view ambiguous. An analysis of *Dream Talk* may be found elsewhere (Cockerill 2003: 106-123).

In Chapter Two, the tentative conclusion was drawn that instances of the auxiliary verb "-ta" which remain in the second versions of Turgenev's first-person narrative stories *The Rendezvous* and *Three Encounters* are mainly used to express the perfective aspect of the original Russian verbs, and that some of these auxiliary verbs are emphasized and appear in the "-te shimatta" form, which clearly shows the completion of the action. We also observed that the present tense verbs in the second versions are often employed in the "-te iru" form, in order to render the past imperfective verbs of the Russian original, and that they express continuous actions or states. In other words, Futabatei regularly changed verb forms from "-te ita" in the first version to "-te iru" in the second version when translating verbs which are past imperfective in the Russian original.

Through these transformations, Futabatei again created a new style which clearly reflected the aspect of the original Russian verbs. The vivid descriptions which resulted allow us to visualize each scene clearly. While in the originals the narrator tells of actions which took place in the past, in Futabatei's second versions the narrator describes actions as they happen. Yet in these second versions the denouements are less effective than in the first versions, due to Futabatei's treatment of verb forms to accentuate aspectual meaning. To what extent did Futabatei continue to accentuate the aspectual forms of the Russian original in his translations of Turgenev's other first-person narrative stories: *Asya* and *The Jew?* What effect did this produce in them? How effective was the denouement?

When Futabatei translated these two stories it seems that he was clearly aware of the existence of the narrator. Booth (1961: 152) defines such narrators as "dramatized narrators", and they are frequently radically different from the implied authors who create them. Was Futabatei aware of the narrator in each story being different from the implied author? For now we may observe that Futabatei employs different Japanese first-person pronouns for the narrator in each story: "watakushi" for the narrator in *Asya* and "boku" in *The Jew*. Each narrator is given a particular style of narration. "-Desu" or "-masu" is the narrative style in *Asya* and the "-da" style is used in *The Jew.* Moreover, in *Asya* and *The Jew* the narrators are introduced to the reader at the beginning of the story, and in *The Jew* even the audience is clearly indicated. In *Dream Talk* Futabatei employs the first-person pronoun "jibun" for the narrator and its style is "-de aru".

We should note that 1896 was the year when Ozaki Kōyō, the leader of the Ken'yūsha group, published his "-de aru" style novel *Tajō takon [Passions and Griefs]*, in which he described in great psychological detail a husband's grief over his wife's death. *Passions and Griefs* is regarded as a major achievement in the history of the "-de aru" style novel. Kōyō was at first strongly against the *genbun itchi* style, and employed a classical Japanese style for the narrative of his works. Later he realized the need for the *genbun itchi* style to describe the spiritual side of a human being and tried it out in several of his stories, though he later turned away from it.

It is worth noting that the beginning of Futabatei's second period of translation activity coincides with the publication of *Passions and Griefs,* which took place throughout 1896. In fact we find "-de aru" endings not only in *Dream Talk,* but also in *A Fortuitous Encounter* (the second version of *Three Encounters*) and in *One-sided Love* (*Asya*).

## *Katakoi [One-sided Love]* (Translated from Turgenev's *Asya*)

The following passage is the beginning of *One-sided Love,* and illustrates the various sentence endings, depending on who is narrating and what is narrated:

> 恰ど私の二十五の時でした、と某といふ男が話し出した、ですから最う餘程以前の事です。私も漸く自由の利く身となつたので、そこで早速外國へ出掛かけましたが、それも當時能く人の言つた教育完成のためではないので、唯何となく浮世の態が見たかつたので。（中略）そこで、私は何の目的が有るでもなく、計畫もなく、唯心に適つた所なら、何處にでも逗留する、新しい面が見たくなれば、直ぐ出立するといふ調子で旅行をしました—新しい面を見たくなればといふのは實際の事で。私には人間の外は何も面白くなかつた。（中略）尤も自然には随分深く感じる方であつたが、自然の美とかいふ、山でも、岩でも、瀑布でも、何でも可いが、尋常たものでないものは、人に纏綿つて長閑にはさして置かぬやうな所があるので、それで好きませんでした。その代り人の面ですな、活きてゐる人の面—言葉にしろ、所作にしろ、笑聲にしろ同じ事だが、—是は私に

取つては無くては叶はぬもので。群聚に交つてゐれば、いつも氣が晴れて愉快になる。人の行く方へ行つたり、人の喚くのに連れて喚いたりするのも面白いが、人の喚くのを見てゐても面白い。人を觀察して樂しむ……と云つて強ち觀察するのでもなく、唯まじりまじり見てゐるのであるが、それが又妙に面白くて、頓と飽くということを忘れて了ふ。ほい、また話が逸れた。(Futabatei Shimei 1964a: 210-211)

[I was then just 25 years old,—the gentleman began—so it happened a long time ago. I had finally reached the age of independence, and straight away I went overseas, not in order to finish my education, as people used to say, but I somehow wanted to see the real world…

So I travelled around without any purpose or plan, I stayed wherever I liked, I left immediately when I felt like seeing new faces. — It was true that I left places in order to see new faces. I was solely interested in people… I was also inclined to sense nature deeply, but I did not like so called natural beauty; anything unusual amongst mountains, cliffs or waterfalls, because they clung to me and did not leave me in peace. Instead, faces, living human faces—their speech, motion and laughter, these are the things that I desperately need. Whenever I am in a crowd, I am always at ease and become happy. I am happy to follow people wherever they go, or I am happy to shout when people shout, or simply to observe how people shout. It is fun to observe people, not to observe, but simply to look closely at them, it brings me joy and I have never tired of doing it. I am sorry that I have wandered from the subject again.]

Futabatei employs the plain "-da" style for the implied author's narrative, ("to nanigashi to yū otoko ga hanashidashita [the gentleman began]"), but this is almost immediately displaced by the language of the dramatized narrator, who employs the polite "-desu/-masu" form for his narrative style. Judging from the styles employed by Futabatei thus far, Futabatei appears to be well aware of the existence of a dramatized narrator who is different from the implied author. Here we should also recall that one of the earlier *genbun itchi* writers, Yamada Bimyō, employed this polite style for his works. However, since the polite form is normally used to address a particular audience, Bimyō's work lacked objectivity. It shows Futabatei's keen sense as a writer that he employed this polite form in a first-person narrative story, but the use of the polite form is not consistent. As may be observed from the passage cited above, there are three different styles mixed in the narrative of *One-sided Love:* the "-desu/-masu" (polite), the "-da" (plain) and the "-de aru" styles. This inconsistency makes the narrative of *One-sided Love* awkward, or it gives the reader the impression that this style is somewhat experimental. When we look more closely, however, we observe that there is some regularity in the use of the three styles. While the polite "-desu/-masu" form is employed when the narrator is conscious of his audience, the "-de aru" style is often used when the narrator is analyzing his own thoughts, as if addressing himself, rather than any particular audience. This is especially so when the narrator is gradually becoming aware of his love for Asya. We may also note that this passage is written mostly using the auxiliary verb "-ta", except for the last few sentences, which in the Russian original are past imperfective. Let us compare Futabatei's translation with the original:

Мне было тогда лет двадцать пять,—начал Н.Н.,—дела давно минувших дней, как видите. Я только что вырвался на волю и уехал за границу, не для того, чтобы «окончить мое воспитание», как говаривалось тогда, а просто мне захотелось посмотреть на мир божий…

Я путешествовал без всякой цели, без плана; останавливался везде, где мне нравилось, и отправлялся тотчас далее, как только чувствовал желание видеть новые лица—именно лица. Меня занимали исключительно одни люди; … Природа действовала на меня чрезвычайно, но я не любил так называемых ее красот, необыкновенных гор, утесов, водопадов; я не любил, чтобы она навязывалась мне, чтобы она мне мешала. Зато лица, живые, человеческие лица—речи людей, их движения, смех,—вот без чего я обойтись не мог. В толпе мне было всегда особенно легко и отрадно; мне было весело идти, куда шли другие, кричать, когда другие кричали, и в то же время я любил смотреть, как эти другие кричат. Меня забавляло наблюдать людей ... да я даже не наблюдал их—я их рассматривал с каким-то радостным и ненасытным любопытством. Но я опять сбиваюсь в сторону. (Turgenev 1964: 71-72)

[I was then about twenty-five years old,—N.N. began.—These matters took place a long time ago, as you can see. I had just reached the age of independence, and went overseas, not in order to "complete my education" as was often said at that time, but simply I felt an urge to see the wide world…

I travelled without any purpose, without any plan, I stayed wherever I liked, and moved on as soon as I felt a desire to see new faces—yes, it was faces I sought. I was interested solely in people: … I was deeply moved by nature, but I did not like her so called beauties, unusual mountains, cliffs and waterfalls. I did not like her to thrust herself upon me, to disturb me. But faces, on the other hand, lively human faces—people's speech, movement and laughter—I could not live without them. I felt especially comfortable and at ease in a crowd, I was happy to go where others went, to shout when others shouted, and at the same time I liked to see how they shouted. It amused me to observe people ... I did not even observe them—I examined them with some sort of joyful and insatiable curiosity. But I am getting off the track again.]

*Asya* is a story of love between the narrator-protagonist and Asya, who is an illegitimate child. Seeley (1991: 153-154) suggests that "the narrator-protagonist embodies some aspects of Turgenev's own personality" and notes that Asya is "said to be drawn from a cousin of his, the illegitimate daughter of his uncle Nikolai". Because of the illegitimacy of her birth, Asya is at first embarrassed when she becomes aware of her love for the narrator-protagonist, but she is courageous enough to summon him to a rendezvous. At this encounter, while Asya is honest and sincerely confesses her love for the narrator, he avoids showing any feeling. Instead he scolds Asya for having spoken of her feelings with her brother Gagin. Later the narrator recounts that he did not realize his love for Asya until she had slipped away from his life. Thus the whole story is made up of the recollections of the narrator- protagonist, who was characterized by Chernyshevsky as "lishnii chelovek" (a superfluous man). Chernyshevsky considers the protagonist to be a liberal, but one who has neither social sense, nor power to act. He vacillates when he needs to make a decision, and makes Asya unhappy (Cited in Satō Seirō 1995: 394).

When Futabatei translated *Asya,* he could not ignore the narrator-protagonist's present time, as he did to a large extent in the second versions of *Three Encounters* and *The Rendezvous*. Hence, all the past imperfective verbs in the first two-thirds of the passage cited above are translated using "-ta" auxiliary verbs. In the original most of these verbs express past experiences which occurred repeatedly. However, once the narrator starts talking about his habitual actions, his preferences for human faces and human animation, Futabatei changes the verb form from "-ta" to "-(r)u".[1]

When we examine all the translations of verbs which are past imperfective in the original, to see whether Futabatei employs "-ta" or "-(r)u" form verbs, a clear pattern in the use of these forms emerges. The "-(r)u" form verbs are employed firstly for the description of scenery, reminding us of similar descriptions in *A Fortuitous Encounter* and the second version of *The Tryst*. The following passage is a description of a little German town on the left bank of the Rhine, where the narrator stays:

> Я любил бродить тогда по городу; луна, казалось, пристально глядела на него с чистого неба; и город чувствовал этот взгляд и стоял чутко и мирно, весь облитый ее светом, этим безмятежным и в тоже время тихо душу волнующим светом. Петух на высокой готической колокольне блестел бледным золотом; таким же золотом переливались струйки по черному глянцу речки; тоненькие свечки (немец бережлив!) скромно теплились в узких окнах под грифельными кровлями; виноградные лозы таинственно высовывали свои завитые усики из-за каменных оград; что-то пробегало в тени около старинного колодца на трехугольной площади, внезапно раздавался сонливый свисток ночного сторожа, добродушная собака ворчала вполголоса, а воздух так и ластился к лицу, и липы пахли так сладко, что грудь поневоле всё глубже и глубже дышала, и слово «Гретхен»—не то восклицание, не то вопрос—так и просилось на уста. (Turgenev 1964: 72-73)
>
> [I liked to stroll about the town at that time; the moon, it seemed, looked down steadily at the town from the clear sky; and the town felt its gaze and stood sensitively and quietly, bathed in its light, in that calm light which at the same time quietly excites the soul.. The cock on the tall Gothic bell-tower shone pale gold, streams of the same gold poured over the dark lustre of the river; slender candles (German people are thrifty) flickered modestly in the narrow windows under the slate roofs; grape vines thrust their twining tendrils mysteriously from behind stone walls; something ran across in the shade near an old well in the triangular market place, suddenly the drowsy whistle of the night watchman rang out, a good-natured dog growled in an undertone, and the air simply caressed one's face, and the lime-trees smelt so sweet that one's chest involuntarily breathed deeper and deeper, and the word "Gretchen"—half exclamation, half question—came naturally to one's lips.]

Compare this with Futabatei's translation:

> その時分(じぶん)町を散歩すると、快(よ)い心地(こころもち)ですわい、澄渡つた空からは月が餘

---

[1] Hereafter the terms "-(r)u" form and "-ta" form will be used frequently in the discussion. The former is taken to mean the "non-ta" form or non-past form, while the latter refers to the placement of the auxiliary verb "-ta" after the verb. In this chapter particular attention is given to the "-te iru" and "-te ita" forms.

念なく町を眺めてゐると、町はまた其を承知してゐながら、森とした中にも何處か人を誘るやうな處もある月の光を浴て、鳴を靜めて控へてゐる。高いゴチック風の鐘樓の屋の棟では、金鷄が蒼味の有る金色を放つてゐれば、薄光りのする河面にも、同じ色の光線が横に流れてゐる、板石葺の家の小窓には（獨逸人は皆險約だから）、細い蝋燭が心細く點つてゐる、葡萄の蔓が石垣越に曲つた頭を密と出してゐる、菱形の廣場の古井戸の邊で、何か物蔭を駈通ると、夜番の睡さうな口笛の音もすれば、氣の善い犬も低く唸る。風は面を撫るやうに吹く、菩醍樹の佳い香が紛々と鼻を撲つて、息氣までが自ら深くなる、そこでグレートヘン（獨逸美人）といふ語が—感嘆の調子でもなく、疑問の調子でもなくて—我知らず口へ出さうになる。(Futabatei Shimei 1964a: 211-212)

> [It is pleasant to wander about the town at that time. From the clear sky the moon looks steadily down on it, and the town is aware of its steady gaze, and stands quietly and breathlessly, bathed in the moonlight, which is peaceful, yet invites the soul. On the tall Gothic bell-tower the gold cock is shining with a pale gold colour. Over the gleaming surface of the river the same gold stream flows by. In the small windows under the slate roofs the slender candles are flickering modestly (as German people are all thrifty), branches of vine thrust out their twining tendrils secretly from behind stone walls. Near the old well in the triangular shaped market place something runs across in the shade, the drowsy whistle of the night guard is heard, a friendly natured dog growls in an undertone. The wind blows as if tenderly stroking one's face, the lime-trees smell so nice that the lungs unconsciously draw breaths deeply, then the word "Gretchen" (German beauty), neither exclamation nor question, naturally comes to the lips.]

As in *A Fortuitous Encounter* and the second version of *The Tryst,* when describing the scenery the past imperfective verbs are translated either by employing the "-te iru" form (which accentuates the aspect of continuous actions or states), or by employing the "-(r)u" form, which expresses the aspect of repetitive actions. It is noticeable that throughout the whole passage Futabatei avoids the use of "-ta" form verbs.

The tense of the narrative in *One-sided Love* thus seems to alternate depending on the nature of what is described, Futabatei employing "-(r)u" form verbs for habitual or repetitive actions and "-te iru" form verbs for the description of scenery. As the story progresses, more examples unfold. "-(R)u" form verbs are observed when the ambivalent (arrogant yet insecure) character of Russians overseas is described, and, more importantly, when Asya's eccentric behaviour is described. The following passage is a description of Asya as first observed by the narrator-protagonist:

> Я не видал существа более подвижного. Ни одно мгновенье она не сидела смирно; вставала, убегала в дом и прибегала снова, напевала вполголоса, часто смеялась, и престранным образом: казалось, она смеялась не тому, что слышала, а разным мыслям, приходившим ей в голову. Ее большие глаза глядели прямо,

светло, смело, но иногда веки ее слегка щурились, и тогда взор ее внезапно становился глубок и нежен. (Turgenev 1964: 77)

[I had never seen a creature more restless than her. Not for a single moment did she sit quietly; she would stand up and run off into the house, and run back again, hum in an undertone, often laugh, and in a very strange way: it seemed she laughed not at what she heard, but at the various thoughts which came to her. Her big eyes gazed directly, brightly and boldly, but sometimes her eyelids narrowed slightly, and then her gaze all of a sudden became deep and gentle.]

私は此娘ほどちよこまかするものを見たことはありません。一分時と動かずには居ません。幾度となく起上つて、家内へ駈込むかとすれば、また駈出して來て、何か中音に唱つて、妄らに高笑をする、それも極く變な風で、耳に聞いた事を笑ふのではなく、心に浮ぶ種々の事を笑ふやうで。大きな眼で、憚る所なく正しく物を視るのが常であつたが、時としては眼を少し細めることもある、其時は眼差が急に柔しく奥床しくなる。 (Futabatei Shimei 1964a: 217)

[I have never seen such a restless creature as this girl. [She] does not sit still even for a single minute. [She] often stands up and runs off into the house, and runs back again, hums in an undertone, so often laughs loudly, in a very strange way, [she] seems to laugh not at what she hears, but at the various thoughts which occur to her. She normally looks out at things boldly and straightforwardly with her big eyes, but occasionally screws them up slightly, and then the expression of her eyes all of a sudden becomes gentle and tender.]

Asya, who is an extraordinary and rather irritating character for the narrator-protagonist, is thoroughly observed and analyzed by him, and in Futabatei's translation all these descriptions are translated using "-(r)u" forms or "-te iru" forms. When we follow these descriptions, we notice a regular feature of Futabatei's translation. When, in the Russian original, Asya's continuous actions are described using past imperfective verbs, Futabatei without exception translates them using the "-te iru" form rather than the "-te ita" form:

1. На уступе сидела, точно, Ася. (Turgenev 1964: 81)

[On the ledge was sitting, in fact, Asya.]

壁の斗出た所には果してアーシヤが蹲踞つてゐます。(Futabatei Shimei 1964a: 221)

[On the projecting part of the wall Asya, in fact, is sitting.]

2. Ася продолжала сидеть неподвижно, подобрав под себя ноги и закутав голову кисейным шарфом; (Turgenev 1964: 81)

[Asya continued sitting motionlessly, with her feet tucked under her, and a muslin scarf wrapped around her head.]

アーシヤは頭をモスリンの頸巻で包むで、足を一所に寄せて、身動をもせずに、尚ほ蹲踞つてゐます。(Futabatei Shimei 1964a: 221)

[Putting her feet close and covering her head with a muslin scarf, Asya is still sitting motionlessly.]

3. Наконец, Ася опорожнила весь свой стакан и, шаловливо покачиваясь, возвратилась к нам. Странная усмешка слегка подергивала ее брови, ноздри и губы; полудерзко, полувесело щурились темные глаза. (Turgenev 1964: 82)
[Finally Asya emptied all her glass, and rocking her head mischievously, walked back to us. A strange grin was slightly lifting her eyebrows, nostrils and lips; her dark eyes were screwed up half cheekily and half happily.]

兎角する内にアーシヤは水呑の水を傾盡して、體を揺てしやならしやならと戻つて來たが、怪しく微笑して眉や鼻や唇を歪めて、浮々してゐる中にも、何處か傍若無人な樣子も有つて、眼を細くしてゐる。(Futabatei Shimei 1964a: 222)

[At last Asya has emptied the glass of water, and swinging her body playfully, has come back to us. [She] smiles strangely, contorting her eyebrows, nostrils and lips, [and] looks happy but at the same time somehow impertinent, and is screwing up her eyes.]

4. За столом она держалась очень чинно, почти чопорно, едва отведывала кушанья и пила воду из рюмки. (Turgenev 1964: 83)
[At dinner she behaved very decorously, almost primly, hardly tasted the food and drank water from her wine glass.]

卓に就いても、大層取澄して、殆ど氣取つてゐるのかと思はれる程で、食物には一寸口を着けたばかりで、只杯で水ばかり飲むでゐる。(Futabatei Shimei 1964a: 223)

[At the dinner table she behaves so decorously that she looks almost prim, she hardly tastes the food and only drinks water from her wine glass.]

5. Я застал ее раз за книгой, одну. Опершись головой на обе руки и запустив пальцы глубоко в волосы, она пожирала глазами строки. (Turgenev 1964: 87)
[I found her once with a book, alone. Leaning her head on both hands, fingers thrust deep into her hair, she was devouring the lines with her eyes.]

或日アーシヤ一人きりで書見をしてゐる所へ往合せましたが、兩手で頭を支へて、指を深く髪毛に埋めて、一心に讀むでゐます。(Futabatei Shimei 1964a: 228)

[One day I found Asya reading a book alone. Supporting her head with both hands and thrusting her fingers deeply into her hair, she is reading eagerly.]

6. Он рассказал мне, что делал в мое отсутствие. Но речи наши не клеились; Ася входила в комнату и убегала снова; … (Turgenev 1964: 91)
[He told me what he had been doing in my absence. But our conversation did not flow easily. Asya kept coming into the room and running out again; …]

ガギンも私の留守中に爲た事の話をしたが、如何も話に氣が乘りません。アーシヤは座舗を出たり、入つたりしてゐます。(Futabatei Shimei 1964a: 232)

[Gagin told me what he had done during my absence, but our conversation does not flow well. Asya comes in and out of the room frequently.]

7. В небольшой комнатке, куда я вошел, было довольно темно, и я не тотчас увидел Асю. Закутанная в длинную шаль, она сидела на стуле возле окна, отвернув и почти спрятав голову, как испуганная птичка. Она дышала быстро и вся дрожала. Мне стало несказанно жалко ее. Я подошел к ней. Она еще больше отвернула голову... (Turgenev 1964: 111)

[In the small room into which I stepped, it was rather dark, and I did not at once see Asya. Wrapped in a long shawl, she was sitting on a chair near the window, turning away from me and almost hiding her head, like a frightened bird. She was breathing rapidly and trembling all over. I felt inexpressibly sorry for her. I walked up to her. She turned her head away even more.]

入つた室は狭い間で、大分薄暗かつたから、アーシヤが何處に居るか、急には分らなかつたが、熟々視れば、長いショールに纒まつて、窓の側の椅子に腰を掛けて面を反けてゐる、物に怖ぢた小禽のやうに、殆ど隱して居るのかと思はれる程に首を蹙めて、息氣を激まして、慄へてゐるそのいぢらしさは、なかなか口では云はれません。私が側へ往つたら、益々面を反けて了つた…… (Futabatei Shimei 1964a: 255-256)

[The room which I entered was very narrow and quite dark, so that I could not find Asya straight away, but when I look around carefully I find her sitting on a chair near the window, turning her head away from me, wrapped in a big shawl. I cannot fully express how pitiful she looks, breathing rapidly and trembling, with her head tucked so deeply, that she appears almost to be hiding, like a frightened bird. When I walk up to her, she has turned her head away even more.]

Except for the last passage (7), Asya's continuous actions are clearly rendered in the present tense, since there are only two possibilities here: "-te iru" and "-te ita". While "-te iru" indicates the present tense, "-te ita" indicates the past tense, and both express the continuous aspect. Significantly, the past perfective verbs in the above quotations from Turgenev's original are all translated using the "-ta" or, occasionally, the "-te shimatta" form. Futabatei describes Asya's actions vividly, as if they are unfolding before the narrator's eyes. First Futabatei changes the tense from past to present by employing the "-te iru" form, so that a clear picture emerges for the narrator and readers, and then he closes the scene by employing the "-ta" or "-te shimatta" form, indicating the completion of the action. Thus the "-ta" form, used here to express Asya's consecutive actions, or the completion of them, carries more aspectual meaning than past tense meaning. Among the passages cited above, passages three and five clearly show the meaning of the "-ta" form which expresses the aspect of completion. It may be observed, especially in chapter four, where the most vivid description of Asya's eccentric actions is given, that the "-te shimatta" form is frequently used. For example, after Asya has daringly climbed onto the ledge of a half-ruined castle and watered a flower, her mood changes abruptly:

> Несколько мгновений спустя оно всё побледнело и приняло сосредоточенное, почти печальное выражение; самые черты ее мне показались больше, строже, проще. Она вся затихла. (Turgenev 1964: 82)
>
> [In a few seconds her face had turned all pale, and it took on a concentrated, almost sad expression; her features themselves seemed [at that moment] larger, sterner and simpler. She quietened down completely.]
>
> 一瞬の間(ま)に最(も)う蒼ざめて了(しま)つて、何か物思はしさうな、殆ど悲しさうな面色(かほつき)となつたのみならず、思做(おもひなし)でもあらうが、其面相(かほだち)も大きく嚴(いか)めしくなつて、艶(つや)も素氣(そツけ)も亡くなつて了つた。全然温順(すツかりおとな)しくなつて了つた。
> (Futabatei Shimei 1964a: 222)
>
> [Her face has turned pale in a moment, it has become melancholy, almost sad, and it may seem only to me that her features have become larger and sterner, they have become very simple and show no charm. [She] has quietened down completely.]

Employing the "-te shimatta" form, Futabatei tries to emphasize the sudden change occurring before the narrator's eyes. To facilitate the reader's visualization of scenes in *One-sided Love,* Futabatei applies the same rule when describing other characters such as Asya's half brother Gagin and their elderly German friend Frau Luise. Their continuous actions, which are depicted using past imperfective verbs in the original, are all translated using the "-te iru" form in Futabatei's version. On the other hand, almost all the past perfective verbs, used to depict successive actions in the original, are translated using "-ta" or "-te shimatta" forms. In short, the actions of characters which unfold before the narrator's eyes are translated in a way which accentuates the aspect of the original verb forms. Consequently "-ta" forms carry more aspectual meaning than tense meaning. In this way Futabatei is able to animate each scene more clearly and vividly for the reader. By contrast, when the "-ta" form is used to express the narrator-protagonist's own actions it changes its value and carries the meaning of the past tense.

As has already been noted, this story opens up with the introduction of the narrator to the reader, and the story, which is made up of the narrator's recollections, follows. The first chapter of the original, in which the background to the story is narrated, is written mostly with the use of past imperfective verbs. Futabatei initially employs the "-ta" form to translate these past imperfective verbs, unless they are used to express habitual or repetitive actions, or to depict scenery. These "-ta" forms, which express past experience, are often reinforced in their reflective meaning by the particular narrative style "-deshita" or "-mashita". In particular, this narrative style is used effectively in chapter VII, where the narrator-protagonist recounts his short trip to the mountains after he has by chance witnessed the encounter between Asya and Gagin. This eavesdropping, which occurs so often in Turgenev's stories, makes the narrator aware of his hitherto unconscious love for Asya. Upset by their apparent "rendezvous", the narrator wanders in the mountains. The narrator recounts only his own actions, hence the style of this chapter is unified and is acceptable for today's readers.

By contrast, the style of other chapters is mixed, since Futabatei consciously varies the style and the form of the verbs. The polite "-desu/-masu" style is used mainly when the narrator is the subject of the sentence and is recollecting his own past, as he is well aware of his audience. Therefore the tense becomes past, employing the "-deshita/ -mashita" forms. The plain "-(r)u" style is often used when the other characters or the scenery are the subject of the sentence. When the narrator describes or analyzes the other characters' actions, or simply describes the setting, the "-(r)u", "-te iru" and "-de aru" forms are used. The "-(r)u" form is employed mainly for repetitive or habitual actions, while the "-te iru" form is used for the description of scenery or the other characters' continuous actions, and the "-de aru" form is used when the narrator-protagonist conveys his own thoughts and analyzes Asya's or Gagin's character. The following is an example of the "-de aru" style:

> Я заглянул в эту душу: тайный гнет давил ее постоянно, тревожно путалось и билось неопытное самолюбие, но всё существо ее стремилось к правде. .... ее душа мне нравилась. (Turgenev 1964: 98)
>
> [I looked into her soul: a secret burden was tormenting her constantly, her inexperienced pride was anxiously losing its way and struggling, but all her being was striving for truth. .... What I liked was her soul.]
>
> 私の觀(み)た所では、此娘(こ)は人知れず始終胸を惱ましてゐるのである、未だ世の味といふものを知らぬから、動(やや)もすれば、修羅(しゆら)を炎(もや)して焦心(いらくら)するやうなもの〻、心は常に眞(まこと)の道を辿らむとする傾(かたむき)を持つてゐるのである。（中略）私の氣に入つたのは實に此娘(このこ)の心である。(Futabatei Shimei 1964a: 239)
>
> [From my point of view, this girl is constantly tormenting her soul. Because [she] has little experience in the real world, she is often outraged and irritated, but her heart inclines to follow the true and honest way. ... What I liked is the heart of this girl.]

Thus, in *One-sided Love,* the past, which the narrator-protagonist tries to seal as past experience by the particular style of his narrative ("-deshita/-mashita"), constantly breaks out, and the characters and scenery emerge as if they insist that the narrator's past has not been completely analyzed and sealed. Futabatei's practice of rendering some of the past imperfective Russian verbs as 'present-tense' form Japanese verbs, in an attempt to retain the aspectual meaning, creates a double stream of time in the translated story. One is the stream of past time, which is given by the narrator-protagonist, and guaranteed by the "-ta" forms, originating in those past imperfective verbs which depict the narrator's actions. The other is the stream of present time which flows in the narrated story, carried by the "-te iru" forms used to render those past imperfective verbs which depict the actions of the other characters. These two streams of time are explicitly divided, but on one occasion they meet, and the narrator steps into the present time of his own narrated story. This is found in passage seven cited above: "...furuete iru sono ijirashisa wa nakanaka kuchi de wa iwaremasen [I cannot fully express how pitiful she looks, breathing rapidly and trembling]". Here the narrator's time becomes the same as Asya's and his viewpoint moves away from his own present time. The narrator slips into the present time which flows in his narrated story.

To sum up, in *One-sided Love* Futabatei seems to focus not on Asya, but on the narrator-protagonist, who is a dramatized narrator, and radically different from the implied author. At first Futabatei gives a stable point of view to the narrator, which is guaranteed by the past form "-ta", but that point of view is constantly challenged by the narrated characters' present time, and finally the narrator's point of view slips into it. As the title *Katakoi [One-sided love]* itself indicates, the narrator-protagonist is unaware, and remains unaware, of his incapacity for love. In this sense the story remains unfinished. Futabatei himself spoke of the significance of the title:

> Do you ask why that story is about one-sided love? Yes, it is one-sided. People might say that this is a rather far-fetched opinion. — Yes, of course, the girl's love should be the ardent one, but I cannot see any evidence that the man's love emerged independently, it seems that he simply responds to her. Well, he is more or less charmed by her, but he is a very ordinary man who has ordinary feelings, and the author does not give him any particular characteristics. That kind of love is described in Russian as "philosophical love"; a feeling shared by everyone. (Futabatei Shimei 1965a: 279 - Emphasis added)

It is significant that Futabatei defines the narrator as "an ordinary man with ordinary feelings" and not as a representative of the type known as "lishnii chelovek [a superfluous man]". When he translated *Asya,* he focused on this ordinary man, and Futabatei described how the "ordinary" narrator responded to Asya's extraordinarily passionate love. While the present time of the narration succeeds in depicting this extraordinary love, the narrator's present time, although not consistently upheld to the end, also succeeds in describing an "ordinary" man's response to it.

Finally a comment must be made on the use of the third-person pronoun and its connection to love-related vocabulary. The use of the third-person pronoun is closely related to the narrative point of view, (a point which will be discussed in more detail in the next chapter). In *One-sided Love,* Futabatei for the first time translated third-person pronouns very clearly:

я повторял сто раз, что **я ее люблю**, я клялся никогда с ней расставаться;… (Turgenev 1964: 116)

[I repeated a hundred times that **I loved her**, I swore never to be separated from her; …]

**彼を愛する**といふことを幾回（いくたび）となく繰返へして、未来永劫離れまいと誓つた、(Futabatei Shimei 1964a: 261)

[I repeated many times that **I loved her** and I swore that [we] won't be separated ever …]

This is uttered by the narrator as he realizes his love for Asya after their fateful meeting. The same phrase is repeated when Asya leaves suddenly, this time as an expression of repentance:

Одно слово ... — но я не сказал его ей, я не сказал ей, что **я люблю ее**... (Turgenev 1964: 119)

[One word ... — but I did not say it to her, I did not tell her that **I loved her**…]

只の一言（ひとこと）……（中略）アーシヤには其一言を聞かさなかつた、**私は彼を愛する**といふことを云はずに了つた…… (Futabatei Shimei 1964a: 265)

[One word ... — I did not say it to Asya, I did not tell that **I loved her**…]

Futabatei also employs the Sino-Japanese word "kenren suru [to love]" which is often used in *Yomihon* (a variety of *gesaku* fiction, generally serious in tone, written during the Edo period):

Послушайте: моя сестра, Ася, в вас **влюблена**. (Turgenev 1964: 107)

[Please listen, my sister Asya **is in love** with you.]

妹が……その……貴君に**眷戀（けんれん）してゐますよ**。(Futabatei Shimei 1964a: 250)

[My sister ... well, ... **is in love** with you.]

Generally third-person pronouns are not used in the translations Futabatei made during his second period of literary activity, and the word "love" is often translated using either old-fashioned Sino-Japanese words or ambiguous expressions from *gesaku* such as "Ore no koto o **nan to ka omotte iru** no ja nai ka? [Is she **thinking especially** of me?]" for "Neuzheli ona menya **lyubit**? [Can she really **be in love with** me?]" Nevertheless, recognizing that

"Ya lyublyu ee [I love her]" are key words in the story, Futabatei translates them as literally as possible, and the third-person pronoun comes out of its own accord, not as the modern "kanojo", but as "kare", which today means "he". We might note that in the third-person narrative *Passions and Griefs*, written in 1896 (the year *One-sided Love* was published), Kōyō frequently employs the third-person pronoun "kare" to indicate both male and female characters.

## *Yudaya-jin*[2] *[The Jew]* (Translated from Turgenev's *Zhid [The Jew]*)

*The Jew* was written in 1846, early in Turgenev's career. About this story Seeley (1991: 94) has written: "Turgenev continues to keep subjectivity at bay by choosing for portrayal a period and setting and events and, presumably, characters from outside the limits of his own experience". Seeley concludes that because of this objectivity and distance from experience, all the main characters become stereotyped. The picture of the protagonist, the Jewish spy who is executed, "makes its impact on the reader in the manner of 'slice of life' journalism".

Satō Seirō (1995: 409) presumes that Futabatei made this translation because of financial difficulties, since he had just resigned from his position at the official gazette bureau. While the translation may have been made for financial reasons, and the original story may be superficial, it is apparent that the narrator in Futabatei's translation gains a more stable point of view than in *One-sided Love*. The narrator of this story is a colonel, a veteran of the Napoleonic wars. He recalls an incident from his life during the 1813 siege of Danzig. Futabatei employs the Japanese first-person pronoun "boku" for the colonel, and the "-no da" style for the narration. The narrator and his audience are explicitly introduced at the beginning of the story by the implied author. Futabatei thus clearly distinguishes the narrator from the implied author by giving them different styles of narration: "-no da" for the narrator and "-da" for the implied author.

After winning a large sum of money at cards, the narrator is approached by a Jew named Girshel, who follows the Russian camp. The Jew offers to bring a beautiful girl to his tent, if the narrator pays for her. He does indeed bring a beautiful Jewish girl named Sara. Although Sara and Girshel take some money, Sara abruptly escapes from the tent on the first visit, and on a subsequent visit she bursts into tears. The young and inexperienced colonel can do nothing but let her go.

In Futabatei's translation the narrator recalls his own actions from a firm present time, and this retrospective viewpoint is clearly indicated by the "-te ita" forms which are used to translate the past imperfective verbs of the original. We may also note that the first-person pronouns are translated faithfully in almost all cases. The following are some typical examples of how the narrator's actions are described in *The Jew*:

1. **Я** <u>молчал</u> и <u>глядел</u> на жида. (Turgenev 1963b: 117)

[**I** <u>remained silent</u> and <u>stared</u> at the Jew.]

---

[2] Note: Futabatei himself intended the characters in this title to have the reading "Yudea-jin" rather than the now accepted "Yudaya-jin".

**僕は**黙つて老夫の面を視て居た。(Futabatei Shimei 1964b: 156)

[**I** was staring at the old chap's face silently.]

2. Пошли толки. **Я** лежал на бурке, пил чай и слушал рассказы товарищей. (Turgenev 1963b: 117)

[The chat began. **I** lay on my felt cloak, drank tea and listened to my comrade's tales.]

其内に話が始まつたから、**僕は**フェルトの上衣を敷いて、臥倒んで、茶を喫みながら、人の話を聽いてゐた。(Futabatei Shimei 1964b: 157)

[In the meantime the conversation began. **I** spread my felt coat and lay on top of it, and was listening to my comrade's chat, while drinking tea.]

3. **Я** стоял перед ней и смотрел на нее молча. (Turgenev 1963b: 118)

[**I** stood in front of her and looked at her silently.]

**僕は**前に立つて黙つて面を視てゐた。(Futabatei Shimei 1964b: 158)

[Standing in front of her, **I** was looking at (her) face silently.]

This firm retrospective point of view does not shift like that of the narrator in *One-sided Love.* The colonel looks back on his past and describes it retrospectively, even when relating how the Jew, who turns out to be the beautiful girl's father, is executed:

**Я** молчал. Гиршель был мне гадок, да и она, его сообщница... (Turgenev 1963b: 130)

[**I** remained silent. Girshel was repulsive to me, and so was she, his accomplice...]

**僕は**黙つてゐた。老父も厭だつたが。同類になつてゐた娘も厭になつて來た。(Futabatei Shimei 1964b: 172)

[**I** remained silent. The old father was repulsive to me and so became his daughter, who was his accomplice.]

By rendering these past imperfective verbs, which express the past continuous actions of the narrator, as "-te ita" forms, retrospectivity is emphasized. On the other hand, the actions of the characters described by the narrator are often portrayed by "-te iru" or "-(r)u" forms, even though the corresponding verbs in the original are past imperfective:

1. **Этот жид, по прозвищу Гиршель**, то и дело таскался в наш лагерь, напрашивался в факторы, доставал нам вина, съестных припасов и прочих безделок; росту был он небольшого, худенький, рябой, рыжий, — беспрестанно моргал крошечными, тоже рыжими глазками, нос имел кривой и длинный и всё покашливал. (Turgenev 1963b: 116)

[**This Jew, whose nickname was Girshel**, was continually hanging around our camp, offering his services as an agent, getting us wine, food supplies and other trifles. He was not tall, he was thin, pock-marked, red-haired—he constantly blinked with his tiny eyes, which were also red, he had a long crooked nose and kept coughing.]

**此奴**は五月蠅用を聞きに來る奴で、酒だの、食物だの、といふやうなものを持つて來るのだ。　背の低い、痩せた、痘瘡のある胡蘿蔔見たやうな色の奴で、小さな、矢張胡蘿蔔色の眼を蒼蠅ぱちぱちやらせて、高い、端の曲つた鼻をして、始終咳ばつかり仕てゐるのだ。(Futabatei Shimei 1964b: 155)

[**This fellow** is constantly and importunately offering his services, and getting wine, food supplies and other things. He is small, thinnish, pock-marked and reddish; he constantly blinks his eyes, which are reddish too, and he has a long crooked nose and is coughing all the time.]

2. Я оглянулся: **Гиршель**. Он был очень бледен, заикался и пришепётывал. (Turgenev 1963b: 118)

[I looked around: it was **Girshel**. He was very pale, stammered and lisped slightly.]

振向いて視ると、**ギルシェリ**だ。非常に蒼然な面をして、物を言ふにも吃つて囁めく。(Futabatei Shimei 1964b: 157)

[[When] I have looked around, it is **Girshel**. He looks very pale and when he talks he stammers and whispers.]

3. Я встал и пошел за ним. **Жид** весь съежился и осторожно выступал по короткой сырой траве. (Turgenev 1963b: 118)

[I stood up and went after him. **The Jew** huddled up and was carefully stepping over the short wet grass.]

ト云ふから、起上つて後に随いて行くと、**老夫奴**小さくなつて、夜露に濡れた短い草の上を竊と歩いて行く。(Futabatei Shimei 1964b: 157)

[As he says this, I stand and follow him. **The old chap** huddles up and is carefully stepping over the short grass, wet by the dew.]

4. Легкий шорох заставил меня оглянуться. **Гиршель** осторожно высовывал голову из-под края палатки. (Turgenev 1963b: 118)

[A slight rustle made me look around. **Girshel** was carefully poking his head under the edge of the tent.]

ごそごそといつたから、振向いて視ると、**老夫**天幕の端から竊と覗いてゐる。(Futabatei Shimei 1964b: 158)

[As I hear a slight rustle, I look around**. The old man** is cautiously peeping at us under the edge of the tent.]

The first and second passages depict Girshel's habitual or repetitive actions, and the verb form Futabatei selects for these actions is "-(r)u", the same as he employed in *One-sided Love*. On the other hand, the third and fourth passages depict Girshel's continuous actions, and for these Futabatei employs the "-te iku" and "-te iru" forms, which are faithful to the aspect, but not the tense, of the original Russian verbs. Girshel's pitiful yet rather comical behaviour (as he shows concern for his daughter, and also before his execution) is emphasized by translating past imperfective verbs into the "-te iru" form:

5. **Несчастный Гиршель** слабо упирался локтями в грудь Силявки, слабо болтал ногами... Глаза его судорожно закатывались... (Turgenev 1963b: 124)

[**Poor Girshel** was feebly prodding his elbows into Silyavka's chest, feebly waving his legs... His eyes were rolling convulsively...]

**ギルシェリ**は辛とシリヤーフカの胸に肘を突張て、足でばたばたやるけれども、毫も力が入つてゐない……眼をきよろきよろさして、いや、見るも哀れな躰さ。(Futabatei Shimei 1964b: 165)

[Girshel is barely prodding his elbows into Silyavka's chest, and kicking his legs, but he is powerless... He rolls his eyes convulsively. It is too pitiful to look at him.]

6. Я приблизился к **Гиршелю**, заговорил с ним; он рыдал, как ребенок, и даже не посмотрел на меня. (Turgenev 1963b: 128-129)

[I came up to **Girshel** and began to speak; he sobbed like a child and did not even look at me.]

僕は**ギルシェリ**の側へ行つて、物を言懸けて見たが、子供のやうに泣いてばかりゐて、面を揚げ得ないのだ。(Futabatei Shimei 1964b: 170)

[I have come up to **Girshel** and tried to speak, but he is sobbing like a child, and he cannot even look at me.]

Thus, when the narrator turns his eyes on Girshel and starts describing his behaviour, in Futabatei's translation the verb form shifts from "-ta" to "-(r)u", the present time of the story begins to flow, and Girshel's actions stand out clearly and vividly. This is also true of other characters such as Girshel's daughter, Silyavka and the soldiers. Their actions, denoted by past imperfective verbs in the original, are also translated as "-te iru" forms:

1. ... я сел подле нее и взял ее смуглую, тонкую руку. Она немного противилась, но как будто боялась глядеть на меня и неровно дышала. (Turgenev 1963b: 119)

[I sat down beside her and took her dark, slender hand. She resisted little, but seemed to be afraid of looking at me, and was breathing unevenly.]

僕が側に坐つて手を—細い淺黒いな—手を把つたけれど、左程厭がりもせん、けれども何となく臆して居て、成るべく僕の面を視ないやうにして、而して息氣を激ましてゐる。 (Futabatei Shimei 1964b: 158)

[I sat down beside her and took her dark, slender hand. She hardly resists, but she seems afraid and she tries not to look at me, and is breathing rapidly.]

2. Она плакала навзрыд... Я ласкал ее, утирал ее слезы; она по-прежнему не противилась, не отвечала на мои расспросы и плакала,—плакала в три ручья. (Turgenev 1963b: 122)

[She was sobbing ... I caressed her, wiped away her tears; as before she did not resist, did not answer my questions, and wept, wept profusely.]

吃逆りあげて泣いてゐる。背を撫でたり泪を拭いたりしてやつたが、矢張厭がりもしない、其代り何と云つて問いても返答をしないで、唯泣いてゐる、—ひた泣に泣いてゐるのだ、— (Futabatei Shimei 1964b: 162)

[She is sobbing. I patted her back and wiped away her tears, as before (she) does not resist, but she does not answer, no matter what I ask, and she is crying— she is wailing...]

3. Он поднимал свою добычу выше головы и смеялся;...Другие два кирасира вьючили лошадей своих сеном, соломой, мучными кулями. (Turgenev 1963b: 123)

[He was holding his booty up above his head and laughing;...the other two cuirassiers were loading their horses with hay, straw and sacks of flour.]

シリヤーフカ奴分捕物を頭より高く差上げて笑つてゐる。（中略）向うの方では兵士が二人ばかり、枯草や藁や粉の袋を自分の騎（の）つて來た馬に駄（つ）むでゐる。(Futabatei Shimei 1964b: 163)

[Silyavka is holding his booty up above his head and laughing—Over there two soldiers are loading the horses on which they have ridden with hay, straw and sacks of flour.]

4. Мы подбежали к солдатам. Они стали в кружок и, представьте, господа! смеялись, смеялись над бедным Гиршелем! (Turgenev 1963b: 130)

[We ran up to the soldiers. They stood in a circle and imagine, gentlemen! laughed, laughed at poor Girshel!]

兵卒共の居る處へ來て見ると、大勢ギルシェリの周圍（まはり）に環立（たか）つて可哀（かわいさう）も何も有りやしない、ワイワイ云つて笑つてゐるんだ。(Futabatei Shimei 1964b: 171-172)

[When we have run up to the place where the soldiers are, a lot of them are surrounding Girshel and they are indeed laughing loudly at him, not pitying him.]

While the third and fourth passages depict the soldiers' actions, the first and second passages depict the actions of the Jewish girl Sara. She behaves timidly towards the narrator, but is greedy for his money. This stereotypical behaviour is presented graphically with the use of "-te iru" forms in Futabatei's translation. Here Futabatei again adopts a foreignizing strategy. However, a domesticating strategy is evident in the way Futabatei translates Turgenev's references to the main characters. Futabatei avoids translating the passage where Turgenev first introduces the name "Girshel", at the very beginning of the story. Futabatei first translates "zhid [the Jew]" literally as "yudea-jin", then employs "oyaji [the old chap]" or "oyaji [the old man]" for "zhid [the Jew]". Futabatei keeps employing these terms even after he abruptly and inexplicably introduces the name "Girshel". While Turgenev alternates "Girshel'" and "zhid [the Jew]" throughout the story, Futabatei alternates "oyaji [the old chap]", "oyaji (using a different Chinese character) [the old man]" or "girusheri (in *katakana*) [Girshel]" during the first half of the story, then uses mainly "girusheri" in the latter part of the story. The terms "oyaji [old chap]" and "oyaji [old man]" (Futabatei even uses "oyaji [the old father]" once the narrator learns that Sara is Girshel's daughter), show the relationship between the characters, but disguise the fact that Girshel is Jewish, a fact central to the story. A similar disguising or softening is found in the way Futabatei translates Turgenev's references to Girshel's daughter Sara. Turgenev first introduces Sara as "zakutannaya figura [a tightly wrapped figure]" and then she is referred to by the narrator as "molodaya zhidovka [the young Jewish girl]". Futabatei translates "zakutannaya figura [a tightly wrapped figure]" firstly as "katsugi o kabutte jitto tatte iru mono [a motionless figure wrapped in a veil]" and then simply as "okatsugi sama [the veiled lady]". After translating "molodaya zhidovka [the young Jewish girl]" quite literally as "yudea-jin no musume [a Jewish girl]", Futabatei keeps employing "musume [girl]" for the third person pronoun "ona [she]". Even when in the original Sara is specifically referred to as "zhidovka [the Jewish girl]", Futabatei simply translates it as "musume [girl]". In the latter part of the story Futabatei translates Sara's name faithfully without omission. However, the Japanese originate word "katsugi [a veil]" and the general word "musume [girl]" not qualified by "yudea-jin no [Jewish]" soften and domesticate Sara's image as a delicate yet cunning Jewish girl. Futabatei later (during the third period of his literary activity) employs the same domesticating strategy with reference to the Jewish character Kain in *Jū no ukiyo [The Hard Life of a Jew],* his translation of Gorky's *Kain i Artem [Kain and Artem].*

In summary, the translated story *The Jew* succeeds in vividly presenting the characters' actions as witnessed by the narrator, through the use of "-te iru" forms to translate past imperfective verbs. The "-ta" forms used to translate past perfective verbs describing the main characters' actions carry more aspectual meaning. On the other hand "-ta" forms which retrospectively depict the narrator's actions, and are faithful renditions of past imperfective verbs, convey more the meaning of tense, and often appear in the "-te ita" form. The dramatized narrator in *The Jew* looks back upon his past objectively, and this firm retrospective viewpoint abides throughout the story. The objectivity of the original narrative is successfully captured in Futabatei's translation. However, the way the characters are named is a significant departure from Turgenev's original and modifies its essence, weakening the Jewish theme. Futabatei adopts a foreignizing strategy in his use of verb forms, but a domesticating strategy in regard to the naming of the characters.

Before turning to Futabatei's translations of the third-person narrative stories *The Portrait, Rudin* and *Petushkov,* let us review what Futabatei achieved through his translation of the first-person narrative stories discussed in this chapter. Although the effect varies in each story, Futabatei succeeds in creating a double stream of time in his translations of the first-person narrative stories *Asya* and *The Jew*. One stream of time is the past, as described by the narrator protagonist, whom Futabatei differentiates from the implied author. The narrator's past is guaranteed by the use of "-te ita" forms, originating in those past imperfective verbs which depict the narrator's own actions. The other is the stream of present time which flows in the narrated story, carried by the "-te iru" forms used to translate those past imperfective verbs which depict the actions of other characters. In *One-sided Love*, these two streams of time meet at the end of the story, and the narrator's present time slips into the present time of the narrated story. In *The Jew* the two streams of time never meet, and the double stream of time guarantees the narrator's objectivity and distance from the events narrated. The narrator seals off his past completely.

In general, we may say that in his translations of Turgenev's first-person narratives, Futabatei adopted a foreignizing strategy in respect of verb forms. Whereas past imperfective verbs are usually translated using "-(r)u" or "-te iru" forms, past perfective verbs are translated employing "-ta" forms. An exception is found in the case of past imperfective verbs used to describe the dramatized narrator's own actions, which are translated using "-ta" forms, often appearing in the "-te ita" form. Consequently these "-ta" forms carry the meaning of the past tense, and impart a clear retrospective point of view to the narrator of the story.

# Chapter 4 — A Third-person Narrative: *The Portrait*

From a purely mechanical point of view, we might expect that when the narrator of a first-person narrative retreats into the background, a third-person narrative would emerge. In this case, the two streams of time created in Futabatei's translations of first-person narratives might diminish or disappear in his translations of third-person narratives. That is, the 'present time' associated with these dramatized narrators might disappear, as might the past tense marker "-te ita" characteristic of the narrator. In this chapter we shall see if this is the case.

The third-person narrative stories which Futabatei translated during the second period of his translation activity were Gogol's *Portret [The Portrait],* Turgenev's novel *Rudin* and his story *Petushkov*. It is significant that the first third-person narrative story to be translated by Futabatei was written by Gogol, rather than by his "favourite" Turgenev, and that *Petushkov* is considered to be, in the words of the prominent Slavist and translator from Russian, Araya Keizaburō (1967), "the most Gogolian story amongst Turgenev's works".

Araya (1967) raises the question: was Turgenev really the Russian writer with whom Futabatei identified most closely, and whom he most admired? If not, why did Futabatei translate so many of Turgenev's stories? In answer to these questions, Araya identifies two opposite tendencies in the works by Turgenev which Futabatei translated, one typified by *The Rendezvous* and the other by *Petushkov.* While *The Rendezvous* is written poetically, depicting all matters, including human affairs, contemplatively, *Petushkov* (and *The Jew*) are written under the strong influence of Russian naturalism. Gogol and Dostoevsky are considered to be two representatives of this type of writing. Araya (1967: 63-65) summarizes the characteristics of Russian naturalism (as typified by *Petushkov*) as follows:

1. The plot typically involves a middle-aged and isolated man falling in love with a young girl and despairing when his love is not reciprocated.
2. The physical descriptions of the main characters frequently portray comical and trivial features, as in the description of Bublitsin in *Petushkov*.
3. Conversation is frequently incoherent and absurd.
4. The story ends with a tragic monologue from the main character.

Araya has drawn the tentative conclusion that amongst those works by Turgenev which Futabatei chose to translate, we clearly see elements of Gogolian stories, and that the Russian writer with whom Futabatei identified most closely was not Turgenev, but Gogol. Araya further suggests (1967: 66-67) that Futabatei may have left *Floating Clouds* unfinished because of a change in his writing style which occurred while he was translating *The Rendezvous,* which shows no traces of Russian naturalism. Araya notes a similarity in the body language found in works by Gogol and Shikitei Sanba, a *gesaku* [light literature] writer of the Edo period, who wrote *Ukiyoburo [The Up-to-date Bath-house]* and *Ukiyodoko [The Up-to-date Barber Shop].* Araya concludes that the styles of Gogol and Sanba met in the works of the young Futabatei. (In this he was in agreement with Shimizu Shigeru (1960), who had earlier noted a phraseological resemblance between Sanba's style and Futabatei's.) Finally Araya raises the question: what are the Gogolian elements in Futabatei's work, and what role do they play? However, he concludes his article without answering this question.

I shall commence my discussion of Futabatei's third-person narrative translations by attempting to answer the question which Araya raised from the point of view of tense and aspect in each translated story. I shall compare the narrator and narrative viewpoint of *Floating Clouds,* which is supposed to be a third-person narrative, with those of third-person narrative stories translated by Futabatei. Although these translations were made almost ten years after *Floating Clouds* Part One first appeared, the comparison will still be useful in helping us understand how Futabatei developed the techniques of a third-person narrative, which was utterly new to Japanese literature at the time. In particular, a comparison of the narrator of *Floating Clouds* with those of *The Portrait, The Mismatch* and *Floating Weed* (translations of *The Portrait, Petushkov* and *Rudin,* respectively), will reveal new insights into which Russian writer most influenced Futabatei's writings.

First of all, we must define the relationship between the narrator, the main character and the author. Protesting against the conventional definition, which distinguishes first-person from third-person narratives on the basis of their grammatical forms, Gerard Genette proposes a different theoretical framework. In his book *Narrative Discourse* he suggests that "the novelist's choice, unlike the narrator's, is not between two grammatical forms, but between two narrative postures (whose grammatical forms are simply an automatic consequence): to have the story told by one of its "characters", or to have it told by a narrator outside of the story" (Genette 1980: 244).

Genette classifies stories into four categories by defining the narrator's status, both by its narrative level (extra- or intradiegetic) and by its relationship to the story (hetero- or homodiegetic). This results in four paradigms:

(1) The extradiegetic-heterodiegetic paradigm, as exemplified by Homer, a narrator in the first degree who tells a story from which he is absent;
(2) The extradiegetic-homodiegetic paradigm, as exemplified by Gil Blas, a narrator in the first degree who tells his own story;
(3) The intradiegetic-heterodiegetic paradigm, as exemplified by Scheherazade, a narrator in the second degree, who tells stories from which she is, on the whole, absent;
(4) The intradiegetic-homodiegetic paradigm, as exemplified by Ulysses in Books IX-XII, a narrator in the second degree, who tells his own story.

Genette (1980: 248) presents this information in tabular form (see Table 6).

***Table 6 : Genette's classification of narratives***

| **LEVEL:<br>RELATIONSHIP** | **Extradiegetic<br>(1st degree narrator)** | **Intradiegetic<br>(2nd degree narrator)** |
|---|---|---|
| *Heterodiegetic*<br>(narrator absent from story as a character) | Homer (1) | Scheherazade (3) C |

| *Homodiegetic* (narrator present in story as a character) | Gil Blas (2) *Marcel* | Ulysses (4) |
|---|---|---|

According to this classification, Genette positions the fictive novelist C, the (second) narrator in *Santeuil* (the original form of *A la Récherche du Temps Perdu*), in the intra-heterodiegetic paradigm, whereas the single narrator of *A la Récherche du Temps Perdu* is in the diametrically opposite category, the extra-homodiegetic. Genette concludes:

> We are dealing here with an absolute reversal, since we move from a situation characterized by the complete dissociation of the instances (first and extradiegetic author narrator: "I"; second narrator, intradiegetic novelist: "C."; metadiegetic hero "Jean") to the inverse situation, characterized by the merging of all three instances in the one single "person": the author-narrator-hero Marcel. (1980: 249)

We may accordingly annotate Genette's table as shown in Table 7, where A= Author, N=Narrator and H=Hero.

Now, using Genette's classification, we may see that all the first-person narrative stories discussed in chapter three are "homodiegetic", and must fall into either category two or four, depending on the narrative level (extra- or intradiegetic). The narrators in *One-sided Love* and *The Jew* are clearly intradiegetic (narrators in the second degree), as they are introduced by the extradiegetic author-narrator as "nanigashi [a certain person—"N.N." in Russian]" and "taisa Nikorai Īryichi [a major Nikolai Il'ich]". The two stories discussed in chapter three fall into category four, the intradiegetic-homodiegetic paradigm, having narrators in the second degree who tell their own stories.

***Table 7 : The relationship between author, narrator and hero in Genette's classification***

| **LEVEL: RELATIONSHIP** | **Extradiegetic** | **Intradiegetic** |
|---|---|---|
| *Heterodiegetic* | Homer<br>A=N≠H | Scheherazade (C)<br>A≠N≠H |
| *Homodiegetic* | Gil Blas (*Marcel*)<br>A=N=H | Ulysses<br>A≠N=H |

The third-person narrative stories we shall discuss in this and the following chapter, and *Floating Clouds,* would fall into categories one or three, being either extraheterodiegetic or intraheterodiegetic, depending on the narrative level. That is, *Floating Clouds* and the other stories are not told by one of the characters. Whether the narrator is of the first or second degree needs to be carefully determined. Does the narrator show himself to be separate from the author, and in what fashion? In this way we may clarify the author-narrator relationship in the third-person narrative.

Booth also dissents from the conventional definition of the relationship between author, narrator and protagonist in first-person and third-person narratives. He writes: "To say that a story is told in the first or the third person will tell us nothing of importance unless we become more precise and describe how the particular qualities of the narrator relate to a specific effect" (Booth 1961: 150). Booth classifies narrators into three categories, according to whether the narrator is dramatized in his own right, and whether his beliefs and characteristics are shared by the author:

1. The implied author,
2. Undramatized narrators,
3. Dramatized narrators.

What differentiates an undramatized narrator from a dramatized one is the extent to which he expresses a different point of view from that of the implied author who creates him. Thus it is possible even in a third-person narrative for a dramatized narrator to remain within the story.

In this context, Kubo Yumi (1984: 98-111) argues that the "controversial" narrator of *Floating Clouds* can be defined as a double of the author who has his own character. In order to make descriptions seem objective, Kubo argues, a narrative device capable of holding a firm narrative point of view needed to be introduced into Japanese literature. The narrator created by Futabatei in *Floating Clouds* is a kind of by-product of the process of creating a modern narrative device which merely holds a point of view, but does not have its own character in the story. Consequently a narrator as a narrative device ought to be separated from the author outside the story. The following is the hypothetical chart drawn by Kubo to show the development of narrators in Japanese literature:

| Katari-te = Author → | Jojutsu-sha 1 = Author → | Jojutsu-sha 2 ≠ Author |
|---|---|---|
| [Narrator] | [Delineator 1] | [Delineator 2] |

Kubo chooses her terminology carefully. She opts for "Katari-te" for the narrators of Edo literature, who are inseparable from the authors, and "Jojutsu-sha" for the narrators of modern Meiji literature, who delineate in the text and who are supposed to be distinct from the authors. According to Kubo's theory, to convert the semi-modern delineator 1 to the modern delineator 2, which functions as a narrative device, it was inevitable that Futabatei would eliminate the existence of the narrator from the text of *Floating Clouds*. First Futabatei deleted the narrator's direct discourse with the reader. Secondly he shifted the verb form from "-(r)u" to "-ta", which carried the meaning of the past tense. In so doing Futabatei took the first steps towards creating a "modern" novel, which put the narrator outside the story.

We may question the extent to which the "semi-modern" delineator 1 has been eliminated from *Floating Clouds*. The question still remains as to whether Futabatei created the narrator of *Floating Clouds* as a double of the author. If the narrator is fully dramatized, and expresses a different point of view from that of the implied author, *Floating Clouds* may fall into Genette's third category, the intraheterodiegetic narrative, in which the narrator is clearly different from the implied author (A≠N≠H). The "modern" story, in which, according to Kubo, the narrator is merely a device to hold a point of view, may conversely fall into

Genette's first category, the extraheterodiegetic paradigm (A=N≠H). Although the narrator is not actually identical with the author, he is a mere narrative device directly manipulated by the implied author.

Now we shall see whether Gogol's *The Portrait* falls into Genette's first (A=N≠H) or third (A≠N≠H) categories. In other words, we shall see whether the narrator is fully dramatized or not. *The Portrait* is the story of a poor but talented young painter, Chartkov, who by chance purchases the portrait of an old man, with eyes that seem incredibly alive. He finds a large sum of money concealed in the frame, but this money leads to the corruption of his talent, as he becomes a fashionable portrait painter, producing works to meet the taste of his wealthy patrons. He comes to the realization that his talent has been corrupted when confronted with a work of spiritual dedication and genius, produced by a friend of his student days. Overcome with jealousy, he uses his wealth to buy as many fine paintings as he can, in order to tear them to shreds. This demonic obsession consumes him completely, leading to madness and death.

The story has a second part, narrated by the son of the artist who produced the seemingly demonic portrait of the old man with the penetrating gaze. The son comes across the painting at an auction and explains its history. His father had painted a notorious moneylender, who was credited with ruining many people's lives. The moneylender had died soon after the work was painted, and the portrait had apparently led to the ruin of many of those who had been unfortunate enough to possess it. The son has come on a mission to destroy the painting, but it mysteriously disappears before he is able to do so.

Gogol produced two versions of this story. The first version was written during 1833 and 1834 and appeared in part one of *Arabesques* in 1835, together with *Nevsky Prospekt [Nevsky Avenue]*. The second version was written during 1841 and 1842, when Gogol was staying in Rome, and it was published in the journal *Sovremennik [The Contemporary]* in 1842. Richard Peace (1981: 116) analyzes the difference between the two versions as follows:

> In revising "The Portrait"... Gogol eliminated many of the more overtly supernatural elements. ... More significantly the identification of the moneylender with Antichrist is absent, while at the same time greater emphasis is placed on the corrupting power of money.

Peace also points out that the second version contains more "naturalistic" descriptions, such as those of the staircase at Chartkov's garret, the comic conversation with the policeman and Chartkov's dealings with a popular newspaper. Futabatei chose to translate the second, more "naturalistic" version.

Futabatei was probably motivated to translate this story by the literary trend of the time, with its interest in portraits, symbolizing the uniqueness of the human personality, and moneylenders, showing the corrupting power of money. The theme of the moneylender was in several instances treated by writers contemporary with Futabatei. Among these we might mention the unfinished masterpiece *Konjiki yasha [The Demon Gold]*, by the leader of the Ken'yūsha group Ozaki Kōyō, in which the hero is betrayed by his fiancée and becomes a heartless moneylender. Part One of that work appeared in the same year as *The Portrait.* Moneylenders are also frequently depicted in the works of Hirotsu Ryūrō, whose *Heme Den [Cross-eyed Den]* (1895) was published two years before *The Portrait.* (Cross-eyed Den commits a murder after borrowing money in the pursuit of love.)

As for the portrait theme, it is significant that *The Portrait* was published soon after Ozaki Kōyō had completed his *genbun itchi* novel *Tajō takon [Passions and Griefs].* Initially Kōyō was opposed to the *genbun itchi* style, and created a pseudo-classical style for his early works, and for his last work, *The Demon Gold.* However, in *Passions and Griefs,* he felt it necessary to adopt the *genbun itchi* style to depict the mentality of the protagonist Ryūnosuke, who grieves over the death of his beloved wife. Written in the "-de aru" style, in which the omniscient narrator's view has more authority, this work clearly depicts the husband's deep sorrow. The portrait theme is used effectively, as Ryūnosuke commissions a large, lifelike portrait of his wife, keeping it by his bedside and constantly talking to it as if his wife were still alive.

Munakata Kazushige (1994: 24-30) points out that around the time that Kōyō published *Passions and Griefs,* there were many novels and articles published concerning portraits. He draws attention to the fact that Ryūnosuke asks that the portrait of his wife be drawn from a photograph, and concludes that what Ryūnosuke seeks for in the portrait is a depiction of his wife's uniqueness and living quality, which coincides with the motif of *The Portrait,* in which the moneylender desperately wishes to leave a living likeness of himself after death.

Gogol's *The Portrait* (in its second version, translated by Futabatei), opens with a description of the picture shop where Chartkov buys the fateful portrait with the enigmatically living eyes:

> Нигде не останавливалось столько народа, как перед картинною лавочкою на Щукином дворе. Эта лавочка представляла, точно, самое разнородное собрание диковинок: картины большею частью были писаны масляными красками, покрыты темнозеленым лаком, в темножелтых мишурных рамах. ... Покупателей этих произведений обыкновенно немного, но зато зрителей—куча. Какой-нибудь забулдыга-лакей уже, **верно**, зевает перед ними, держа в руке судки с обедом из трактира для своего барина, который, **без сомнения**, будет хлебать суп не слишком горячий. Перед ним уже, **верно**, стоит в шинели солдат, этот кавалер толкучего рынка, продающий два перочинные ножика; торговка-охтенка с коробкою, наполненною башмаками. **Всякой восхищается по-своему**; мужики обыкновенно тыкают пальцами; кавалеры рассматривают серьёзно; лакеи-мальчики и мальчишки-мастеровые смеются и дразнят друг друга нарисованными карикатурами; старые лакеи во фризовых шинелях смотрят потому только, чтобы где-нибудь позевать; а торговки, молодые русские бабы, спешат по инстинкту, чтобы послушать, о чем калякает народ, и посмотреть, на что он смотрит. В это время невольно остановился перед лавкою проходивший мимо молодой художник Чартков. (Gogol 1973b: 79-80)
>
> [Nowhere were so many people standing as in front of the picture shop in Shchukin Court. The shop, indeed, presented the most heterogeneous collection of marvels: the pictures were painted for the most part in oil colours, covered with dark-green varnish, in dark-yellow tinsel frames. ... Buyers of these works are normally few, but there are heaps of spectators. Some debauchee lackey is, **I suppose**, already gaping before them, holding in his hand a set of dishes from the eating house for his master, who, **without doubt**, will drink his soup not very warm. In front of him, **I suppose**, a soldier in a great coat is standing, this cavalier of the second-hand goods market normally sells

two penknives; and a market woman from Okhta with a box full of shoes**. Each one admires them in his own way**: the peasants usually poke their fingers at them; the cavaliers examine them seriously; the footboys and apprentices laugh and tease each other over the painted caricatures; the old lackeys in frieze overcoats look at them simply to have something to gape at; and the market women, young Russian peasant women, hurry here by instinct, to hear what people are gossiping about, and to see what they are looking at. At this moment, a young artist, Chartkov, who was passing by, involuntarily stopped in front of the picture shop.]

何處と云つて、シチウキン長屋の繪屋の前ほど、人の群聚る處は有るまい。それも其筈で、此處には種々珍らしい物がある。繪は大抵油繪で、青黒い漆を塗つて、濁黒い金縁を附けてある。（中略）かうした繪ではあるが、買手は少ない、其代り見物は常も山を成してゐる。道草を喰ふことの甚い好きさうな誰家の僕が店頭で欠びをしてゐるが、辨當の入つた仕出屋の岡持を提げてゐるからは、旦那殿は餘り熱くない肉羹を吸はれるに**違ひない**。其前に立つてゐるのは外套を着た兵士、常も古着市へ小刀二挺を賣りに行くと云ふ先生で、其次は半靴を一杯詰めた箱を抱へた女 商人お泣といひさうな女である。**さて覽方だが、これが人に由つて違ふ**。百姓は兎角指を指したがる。兵士は眞面目な面をして見る。丁稚小僧は鳥羽繪を覽て高笑をして調戯ひ合ふ。フリーズ（織物の名）の外套を着た年老つた僕は何處かで閑を潰したいばかりで視てゐる。若い嚊衆は人が饒舌てゐる事なら、何でも聽きたい、視てゐるものなら、何でも視たい、といふ一心で嗅付けて急いで來る。

此時チャルトコフといふ通りすがりの若い畫家が何心なく店頭に立止つた。
(Futabatei Shimei 1964a: 316)

[Nowhere are so many people crowding as in front of the picture shop in Shchukin tenement house. It is no wonder, as various marvels are presented here. The pictures are almost all oil paintings, covered with dark-green Japanese lacquer in murky gold frames. ... Pictures are such, and buyers are few, but spectators are always crowding around. Some servant who likes loitering on the way is yawning in front of the shop. As he is holding a take-away lunch box from the caterer his master **must suck** not very warm soup. The fellow standing in front of him is a soldier in a great coat, who always goes to sell two penknives at the second-hand clothes shop. The next is a woman, whom we might call market woman Onaki [Mrs. Sobbing] with a box full of shoes. **Now the way of looking at the pictures varies**, depending on the person. The peasants tend to poke their fingers at them. The soldiers gaze at them seriously. The apprentices laugh and tease each other over the Toba-style caricatures. The old servants in frieze (the name of the material) overcoats are looking at them simply to kill time. The young peasant women hurry here by instinct only to want to listen to what people are gossiping about and to see what people are looking at.

At this moment a young artist called Chartkov, who was passing by, has involuntarily stopped in front of the shop.]

The beginning of *The Portrait* is striking in two ways. Firstly, its sentence endings are all "-(r)u" form verbs, except for the last one. Secondly, there is an abundant use of words rooted in Japanese culture. Whereas the first paragraph of Gogol's original uses a mixture of past and present tense verbs, Futabatei uses "-(r)u" form verbs throughout, until the last sentence, when the main character is introduced with a "-ta" form verb. In the original, all the main clause verbs in this passage are imperfective, until the appearance of Chartkov in the final sentence. Gogol employed imperfective verbs to describe the picture shop, where the portrait of the moneylender lies buried beneath other miscellaneous pictures. A detailed description of the pictures in the shop is followed by a similarly detailed, fragmented and sarcastic description of the viewers outside the shop. Initially, when past imperfective verbs are used, the description is relatively neutral. Once the shift is made to the present imperfective, the narrative becomes personal. Together with words such as "verno [probably]", "bez somneniya [without doubt]", and "Vsyakoi voskhishchaetsya po-svoemu [Each one admires them in his own way]", the present imperfective verbs imply the presence of the narrator. The narrator in *The Portrait* appears every so often in the text to make comments on the protagonist's actions and even to speak on his behalf. The following two passages contain typical examples of the narrator's voice, offering comment, or speaking on behalf of the protagonist:

1. Чартков вступил в свою переднюю, нестерпимо холодную, как всегда бывает у художников, чего впрочем они не замечают. (Gogol 1973b: 84)

[Chartkov entered his anteroom, which was unbearably cold, as is always the case at artists' homes, though they do not notice it.]

2. Наконец, овладело им невольное размышление: он стал думать о том, кому бы нужны были эти произведения. Что русской народ заглядывается на *Еруcланов Лазаревичей*, на *объедал и обпивал*, на *Фому и Ерему*, это **не казалось** ему удивительным: изображенные предметы были очень доступны и понятны народу; но где покупатели этих пестрых, грязных, масляных малеваний? кому нужны эти фламандские мужики, эти красные и голубые пейзажи, которые показывают какое-то притязание на несколько уже высший шаг искусства, но в котором выразилось всё глубокое его унижение? Это, **казалось**, не были вовсе труды ребенка-самоучки. (Gogol 1973b: 80)

[In the end he was overcome by involuntary meditation: he began wondering who needed these works. **It did not seem** surprising to him that Russians are lost in admiration of the paintings of the 'Eruslanov Lazarevich's' of this world, of people who had eaten and drunk well, of 'Foma and Erema'; these subjects were very accessible and easily understood; but where are the buyers of these motley, dirty oil daubs? Who needs these Flemish peasants, these red and blue landscapes, which display some pretension to a somewhat higher level of art, but in which was expressed its deeper degradation? They, **it seemed**, were not at all the works of a self-taught child.]

While passage one incorporated a comment directly from the narrator, in passage two the narrator appears to speak on behalf of the protagonist. The word "kazalos' [it seemed]" plays a significant role in this passage. Boris Uspensky (1970: 5-134) classifies the fields in which the point of view manifests itself in a literary text into four: the level of value, the level of phraseology, the level of spatial and temporal characteristics and the level of psychology. At the level of psychology Uspensky lists two possible ways of describing the actions of characters in the literary text. One way is to describe them from the point of view of an extraneous observer. The other is to describe them from the point of view of themselves, or that of an all-seeing observer. Whereas the former is an external point of view (in relation to the depicted character), the latter is an internal point of view. In the latter case, the author puts himself in the position of an omniscient observer. When the character's inner state is depicted, we often encounter *verba sentiendi* [verbs of perception], such as "on podumal [he thought]", "on pochuvstvoval [he felt]", "emu pokazalos' [it seemed to him]", "on znal [he knew]", "on vspomnil [he remembered]". On the other hand, in the same text we also encounter modal words such as "vidimo [evidently]", "ochevidno [obviously]", "kak budto [as if]", "kazalos' [it seemed]", which are significant signs of the point of view of the extraneous observer. *Verba sentiendi* and modal words may appear together in such expressions as "On, kazalos', dumal... [Apparently he thought...]" and "N.N. kak budto khotel... [It would seem N.N. wanted...]". Uspensky (1970: 115) defines these modal words as "slova ostraneniya [words of detachment]", since they function "to justify the use of the verbs of inner condition with regard to a person who is depicted from some detached ["ostranennyi"] point of view". These modal words "play the role of a special operator, which allows one to translate an expression describing inner thoughts into the level of objective description".

We may thus see that by using these modal words, especially "kazalos' [it seemed]" and "kak budto [as if]", the narrator of Gogol's *The Portrait* is able to objectively describe the inner thoughts of the protagonist Chartkov. Conversely speaking, these modal words reveal the existence of the narrator in the text. The following passage is a description of Chartkov's inner state, following a strange dream in which the moneylender climbs out of his portrait and drops a bundle of money.

> 3. При всем том он всё-таки не мог совершенно увериться, чтобы это был сон. Ему **казалось**, что среди сна был какой-то страшный отрывок из действительности. **Казалось**, даже в самом взгляде и выражении старика **как будто** что-то говорило, что он был у него эту ночь; рука его чувствовала только-что лежавшую в себе тяжесть, **как будто бы** кто-то за одну только минуту пред сим ее выхватил у него. Ему **казалось**, что если бы он держал только покрепче сверток, он, верно, остался бы у него в руке и после пробуждения. (Gogol 1973b: 92)
>
> [For all that, he still couldn't convince himself completely that it was a dream. **It seemed** to him that in the dream there was a kind of strange fragment from reality. **It seemed** that even in the old man's gaze and expression, it was **as if** something said that he was at his place last night; his hand felt the weight which had just been lying in it, **as if** someone had just snatched it from him. **It seemed** to him that if he had held on to the bundle just a little more strongly, it would have remained in his hand after waking.]

Employing a narrator who does not appear as a character in the text, yet shows his existence with these modal words, Gogol describes the protagonist's inner thoughts and state objectively. This narrator, although not given a persona like the narrator-protagonists in Turgenev's stories, has his own voice and style, which are explicitly shown by the present imperfective verbs and these modal words. If we apply the system of classification developed by Genette, the narrator of *The Portrait* falls into category (3), intradiegetic-heterodiegetic, a narrator in the second degree who tells stories from which he is on the whole absent. In Booth's terminology he is a "dramatized narrator". It is interesting to see how Futabatei translated these passages with the narrator's modal words. The following are Futabatei's translations of passages 2 and 3:

2. 　　一其の内に我にもなく考へ込んだ。一體まアこんな繪が何になるであらう？成程露西亜人のことであるから、エルスラーヌイ、ラザレーウィチーとか、衣服を飲み食した人とか、フォーマにエレーマとかいふものは見もしよう、夫は**解つてゐる**。畫いてある物が誰にも解り易すいものであるから。けれども、こんなに妄に油顏料を塗散らした汚ならしい繪を誰が買はう？あの南歐羅巴の百姓だの、景色畫の赤いのだの、青いのだのとなると、最う幾らか高尚がつて美術めかしてゐるけれど、其實は大に美術を辱しめたものである、こんなものが一體何になるのであらう？子供が我流に漫畫をしたものとも**見えない**、一 (Futabatei Shimei 1964a: 317)

[...In the meantime, he began meditating involuntarily. I wonder what the use of these paintings is. Indeed it is understandable that Russian people look at *Eruslanov Lazarevich*, at people who drank and ate clothes, at *Foma and Erema.* Yes, **I understand** it, since the subjects depicted here are easy for everyone to understand. Yet, who, I wonder, will buy these motley, dirty oil paintings? As for the southern European peasant and these red and blue landscapes, although they show some pretension to a higher level of art, in fact they deeply disgrace art. What on earth is the use of these paintings? **It does not seem** that they are entirely self-taught scribblings by children.]

3. 　　けれども、どうも夢のやうには思はれない。夢のやうな中にも、何處か恐ろしい現が雜つてゐるやうな所があるばかりか、老人の眼付面色を見れば、何とか言**つてゐるやうである**。或は昨夜出て來た事を言つてゐるのかも知れぬ。また手には今しがたまで何か重い物を持つてゐた覺えがあつて、誰かゞ只今それを持つて去**つたやうな氣がする**。最う少し緊り握つてゐたら、眼が覺めても手の中は金包が屹度殘つてゐたらうものをとさへ**思はれる**。(Futabatei Shimei 1964a: 329)

[None the less, it doesn't seem it's entirely a dream. Not only does it seem that there is some strange fragment from reality in the dream, but also the old man's gaze and

> expression **seem to** say something. They may suggest that he has come out last night. My hand also **feels as if** it has been holding something heavy and someone has just now snatched it away from me. **It seems** that if I had held it a little more strongly, the bundle of money would have remained in my hand after waking.]

In passage 2, except for the first sentence, Futabatei employs "-(r)u" form verbs all the way through, and passage 3 is translated entirely using "-(r)u" form verbs. The word "kazalos' [it seemed]" is faithfully translated as "omowa reru" or "mieru" [it seems], so that everywhere we find a direct manifestation of Chartkov's inner thoughts. Futabatei has transformed Gogol's narrative passages into Chartkov's monologues.

We may also observe in these passages that Futabatei is still adhering to the practice he developed when translating Turgenev's stories, that of translating some past perfective verbs into "-ta" form verbs, while past imperfective verbs are translated as "-(r)u" form verbs. In translating past imperfective verbs as "-(r)u" form verbs, Futabatei achieves two effects. One is to depict Chartkov's inner thoughts, the other is to emphasize the narrator's presence in the story. In the process the story takes on the appearance of a description by an on-the-spot commentator.

When all Futabatei's translations of imperfective verbs are examined, it is further evident that he employs "-(r)u" form verbs not only for the description of continuous actions or states, but also for habitual or repeated actions. The following are typical examples of each:

1. Description of a state or of the setting

> Красный свет вечерней зари оставался еще на половине неба; еще домы, обращенные к той стороне, чуть озарялись ее теплым светом; а между-тем уже холодное синеватое сиянье месяца становилось сильнее. Полупрозрачные легкие тени хвостами падали на землю, отбрасываемые домами и ногами пешеходцев.
> (Gogol 1973b: 83)
>
> [The red colour of the evening glow still remained in half of the sky; the houses facing in that direction were slightly lit up by its warm light; meanwhile the cold bluish moonlight was already getting stronger. The light half-transparent shadows cast by houses and the legs of pedestrians fell on the ground like tails.]
>
> 空は未(ま)だ半ば夕焼に赤らむで、西を向いた家は皆その暖かさうな反映(てりかへし)を受けてゐる一方には、冷(ひややか)に蒼味(あをみ)を帯びた月影が次第に煌(きら)めいて來る。家や往來の人の足は朦朧(ぼんやり)した淡(うす)い影を尾のやうに地に曳(ひ)いてゐる。(Futabatei Shimei 1964a: 320)
>
> [The sky is still half reddened in the evening glow, the houses facing to the west have its reflected light, meanwhile the cold bluish moonlight is gradually getting brighter. The houses and the legs of pedestrians cast their dim and light shadows on the ground like tails.]

2. Description of continuous actions

Произнесши это, художник вдруг задрожал и побледнел; на него глядело, высунувшись из-за поставленного холста, чье-то судорожно искаженное лицо. Два страшные глаза прямо вперились в него, как бы готовясь сожрать его; на устах написано было грозное повеленье молчать. Испуганный, он хотел вскрикнуть и позвать Никиту, который уже успел запустить в своей передней богатырское храпение; но вдруг остановился и засмеялся. (Gogol 1973b: 86-87)

[Having said this, the artist suddenly began shivering and turned pale; someone's convulsively distorted face, thrust out from the canvas which had been put there, was staring at him. Two fearful eyes fastened upon him, as if preparing to devour him; upon the lips was written a threatening order to keep silent. Frightened, he wanted to cry out and call Nikita, who had already managed to start snoring like a knight in his anteroom, but suddenly he stopped and burst out laughing.]

といふかと思ふと、慄然(ぶるぶる)と胴震(どうぶるひ)をして蒼くなつた。其處に置いてある布地の影から、誰やら無氣味な面(かほ)を出して、此方(こちら)を睨んでゐる。恐ろしい眼で喰付きさうに睨み詰めてゐて、聲を立てると料簡があるぞといひさうな口付をしてゐる。愕然(ぎよつ)として、僕(ぼく)を、既(も)う入口の間(ま)で蟒蛇(うはばみ)のやうな鼾(いびき)をかいてゐたニキータを呼ばうとしたが、廢(や)めて笑ひ出した。(Futabatei Shimei 1964a: 324)

[Having said this [he] shivers and has turned pale. Someone is thrusting his uncanny face from the standing [canvas] cloth, and staring at this person [me]. He is staring at him [me] with his fearful eyes as if they are ready to devour him [me], and his lips seem to be saying he would do so if he [I] break[s] his [my] silence. Terrified, he was just about to call his servant Nikita, who was snoring loudly like an anaconda, [but] he has stopped and has burst out laughing.]

3. Description of repeated actions

Казалось, весь город хотел у него писаться. У дверей поминутно раздавался звонок. ... Со всех сторон только требовали, чтоб было хорошо и скоро. ... Дамы требовали, чтобы преимущественно только душа и характер изображались в портретах, чтобы остального иногда вовсе не придерживаться, округлить все углы, облегчить все изъянцы и даже, если можно, избежать их вовсе. ... Мужчины тоже были ничем не лучше дам. (Gogol 1973b: 106)

[It seemed that the whole city wanted him to paint them. The door bell rang continually. ... From all sides all people wanted was that he paint well and quickly. ... The ladies demanded that principally only the soul and character should be depicted in the portraits, that other aspects not be adhered to, that corners be rounded, defects be lightened or, if possible, avoided entirely. ... The men too were no better than the ladies.]

> 市内擧つて肖像を畫いて貰ひに來るかのやうに、入口の呼鈴は間斷なく鳴る。（中略）來る人も來る人も、皆手際善く而して急いで畫て呉れろと云ふから、（到底も念を入れてはゐられない。）（中略）貴婦人達は何でも心意氣の面白い所を專一にして、他の所は、品に寄つては、顧はずに置いて呉れろ、それから、角々を圓く、疵を目立たぬやうにして、成らう事なら、全で削つて貰ひたい、（何でも熟々視入られても恥かしからぬ、惚れて了はれても大事ないから、そのやうな面に畫いて貰ひたいと言はれる。）（中略）紳士方も貴婦人達に劣らない、（グツと威張つて首をヒン捩つた所を畫いて呉れろと云ふ方もあれば、神々しく眼を釣揚げて天を睨むだ所をといふ方もある。）(Futabatei Shimei 1964a: 343-344)
>
> [The door bell rings continually, as though the entire town is coming and asking to have their portraits painted. ... All the customers demand to be painted beautifully and quickly (it is impossible to work attentively). ... The ladies demand that he paint solely an interesting disposition, that he leave the other parts depending on the quality, round off all corners, lighten all defects, and if possible delete them all (they demand to be portrayed very well so that the portraits will be gazed at intently, even fallen in love with). ...The gentlemen are no better than the ladies, (one demands to be painted turning his neck pompously, another demands to be painted turning his eyes up importantly and gazing at the sky).]

The description of scenery in the first passage is lyrical and melancholy, like that described by Turgenev. However, Gogol's protagonist, unlike Turgenev's, is not allowed to empathize with the beautiful scenery. On the contrary, we sense the narrator's intention is to force Chartkov to realize the stark contrast of his poverty and the stupidity of his impulsive purchase of the portrait, which has left him penniless. A similar ironic contrast is found in Futabatei's first novel *Floating Clouds:*

> 庭の一隅に栽込んだ十竿ばかりの繊竹の、葉を分けて出る月のすゞしさ。月夜見の神の力の測りなくて、斷雲一片の翳だもない、蒼空一面にてりわたる清光素色、唯亭々皎々として雫も滴たるばかり。初は隣家の隔ての竹垣に遮られて庭を半より這初め、中頃は縁側へ上ツて座舗へ這込み、稗蒔の水に流れては金瀲灔、簷馬の玻璃に透りては玉玲瓏、座賞の人に影を添へて孤燈一穗の光を奪ひ、終に間の壁へ這上る。(Futabatei Shimei 1964a: 20)
>
> [The splendid moon has risen, outlining the leaves of ten slim bamboo trees planted in the corner of the garden. Limitless in its power, the moon lights up the whole sky, in which is not a single cloud; its radiant, white illumination seems to pour down glistening drops of light to the earth below. At first the bamboo fence between the

> houses holds back the moonbeams and they extend only half way across the garden. As the moon rises in the sky, the moonbeams creep up to the verandah and pour into the room. The water in the bonsai pot there shimmered in the light; the glass wind chime tinkled and glittered. Then the moonlight silhouettes the two young people and steals the brightness from the single lamp in the room. Finally it climbs up the wall.] (Ryan 1967: 217 – modified)

Although the narrator of *Floating Clouds* is more loquacious than that of *The Portrait* and comments excessively on Osei's pretension, revealing his existence in the novel, both narrators mock their protagonists and use their poetical descriptions ironically. Employing many obscure words of Chinese origin, which Ozaki Satoakira (1967: 126-127) lists as the most difficult used in *Floating Clouds,* such as "seikō soshoku [white and bright moonlight]", "teitei kyōkyō [distant and radiant light]" and "kinren'en [shimmering or glittering light]", the narrator of *Floating Clouds* describes the scenery in the midst of which Bunzō awkwardly confesses his love for Osei. Osei replies to Bunzō's question obliquely, suggesting that the only one more important than her parents is not a person, but truth. In combination with this serious, yet absurd and rather comical conversation, the lofty style used to describe the scenery, with its obscure Chinese vocabulary, produces a mocking effect. Although Tanaka Kunio (1998: 157-163) points out the similarity in structure between the description of a garden at night in *A Chance Encounter* and that in *Floating Clouds,* the effects are utterly different, even opposite. In *A Chance Encounter* the narrator-protagonist describes scenery with which he is in complete empathy, and which amplifies his psychological state. In *Floating Clouds,* the protagonists do not appreciate the background scenery and are ironically contrasted with it. We might even suggest that all these ornate words of Chinese origin are employed merely to symbolize the sophisticated but superficial appreciation of the garden by the protagonists, their alienation from its beauty.

In spite of his declared principle that Chinese words which are not in general use should not be employed in a novel, Futabatei deliberately used these obscure Chinese words. This became the target of criticism by the most influential contemporary critic, Ishibashi Shian, and Futabatei's rival Yamada Bimyō, who accused him of meaningless pedantry. However, this "meaninglessness" has an effect. If the reader takes in the approximate sound of these obscure words, and unconsciously skips over their meaning, he finds himself experiencing the same superficial appreciation of the garden as the protagonists. This may be the very irony which the cynical narrator of *Floating Clouds* intends to achieve.

We may also draw attention to the verb forms used in these descriptions. While in the description from *Floating Clouds* "-(r)u" form verbs are used, in *The Portrait* use is made of "-te kuru" and "-te iru" forms, which emphasize aspectual meaning. One depicts change, the other states of being. In both cases the verb forms also carry the meaning of the present tense. The original Russian verbs, however, are past imperfective. When Futabatei converted these past imperfective verbs into "-(r)u" form verbs (more precisely "-te kuru" and "-te iru" form verbs), he shifted the narrator's role closer to that of *Floating Clouds,* that of an on-the-scene witness. In the description of scenery, then, Futabatei retained the aspect of the verbs, but changed their tense, stressing the presence of the narrator in the story.

Let us now turn to Futabatei's treatment of descriptions of continuous actions. Futabatei's regular practice of changing the tense of past imperfective verbs is frequently observed in translating the verb "glyadet' [to stare]". We may also observe in the passage cited above that as well as changing the tense form of past imperfective verbs, Futabatei employs "-ta" form verbs to translate past perfective verbs. As a consequence of these two concurrent practices, the "-ta" form verbs carry more aspectual meaning than past tense meaning: "aoku natta [has turned pale]", "warai dashita [has burst out laughing]". As for those sentences ending with "-te iru" form verbs, it becomes harder to judge whether these are the words of the narrator, or the inner voice of the protagonist Chartkov. The following is a recent translation of the same passage carried out by Yokota Mizuho:

> こう言ったかと思うと、絵かきは急に顔色を変え、ぶるぶる震えだした、そばに置いてあった画布(カンバス)のかげから、だれだか、ひきつったようにゆがんだ無気味な顔を突きだして、**彼のほうを**にらみつけていたのだ。ものすごいふたつの目が、いまにも取って食いつくしてしまうぞとばかり、ぴたりと視線をむけ、声をたてたら、ただではおかないぞという口つきをしていた。ぞっとした**彼は**、もう隣りの控え室で大いびきをかいて寝こんでいたニキータを呼ぼうとして思わず大声をあげるところだったが、急に思いとどまって笑いだした。(Gogol 1983: 86-87)

> [Having said this, the artist suddenly turned pale and began shivering. From the canvas standing beside him, someone had thrust out his convulsively distorted face and he was staring **at him**. Two fearful eyes fastened straight upon him, as if they were ready to devour him, his lips appeared to be saying he would punish him if he broke silence. Terrified, **he** was just about to call Nikita, who was snoring loudly in the adjoining anteroom, when he suddenly stopped and began laughing.]

Together with the use of the third-person pronoun "kare [he]", Yokota employs "-ta" form verbs throughout this passage for both past perfective and past imperfective verbs. When we compare the two renditions of the phrase "na **nego** glyadelo [(someone's face) was staring at **him**]", "**kochira** o nirande iru [(someone) is staring at **me**]" and "**kare** no hō o niramitsukete ita no da [because (someone) was staring at **him**]", the difference between the two translations becomes clear. In Yokota's recent translation, it is clear that the whole sentence is the utterance of the narrator, explaining the fear seizing Chartkov, since the sentence ending "-no da" (the particle "no" combined with the auxiliary verb "da") carries the meaning of judgement or explanation by the speaker. The third-person pronoun employed in this sentence also indicates an extraneous observer. Moreover, in Yokota's translation, this observer is positioned outside the story, as shown by the constant use of "-ta" form verbs to render all the past tense verbs in the original, so that the narrator's point of view is close to the omniscient one. In Futabatei's translation, however, the narrator positions himself in the story and observes Chartkov as an on-the-spot commentator, as was the case in the description of the setting. Moreover, in this passage Futabatei's rendition of the third-person pronoun "na nego [at him]" is "kochira o [in this direction (at me)]". Therefore this sentence may be understood either as a comment made by the narrator inside the story, or as Chartkov's monologue. In either case, the narrator's point of view is not omniscient, but limited. The narrator follows the incident as it unfolds before his eyes.

Although Yokota's translation is by far the more accurate in terms of its rendition of verb forms and of the third-person pronoun, the narrative point of view in Futabatei's translation is closer to that of the original. Futabatei emphasizes the narrator's viewpoint, which often appears inside the story in the original. As a matter of fact, Gogol himself uses present tense verbs at a climax in the story, when, in Chartkov's dream, the old moneylender emerges from his portrait. The verbs used here are "videt' [to see]" and "glyadet' [to look at, to gaze upon]":

> Со страхом вперил он пристальнее глаза, как бы желая увериться, что это вздор. Но наконец уже в самом деле... он видит, видит ясно: простыни уже нет ... портрет открыт весь и глядит мимо всего, что ни есть вокруг, прямо в него, глядит просто к нему во внутрь ... У него захолонуло сердце. И видит: старик пошевелился и вдруг уперся в рамку обеими руками. Наконец приподнялся на руках и, высунув обе ноги, выпрыгнул из рам... (Gogol 1973b: 89)
>
> [With fear he fastened his eyes more intently, as if wishing to convince himself that it was nonsense. But in the end in actual fact ... he sees, sees clearly: the cover is no longer there... the portrait is all exposed and is staring, disregarding everything else around, straight at him, is staring into his soul ... His heart froze. And he sees: the old man has stirred and has suddenly rested both his hands against the frame. Finally he has raised himself on his arms and, thrusting out both legs, has jumped from the frame...]

In this climax, all imperfective verbs are employed in the present tense form, while all perfective verbs appear in the past tense. While the former describe continuous actions, the latter describe sequential actions. The protagonist then has two more dreams, and is thrown into deeper and deeper confusion as he wakes from each successive dream. Each time, just before Chartkov wakes from his fearful dreams, Gogol inserts sentences written with present imperfective verbs:

> И видит он: это уже не сон; черты старика двинулись, и губы его стали вытягиваться к нему, как будто бы хотели его высосать ... с воплем отчаянья отскочил он и проснулся. (Gogol 1973b: 91)
>
> [And he sees: this is no longer a dream; the old man's features have moved, and his lips have begun to stretch out towards him, as if they wanted to suck him out. ... with a wail of despair he jumped away and woke up.]
>
> Он вперил глаза в щель и пристально глядел на простыню. И вот видит ясно, что простыня начинает раскрываться, как будто бы под нею барахтались руки и силились ее сбросить. «Господи, боже мой, что это!» вскрикнул он, крестясь отчаянно, и проснулся. (Gogol 1973b: 91)
>
> [He fastened his eyes upon the crack and intently gazed at the cover. And now he sees clearly, that the cover is beginning to open, as if hands were floundering around under it and trying to throw it off. "Oh Lord, my God, what is this!" he cried, crossing himself desperately, and woke up.]

Clearly differentiating "videt' [to see]", which is used to describe the passive action of the threatened Chartkov, from "glyadet' [to gaze (upon), to stare (at)]", which is used to describe the active intimidation by the old man in the portrait, Gogol opts for the present tense for these verbs of seeing, so that the crucial dream scene is visualized more immediately. Concerning the use of the present tense at climactic moments in the story, it is generally acknowledged as the "historic present". Terence Wade defines it as follows:

> The use of the present tense with past meaning brings the action more graphically before the mind's eye of the reader or listener. It is a device commonly found in literary works and is much more widely used in Russian than in English. (Wade 1992: 287)

Kindaichi Masumi (1994: 249-292) refers to Gogol's use of this form as "danwa retorikku no rekishiteki genzai [the historic present in discourse rhetoric]". Kindaichi defines the rhetorical use of the historic present in literary works as the use generally known as the historic present. Its effect is to bring a graphic image to the reader's mind and to heighten the tension in the story. He cites Pushkin, Lermontov and Gogol as Russian writers who employed the historic present in this category.

Analyzing all instances of the historic present in Pushkin's works (only fifteen instances), and some in Lermontov's and Gogol's works, Kindaichi draws out general features of its use as follows. Firstly, the number of consecutive verbs used in each instance is no more than five. Secondly, they are generally used either in first-person narrative stories, or in direct speech cited within the narrative. In other words, they are used in a context where the narrator is seen to exist concretely, and narrates to the reader or listener. Thirdly, instances of its usage can be classified into the following five groups:

1. When verbs of seeing introduce its use
2. In association with the adverb "vdrug [suddenly]"
3. When verbs of motion are employed
4. To describe the immediate setting
5. To describe past habitual actions, in association with the particle "byvalo [it used to happen]"

Concerning Gogol's use of the historic present, while Kindaichi (1994:281) admits it needs further research, it is used in a context where the narrator exists concretely in the story, and verbs of sight are frequently employed. Kindaichi's observations are born out by the above cited instances from *The Portrait,* where imperfective verbs of sight are used predominantly, and the number of verbs used consecutively is no more than five. Most importantly, they are used in the narrator's monologue.

One feature of the use of the historic present in *The Portrait,* however, does not fit Kindaichi's generalizations. Analyzing several instances, Kindaichi comes to the conclusion that the historic present is mainly used to depict sequential actions. In *The Portrait,* however, we have seen that the historic present is used to depict continuous actions, while sequential actions are described using past perfective verbs. In clearly differentiating the use of each verb form, Gogol stressed the aspectual meaning rather than the tense meaning.

Past perfective verbs are used less to express past tense than perfective aspect, as Futabatei did with "-ta" forms in his translations.

Writing about the relationship between verbal forms in Russian and the temporal position of the author, Boris Uspensky points out the simultaneity [sinkhronizm] rendered by present imperfective verbs. Uspensky cites *Ledi Makbet Mtsenskogo uezda [Lady Macbeth of Mtsensk Province],* written by Nikolai Leskov, who is known as a writer with stylistic characteristics reminiscent of Gogol:

> Катерина Львовна закрыла окно ... да и легла. ... Спит и не спит Катерина Львовна, а только так ее омаривает, так лицо потом и обливается, и дышится ей ... Чувствует Катерина Львовна ... Наконец кухарка подошла и в дверь постучала: «Самовар»—говорит, ... Катерина Львовна ... насилу прокинулась ... А кот ... трется ... Катерина Львовна заворошилась ... а он ... лезет: ... (Uspensky 1970: 94)

> [Katerina L'vovna shut the window ... and then lay down ... Katerina L'vovna sleeps and yet does not sleep, she is so hot that her face is bathed in perspiration, and she is short of breath ... Katerina L'vovna feels ... Finally a kitchen maid came and knocked at the door: "Samovar" she says, ... Katerina L'vovna ... hurried out with difficulty ... And the cat ... is rubbing itself [against her] ... Katerina L'vovna stirred ... and he ... comes crawling: ...]

Uspensky (1970: 96) defines the roles of present imperfective and past perfective verbs as follows:

> It is clear that the present tense signals here the fixation of the point of view from which the description is made: we may say that each time the present tense form is used, the author's position is synchronous [with that which is described], ... Meanwhile, verbs in the past tense register the transition to each new description from the synchronous position, that is, to each subsequent fixation of the point of view.

Uspensky (1970: 101) concludes: "The opposition of aspectual forms appears in the field of poetics as an opposition between the synchronous and retrospective positions of the author". Contrasting the retrospective effect rendered by the past perfective, Uspensky stresses that the imperfective verb in general has the effect of creating a synchronous author's (or narrator's) position within the story he tells.

We may thus see that in Chartkov's first dream, Gogol employs the present imperfective verbs of seeing "vidit [sees]" and "glyadit [is staring]" to assist the reader to visualize these continuous actions, and to create the synchronous position of the narrator. Again in the second and third dreams, the verb "vidit [sees]" is used repetitively together with the conjunction "kak budto by [as if]", to graphically portray Chartkov's fear, and to emphasize the narrator's existence in the story.

Let us now compare the two translations of the first dream written by Futabatei and Yokota:

Futabatei:

慄然としながらそれを凝視めた其様子は、宛と其様な馬鹿な事のない事を確めたいやうな鹽梅であつたが、其内に上敷の布がいつしか脱れて、肖像畫が露になつて、四邊の物には眼も觸らさず、宛然洞穿きさうな眼付で、直と**此方を**凝視めてゐるのが、紛ふ方なく、まざまざと見える……**と思ふと**、胸が冷りとした。頓て老人は動き出して、額縁に兩手を掛けて身を動かしたか**と思うと**、足を二本ぬつと出して、額を踊り出た…… (Futabatei Shimei 1964a: 326)

[The way he gazed upon it with fear, it looked as if he wished to assure himself that there should not be such an absurd thing, but in the end it is unmistakably clearly seen that the sheet covering it slips down, the portrait is now uncovered, and without paying attention to anything else it is staring straight **at me** with eyes so sharp they seem to penetrate ... **as I realize this** my heart has frozen. Soon the old man starts moving and I realize that he is resting both his hands against the frame, thrusting both legs out, and has jumped out from the frame.]

Yokota:

ぞっとしながらも**彼は**じっと目をこらしていたが、それはまるで、そんなばかなことがと、事実を確かめたいと念じているようだった。だが、やがて、もう現実に……**彼は**見た、まざまざと見ていた、敷布はもうなくなり、……肖像画はすっかりむきだしになり、あたりのものにはいっさい目もくれず、まともにぴたりと、腹のなかまで見とおすように**彼を**にらみつけている……。**彼の**心臓はひやりとした。見ていると、老人は急に両手を額縁にかけて身動きしはじめ、やがて、両手で体をもちあげると、両足を突きだして、額縁のなかから跳びだしてきた…。(Gogol 1983: 91)

[Despite his fear **he** fastened his eyes intently; it looked as if he wished to assure himself that there should not be such an absurd thing. But in the end, indeed ... **he** saw, he saw clearly: there is no longer a sheet,... the portrait is revealed completely, without paying any attention to other things nearby it is staring straight **at him**, as if its eyes are penetrating him. **His** heart froze. While he was watching, the old man suddenly rested his hands against the frame and stirred; soon he raised himself a little on his arms, then thrusting both legs out he was jumping towards him from out of the frame.]

When we compare these two translations, again the first thing that strikes us is that the impression produced by Futabatei's translation is more intense and immediate than that produced by Yokota's, in spite of the literalness of the latter. A single unfaithful rendition of a verb form in Yokota's version makes the whole translation entirely different from the original. For "On vidit, vidit yasno...[he sees, he sees clearly]", he writes "kare wa mita mazamazato mite ita [he saw, he saw clearly]". It is evident that Yokota intended to translate the whole passage from a retrospective point of view. By employing the "-te ita" form, Yokota shifts the tense form from present to past. The only "-(r)u" form verb used in the whole passage, "niramitsukete iru [(he) is staring]", is embedded in a sentence governed by a "-te ita" form verb. The predominant verb form in Yokota's translation thus becomes "-ta", carrying the meaning of the past tense, rather than the perfective aspect.

In Futabatei's translation, on the other hand, the key phrase "On vidit, vidit yasno...[he sees, he sees clearly]" is translated as "magau kata naku, mazamazato mieru [it is unmistakably and clearly seen]". Although the punctuation and the third-person pronoun are not rendered literally, Futabatei keeps the tense form as it appeared in the original. In fact Futabatei changed the punctuation so much that only one full stop appears in his translation, so it is hard to judge in this passage which tense is dominant. However, when we read Futabatei's rendition of the whole dream sequence, it becomes obvious that he tended (with very few exceptions) to render past imperfective verbs using "-(r)u" or "-te iru" form verbs, and past perfective verbs using "-ta" or "-te" form verbs. The following is the continuation of the passage cited above, first in Gogol's original, then in Futabatei's translation. We can clearly see how conscious of the verb forms Futabatei was.

> Сквозь щелку ширм видны были уже одне только пустые рамы. По комнате раздался стук шагов, который наконец становился ближе и ближе к ширмам. Сердце стало сильнее колотиться у бедного художника. С занявшимся от страха дыханьем он ожидал, что вот-вот глянет к нему за ширмы старик. И вот он глянул, точно, за ширмы с тем же бронзовым лицом и поводя большими глазами. (Gogol 1973b: 89)

> [Through the chink in the screen only the empty frame was visible. In the room the sound of footsteps resounded, which finally came closer and closer to the screen. The poor artist's heart began to pound more heavily. With breathless fear he anticipated that the old man would any moment look in at him from behind the screen. And the next moment he indeed looked from behind the screen with that same bronze face, opening wide his big eyes.]

> 衝立の隙間から覗いて視ると、空(から)になつた額ばかり見える。すると、室の内に跫音(あしおと)がして、段々衝立の傍(そば)へ來る。美術家は胸で早鐘を撞(つ)き出した。恐ろしいので息氣(いき)を凝(こら)して、今にも老人が衝立の向ふから面(かほ)を出しさうに思つて居ると果して例の青銅色(からかねいろ)の面がぬつと出て、衝立の内を覗いて、大きな眼でじろじろ視廻す。(Futabatei Shimei 1964a: 326)

> [When (he) peeps through the chink in the screen, only the empty frame is seen. Then in the room footsteps are heard, they come closer and closer to the screen. The artist's heart has begun beating fast. Breathless with fear (he) anticipates that the old man will glance through the screen at any minute, as expected, that bronze face appears, peeps through the screen and stares up and down with its big eyes.]

Clearly distinguishing between imperfective and perfective verbs, Futabatei employs "-(r)u" form verbs for the former, and "-ta" or "-te" form verbs for the latter. Here the predominant form is "-(r)u", which carries the meaning of the continuous aspect. In this context, the "-ta" form verbs used to translate past perfective verbs seem to lose their past tense meaning, conveying rather the meaning of the perfective aspect.

The treatment of third-person pronouns appears to contribute to the vividness of this passage as well. Futabatei does not indicate the third-person pronouns, which nowadays would be translated using "kare". Okumura Tsuneya (1954: 70-71) notes that Futabatei used "kare" only once to translate the third-person pronoun referring to Chartkov. Comparing translations by Futabatei and Hirai Hajime (1937), Okumura observes that for the most part Futabatei simply omits third-person pronouns. He considers the use of "kare" to be innovative and logical, compensating for the "illogical" absence of such a pronoun in Japanese, and contributing to the evolution and modernization of the Japanese language. However, it is hard to see what is "illogical" about the absence of a third-person pronoun in Japanese, which has its own internal consistency.

When we compare Futabatei's translation of the dream sequence with the Russian original, we see that Futabatei does occasionally translate third-person pronouns, though not necessarily as third-person, but often as pseudo first-person pronouns. Some in the accusative case are translated as "kochira o [in this direction (at me)]" (four instances), some in the nominative and dative cases as "jibun wa/ga [I]" (three instances). A further three instances in the nominative case are translated by the nouns "kono otoko wa [this man]" and "gaka wa [the artist]". Initially Futabatei translates the third-person pronoun as "gaka [the artist]" to specify the subject of the actions from the narrator's point of view. Then, by not translating the third-person pronouns, or by translating them as "kochira o [at me]" or "jibun wa/ga [I]", he shifts the point of view from the narrator to the protagonist. Towards the end, most of the hallucinatory dream sequence is translated as Chartkov's inner thoughts. Futabatei even introduces the phrase "to omou to [as (I) realize]" to strengthen Chartkov's point of view.

Futabatei's treatment of third-person pronouns referring to the protagonist follows a progression. While these pronouns are for the most part omitted, Futabatei also substitutes a succession of nouns for them. First he employs "gaka [the painter]" to refer to the poor and unknown Chartkov, then the name "Charutokofu [Chartkov]" and "bijutsuka [the artist]", when he becomes rich and popular. (As already noted, during the dream sequence "kochira (o) [at me]" and "jibun [I]" are used.) The substitution of nouns for the third-person pronouns (thirty-three instances) together with the faithful rendition of nouns such as "khudozhnik [the artist]" and "Chartkov" make Futabatei's translation sufficiently accurate. Nothing is "vacant" or "illogical", yet his zero-rendition of third-person pronouns facilitates shifts in the narrative point of view, corresponding to similar shifts in the original, shown by the use of present tense verbs. Although the use of "kare" might have been innovative and indispensable in reproducing the original without omission, the notion that it is needed to translate "logical" western languages, and even to overcome some logical defect in the Japanese language, is open to question. Some scholars and translators consider that the less third-person pronouns are translated, the more natural the result. Yanase Naoki (2000) is one such scholar, suggesting that needless translations of third-person pronouns should be eliminated.

Finally, let us consider Futabatei's translation of past imperfective verbs depicting habitual actions. Gogol's frequent use of past imperfective verbs for this purpose is first observed in the description of Chartkov's inclination towards the life of a fashionable artist.

As already noted in the discussion of the dream sequence, Gogol often inserts modal words such as "kazalos' [it seemed]" or "slovom [in a word]" to indicate the presence of the narrator. "Slovom" is particularly used when the garrulous narrator is characterizing Chartkov by his habitual actions:

> **Иногда** хотелось, точно, нашему художнику кутнуть, щегольнуть, **словом**, кое-где показать свою молодость. Но при всем том он мог взять над собою власть. ... **Иногда** становилось ему досадно, **когда** он видел, как заезжий живописец, француз или немец, **иногда** даже вовсе не живописец по призванью, одной только привычной замашкой, бойкостью кисти и яркостью красок производил всеобщий шум и скапливал себе в миг денежный капитал. Это приходило к нему на ум **не тогда, когда**, занятый весь своей работой, он забывал и питье, и пищу, и весь свет, **но тогда, когда** наконец сильно приступала необходимость, **когда** не на что было купить кистей и красок, **когда** неотвязчивый хозяин приходил раз по десяти на день требовать платы за квартиру. (Gogol 1973b: 85-86)
>
> [**Sometimes** our artist wanted to go on a binge, to dress foppishly, **in a word** to show off his youth somewhere. But for all that he was able to take himself in hand. ...**Sometimes** he became vexed, **when** he saw how a visiting painter, French or German, **sometimes** not even a painter by profession, simply by an acquired manner, by the glibness of his brush and the brightness of his colours, created a universal sensation and accumulated in an instant monetary capital. This came to mind **not when**, totally consumed by his work, he forgot clothes, food and the entire world, **but when** finally need besieged him, **when** there was no money to buy brushes and paints, **when** the importunate landlord came ten times a day to demand the rent for his apartment.]

Repeatedly employing similar sounding words, "inogda [sometimes]", "kogda [when]", "togda, kogda [at that time when]", Gogol's narrator adds more and more detailed commentary, until the detail itself becomes comical. Futabatei sensed the unique tone of the narrator and translated this whole passage using "-(r)u" or "-te iru" form verbs to synchronize with the narrator's voice. Futabatei also employs vulgar colloquial expressions common in the Edo period, a feature which was harshly criticized by the prominent translator Yonekawa Masao (1963: 90-91).

> **成程、我(こち)の美術家は**時とすると、一寸洒落た風をして酒でも飲むで遊び行(ある)いて、**まア早く云へば一花を遣(や)つて見たく思ふこともないではないが、**それでも**感心に**辛抱してゐる。（中略）ではあるが、佛人なり、獨逸人なり、何處か外國から來た畫家なら未(ま)だしも、全然(まるつきり)畫家でも無い者までが、ほんの慣熟(なれ)で、筆の達者(たつしや)な所や、繪の具の華美(はで)な所で世上を騒がして、瞬く間に大金を儲けるのを見ると、忌々(いまいま)しくなる**時もある**。仕事に浮身を窶(やつ)して、糊口の事も世間の事も忘れて了つてゐる時には、そんな事はないが、甚(ひど)く逼迫して筆や顏料(ゑのぐ)を買う事も出來ぬ所へ、家主(いへぬし)が執着(しつこ)く日に十度(じつたび)も家賃の催促に來る時などには、そんな心地(こころもち)のする**こともある**。(Futabatei Shimei 1964a: 322-323)

> [**Indeed**, **our artist** sometimes wants to dress foppishly and go on a binge, **in short**, **there are times when he feels like enjoying himself sumptuously**, but **to my admiration** he has been patient. ... However, when he sees a French or German painter from overseas, even someone who is not a painter at all, with an acquired manner, with glibness of brush and brightness of colour, make a sensation and pile up a lot of money in an instant, he **sometimes becomes** vexed. This **happens not when** he forgets food and drink, and the entire world, being engrossed in his work, **but when** his finances get tight and he hardly has any money even to buy a brush or colours, and on top of that the landlord comes as often as ten times a day to ask him to pay the rent.]

The phrase criticized by Yonekawa as unsuitable is "hana o yatte mitaku omou koto mo nai de wa nai ga [there are times when he feels like enjoying himself sumptuously]", which Futabatei offers for "koe-gde pokazat' svoyu molodost' [to show off his youth somewhere]". The word "hana o yaru" indeed, has sexual connotations implying visits to prostitutes, and may be unsuitable in a serious translation. It should be noted, however, that this phrase is uttered by the rather garrulous narrator and follows the word "slovom [in a word]", which is colloquially translated as "mā hayaku ie ba [in short]". Futabatei even appends the words "kanshinni [to my admiration]" and "naruhodo [indeed]" to emphasize the narrator's direct comments. Generally speaking, Futabatei employed quite a few "frivolous" words commonly used by Edo *gesaku* writers, especially when the narrator's tone of voice is clearly indicated, such as in the introduction to the story, when the main characters are introduced, and when describing Chartkov's habitual actions and the change that came over them. Table 8 shows how Futabatei "freely", sometimes mistakenly, translated some phrases from the original, adding a strong Japanese touch and some comical tone:

***Table 8***

| | |
|---|---|
| 1. торговка-охтенка<br><br>[a market woman from Okhta] | をんなあきうど なき<br>女商人お泣<br><br>[a market woman Mrs. Sobbing] |
| 2. карикатурами<br><br>[(over) caricatures] | と ば ゑ み<br>鳥羽繪(を覧て)<br><br>[(looking at) Toba-style caricatures] |
| 3. О нем заговорили печатно—это было для него новостию;<br><br>[They started talking about him in the press—that was a novelty for him] | 新聞紙上で自分の評判をされる——つひぞ 喰べ附けない事である<br><br>[He is getting positive press coverage—he is not accustomed to such fare.] |
| 4. пробуя сообщить грациозные движения руке<br><br>[trying to impart graceful movements to his hand] | しな<br>是れ手振に品を遣らうと試みたものである。<br><br>[This is to try out a flashy hand gesture.] |

<table>
<tr><td>5. Он глядел на него глупо,<br><br>[He looked at it stupidly,]</td><td>ほんがりとして視てゐる眼の前には、<br><br>[looking at something in front of him with mouth and eyes wide open.]</td></tr>
<tr><td>6. Нет, я не понимаю напряженья других сидеть и корпеть за трудом.<br><br>[No I can't understand the exertions of others to sit and sweat over their work.]</td><td>私（わたくし）には如何（どう）も人を坐らせて置いて、のツつそツつして肖像を畫いてゐる人の心持がらんすな、<br><br>[I can't understand someone who sits you down and paints with his body stretched or bended.]</td></tr>
<tr><td>7. Уже начинал он верить, что всё на свете делается просто,<br><br>[He had already begun to believe that everything in the world happens simply,]</td><td>世の中の事にすぢりもぢツた事は一ツもない、（中略）などと思つてゐる。<br><br>[He thinks that there is nothing complicated in this world, …]</td></tr>
</table>

Except for the sixth example, all these expressions originating in Edo *gesaku* (light literature) appear in the narrative, adding a distinctive tone to the narrator's voice. As Yonekawa points out, "onna akiudo Onaki [a market woman Mrs. Sobbing]" is obviously a mistranslation, "okhtenka [a woman from the village of Okhta]" being mistaken for a female noun based on "okhti", which expresses feelings of disappointment. As well as this mistranslation, Yonekawa denigrates all the colloquial expressions cited above as "vulgar" appropriations from Edo *gesaku*, which are difficult for us as contemporary readers to understand, and frivolous. However, Futabatei employed these distinctive expressions because readers at that time could appreciate them. He uses them only when the narrator positions himself inside the story and describes Chartkov's actions as an outsider, adding comic effect. When Chartkov's fateful dream and his downfall are described, Futabatei does not use such expressions at all. They appear to be used only to reproduce the tone of Gogol's narrator, who chatters away and piles detail upon detail until he realizes the detail is becoming excessive.

To reproduce the self-multiplying details supplied by Gogol's narrator, Futabatei constantly uses "-(r)u" or "-te iru" form verbs. In the passage cited above, "toki **mo aru** [there are times when]" and "koto **mo aru** [there is a case when]" not only synchronize the narrator's position but also echo the repetition of similar-sounding words "inogda [sometimes]", "kogda [when]", "togda, kogda [at the time when]", which are used in the narrator's description of ever multiplying details. Similarly, in the description of repeated actions cited earlier, where Gogol's narrator describes the demands which Chartkov's wealthy clients place upon him, the word "trebovali [demanded]", which significantly is past imperfective, appears five times. Apart from the repetition of the key word "treboval(i) [demanded]", Gogol's narrator again shows his characteristic way of speaking, using the modal words "kazalos' [it seemed]" and "slovom [in short]". Although in Futabatei's translation the word "slovom [in short]", which appears twice in the original, is not clearly rendered, the key repetitions of "treboval(i) [demanded]" are rendered into the honorific expressions "to iwa **reru** [(ladies and gentlemen) demand]" and "**kata** mo aru [there is a lady (or a gentleman) who demands]", which appear in turn. The most significant factor here, remains, however, the "-(r)u" form chosen for the verb.

As Kindaichi has pointed out in his thesis, one of the uses of the historic present observed in the works of Pushkin, Lermontov and Gogol is to describe past habitual actions. Uspensky points out that present imperfective verbs have the effect of creating a synchronous position of the author. If past habitual or repetitive actions, which are normally described employing past imperfective verbs, may be emphasized by the use of the historic present even in Russian, it is quite rational for Futabatei to select "-(r)u" form verbs when translating past imperfective verbs depicting past customary actions. In so doing Futabatei emphasized the narrator's synchronous position and portrayed past habitual actions graphically, as if they were present actions. In other words, Futabatei emphasized the aspectual meaning of repetition and eliminated the past tense meaning.

So in *The Portrait* the predominant verb form is "-(r)u", and more specifically "-te iru", which carries the aspectual meaning of describing states, continuous actions and repetitive customary actions. The aspectual meaning of state is observed when the background setting is described. Continuous actions are shown strongly during the dream sequence. Repetitive or customary actions are observed when the change in Chartkov's customary behaviour comes about as a result of finding money in the portrait frame. All these descriptions are made from a synchronous narrative position, and there is a clear attempt to reproduce the tone of speech of Gogol's narrator. Consequently "-ta" form verbs, appearing in a text where the predominant verb forms are "-(r)u" or "-te iru", carry the aspectual meaning of completion of actions. Such "-ta" form verbs generally appear in isolation, and correspond to past perfective verbs in the original. The aspectual meaning of these "-ta" form verbs is especially clear in the first half of the story, and often emphasized by the use of the "-te shimatta" form, as observed earlier in Futabatei's translations of Turgenev's stories.

However, there remain several instances of the use of "-ta" form verbs to indicate the past tense, especially in the form "-te ita". In Part One of *The Portrait* there are thirteen instances of "-te ita" forms, and eight of them are renditions of past imperfective verbs. They are often employed together with adverbs of duration. The following passages contain such instances of the use of "-te ita" forms:

> 1. Наконец ему сделалось даже страшно ходить по комнате; ему казалось, как будто сей же час кто-то другой станет ходить позади его, и **всякий раз** робко оглядывался он назад. (Gogol 1973b: 88)
>
> [Finally it even became terrifying for him to walk about the room; it seemed to him as if at any moment someone else would start walking behind him, and **all the time** he kept looking back timidly.]
>
> 結局(はて)は室(へや)の内を一人で歩くのも無氣味になる。今にも誰やら後から跟随(つい)て來さうに思はれるので、**動(と)もすれば**怖々(おづおづ)振返つて、後を視てゐた。
> (Futabatei Shimei 1964a: 325-326)
>
> [Finally it has become terrifying for him to walk alone in the room. It seems to him as

if someone will start following him, he **often** turned back timidly, looking around.]

2. **Долго** глядел он, высунувши голову в форточку. Уже на небе рождались признаки приближающейся зари; ... (Gogol 1973b: 92)

[**For a long time** he gazed, sticking his head out through the small ventilation window. Already in the sky the signs of the approaching dawn were appearing; ...]

小窓から首を出して、畫家は**久らく**眺めてゐた。空は段々拂曉近い景色に爲つて來る。(Futabatei Shimei 1964a: 329)

[Sticking his head through the small window, he gazed **for a while**. The sky is changing its colour close to the dawn...]

3. **С минуту** неподвижный и бесчувственный стоял он посреди своей великолепной мастерской. Весь состав, вся жизнь его была разбужена в одно мгновение, как будто молодость возвратилась к нему, как будто потухшие искры таланта вспыхнули снова. (Gogol 1973b: 113)

[**For about a minute** he stood motionless and insensible in the middle of his splendid studio. His whole being, his whole life was aroused in an instant, as if his youth had returned to him, as if the extinguished sparks of his talent had burst into flame again.]

我家の立派な畫の間の中央に突立つたまゝ**暫らくは**身動きもせず茫然としてゐた。恰も一瞬の間に蘇生つたやうな、若返つたやうな、才思の油が竭きて暗くなつたのが再びぱツと明くなつたやうな心地がする。(Futabatei Shimei 1964a: 351)

[In the middle of his splendid studio he was standing **for a while** motionlessly and insensibly. He feels as if he is brought back to life, as if youth returns to him, as if the burnt out oil of his talent bursts into flame again.]

If we study these examples carefully, we note that these "-te ita" forms, although they explicitly indicate the past tense, do not guarantee a retrospective narrative viewpoint as they did in Futabatei's translations of Turgenev's first-person narrative stories. While, in the first-person narratives, the "-te ita" forms are used specifically to describe the narrator-protagonist's actions, and to maintain a retrospective viewpoint, in the third-person narrative of *The Portrait* they are employed simply to indicate the span of the protagonist's continuous actions. We thus find the answer to the question we posed at the beginning of this chapter: the "-te ita" form does appear in the text of *The Portrait,* but is not used to maintain a dramatized narrator's retrospective point of view, as in Futabatei's translations of first-person narratives. The dramatized narrator of *The Portrait* maintains a synchronous point of view in that third-person narrative. Emphasized by adverbs such as "dolgo [for a long time]" or "s minutu [for about a minute]", the past imperfective verbs in the original indicate the specific time span during which the action continues. In Futabatei's translation "-te ita" forms indicating these time spans appear in isolation among sentences ending with "-(r)u" or "-te iru" form verbs. After a momentary skip back to the recent past, the reader is brought back to the present time which flows in the story, guaranteed by the "-(r)u" and "-te iru" form verbs indicating the synchronous position of the narrator.

The narrator's synchronous position is firm throughout Part One of *The Portrait.* Only when the protagonist's death is described does the narrator reveal his retrospective point of view:

> К счастию мира и искусств, такая напряженная и насильственная жизнь не могла долго продолжаться: размер страстей был слишком неправилен и колоссален для слабых сил ее. (Gogol 1973b: 116)
>
> [Fortunately for the world and for art, such a strained and violent life could not long continue: the extent of its passion was too irregular and too colossal for its weak forces.]
>
> 此世に取つて、又美術に取つて、幸福な事には、かう無理に、張詰めた氣では永く生存(ながら)へることが出來なかつた。人間の弱い命根では、この度外(どはづ)れな、凄まじい妄執に耐(た)へ得なかつた。(Futabatei Shimei 1964a: 353)
>
> [Fortunately for the world and for art, being so violently strained he could not live long: the obsession was too excessive and too colossal for the weak forces of a human being.]

Except for the modification of the inanimate subject ("takaya ... zhizn' ne mogla dolgo prodolzhat'sya [such a ... life could not long continue]", which is rendered as "nagaku nagaraeru koto ga dekinakatta [he could not live long]"), Futabatei employs "-ta" forms in an attempt to reproduce the past tense of the original Russian verbs. In the original, the narrator at this point abandons his garrulous and playful tone, and concludes on a serious note. To reproduce this serious tone, Futabatei positions the narrator outside the story, and allows him to conclude the narration from a retrospective point of view.

Let us summarize what we have learnt about Futabatei's translation of *The Portrait.* In *The Portrait,* Futabatei for the first time created a story, where the dramatized narrator consistently maintains a synchronous point of view. The almost constant rendition of the original past imperfective verbs into "-(r)u" or "-te iru" form verbs (emphasizing aspect) resulted in a present tense narrative, with "-ta" form verbs carrying perfective aspectual meaning rather than past tense meaning. The verbose, mocking tone of Gogol's narrator is reproduced, often by employing the vocabulary of Edo *gesaku* [light literature] writers. In Futabatei's translation the narrator's voice more often gives way to the protagonist's inner thoughts than in Gogol's original. These characteristics of *The Portrait* may also be observed in *Floating Clouds.*

Similarities between *Floating Clouds* and Gogol's works have been noted before. Many articles have been written about the beginning of *Floating Clouds.* Seki Ryōichi (1967: 308-

317) initiated the discussion by pointing out the similarities between Futabatei's opening and that of Chapter Two of Tsubouchi Shōyō's novel *Kyōwaranbe [Children in the Capital City]*. Subsequently Hatano Kazuhiro (1982: 64-80) and Isahaya Yūichi (1982: 51-61), both slavists, simultaneously published articles pointing out the similarities between the opening of *Floating Clouds* and that of Gogol's *Nevsky Avenue.* While Isahaya simply finds stylistic and structural resemblance between these two openings, Hatano finds many stylistic similarities between *Floating Clouds* and Gogol's stories in general. Hatano pinpoints the role of the narrator, who appears to be a dunce and evokes laughter (a stylistic device know by slavists as *skaz*). A year later Shimizu Shigeru (1983: 34-51) responded, suggesting that *Nevsky Avenue* and *Children in the Capital City* had both impacted on the beginning of *Floating Clouds.* He also suggested that Shōyō, in writing *Children in the Capital City,* had himself been influenced by an early translation Futabatei had made of an (as yet unidentified) work by Gogol. Futabatei had shown the translation to Shōyō, who was at that time his teacher. Janet Walker (1995: 36) also concludes that *Nevsky Avenue* "provided Futabatei with a model for a prologue or introduction that situated two characters in an urban milieu in the modern world that is unstable because of the coming of a new economic, social and spiritual order". These various articles base their arguments on the detailed description of various kinds of moustaches and whiskers, and the introduction of two main protagonists with opposite characters, features common to *Floating Clouds* and *Nevsky Avenue.*

Although *The Portrait* lacks this direct resemblance, the detailed description of various kinds of pictures and viewers in the introduction to *The Portrait* is similar to the detailed description of clothes and whiskers in *Floating Clouds.* Moreover, the situation into which the narrator introduces the protagonists in *Floating Clouds* is closer to that in *The Portrait* than to that in *Nevsky Avenue.* The following passages show how the protagonists are introduced in each of these works:

*Floating Clouds:*

途上人影(ひとけ)の稀れに成つた頃、同じ見附の内より兩人(ふたり)の少年(わかもの)が話しながら出て參つた。(Futabatei Shimei 1964a: 5)

[I notice two of our young men, engrossed in conversation, have come through the gate now that the crowd has thinned out.]

*The Portrait (Shōzōga):*

此時チャルトコフといふ通りすがりの若い畫家が何心なく店頭(みせさき)に立止つた。(Futabatei Shimei 1964a: 316)

[At this time a young artist named Chartkov, passing by the shop, has stopped involuntarily.]

*The Portrait (Portret):*

В это время невольно остановился перед лавкою проходивший мимо молодой художник Чартков. (Gogol 1973b: 80)

[At this time a young artist who was passing by, Chartkov, stopped involuntarily in front of the shop.]

*Nevsky Avenue:*

«Стой!» закричал в это время поручик Пирогов, дернув шедшего с ним молодого человека во фраке и плаще. «Видел?» (Gogol 1973b: 15)

["Stop!", shouted lieutenant Pirogov at that moment, tugging a young man in a tail-coat and cloak who was walking with him. "Did you see that?"]

While in both *Floating Clouds* and *The Portrait* the protagonists are introduced by the narrator with a comment on their appearance, in *Nevsky Avenue* the protagonists are introduced engrossed in conversation, without any comment by the narrator. On the other hand, what is common to both *The Portrait* and *Nevsky Avenue* is the verb form employed when the protagonists are first introduced, which is past perfective. In both stories Gogol shifts the verb form from present to past at this point. Futabatei, however, continued employing present verb forms until the very last in *The Portrait,* maintaining the narrator's synchronous point of view. Interestingly, the verb forms and narrative point of view in Futabatei's translation of *The Portrait* coincide with those in *Floating Clouds* Part One.

As shown in the first chapter of this study, Futabatei began employing "-ta" form verbs to show past tense under the direct influence of his translations of Turgenev's stories, *The Tryst* and *A Chance Encounter.* Whereas in Part One of *Floating Clouds*, which is colloquial in style (resembling the style of Edo *gesaku*), "-ta" form verbs carry mainly aspectual meaning, in Part Two, more typically the meaning of the past tense. In consequence, the narrator (who in Part One is ever present, with his own distinctive voice, and even his own body) shifts outside the story in Part Two. In Part Two, "-(r)u" form verbs are used mainly to express the protagonist's (Bunzō's) inner thoughts. Then, in Part Three, "-(r)u" form verbs begin to appear more frequently again, as more space is given to the expression of Bunzō's inner thoughts and descriptions are made from Bunzō's point of view. In short, the narrative point of view in *Floating Clouds* shifts from synchronous to retrospective. While the deeds of the protagonists are depicted objectively by the narrator from his retrospective point of view, employing "-ta" form verbs, the inner thoughts of the protagonists, Bunzō and Osei, and observations made from their point of view, are depicted subjectively, employing "-(r)u" form verbs. Hence, in *Floating Clouds* Part Three, the points of view become dual, and the narrator of *Floating Clouds* has lost the stance from which he was able to make mocking comments about the protagonists.

Thus *The Portrait,* which was written almost ten years after the publication of *Floating Clouds* Part One, shows the path *Floating Clouds* could have taken. If Futabatei had not shifted the verb forms denoting the protagonist's actions from present to past, had he maintained the narrator's synchronous position, Japan's "first modern novel" would have maintained a single narrative point of view. Then the narrator's point of view could easily have slipped into the protagonist's point of view to express his inner thoughts. Then, too, the narrator could have maintained his original, garrulous tone of voice, capable of criticizing and joking at his protagonists' expense.

Noguchi Takehiko (1994) has noted that in *Floating Clouds,* the further the novel progresses, the more frequently and prominently "-ta" auxiliary verbs are employed. Referring to the final paragraph of *Floating Clouds* Part Three, Noguchi emphasizes that not only the Edo *gesaku* style, but even the "author" himself, has disappeared from the novel, due to the constant use of "-ta" auxiliary verbs. In Part Three, Noguchi argues, any indication of the author's subjectivity (that there is a person narrating) is eliminated, and the author is now omnipresent in the novel, and present in each main character. "The author no longer exists as a narrator, but narrates from a certain fictitious point of view. This must be the style of a third-person narrative." (Noguchi 1994: 233-234) Making the connection with the first version of *The Tryst,* in which nearly all sentences end with the auxiliary verb "-ta", Noguchi concludes:

> The style of the first version of *The Tryst,* in which all the sentence structures 'converge' upon the sentence endings "-ta", is similar to the style Futabatei finally reached in Part Three of *Floating Clouds. The Tryst* is a first-person narrative, in which the subject "jibun" [I] governs the "-ta" endings. *Floating Clouds* is a third-person narrative, in which the protagonist Bunzō governs them. There is no difference in the use of "-ta" endings between them. In any case "-ta" refers to a person. It is the very sentence ending that manifests the third-person narrative discovered by modern Japan. (Noguchi 1994: 264)

The role of "-ta" auxiliary verbs is indeed significant in *Floating Clouds,* and the direct influence of the first version of *The Tryst* on *Floating Clouds* is apparent. The innovation in the use of the "-ta" form, however, lay not in its referring to a person, as suggested by Noguchi, but in its use as a past tense marker. Moreover, Noguchi's analysis lacks detailed examination of the frequency of "-ta" form verbs in each chapter. The frequency of "-ta" form verbs does not increase all through the novel. It increases significantly in Part Two, but then drops away somewhat in Part Three. Table 9 shows the number of "-ta" and "-(r)u" form verbs appearing in each part of *Floating Clouds,* as recorded by Ozaki (1967: 68):

***Table 9***

| | Part One | Part Two | Part Three | Total |
|---|---|---|---|---|
| "-ta" form verbs | 29 | 178 | 117 | 324 |
| "-(r)u" form verbs | 140 | 79 | 111 | 330 |

Amongst the chapters in Part Two (i.e. chapters seven to twelve), chapters seven, nine, ten and twelve show the predominant use of "-ta" form verbs. In Part Three (chapters thirteen to nineteen), on the other hand, chapter seventeen is the only chapter which shows predominant use of "-ta" form verbs. In the final chapter, from which Noguchi's quotation is taken, the predominant verb form is in fact "-(r)u". So Futabatei's use of "-ta" form verbs is most stable in Part Two, and the use of "-(r)u" form verbs revives in Part Three, not to express the narrator's point of view, but to express that of the main characters.

It should also be pointed out that Noguchi identifies the narrator of *Floating Clouds* directly with the author. Because of this identification, the narrator of *Floating Clouds* is regarded as a pre-modern feature, which accounts for the presence of the Edo *gesaku* style in the "modern" novel. Consequently, according to Noguchi's argument, such a narrator must be eliminated, a process facilitated by the use of "-ta" form verbs.

Yet the narrator of *Floating Clouds* has much in common with the narrator of *The Portrait,* not least, the fact that he is not identical with the author. Futabatei's "modern" novel *Floating Clouds* began under the strong influence of Gogol's works. Futabatei may have been influenced by *Nevsky Avenue* when he wrote the introduction of *Floating Clouds,* as many scholars have suggested, or he may have been influenced by *The Portrait,* as suggested in this study. Both Gogol and Futabatei begin their works by setting a dramatized narrator inside the story to make synchronous descriptions. Consequently the verb form employed by them was the present tense form with much emphasis on the aspectual meaning of continuity. The narrator of *Floating Clouds* initially took the stance of being able to mock and laugh at the protagonist, Bunzō. However, when Futabatei translated Turgenev's first-person narrative stories, this influenced the narrative of *Floating Clouds.* Frequent use of "-ta" form verbs led to the narrator's position moving from inside to outside the story, and induced a retrospective point of view.

Without doubt "-ta" form verbs played a significant role in *Floating Clouds,* but whether this was a positive role deserves consideration. If the ultimate goal of *Floating Clouds* was to create a third-person narrative with an omniscient point of view, then the "-ta" form verbs certainly played a positive role. However, if Futabatei's intention was to create a modern novel modeled on one of Gogol's third-person narrative stories such as *The Portrait,* with a dramatized narrator, then "-ta" form verbs with past tense meaning intervened, and changed the structure of the story, by shifting the narrator's position. In this sense, behind the creation of *Floating Clouds,* there was a struggle between the conflicting influences of Gogol's and Turgenev's narrative styles. It may well be that Futabatei left *Floating Clouds* unfinished, because he was unable to resolve this conflict.

# Chapter 5 — Third-Person Narratives: *Floating Weed* and *The Mismatch*: The Restoration of "-ta" Expressing the Past Tense

## *Ukikusa [Floating Weed]* (Translated from Turgenev's *Rudin*)

The remaining two translations from works by Turgenev made during Futabatei's second period are *Floating Weed* (translated from *Rudin*) and *Kusare-en [The Mismatch*[1]*]* (translated from *Petushkov*). Both are third-person narrative stories in which the narrator does not appear as one of the characters. We should pay particular attention to the use of verb forms in *Floating Weed,* as this is Futabatei's first translation of a third-person narrative story by Turgenev.

In an essay written for volume three of the most recent edition of Futabatei's complete works, Komori Yōichi (1985: 3-5) makes reference to the use of "-ta" and "-(r)u" forms in Futabatei's translations. Komori first notes that Futabatei's frequent use of "-ta" form verbs in Part Three of *Floating Clouds* seems to prove Roland Barthes' theory that modern prose works possess the past tense and third-person pronoun as their fictitious symbol. However, when we follow the shifts in Futabatei's translation style, Komori continues, it turns out that Futabatei took the opposite direction in the use of "-ta" forms, and even in the use of the third-person pronoun. In the second version of *The Tryst* Futabatei used "-ta" forms for sentence endings less frequently than in the first version, though the shift in verb forms from "-ta" to "-(r)u" does not necessarily mean that he shifted the tense form from past to present. Komori goes on to consider the views of Yanabu Akira (1983: 101) who suggests that while "-ta" and "-(r)u" forms may appear to express past and present tense respectively, in fact their functions in translation are somewhat different. The "-ta" form functions to objectify the actions unfolding in front of the speaker (= the narrator), while the "-(r)u" form, and particularly the "-te iru" form, is a sign for the narrator's participation in or witnessing of the scene. Agreeing fully with Yanabu's position, Komori applauds Futabatei's shift in verb forms from "-ta" to "-te iru" in the second version of *The Tryst,* as this shift strengthens the position of the sportsman-narrator in the story. This choice of verb forms, Komori observes, is consistent throughout Futabatei's translations of works by Turgenev such as *Dream Talk, Floating Weed, The Jew* and *The Mismatch.* In these works "-ta" forms are used to advance the plot, while "-te iru" forms are used to describe the setting. Komori concludes that Futabatei's sentence endings were appropriate for translating Turgenev's works, resulting in a narrator's point of view which is limited like that of the other characters. In Turgenev's first-person narratives the narrators participate in and witness incidents, which they then objectify and report to the reader.

As observed in Chapter Three of this study, the narrator of *The Jew* is, indeed, a character

---

[1] "Kusare-en" means "an unfortunate but inescapable relationship". It is one of those words which are very difficult to translate adequately. The root "kusaru" means both "rotten" and also "tie together". The word is commonly used jokingly between friends to suggest a relationship which is not going very well, but which is destined by fate. In order to avoid a long and awkward title, I have translated it here as "The Mismatch".

in the story. "-Ta" and "-te iru" forms play a role in presenting the incidents which unfold in front of the narrator. However, the narrator's actions are often described using "-te ita" form verbs, which clearly carry the meaning of the past tense. This use of verb forms creates two streams of time in the stories. The narrator of *The Jew* remains in his own present time.

These "-te ita" forms describing the narrator's actions disappear in *The Portrait,* the translation of Gogol's third-person narrative. In *The Portrait* Futabatei for the first time used "-ta" and "-(r)u" or "-te iru" forms primarily to express aspectual meaning. The narrator of *The Portrait* does not participate as a character in the story, but witnesses and reports incidents which unfold in front of him. In *The Portrait* "-ta" and "-te iru" forms are used exactly as Yanabu defined, and "-te ita" forms are used only in a few instances, to describe those of the protagonist's actions which continue for a certain period of time within the story.

Do all "-ta" and "-te iru" forms in *Floating Weed* function as Komori has suggested? More specifically, will "-te ita" forms describing the narrator's actions disappear in *Floating Weed* as they disappeared in *The Portrait?* It is worth initially citing Futabatei's own comments on the narrative points of view in works by Dostoevsky and Turgenev:

> I am intending to write something, but I haven't settled my viewpoint towards various phenomena in the world. So I am still vacillating. ... (In other words), there are two ways of observing these phenomena. If I may refer to the attitudes of [other] writers, Dostoevsky and Turgenev seem to represent these two methods of observation. In Dostoevsky's works, the author almost identifies himself with the main characters in his works, and we cannot perceive the author, but [only] the main characters. In Turgenev's works the author certainly exists apart from the main characters. To a certain extent the author seems to criticize the characters in his works. (Futabatei Shimei 1965a: 165)

The above comments appeared in an interview published under the title "*Sakka kushin dan [An Account of a Writer's Labours]"* in May 1897, the very month when Futabatei began publishing *Floating Weed.* This brief comment seems to precisely define the narrator-character relationship in *Rudin.* (Futabatei appears not to distinguish between author and narrator.) In *Rudin* Turgenev establishes a narrator who is not one of the characters, but a mere device to hold the narrative point of view and develop the plot. Futabatei was at first reluctant to acknowledge this new Turgenevan narrator, as he often addresses the reader in a similar fashion to the narrator of *Floating Clouds:*

> 1. **Кстати, читатель, заметили ли вы**, что человек, необыкновенно рассеянный в кружке подчиненных, никогда не бывает рассеян с лицами высшими? Отчего бы это? Впрочем, подобные вопросы ни к чему не ведут. (Turgenev 1963c: 247)
>
> [**By the way, reader, have you noticed** that a person who is exceptionally absent-minded in the circle of his subordinates, is never absent-minded with persons of a higher rank? Why might that be? However, such questions lead nowhere.]
>
> **一躰**自分より身分の卑(ひく)い者の前でおそろしく打寛(うちくつろ)ぐ者に限つて、身分の上の人の前へ出ると、打寛がぬものである。これは如何(どう)した譯(わけ)であらう？

併し、こんな不審を起したとて、何の益にも立たぬことである。(Futabatei Shimei 1964b: 15)

[**Generally speaking**, a person who is exceptionally relaxed with his inferiors tends to be tense with his superiors. I wonder why this is. But it is no use harbouring such questions.]

The sentence endings "mono de aru" and "koto de aru" indicate that the comment is addressed directly to the reader by the narrator, but Futabatei drops the word "chitatel' [reader]" from his translation. This word appears three times in Turgenev's original and Futabatei does acknowledge its presence in the two other instances:

2. Михайло Михайлыч, **уже знакомый читателю**, вошел в кабинет. (Turgenev 1963c: 276)

[Mikhailo Mikhailych, **to whom the reader has already been introduced**, entered the study.]

**諸君お知己の**レジネフが座舗へ入つて來た。(Futabatei Shimei 1964b: 45)

[Lezhnev, **to whom everyone has already been introduced**, entered the room.]

3. Вернувшись домой, тотчас после встречи с Лежневым, Рудин заперся в своей комнате и написал два письма: одно—к Волынцеву (**оно уже известно читателям**) и другое—к Наталье. (Turgenev 1963c: 332)

[On returning home, immediately after his meeting with Lezhnev, Rudin locked himself in his room and wrote two letters: one to Volyntsev (**the readers are already familiar with it**) and the other to Natal'ya.]

ルーヂンはレジネフに別れてから程なく家へ歸ると其儘、部屋に閉籠つて、ワルィンツーォフへ贈るのとナターリヤへ贈るのと二通手紙を書いた（**ワルィンツォーフへの手紙は讀者御存じの通りである**）。 (Futabatei Shimei 1964b: 111)

[On returning home, soon after the parting with Lezhnev, Rudin locked himself in his room and wrote two letters: one is addressed to Volyntsev the other to Natal'ya (**the letter to Volyntsev is already known to the reader**).]

It is only in the translation of the third passage that an exact translation of "chitatel' [reader]"— "dokusha [reader]" appears. This gradual shift towards recognizing the word "reader" indicates Futabatei's gradual recognition of the author behind the narrator. In chapter twelve, towards the end of the novel, where the protagonist's vagrancy is described, Turgenev inserts the following comment from the narrator:

> **Один мой знакомый**, много покатавшийся на своем веку по России, сделал замечание, что если в станционной комнате на стенах висят картинки, изображающие сцены из «Кавказского пленника» или русских генералов, то лошадей скоро достать можно;... (Turgenev 1963c: 352)
>
> **One of my acquaintances**, who has travelled a lot about Russia during his lifetime, made the observation, that if the pictures hanging on the station room walls show scenes from *The Prisoner of the Caucasus,* or Russian generals, it will be possible to get [fresh] horses quickly;...]

Futabatei translated this passage as follows:

> **作者の一知己に**若い頃多く露西亞を旅して行(ある)いたものがある。其人の云ふのに、若し立場(たてば)にカフカーズ捕虜譚(ものがたり)の一節か、又は露國の陸軍將官を描(か)いた額が掛つてゐれば、直(ち)き馬が雇はれるけれど、— (Futabatei Shimei 1964b: 134)
>
> [**There is a person among the author's acquaintances** who travelled around Russia in his youth. This person made the comment, that if the pictures which hang on the wall of the station describe scenes from *The Prisoner of the Caucasus* or Russian generals, the horses may be hired quickly, but ...]

Here Futabatei explicitly suggests that the narrator is in fact the implied author. If we apply the classification developed by Genette, *Rudin* falls into category one, the extradiegetic-heterodiegetic, with a narrator in the first degree, who tells a story from which he is absent. The author-narrator-hero should be A=N≠H. In contrast to the narrators in *The Portrait* and *Floating Clouds* [A≠N≠H], the narrator in *Rudin* keeps his distance from the protagonist, Rudin, and his voice never slips into the protagonist's voice. Futabatei clearly understood the relationship between author and characters in *Rudin,* where the author controls and criticizes the main characters as an extraneous narrator. In the process of translation he came to the conclusion that the narrator is identical with the implied author.

Frank Seeley has noted the importance of the narrative point of view in *Rudin.* Comparing *Rudin* with Lermontov's *A Hero of Our Time,* he isolates three distinct viewpoints with regard to their heroes: that of the hero himself, that of the hero's friend, and that of the narrator.

> But Turgenev varies and complicates Lermontov's scheme. In the earlier novel, the most revealing view of the hero is his own, the least important that of the 'editor', with that of the friend somewhere in between. In *Rudin* it is the other way round: it is the narrator's point of view which takes up the most space and is most important, while the protagonist's view of himself takes up least space and is least important; the viewpoint of the friend is again intermediate in scope, ... (Seeley 1991: 170)

So in *Rudin* the voice of the narrator, whose view directly represents the author's view, dominates and controls the main characters.

*Rudin* was the first of Turgenev's novels to be published in *Sovremennik [The*

*Contemporary],* in 1856. Rudin is a "superfluous man" (lishnii chelovek)[2], with "intellect"[3], but no means. Modeling the protagonist on his friend Bakunin, Turgenev first undertook the novel as "another study of a superfluous man's failure in love" but it was significantly amplified and modified and "developed into a full-length portrait of a many-faced and more impressive figure" (Seeley 1991: 168).

The plot of the novel is extremely simple. To the country estate of Dar'ya Mikhailovna comes a stranger, Dmitrii Nikolaevich Rudin, and he quickly captivates the visitors to Dar'ya's salon with his eloquence. Rudin has considerable influence and control over the lives of people in Dar'ya's circle, especially Dar'ya's daughter Natal'ya, who is only seventeen years old. However, unable to understand his own feelings, Rudin cannot return Natal'ya's love, or appreciate the value of her willingness to support his ideas. He leaves Dar'ya's estate in disgrace and despair. In an epilogue, Turgenev shows many of Rudin's attempts to put his ideas into practice, as recounted to Lezhnev in a final and unexpected meeting. Finally, in 1860, an account of Rudin's death was added, the most "quixotic" passage of the novel:

> Turgenev takes the story to a precise historical moment. On 26 June 1848 Rudin is on the barricades in Paris at the time of the revolution. He is shot through the heart—after the revolution has failed. ... Rudin dies fighting for a foreign cause, on foreign soil. (Knowles 1988: 55)

The meaninglessness of Rudin's death is accentuated by the fact that those around him do not even realize he is Russian, thinking he is a Pole. According to Knowles (1988: 54), "Turgenev's Rudin is ultimately a failure". Japanese readers, and even Futabatei, seem to regard *Rudin* simply as an account of a man's failure in life, rather than of a superfluous man's failure in love. Many comments made by critics and by young writers contemporary to Futabatei show how they were moved by Rudin's farewell letters, and by his final chance encounter with Lezhnev. The following fragment, written by Tayama Katai, a representative of the naturalist school of writers, gives some insight into the state of mind of those upon whom *Floating Weed* made an impression:

> Amongst all the translations made by Futabatei, I was most impressed and influenced by *Floating Weed,* serialized in the journal *Taiyō*. ... There was a phrase, "a person with a cool head and a warm heart", in it. I was very fond of this phrase, and every so often referred to it. There was also a scene where Rudin went to see Volyntsev before they parted. It put me in a pensive mood. Rudin's letters always became a subject of our conversations. "Let us clink glasses. There is little left us now." Copying the words exchanged between Lezhnev and Rudin, we clinked glasses of beer more than once. (Cited in Yasuda 1976: 63)

Japanese readers interpreted *Floating Weed* as a story of reconciliation between old

---

[2] The term "superfluous man" is applied to many protagonists of Russian literature from Pushkin's Onegin and Lermontov's Pechorin to Goncharov's Oblomov. Use of the term became widespread following the publication of Turgenev's "The Diary of a Superfluous Man" in 1850.

[3] Knowles (1988: 53) compares three superfluous men: Pushkin's Eugene Onegin, Lermontov's Pechorin, and Turgenev's Rudin. Onegin displays the primacy of the aesthetic, Pechorin that of the will, and Rudin that of the intellect.

friends, rather than as a full portrait of a superfluous man. Moreover, while Futabatei was in Russia as a correspondent for the *Asahi shinbun, Floating Weed* was republished (in 1907), and regarded as a work belonging to the naturalist school. In the journal *Teikoku Bungaku [Imperial Literature], Floating Weed* was compared favourably with *Kesshōki [An Account of Bloodied Laughter],* Futabatei's translation of Andreyev's *Krasnyi smekh [Red Laughter],* which appeared around the same time:

> It is inevitable that *An Account of Bloodied Laughter* has become a target of the "not red laughter" [cynical laughter] of literary critics, who make many superficial observations. However, this work *Floating Weed* belongs to the naturalist school of writing, and it is so easy to understand that surely all readers will read through it with great interest. (Cited in Futabatei Shimei 1964b: 376)

*Floating Weed* was perceived, then, as having something in common, thematically and stylistically, with the works of the naturalist school. On the other hand, some scholars have pointed out the similarity between Rudin and Bunzō, the protagonist of *Floating Clouds,* both of whom may be seen as "superfluous men". The Russian scholar, Raisa Karlina, notes the similarity in the titles of *Ukigumo [The Floating Clouds]* and *Ukikusa [The Floating Weed],* the latter connoting a precarious life. Karlina (1962: 31-35) sees the undoubted influence of Rudin's image on Bunzō, though she considers Futabatei's creation of a Japanese superfluous man to be far less significant in terms of its social depth, than was the case with Rudin. While Rudin is interested in broad social issues, and his thoughts are directed towards the common weal, Bunzō has no greater purpose and pays no attention to the welfare of people beyond those who immediately surround him. The Japanese superfluous man lacks a "cause", indispensable for his Russian counterpart. Karlina considers Futabatei's understanding of Rudin to be unbalanced, with emphasis being placed on his failure rather than his idealism. Satō Seirō (1995: 408) points to Futabatei's account of his own life, as recorded by his disciple Mozume Yoshiko, where he states: "Watashi wa dōmo Rūjin no omokage ga aru [I have something in common with Rudin]", and suggests that Futabatei saw his own image in the depictions of Bunzō and Rudin, the image of one who had failed in his personal life. It is thus possible to see a thematic link between *Floating Weed* and works of the naturalist school of Japanese writers, who tended to describe the dark and negative side of their own personal lives.

Before turning to a stylistic analysis of *Floating Weed,* it is worth citing an interesting observation Knowles makes about the genesis of *Rudin:*

> The final impetus for actually writing the novel after all the prevarications of previous years was probably provided by a visit to Spasskoe by three of his friends, who convinced him that it was his duty to his country to write his novel. The four spent most of the time completing and producing a short play, "Shkola gostepriimstva" ("The School for Hospitality"). This helps to explain why *Rudin* strikes many readers as rather <u>theatrical</u> in its construction, with each chapter resembling a "scene", and dialogue moving the action along. (Knowles 1988: 49 — Emphasis added)

Indeed, the story pivots around the salon of Dar'ya Mikhailovna. Every so often the main characters gather in her salon and the dialogues between them provide a fitting setting for

Rudin's eloquence. Especially noteworthy is the dialogue between Rudin and the misogynist Pigasov. The following passage describes the first gathering at Dar'ya Mikhailovna's salon, and is followed by Futabatei's translation:

> *Салон* уже начался. На широкой кушетке, подобрав под себя ноги и вертя в руках новую французскую брошюру, расположилась хозяйка; у окна за пяльцами сидели: с одной стороны дочь Дарьи Михайловны, а с другой m-lle Boncourt—гувернантка, **старая и сухая дева лет шестидесяти**, с накладкой черных волос под разноцветным чепцом и хлопчатой бумагой в ушах; в углу, возле двери, поместился Басистов и читал газету, подле него Петя и Ваня **играли в шашки**, а прислонясь к печке и заложив руки за спину, стоял господин небольшого роста, взъерошенный и седой, с смуглым лицом и беглыми черными глазками—некто Африкан Семеныч Пигасов. (Turgenev 1963c: 247-248)
>
> [The *salon* had already begun. The lady of the house settled herself on a wide couch, with her legs tucked under her and flicking through a new French brochure; by the window, at a tambour, sat, on one side, Dar'ya Mikhailovna's daughter, and, on the other side, Mlle. Boncourt, the governess, **a dry old maid of about sixty**, with false hair of a black colour under a motley cap and cotton in her ears; in the corner near the door Basistov had located himself and was reading a newspaper, near him were Petya and Vanya, **playing draughts**, and leaning against the stove and putting his hands behind his back, stood a man of low stature, with a dark-complexioned face covered by dishevelled grey hair and with eyes that darted around—a certain Afrikan Semenych Pigasov.]
>
> （一、最(も)う家内の人々は寄集つてゐる。）ソロン集會が始まつてゐるのである。主婦(あるじ)のダーリヤは大きな臥椅子(ねいす)に憑(よ)つて、足を縮めて、手に新版の佛蘭西の小本(こほん)を持つてゐる。窓の側には縫架(ぬいわく)を中間(なか)に相對(むかふまへ)にナターリヤと女教師のＭｌｌｅ.Boncourt(マドモアゼール ボンクール)とが座つてゐたが、**此女教師というのは、今まで男を持たずに押通して來た六十ばかりの干乾(ひから)びたやうな老婆(ばあさん)**で、間色(まだら)の頭巾(づきん)を冠つて、兩方の耳に綿花(わた)を挿むでゐる。隅の戸の側にはバシストフが座つて新聞を讀んでゐる。その側(そば)にはペーチヤとワーニヤが**将棋を弄(さ)してゐる**。暖爐の前には蓬々(もじやもじや)とした白髪頭(しらがあたま)の、色の淺黒い、黒眼勝(くろめがち)のきよときよとした眼の、背(せい)の低い男が兩手を後に廻して立つてゐる。是はアブリカン、セミヨーヌイチ、ピガーソフとかいふ男で。(Futabatei Shimei 1964b: 15)
>
> [(... , people have already gathered.) The *salon* (the gathering) has begun. The lady of the house, Dar'ya, settles herself on a wide couch, tucking her legs under her and holding a new French brochure in her hands. By the window, facing each other, with a tambour between them, Natal'ya and the governess, Mlle. Boncourt, sat, **this governess is a dried-up old woman of about sixty, who has been obstinately alone, without a man**, wearing a motley cap and putting cotton in her ears. In the corner near

> the door sits Basistov, reading a newspaper. Near him are Petya and Vanya **playing *shōgi* [Japanese chess]**. In front of the stove a man of low stature is standing, with a dark-complexioned face covered by dishevelled and grey hair and roving blackish eyes. This is a certain Afrikan Semenych Pigasov.]

While in the original Russian text the description of people gathering in the salon employs past imperfective verbs to convey the meaning of continuous actions in the past, in Futabatei's translation the corresponding description constantly employs "-te iru" forms. Consequently the description becomes more immediate and vivid, as though, as has been suggested by Knowles, the reader is witnessing a theatrical scene. Here Futabatei follows the same practices as he had done in translating Gogol's third-person narrative *The Portrait.* When we examine the text of *Floating Weed* up to the passage cited above, we find that, as in *The Portrait,* he translates past imperfective verbs expressing states and continuous actions mainly as "-te iru" forms. He translates some past perfective verbs as "-ta" forms, with the emphasis on the aspectual meaning of completion. It would appear, then, that the narrator of *Floating Weed* allows his presence to be felt in a similar way to the narrator of *The Portrait.* The free, and slightly vulgar translation of the reference to the governess Mlle. Boncourt ("staraya i sukhaya deva let shestidesyati [a dry old maid of about sixty]") as "kono jokyōshi to yū no wa, imamade otoko o mota zu ni oshitōshite kita rokujū bakari no hikarabita yōna bāsan de [this governess is a dried-up old woman of about sixty, who has been obstinately alone, without a man]" may prove Futabatei's intention of indicating the presence of a garrulous narrator similar to Gogol's. Futabatei also employs the Japanese term "shōgi [Japanese chess]" for "shashki [draughts]", this domestication at the phraseological level suggests a similar translation strategy to that adopted in *The Portrait.* It would appear, however, that Futabatei gradually sensed the difference between the narrators in *The Portrait* and *Rudin,* resulting in a shift in the narrative point of view in *Floating Weed.* This shift is apparent when Futabatei translates the description of the guests' reactions to Rudin's eloquence, which follows the description of the *salon*:

> Люди внесли ужин, и, полчаса спустя, все разъехались и разошлись. **Дарья Михайловна** упросила Рудина остаться ночевать. **Александра Павловна**, возвращаясь с братом домой в карете, несколько раз принималась ахать и удивляться необыкновенному уму Рудина. **Волынцев** соглашался с ней, однако заметил, что он иногда выражается немного темно... то есть не совсем вразумительно, прибавил он, желая, **вероятно**, пояснить свою мысль; но лицо его омрачилось, и взгляд, устремленный в угол кареты, **казался** еще грустнее.
>
> **Пандалевский**, ложась спать и снимая свои вышитые шелком помочи, проговорил вслух: «Очень ловкий человек!»—и вдруг, сурово взглянув на своего казачка-камердинера, приказал ему выйти. **Басистов** целую ночь не спал и не раздевался, он до самого утра всё писал письмо к одному своему товарищу в Москву; а **Наталья** хотя и разделась и легла в постель, но тоже не на минуту не уснула и не закрывала даже глаз. Подперши голову рукою, она глядела пристально в темноту; лихорадочно бились ее жилы, и тяжелый вздох часто приподнимал ее грудь. (Turgenev 1963c: 270)

> [The servants brought in supper, and half an hour later, everyone had departed and dispersed. **Dar'ya Mikhailovna** begged Rudin to remain and pass the night.

**Aleksandra Pavlovna**, as she was on the way home with her brother in a carriage, several times exclaimed "ah!" and marvelled at Rudin's extraordinary intellect. **Volyntsev** agreed with her, but noted that he sometimes expressed himself somewhat vaguely... that is to say not quite intelligibly, he added, **no doubt** wishing to explain his thoughts, but his face became clouded and his gaze, fixed on a corner of the carriage, **seemed** even more melancholy.

**Pandalevsky**, going to bed and taking off his silk-embroidered braces, said aloud: "A very smart fellow!", and suddenly, casting a stern glance at his valet, ordered him to leave the room. **Basistov** did not sleep all night and did not undress, he was up till morning writing a letter to one of his friends in Moscow; while **Natal'ya**, although she undressed and went to bed, did not go to sleep either, even for a minute, and did not even close her eyes. Propping her head on her arm, she gazed intently into the darkness, her veins were throbbing feverishly and a deep sigh often lifted her bosom.]

晩餐を運び込むでから、半時も經つと、皆おもひおもひに歸つて了つたが、ルーヂンだけは引留められて泊ることになつた。**アルクサンドラ**は弟と一つ馬車で歸りながら幾度かルーヂンの奇才に驚嘆した。**ワルィンツォーフ**も姉に尤も同じだけれど、併しルーヂンの所説は折々少し胡亂になる……ソノ判然しないと、**多分**思ふ所を明に云はうと思つた**のであらう**、言葉を足して云つた。けれども顔色も冴えんで、馬車の隅を凝視めて、**さも憂はしさうな**眼付をしてゐた。

**パンダレーフスキイ**は寢やうとして絹絲で繍をしたヅボン釣を外しながら、口へ出して「中々味を遣るわい！」と云つたが、偶然恐ろしい面をして室僕を睨付けて、彼方へ行けと言つた。**バシストフは**終夜眠らず衣服をも脱がず、一心にマスクワの友人に贈る手紙を書いてゐた。**ナターリヤは**衣服を脱いで臥床には就いたが、同じくまんじりともせず、又眠やうともしなかつた。手で頭を支へて、暗黒を凝然と諦視てゐたが、脈は烈しく搏つて、幾度となく深い溜息が胸を突いて出た。(Futabatei Shimei 1964b: 39-40)

[Half an hour after supper was brought in, everyone had dispersed in different directions, and only Rudin was begged and reminded to stay overnight. **Aleksandra**, while she was on her way home in the carriage with her brother, several times marvelled at Rudin's extraordinary talent. **Volyntsev** almost agreed with her, but [considered that] Rudin's thoughts occasionally became obscure... that is they became incomprehensible, he added, **probably** wishing to explain what he thought. However, his face was gloomy and his eyes, fixed on a corner of the carriage, **seemed** more melancholy.

**Pandalevsky**, going to bed and taking off his silk-embroidered braces, said aloud: "He's a clever fellow", but suddenly, casting a stern glance at his page, ordered him to go away. **Basistov** did not sleep the whole night, and did not undress, he was eagerly writing a letter to his friend in Moscow. **Natal'ya**, although she undressed and lay down, did not sleep either, even for a minute, and she did not even try to sleep. Propping up her head with her arm, she was staring intently at the darkness, her veins were throbbing feverishly and every so often a deep sigh escaped from her chest.]

This is the first instance when past imperfective verbs expressing continuous actions in the original are rendered successively as "-te ita" or "-ta" forms. Turgenev contrasts the overwhelmingly positive impression Rudin had made on Aleksandra and Natal'ya with the more negative and antagonistic reactions from Volyntsev and Pandalevsky, both of whom would later become rivals for the affections of Natal'ya and Dar'ya. Futabatei's translation of this passage is more literal and accurate than his translation of earlier passages, with fewer insertions and omissions. The description of Pandalevsky could have been handled more comically, but Futabatei's translation remains restrained.

Futabatei's translation of this passage is quite meticulous in respect of verb forms. While in the original the description of the characters' reactions employs both imperfective and perfective past tense verbs, in Futabatei's translation both are rendered as "-ta" forms, the distinction between them being subtly indicated by use of "-te shimatta" forms for perfective and "-te ita" forms for imperfective. This is very similar to Futabatei's strategy when making his first translations from Turgenev's first-person narratives *The Rendezvous* and *Three Encounters*. In those translations (*The Tryst* and *A Chance Encounter*) the use of "-ta" forms in a first-person narrative results in a clear retrospective point of view. In the passage just cited from *Floating Weed*, the use of "-ta" forms in a third-person narrative establishes an omniscient narrative point of view.

In *Rudin*, itself a third-person narrative, the narrator positions himself outside the story, and depicts every character in the story from an omniscient point of view. In the passage just cited the narrator even shows us Volyntsev's inner thoughts, prefaced by the modal word "veroyatno [probably]", which does not, however, make explicit the narrator's presence in the story, as it did in *The Portrait*. This is a passage where Turgenev's direct manipulation of his characters is explicitly shown. Hence Futabatei was impelled to shift the narrative point of view in his translation, from inside the story to external to the story. This sudden shift of viewpoint in *Floating Weed* is paralleled by a similar shift in *Floating Clouds* Part Two, resulting from a change in verb forms:

> 奥の間の障子を開けて見ると、果して昇が遊(あそび)に來てゐた。加之(しか)も**傲然と**火鉢の側(かたはら)に大胡坐(おほあぐら)をかいてゐた。その傍(そば)にお勢が**ベツタリ坐ツて**、何かツベコベと**端手(はした)なく**囀ツてゐた。少年の議論家は素肌の上に上衣(うはぎ)を羽織ツて、**仔細らしく**首を傾(かし)げて、ふかし甘薯(いも)の皮を剥いて居、お政は**囂々敷(ぎやうぎやうしく)**針箱を前に控へて、**覺束(おぼつか)ない手振りで**シヤツの綻を縫合はせてゐた。
> (Futabatei Shimei 1964a: 80)
>
> [He slid open the door of the sitting room. There was Noboru, **arrogantly** sitting cross-legged beside the *hibachi* [charcoal burner]. Osei **was sprawled** beside him, chattering **foolishly** away. Our young dialectician was concentrating on peeling the skin from a sweet potato **with an air of importance**, his head cocked to one side. He wore a coat with nothing underneath. Omasa was **awkwardly** stitching the torn shirt, **pompously** putting the sewing box before her.] (Ryan 1967: 284— Modified)

Both passages depict the actions (mainly continuous) of the main characters with the frequent use of "-te ita" forms. This results in the point of view in both cases being located outside the story. However, while in *Floating Weed* the main characters' actions are shown impartially, objectively revealing their attitude towards Rudin, in *Floating Clouds,* which is supposed to have been influenced by Gogol's stories, all the main characters' actions are depicted in an equally comical or absurd light. All are caricatured through the malicious eye of the narrator. The words highlighted in the passage clearly demonstrate the narrator's satirical attitude. Even the protagonist Bunzō cannot escape the narrator's satire. In the passage from *Floating Clouds* the narrator shows his presence through his satirical comments, in spite of the fact that all verbs are of the form "-te ita".

Thus the shift in narrative point of view in *Floating Weed* is induced by the nature of Turgenev's third-person narrative, in which the narrator positions himself outside the story, and manipulates the characters directly. On the other hand, the shift in the narrator's point of view in *Floating Clouds* did not occur as a logical consequence of the story, but happened accidentally under the influence of Futabatei's translation of Turgenev's first-person narratives, in which "-ta" form verbs are used consistently to translate all Russian past tense verbs. In *Floating Clouds* the narrative point of view should have remained inside the story, and consequently the verb form should have remained "-te iru".

Having once shifted the narrator's point of view, Futabatei once again employs "-te iru" forms to describe the continuous actions of the main characters gathered in Dar'ya's salon. Furthermore, the habitual or repetitive actions of the main characters who come under Rudin's influence are also described using "-te iru" forms. The following are some examples of the description of such habitual actions:

> Прошло два месяца с лишком. В течение всего этого времени Рудин почти не выезжал от Дарьи Михайловны. Она не могла обойтись без него. ...
>
> — Не люблю я этого умника,—говаривал он [Пигасов],— выражается он неестественно, ни дать ни взять, лицо из русской повести; скажет: «Я», и с умилением остановится... «Я, мол, я...» ...
>
> Пандалевский побаивался Рудина и осторожно за ним ухаживал. ...
>
> После самой Дарьи Михайловны Рудин ни с кем так часто и так долго не беседовал, как с Натальей. ...
>
> Не как девочка болтала Наталья с Рудиным... (Turgenev 1963c: 287-289)
>
> [More than two months had passed. During all this time Rudin had hardly been away from Dar'ya Mikhailovna's place. She could not manage without him. ...
>
> —I don't like that smart fellow—he [Pigasov] would say—He expresses himself unnaturally, just like a character in a Russian tale; he'll say "I" and stop, overcome with emotion... "I," he says, "I" ...
>
> Pandalevsky was rather afraid of Rudin and carefully tended to his needs. ...

> Apart from Dar'ya Mikhailovna herself, there was no-one with whom Rudin conversed so often or so long as Natal'ya. ...
>
> It was not as a little girl that Natal'ya chatted with Rudin...]
>
> 二月《ふたつき》餘り經つたが、此間《このあひだ》ルーヂンはダーリヤの家《ところ》に殆ど居ずくまりであつた。ダーリヤは最《も》うルーヂンでなければ夜も日も明けぬ。（中略）
> ピガーソフは此様《こん》な事を云つてゐる、「私《わし》は彼《あの》才子は嫌《きらひ》だ。厭《いや》に物を云ふ、宛《まる》で小説中の人物か何ぞの様に、しんみりとなつて私《わたくし》はといふ……私は、私は……つて、（長口上《ながこうじやう》を並べ立てる。）（中略）
> パンダレーフスキイはルーヂンを憚つて怯《おそ》る怯る機嫌を取つてゐる。（中略）
> 主婦《あるじ》を除いてはルーヂンは一番ナターリヤと話を屢《よ》くする、而《さう》して長く話してゐる。（中略）
> ナターリヤは子供になつて話をしてゐるのではない。(Futabatei Shimei 1964b: 58-60)
>
> [More than two months had passed, and during this period Rudin had almost all the time stayed at Dar'ya's house. Dar'ya cannot manage without Rudin. ...
>
> Pigasov is saying the following: "I don't like that clever person. He talks too much. Just like a character in a novel, he says "I" in a quiet tone. "I" after "I", (he makes a long speech) ...
>
> Pandalevsky is afraid of Rudin and cautiously ingratiates himself with him. ...
>
> Except for the lady of the house, Rudin talks to Natal'ya most often and longest. ...
>
> Natal'ya chatters to him not as a child. ...]

The past imperfective verbs expressing habitual or repetitive actions in the original are constantly translated as "-te iru" forms in *Floating Weed,* just as Futabatei had done earlier in *The Portrait.* In both translations the use of the "-te iru" form enables Futabatei to describe the characters' habitual actions more graphically and vividly, in the case of *Floating Weed* creating a theatrical effect. What distinguishes *Floating Weed* from *The Portrait,* however, is the clear indication of time.

In the first extract cited above, Futabatei translates the first two sentences employing "-ta" forms (tatta, izukumari de atta), though in the original both perfective and imperfective past tense forms appear (Proshlo, ne vyezzhal). We should pay particular attention to the translation of "ne vyezzhal [had not been away]" as "izukumari de atta [had stayed almost all the time]", as by now it has become clear that when past imperfective verbs are translated as "-ta" or "-te ita" forms, Futabatei's intention is to explicitly indicate the external position of the narrator. Associated with this explicit marking of past time are several clear indications of temporal setting within *Rudin.* Janet Walker (1995: 30) suggests that the precise indication of time in the opening passage of *Floating Clouds* may be attributed to the influence of Turgenev, who "regularly indicates the historical time of his novels". The crucial issue here is how these indications of time affect the narrative point of view in each work. Let us compare the openings of *Floating Clouds, Floating Weed* and *Rudin:*

> **千早振る神無月も最早跡二日の餘波となツた廿八日の午後三時頃に、** 神田見附の内より、塗渡る蟻、散る蜘蛛の子うようよぞよぞよ沸出でゝて來るのは、孰れも 頤 を氣にし給ふ方々。(Futabatei Shimei 1964a: 4)

> [**It is three o'clock in the afternoon of a late October day**. A swirling mass of men stream out of the Kanda gate, marching first in antlike formation, then scuttling busily off in every direction. Each and every one of these fine gentlemen **is primarily interested in getting enough to eat** / (shows their dignity by their fine moustache). (Ryan 1967: 197—with correction of bold words in brackets)

> **夏の靜かな朝の事であつた。**晴やかな空に日最う高く昇つてゐたが、野は未だ露に煌めいて、今しがた靄の霽れた谷間からは何處となく良い匂のする涼風が通つて、しつとり濡れた森の中には早起の小禽が面白さうに囀づる聲がする。(Futabatei Shimei 1964b: 4)

> [**It was a quiet summer morning**. The sun has already risen quite high in the clear sky, the field is still glittering with dew, from the valley where the mist has just cleared a fresh breeze blows somewhat fragrantly, in the damp forest the cheerful twittering of the early-rising birds is heard.]

> **Было тихое летнее утро**. Солнце уже довольно высоко стояло на чистом небе; но поля еще блестели росой, из недавно проснувшихся долин веяло душистой свежестью, и в лесу, еще сыром и не шумном, весело распевали ранние птички. (Turgenev 1963c: 237)

> [**It was a quiet summer morning**. The sun stood already quite high in the clear sky; but the fields were still shimmering with dew, a fresh and fragrant breeze blew from the valleys just awakened, and in the forest, still damp and quiet, the early rising birds were merrily singing.]

Although the opening passages of both *Floating Clouds* and *Floating Weed* contain clear indications of time, and the indication in *Floating Clouds* is even more precise than that in *Rudin*, it does not affect the narrative point of view of *Floating Clouds.* The narrator of *Floating Clouds* appears to be located in the same time continuum in which the plot of the novel unfolds. In *Floating Weed,* on the other hand, the indication of time does immediately affect the narrator's position. By rendering "bylo [was]" as "-de atta [was]", Futabatei positions the narrator of *Floating Weed* outside the story. Even though the description which follows uses "-(r)u" forms, the narrator remains distanced from it. The same may be said of the descriptions of the characters' habitual actions cited above. First Futabatei positions the narrator outside the story by opting for the "-ta" form to translate a past imperfective verb, then shifts the verb form to "-te iru" for those past imperfective verbs which describe the habitual or repetitive actions of the main characters. Throughout *Floating Weed* Futabatei maintained the practice of translating past imperfective verbs depicting states and habitual or repetitive actions as "-te iru" forms. The only exception is the translation of past imperfective verbs describing the continuous actions of the main characters as "-te ita" forms. This latter practice, together with the precise indication of the temporal setting, clearly indicates the extraneous position of the narrator, as shown in the following passage from the final chapter:

> Минуло около двух лет. Настали первые дни мая. На балконе своего дома сидела Александра Павловна, но уже не Лепина, а Лежнева; она более года как вышла замуж за Михайла Михайлыча. Она по-прежнему была мила, только пополнела в последнее время. Перед балконом, от которого в сад вели ступени, расхаживала кормилица с краснощеким ребенком на руках, в белой шинельке и с белым помпоном на шляпке. Александра Павловна то и дело взглядывала на него. Ребенок не пищал, с важностью сосал свой палец и спокойно посматривал кругом. Достойный сын Михайла Михайлыча уже сказывался в нем.
> Возле Александры Павловны сидел на балконе старый наш знакомый, Пигасов. (Turgenev 1963c: 342)
>
> [About two years had passed. The first days of May had come. Aleksandra Pavlovna, no longer Lepina, but Lezhneva, was sitting on the balcony of her home; it was more than a year since she had married Mikhail Mikhailych. She was as lovable as before, she had just put on a little weight lately. In front of the balcony, from which some steps led into the garden, a wet-nurse was walking back and forth with a rosy-cheeked baby in her arms, in a little white coat, with a white pom-pom on his cap. Aleksandra Pavlovna was incessantly looking at him. The baby did not cry, but sucked his thumb importantly and was calmly looking around. A worthy son of Mikhail Mikhailych could already be seen in him.
> On the balcony beside Aleksandra Pavlovna our old friend Pigasov was sitting.]
>
> 二年許(ばかり)經つた。五月初旬の事であつたが、觀樓(ものみ)へ出て、アレクサンドラ、パーウロウナ、其頃は最(も)うリーピナではなくて、レヂネフが坐つてゐた。レヂネフの所へ嫁(き)てから最う一年餘にもなるのである。相變らず美しいが、此頃は少し肥つたやうで。觀樓(ものみ)には階(きざはし)が附いてゐて、それを降りると庭になつてゐる。乳母が小さい白い外套を被て、白い房の附いた帽子を戴(かぶ)つた、頰の紅い赤兒を抱いて、觀樓の前を彼方此方(あちこち)と歩いてゐたが、アレクサンドラはともすれば其兒の方を見遣つてゐた。赤兒は泣きもせずに、眞面目くさつて自分の指を吸ひながら、おつとりと四邊(あたり)を視廻してゐた。どうしてもレジネフの息子に違ひない。
> アレクサンドラの側(そば)には、例のピガーソフが坐つてゐた。(Futabatei Shimei 1964b: 122)

[About two years had passed. It was at the beginning of May, on the balcony Aleksandra Pavlovna was sitting, no longer Lepina, but Lezhneva. Already more than a year has passed since she married Lezhneva. She is as beautiful as before, she seems to put on weight lately. There are stairs leading to the garden. A wet-nurse was walking around carrying a rosy-cheeked baby in her arms, in a white cloak, with a white pom-pom on his on his cap, and Aleksandra was incessantly looking at him. The baby did not cry, but was calmly looking around, sucking his thumb importantly. Without doubt, this must be Lezhnev's son.
Beside Aleksandra, that Pigasov was sitting.]

Where scenery is described using past imperfective verbs in the original, Futabatei opts for "-te iru" forms. However, when past imperfective verbs are used to describe the continuous actions of the characters, Futabatei opts for "-te ita" forms. These "-te ita" forms, together with the clear indication of the past by "-de atta [It was]" for "nastupili [had come]", place the action in the past. Consequently the narrative point of view becomes retrospective and omniscient. The narrator positions himself outside the story and takes up a vantage point from which all the incidents in the story may be seen to unfold. The style which Futabatei created towards the end of his translation is quite similar to the style of the Japanese naturalist writers. The following is a quotation from the story *Futon [The Quilt],* which is regarded as the most typical of the works of naturalist fiction, and was written by Tayama Katai ten years after the publication of *Floating Weed.* Tayama Katai, as already mentioned, worshiped Futabatei and his translations of Turgenev's works.

あくる日は日曜日の雨、裏の森にざんざん降つて、時雄の爲めには一倍に侘しい。欅の古樹に降りかゝる雨の脚、それが實に長く、限りない空から限りなく降つて居るとしか思はれない。時雄は讀書する勇氣も無い、筆を執る勇氣もない。もう秋で冷々と背中の冷たい籐椅子に身を横へつゝ、雨の長い脚を見ながら、今回の事件から其身の半生のことを考へた。かれの經驗にはかういふ經驗が幾度もあつた。一歩の相違で運命の唯中に入ることが出來ずに、いつも圏外に立たせられた淋しい苦悶、その苦い味をかれは常に味つた。文學の側でも左様だ、社會の側でも左様だ。戀、戀、戀、今になつてもこんな消極的な運命に漂はされて居るかと思ふと、其身の意氣地なしと運命のつたないことがひしひしと胸に迫つた。ツルゲーネフの所謂　Superfluous man！だと思つて、其主人公の儚い一生を胸に繰返した。
寂寥に堪へず、午から酒を飲むと言出した。（中略）徳利に酒が無くなると、只、酒、酒と言ふばかりだ。そしてこれをぐひぐひと呷る。氣の弱い下女は何うしたことかと呆れて見て居つた。男の兒の五歳になるのを始めは頻りに可愛がつて抱いたり撫でたり接吻したりして居たが、何うした具合でか泣出したのに腹を立てて、ピシヤピシヤと其尻を亂打したので、

> 三人の子供は怖がつて、遠巻にして、平生に似もやらぬ父親の赤く酔つた顔を不思議相に見て居た。（中略）時雄はふらふらと危く小便を仕て居たが、それがすむと、突如 轄 と厠の中に横に寝てしまつた。細君が汚がつて頻りに揺つたり何かしたが、時雄は動かうとも立たうとも爲ない。そうかと謂つて眠つたのではなく、赤土のやうな顔に大きな鋭い目を明いて、戸外に降り頻る雨をじつと見て居た。(Tayama Katai 1968: 77-78)

> [The next day is Sunday and it has rained, the steady downpour in the woods behind the house seeming twice as miserable as usual, and all for Tokio's benefit. The rain falling onto the old keyaki [zelkova] tree comes from a long distance away, it seems to rain endlessly from the endless sky. Tokio has not the mettle either to read books or to write. He has just lounged in his wisteria chair—cold to the back now that it is coming into autumn—and has gazed at the streaming rain, thinking, in the light of this incident, how his life has been till now. He had already suffered similar experiences. He invariably tasted the bitterness of lonely torment, the torment of forever being made to stand on the outside of things and, because of some wrong steps, never being able to enter into the heart of destiny. It is the same with literature, the same with society. Love, love, love... Is he still being tossed, even now, by the waves of a negative fate? The thought has left him overcome by his wretchedness and by the ineptitude of fate. "I am Turgenev's 'superfluous man'", he thought, and went over in his mind the transient life of the protagonist.
> Overwhelmed by loneliness, he started asking for *sake* during the day. ... Each time when he drinks a bottle of *sake*, what he says is only "*sake*, *sake*", and he gulps it down. The timid housemaid was looking at him, stunned by her master's behaviour.
> At first Tokio was holding, patting and kissing his five-year-old boy, but he got so upset when the boy somehow began crying, that he started smacking the boy's bottom. Three of his other children were frightened by this, and surrounded him at a distance. They were dumbly looking at their father's red and drunken face, which appeared strange to them. ...
> ... Tokio was urinating unsteadily on his feet. When he had finished urinating, he suddenly fell and lay down on the toilet floor. His wife was annoyed and shook him several times, but he does not move or stand up, and yet he was not asleep. With his sharp eyes wide-open in his face red like clay, he was looking at the rain steadily falling down outside.][4]

This passage depicts the state of a financially poor but established writer, Tokio, who has just discovered that he has been betrayed by his female disciple Yoshiko. Tokio finds that Yoshiko had not seriously devoted herself to the literary work which Tokio had encouraged her to undertake, that of an independent woman in a new era. Instead she had taken Tokio's advice literally and fallen in love with the divinity student Tanaka. Tokio feels himself betrayed by Yoshiko, not only as a mentor, but as a middle-aged man who has himself fallen

[4] In making this translation I have consulted Kenneth Henshall's translation (Tayama Katai 1981: 48).

in love with the young woman. Tokio's state, as depicted here, may seem more comical, even ludicrous, rather than miserable or sorrowful. However, by employing "-te ita" forms, the narrator of *Futon* describes Tokio's despairing continuous actions retrospectively, as he does the other characters' actions. Consequently the narrative point of view is placed outside of the story, and events are depicted omnisciently. Here the narrator's position is so close to the implied author's that we cannot expect the same comic, mocking effect produced by a narrator who is distinct from the implied author, as is the case in Gogol's stories. Moreover, in this typical work of naturalist fiction, the protagonist Tokio is often considered to be modeled very closely on the author Katai himself, despite the use of the name "Tokio", and the third-person narrative structure (Keene 1984: 264). The narrative becomes overly serious if the author cannot afford to objectify himself. The image of the middle-aged writer despairingly comparing himself with "the fugitive life" of a protagonist from a novel by Turgenev may easily be taken for that of Katai himself, and the novel must be *Rudin.* We have already noted how passionately Katai read *Floating Weed,* which develops a similarly serious tone towards the end. In both *Futon* and *Floating Weed* an omniscient narrative point of view is created by the use of "-te ita" forms to describe the main characters' continuous actions. The use of "-(r)u" or "-te iru" forms in the description of the setting does not affect this stable narrative point of view. However, while in *Futon* the omniscient narrative point of view is stable throughout the story, in *Floating Weed* the narrative point of view gradually shifts from inside to outside the story, coinciding with the shift in the translation of past imperfective verbs describing continuous actions from "-te iru" to "-te ita".

This shift in verb forms is first observed in the description of the characters' reactions to Rudin's eloquence. Later we may observe the use of "-te ita" forms to describe continuous actions when Natal'ya becomes aware of her love for Rudin, when Rudin confesses his love for Natal'ya, and when their love is brought to an end by the eavesdropper Pandalevsky reporting the situation to Dar'ya Mikhailovna. In these climactic scenes both "-te ita" and "-te iru" forms are used to describe the characters' continuous actions. Unlike other stories hitherto translated by Futabatei, present imperfective verbs are not employed in the description of these climactic scenes in the original, so the verb forms of the original are not directly contributing to the use of "-te iru" forms in the translation. The sole factor determining the choice between "-te iru" and "-te ita" is the narrator's point of view in the story. As Futabatei gradually identifies the narrator more closely with the implied author, the use of "-te ita" forms to translate past imperfective verbs expressing continuous actions becomes dominant over the use of "-te iru" forms in these climactic scenes.

The following passage is taken from the farewell scene in which Rudin departs from Dar'ya Mikhailovna's estate, and illustrates Futabatei's use of "-ta" and "-te ita" forms to establish an omniscient narrative point of view.

> Басистов <u>не скрывал</u> своей горести. Наталья явно <u>избегала</u> Рудина. Она <u>старалась</u> не встречаться с ним взорами; однако он <u>успел</u> всунуть ей в руку свое письмо. За обедом Дарья Михайловна еще раз <u>повторила</u>, что надеется увидеть его перед отъездом в Москву, но Рудин ничего <u>не отвечал</u> ей. Пандалевский чаще всех с ним <u>заговаривал</u>. Рудина не раз <u>подмывало</u> броситься на него и поколотить его цветущее и румяное лицо. M-lle Boncourt частенько <u>посматривала</u> на Рудина с лукавым и странным выражением в глазах: у старых, очень умных легавых

собак можно иногда заметить такое выражение... «Эге!—казалось, говорила она про себя,—вот как тебя!»

... До самой станции говорил Рудин о достоинстве человека, о значении истинной свободы,—говорил горячо, благородно и правдиво,—и когда наступило мгновение разлуки, Басистов не выдержал, бросился ему на шею и зарыдал. У самого Рудина полились слезы; но он плакал не о том, что расставался с Басистовым, и **слезы его были самолюбивые слезы**. (Turgenev 1963c: 335-336)

[Basistov did not conceal his grief. Natal'ya was clearly avoiding Rudin. She tried not to meet his eyes, though he did manage to slip his letter into her hand. At dinner Dar'ya Mikhailovna once again repeated that she hoped to see him before her departure for Moscow, but Rudin did not reply to her. Pandalevsky spoke to him more often than anyone else. More than once Rudin felt the urge to hurl himself at him and punch his rosy and blooming face. Mlle. Boncourt often looked at Rudin with a knowing and strange expression in her eyes: in old and very intelligent setter dogs one may observe such an expression... "Oho!", she seemed to be saying to herself, "Serves you right."
... All the way to the station Rudin spoke about the dignity of man, about the meaning of true freedom,—he spoke ardently, nobly and truthfully,—and when the moment came to part, Basistov could bear it no longer, threw himself on his shoulder and began to sob. Rudin's tears began to flow as well, but he wept not because he was parting with Basistov, and **his tears were tears of self-love**.]

バシストフは頭(てん)から別を惜むでかゝり、ナターリヤは人目をも憚らず公然(あからさま)に迯(に)げ廻つて、成るべく眼を視合さぬやうに構へてゐたが、それでもルーヂンは辛うじて手紙だけは渡した。食事の時にダーリヤは重ねてマスクワへ上(のぼ)る迄には最(も)一度會ひたいと云つたけれど、ルーヂンは何とも返答をしなかつた。パンダレーフスキイは人よりも餘計にルーヂンに物を云懸けたが、ルーヂンは此男の得意らしい紅顏(あからがほ)を視ると、飛蒐(とびかか)つて打倒(ぶちのめ)したく思ふことも幾度(いくたび)か有つた。Ｍｌｌｅ．Boncourt(マドモアゼール ボンクール)は何か擽(くすぐつ)たいやうな可異(をかし)な眼付でルーヂンの面(かほ)をじろじろ視てゐた。年功を積んだ悧恰な探犬(さぐりいぬ)は如何(どう)かすると此樣(こん)な眼付をすることがある。眼が物を云つたら、「そら見たことか！」とでもいひさうである。
（上略）ステーションへ着くまでルーヂンは人の人たる所以、眞の自由の貴(たつと)き所以を熱心に説き立てゝ、随分高尚なことも道理(もつとも)なことも云つた。卒分袂(いざわかれ)といふときバシストフは耐りかねて、ルーヂンの首にしがみ付いて泣出したので、ルーヂンも泣きは泣いたが、併しバシストフに分れるのが辛くて泣いたのではない。**彼の涓(なみだ)は利己の涙であつた**。(Futabatei Shimei 1964b: 114-115)

> [Basistov was deeply sorry for the separation, Natal'ya openly ran away from Rudin without avoiding others' eyes, tried not to have eye contact with him, though Rudin just managed to pass his letter to her. At dinner, Dar'ya once again said to Rudin that she wished to see him before she had departed for Moscow, but Rudin did not reply. Pandalevsky talked to Rudin more often than any other person. Several times Rudin felt the urge to throw himself upon him and punch him when he saw the man's blooming and rosy face. Mlle. Boncourt was staring at Rudin's face with a peculiar and titillated look in her eyes. Old, experienced and clever setter dogs sometimes show the same expression in their eyes. If eyes can talk, they seem to say: "Hey! (Look at you.) It serves you right."
> ... Until they arrived at the station, Rudin talked passionately about the dignity of man and the value of true freedom, he talked about noble and rational things. At the time of parting, Basistov could not bear it and threw himself upon Rudin's neck and began sobbing. Although Rudin cried as well, he cried not because he could not bear to part with Basistov. **His tears were tears of self-love**.]

Generally speaking, in *Floating Weed* Futabatei's translation comes gradually to correspond more closely to the original in its narrative posture. At the beginning of the work omissions and interpolations are often observed in an attempt to maintain the narrator's position within the story, but towards the end of Futabatei's translation the narrator's position corresponds quite precisely to the original and this is reflected in the choice of verb forms. In the passage cited above Futabatei opts for "-ta" forms for past perfective verbs and "-ta" and "-te ita" forms for past imperfective verbs. The "-(r)u" forms are employed only for the present form predicative "mozhno zametit' [one may observe]", by which device the implied author directly inserts his own comments about the characters in his novel. In *Rudin* Turgenev employs present tense verbs exclusively for the purpose of voicing his opinions of the characters or of events in the narrative. Hence the narrative of *Floating Weed* (as exemplified by the above passage) gradually becomes dominated by "-ta" forms, expressing the meaning of the past tense, and reflecting an omniscient point of view.

Another observation which may be made about this passage is that Futabatei for the first time uses the third-person pronoun "kare [he]", in the same way that it is currently used in modern Japanese. Futabatei's translation of the last sentence "i slezy **ego** byli samolyubivye slezy [and **his** tears were tears of self-love]" is corresponds very closely to the original: "**Kare** no namida wa riko no namida de atta [**His** tears were tears of self-love]". This rendition clearly demonstrates that Futabatei has finally apprehended the author-narrator relationship in *Rudin,* since both the third-person pronoun " kare no [his]" and the predicative "-de atta [were]" evidently show the extraneous position of the narrator, who is identified closely with the implied author.

Thus we see that in *Floating Weed* Futabatei at first follows the same translation practices as he did in *The Portrait,* creating a graphic and theatrical presentation of the action, scene by scene, by the use of "-te iru" forms for those past imperfective verbs expressing states, habitual actions and, in particular, the continuous actions of the main characters. However, in the process of working on his translation, Futabatei begins to use "-te ita" forms to translate those past imperfective verbs which describe the continuous actions of the characters, coinciding with his decision to regard the narrator as identical with the implied author. In the end *Floating Weed* gains a stable, omniscient narrative point of view by the predominant use of "-te ita" forms in preference to "-te iru" forms, the former nowadays being more standard renditions for past imperfective Russian verbs. The narrative style thus developed in *Floating Weed* may have in turn influenced the narratives of the naturalist writers, in which there is a tight relationship between the narrator and the author, supporting an omniscient point of view.

## *Kusare-en [The Mismatch]* (Translated from Turgenev's *Petushkov*)

The second story to be discussed in this chapter is *The Mismatch*, Futabatei's translation of *Petushkov,* one of Turgenev's early stories. *Petushkov* was written in 1847, one year later than *Zhid [The Jew],* and was written concurrently with *Zapiski okhotnika [A Sportsman's Sketches]*. As has already been noted, *Petushkov* is the most Gogolian of Turgenev's stories. Araya and Seeley both note that the urban middle-class setting, the comical vein (especially in the dialogue), and the physical descriptions of the characters are distinctly Gogolian. However, while Seeley (1991: 96) regards the theme of the story, the middle-aged Petushkov's love, "an obsession that degrades and morally destroys its bearer", to be typical of Turgenev, Araya (1967: 64) considers the middle-aged and isolated man's unreciprocated love for a young girl to be a motif more characteristic of Gogol's stories.

There is indeed some discord between the Turgenevan and Gogolian elements in *Petushkov,* which carry over into Futabatei's translation. This discord is evidenced stylistically in the sentence endings, which reflect the narrative point of view. Seeley (1991: 85) points out that, following works by Lermontov and Gogol, Turgenev in three of his first five stories adopted the distancing device of hiding the author behind one or more narrators. He discarded the idea of presenting his stories as a collection, and thus has no need to interpolate an 'editor'. While Turgenev employs an anonymous "I" in *Three Encounters, Petushkov* is told by an omniscient author, as was Turgenev's first novel *Rudin.*

As typically seen in other works by Turgenev, the opening of *Petushkov* establishes the temporal setting with a date, in this case only approximate:

> В 182... году в городе О... проживал поручик Иван Афанасьевич Петушков. Он происходил от бедных родителей, пяти лет остался круглым сиротой и попал на руки к опекуну. Имущества у него, по милости опекуна, не оказалась никакого; он перебивался пополам с грехом. ... Вся жизнь Петушкова прошла чрезвычайно однообразно; под сорок лет он был еще молод и неопытен, как ребенок. Знакомых он дичился, а с теми, на участь которых мог иметь влияние, обходился весьма кротко ...
> За людьми, осужденными судьбою на жизнь однообразную и невеселую, часто водятся разные привычки и потребности. Петушков по утрам, за чаем, любил кушать свежую белую булку. Без этого лакомства он жить не мог. ... (Turgenev 1963b: 133)
> [In 182... in the town of O... there lived a lieutenant Ivan Afanas'evich Petushkov. He was born of poor parents, at the age of five was left a complete orphan, and fell into the hands of a guardian. Thanks to this guardian, he was left with no property whatsoever; and barely made ends meet. ... Petushkov's whole life passed extremely monotonously; as he approached forty he was still as young and inexperienced as a

child. He was shy of his acquaintances, but he treated those over whose fate he had some influence, very gently. ...

People condemned by fate to a monotonous and joyless existence, are often subject to various habits and wants. Petushkov liked to eat a fresh white bread roll in the mornings with his tea. He could not live without this sweet delicacy. ...]

千八百二十何年のこと。何とやら町にイワン、アフファナーシエウィチ、ペツシコーフといふ陸軍の中尉があつた。貧家に生れて、早く兩親に死なれ、五年間も煢獨でゐた擧句、後見の手に渡り、其又後見のお蔭でなけなしの財産を皆無にして了つたから、随分果敢ない世を渡つて來た。（中略）一、誠に穩かな世を渡つて來た人であるから、四十になつても未だ何處か若々としてゐる代り、大のお坊さんで極く愛度氣ない、相識が有つても逢ふのを厭がつて、目下の者には極く柔しくする。

一本調子の面白くない世を渡る人にはえて有りがちの一癖、何や彼や無くては濟まされぬ物の數ある中に、毎朝々茶に出來立ての白い捻麵包を味ふのが大の好で、此君なくては一日も居られないのである。(Futabatei Shimei 1964b: 206)

[It was in 182.. . In a certain town there lived a lieutenant Ivan Afanas'evich Petushkov. He was born in a poor family, his parents died early, after (he was) left alone for five years, finally fell into the hands of a guardian, and thanks to another guardian, lost all the little property he had, so he lived a pretty modest life... …, because he has spent his life very quietly, he looks still young and is extremely inexperienced for his forty years, and he avoids his acquaintances, though he treats his subordinates quite gently.

People who spend their life monotonously and joylessly often have habits and certain things without which their life cannot continue. [In Petushkov's case] he likes to eat a fresh white bread roll with his tea every morning, and he cannot live without this dear [delicacy].]

What is observed in this opening passage, in both the original and the translation, is the clear indication of the narrator's position, which is shown by the past imperfective verbs "prozhival [lived]" and "perebivalsya [made ends meet]" in the original, and by the corresponding words "(chūi ga) atta [there was (a lieutenant)]" and "hakanai yo o watatte kita [lived a modest life]" in Futabatei's translation. These "atta" and "-te kita" forms used to translate the past imperfective verbs clearly indicate the past tense, and position the narrator outside the story. Consequently the narrative point of view becomes retrospective and omniscient.

Futabatei then shifts the verb forms from "-ta" to "-(r)u" for the description of Petushkov's features and character, which are described using past imperfective verbs in the original. We have already seen a similar shift of verb forms in *The Portrait* and *Floating Weed.* Following the comment on Petushkov's youthfulness and inexperience, Turgenev inserts a comment written in the present tense: "Za lyud'mi, osuzhdennymi sud'boyu na zhizn' odnoobraznuyu i neveseluyu, chasto vodyatsya raznye privychki i potrebnosti [People condemned by fate to a monotonous and joyless existence are often subject to various habits and wants]". Since Turgenev sets the narrative point of view outside the story, we do not find a narrator of the Gogolian type in *Petushkov,* and the comment just cited is taken to come from a narrator outside the story, whose position is close to the implied author's. In Futabatei's translation, this comment is combined with the description of Petushkov's humble indulgence of eating a fresh white bread roll every morning, which leads to his fateful love interest early in the story.

In *The Mismatch* Futabatei combines sentences more often than in any previous translation. The number of full stops in the whole story is reduced by almost half when compared with the original. In chapter three it is reduced to a third. This reduction of the number of full stops (by means of the conversion of full stops into commas) is often observed in passages describing conversations, bringing a colloquial style into the narrative. Futabatei's translation of the extraneous narrator's comment, cited above, is a good example of this colloquial style, with its excessive use of commas and its particular vocabulary, such as "ete ari gachi no ippeki [a habit often found/classic Chinese]", "dai no suki [big favour/classic Japanese]" and "kono kimi [this dear delicacy/semi-modern Japanese indicating a demimondaine]". This colloquial style, suggestive of a raconteur, seems to cause Futabatei to be confused about the position of the narrator in *Petushkov*. Because of the Gogolian comic element, Futabatei finishes this sentence with "ichinichi mo ora re nai no de aru [cannot live even a day], which corresponds to the past imperfective "zhit' ne mog [could not live]". In consequence, Futabatei unintentionally sets the narrator inside the story.

Satō Seirō (1995: 414) points to Futabatei's notable use in *The Mismatch* of the "-no de aru" ending, which was developed by Ozaki Kōyō, and nowadays is widely used to state the speaker's explanation or judgement. However, the use of the "-no de aru" form is observed with similar frequency in Futabatei's other third-person narrative translations: *The Portrait* and *Floating Weed.* Firstly, in *The Portrait*, (where the narrative point of view reflects Gogol's choice of an implied immanent narrator in the original), the "-no de aru" form is often used to express the protagonist's inner thoughts, since the narrator's point of view often merges with Chartkov's point of view. Secondly, we may observe that the narrator's comments, distinctly shown by the use of present imperfective verbs in the original, are rendered by employing the "-mono de aru" form, a variant of the "-no de aru" form, which emphasizes the speaker's general comment or opinion. Thirdly, when "-(mo)no de aru" forms are employed to translate past perfective or imperfective verbs, they tend to reveal the narrator's presence, by adding either emphasis or explanation. The following passage from *The Portrait* is a typical example of effective translation of narrative comment using "-te iru" and "-no de aru" forms, (expressing present tense and narrator's explanation respectively). The original Russian contains past imperfective verbs:

> .. тогда пробегала даже мысль, пробегающая часто в русской голове: бросить всё и закутить с горя на-зло всему. И теперь он почти был в таком положении. (Gogol 1973b: 86)
>
> [...then the thought even passed through his head, as it often passes through a Russian head: to abandon everything and to drown one's sorrows to spite everything. And

now he was almost in such a state. ..]

露西亜人には珍しからぬ事であるが、そんな時には寧そ何も彼も放擲つて了つて、暴に酒でも飲んで遣らうかと思ふこともあるが、今は殆ど然うした心地に成つてゐる**のである**。(Futabatei Shimei 1964a: 323)

[It often is found amongst Russian (people) that at such a moment he has a thought of abandoning everything and going drinking out of desperation. And now he is almost in such a state. ]

The narrator in *The Portrait* is present in the story, so it made sense for Futabatei to employ the "-te iru" form to express the meaning of the present tense when translating past imperfective verbs in this passage. In *The Portrait*, Futabatei employed the "-no de aru" form to translate both past imperfective and past perfective verbs without distinction.

In *Floating Weed*, on the other hand, where Turgenev sets the narrator outside the story, and every so often inserts the narrator's direct comments (employing present imperfective verbs), "-no de aru" forms are employed mainly to translate past imperfective verbs. In this work the number of "-no de aru" forms used for past imperfective verbs is more than twice the number of instances used for past perfective verbs. The following are typical instances of the use of "-no de aru" forms to translate past imperfective and perfective verbs:

1. Он и теперь жил у богатой помещицы, Дарьи Михайловны Ласунской, в качестве приемыша или нахлебника. (Turgenev 1963c: 241)

[He still lived with a rich lady landowner, Dar'ya Mikhailovna Lasunskaya, as an adopted child or parasite.]

今もダーリヤ、ミハイロウナ、ラスンスカヤといふ金満の女地主の所に養子とも附かず、食客とも附かず、厄介になつてゐる**のである**。(Futabatei Shimei 1964b: 9)

[And now he lives with a rich (female) landowner, Dar'ya Mikhailovna Lasunskaya, as either an adopted child or a parasite.]

2. Краска бросилась в лицо Рудину. Неожиданная восторженность Натальи его поразила; но последние слова ее уязвили его самолюбие. (Turgenev 1963c: 324)

[Colour rushed to Rudin's face. Natal'ya's unexpected enthusiasm struck him, but her last words wounded his pride.]

ルーヂンは面色忽ち朱を濺いだ。ナターリヤが思懸けず憤然となつて度肝を抜かれてゐたが、最後の一句を聞くとグツと、癪に障つた**のである**。

(Futabatei Shimei 1964b: 102)

[Rudin blushed instantly. As Natal'ya became unexpectedly enthusiastic, Rudin was struck, out of his wits, but when he heard her last words, he was deeply offended at them. ]

Whilst the "-no de aru" forms employed to translate past imperfective verbs tend to express the implied author's explanations, the "-no de aru" forms used to translate past perfective verbs are used mainly to place emphasis on the successive and instantaneous actions of the main characters. The predominant use of the "-no de aru" form to translate past imperfective verbs conveying the implied author's explanations results in that author's presence being explicitly shown in *Floating Weed.* Almost all the past imperfective verbs for which "-no de aru" forms are employed convey the meaning of a state or habitual action. Consequently these past imperfective verbs are frequently translated as "-te iru no de aru", a present tense form. On the other hand, only two instances are observed where "-te ita no de aru" forms are used to translate past imperfective verbs, and one of these, interestingly, depicts a continuous action:

Рудин говорил о том, что придает вечное значение временной жизни человека. (Turgenev 1963c: 269)

[Rudin was talking about that which gives eternal meaning to the fleeting life of a human being.]

ルーヂンは人の露の命が如何(どう)して不滅のものになるか、其理由を説いてゐたのである。
(Futabatei Shimei 1964b: 38)

[Rudin was explaining the reason, how the fleeting life of a human being became eternal.]

This is the second instance in *Floating Weed* when a past imperfective verb is translated using a "-te ita" form, clearly expressing the sense of the past tense. Hereafter Futabatei constantly employed "-te ita" forms for past imperfective verbs expressing the continuous actions of the main characters. This "-te ita no de aru" form seems to reveal Futabatei's growing awareness of the narrator's position, which is outside the story.

Although in *Floating Weed* "-te ita no de aru" forms appear rarely (only twice), and the "-te iru no de aru" form is dominant (eleven instances), in *The Mismatch* Futabatei employed the "-te ita no de aru" form more consciously three times, with a distinct indication of time. The "-te iru no de aru" form appears only once. Moreover, the "-no de aru" form, whose frequent occurrence is noted by Satō Seirō, in fact appears only eight times in all in *The Mismatch,* compared with nineteen instances in *The Portrait* and forty instances in *Floating Weed.* Yet the use of the "-no de aru" form in *The Mismatch* seems to have some distinctive features which differentiate it from its use in *The Portrait* and *Floating Weed.* The following are the three instances of the "-te ita no de aru" form which are observed in *The Mismatch:*

1. **Однажды** Петушков (которому, по вышеозначенным причинам, вне дома Прасковьи Ивановны приходилось плохо) сидел в задней, Василисиной, комнате и хлопотал над каким-то доморощенным снадобьем, не то вареньем, не то настойкой. Хозяйки не было дома. Василиса сидела в булочной и попевала песенку. (Turgenev 1963b: 147-148)

[**One day** Petushkov (who, for the above-mentioned reasons, found it uncomfortable outside Praskov'ya Ivanovna's house,) was sitting in Vasilisa's room at the back and was busying himself over some home-made brew, somewhere between a jam and a liqueur. The mistress of the house was not at home. Vasilisa was sitting in the bakery and singing a song to herself.]

前回の理由で叔母さんの家に居るのが一番居心が善いので、尚のこと入浸りになつてゐる**或日のこと**、裏のワシリーサの部屋で、ジャムとも附かず煮浸しとも附かぬ妙な物を拵らへてゐたが、其日は叔母さんは留守で、ワシリーサは店で歌を唱つてゐた**のである。**(Futabatei Shimei 1964b: 221)

[For the reason mentioned in the last chapter, he found it most comfortable staying with [Vasilisa's] aunt, so he stayed there all the time, and **this was one of those days** when he was in Vasilisa's room, and making something strange, either jam or syrup; that day the aunt was not at home, and Vasilisa was singing a song in the shop.]

2. Она **всё утро** жаловалась на скуку. **Судя по выражению лица Ивана Афанасьича**, в его голове вертелась мысль необыкновенная и для него самого неожиданная. (Turgenev 1963b: 152)

[**All morning** she was complaining of boredom. **Judging by the expression on the face of Ivan Afanas'ich**, some extraordinary and for himself quite unexpected thought was turning over in his head.]

**今朝は**ワシリーサは始終辛氣だ辛氣だと云續けに云つてゐ、ペツシコーフはペツシコーフで、何か思掛けぬ奇想が浮んだのを胸に秘めてでもゐるやうな面色をしてゐた**のである。**(Futabatei Shimei 1964b: 227)

**This morning** Vasilisa was complaining all the time of feeling dull, while Petushkov was displaying a queer expression, as if he was hiding a secret thought; the most unexpected and extraordinary thought ever had.]

3. Прасковьи Ивановны уже не было на свете. Хозяйством заведовала ее племянница Василиса вместе с мужем своим, рыжеватым и подслеповатым мещанином Демофонтом. (Turgenev 1963b: 177)

[Praskov'ya Ivanovna was no longer of this world. Her niece Vasilisa was managing the business together with her husband, a reddish-haired and weak-sighted petty bourgeois Demofont.]

**其頃は**麺包店の叔母さんも最う故人の数に入つて、姪のワシリーサが頭髪の赤ツちやけた始終睡さうな面をしてゐる亭主のデモフォントと後を引受けてゐた**のである**。(Futabatei Shimei 1964b: 256)

[**At that time** the mistress of the bakery had already passed away, and her niece Vasilisa had been managing it together with her husband Demofont, a reddish-haired man who always looked sleepy.]

Close examination of these instances reveals the following features common to all of them. Firstly, Futabatei translated the indication of time shown in the original fairly clearly in the first two instances, and in the third instance he even inserted an indication of time which is not found in the original. Secondly, the past imperfective verbs translated by the "-te ita no de aru" form all depict the continuous actions of the main characters. Finally, and most importantly, the "-no de aru" forms employed in these instances reveal the narrator's extraneous position. The second instance demonstrates this specific function most clearly. Instead of translating the narrator's direct comment "Sudya po vyrazheniyu litsa Ivana Afanas'icha [Judging by the expression on the face of Ivan Afanas'ich]", Futabatei simply added the "-no de aru" form to show the subject who judges Petushkov's facial expression, the extraneous narrator.

Thus the use of "-no de aru" in *Petushkov* is not notable for its frequency, but is notable in its specific function of denoting the extraneous narrator in the form of "-te ita no de aru". This form appears to correct Futabatei's apparent misconceptions about the narrator's position at the beginning of *The Mismatch*.

The following passage is a description of Petushkov's sorry state, after he has been abandoned by Vasilisa. It illustrates Futabatei's use of the "-te iru no de aru" form to translate past imperfective verbs.

Прошла еще неделя. Петушков перестал даже разговаривать с своим Онисимом, перестал выходить. С утра до вечера лежал он на диване, закинув руки за голову. Стал он худеть и бледнеть, ел он неохотно и торопливо, трубки вовсе не курил. Онисим только головой покачивал, глядя на него.
— А ведь вам нехорошо, Иван Афанасьич,—говорил он ему не раз.
—Нет, ничего,—возражал Петушков. (Turgenev 1963b: 172)

[One more week passed by. Petushkov even stopped talking to his Onisim, and stopped going out. From morning to evening he lay on the couch, his hands behind his head. He began to lose weight and to become pale, ate unwillingly and hurriedly, and did not smoke a pipe at all. Onisim just shook his head, looking at him.
—You're really not well, Ivan Afanas'ich—he said to him more than once.
—No, I'm all right—objected Petushkov.]

**それから一週間ばかりもすると**、最うオニシムと話もしなくなつて、頓と

> 外へは出なくなつた。朝から晩まで兩手を頭の下にかツて、長椅子に臥(ね)ころんでばかりゐる。段々疲れて、血色も惡く、食卓に向つてもさも不味(まづ)さうにして、匆々(そこそこ)にナイフを擱(お)いて了(しま)ふ。煙草さへ全く喫(の)まなくなつた。オニシムは其樣子を視(み)て唯首を掉(ふ)るばかり**である**。
> をりをり氣にして、「如何(どう)かさツしやいましたか？」と問(たづ)ねてみるが、唯いゝえとばかり云つてゐる**のである**。(Futabatei Shimei 1964b: 250)

> [**A week later** (Petushkov) no longer talks to Onisim and has stopped going out completely. From morning to evening he is lying on the couch, putting his hands under the head. He gradually weakens and turns pale; although he sits at the dinner table, he is unwilling to eat and quickly puts his knife down. He has even stopped smoking entirely. Onisim is simply shaking his head as he looks at him. Occasionally he is concerned about (Petushkov) and asks (him)—Is something wrong with your?—but (Petushkov) says only "No".]

Here the "-no de aru" form is employed to translate the past imperfective verb "vozrazhal [objected]" in the form "itte iru no de aru [says]", indicating repetitive action. Although the aspectual meaning is emphasized by "-te iru", the narrator's extraneous position is indicated by the use of "-no de aru" and further strengthened by the clear indication of time.

As for the "-(r)u" form verbs which create some variation from the monotonous and repetitive use of "-ta" forms, Futabatei again applies much the same practice as he had in *The Portrait* and *Floating Weed.* He again chooses to use "-te iru" forms for most past imperfective verbs describing states, habitual actions and continuous actions. The passage cited above demonstrates this practice very clearly: "-ta" forms are used to translate past perfective verbs and "-te iru" or "-(r)u" forms for past imperfective verbs. The resulting translation style is identical with that of Part One of *The Portrait,* in which the dominant tense form is present, and "-ta" forms function as aspect markers. However, unlike *The Portrait* (and similarly to *Floating Weed*) some of the past imperfective verbs describing continuous actions of the main characters are consciously translated as "-te ita" forms, particularly in the latter part of *The Mismatch.* As observed already, these "-te ita" forms tend to be employed together with the "-no de aru" form, and with a clear indication of time. There are nine instances of "-te ita" forms in *The Mismatch.* Five of them are accompanied by a clear indication of time, and three are employed together with the "-no de aru" form. The following passage describes Petushkov's depression after having returned to his tranquil but monotonous life, following his own impulsive decision to leave Vasilisa behind in the bakery:

> Он вышел из дому, но ни к кому не зашел. Проходил по улицам. Обратил внимание на заходящее солнце. Наконец, часу в девятом воротился домой. Он улыбался; он беспрестанно пожимал плечами, как бы дивясь своей глупости. «Ведь вот,—думал он,—что значит твердая воля...»
> На другой день Петушков встал довольно поздно. Ночь он провел не совсем хорошо, до самого вечера не выходил никуда и скучал страшно. (Turgenev 1963b: 157)

[He left the house, but he did not call in on anyone. He walked about the streets. He observed the setting sun. Finally, some time after eight o'clock, he returned home. He kept smiling and shrugging his shoulders, as if marvelling at his own stupidity. "Yes,—he thought,—That's what it means to have a strong will...
The following day Petushkov got up rather late. He had not slept very well, did not go out anywhere till evening and pined terribly.]

で、家を出たが、何處（どこ）へ行くでもなかつた。町を彷徨（うろつ）いて、入日（いりひ）を眺めなどしてゐたが、戻つて來たのは**彼是九時ころ**でもあつたらう。莞爾々々（にこにこ）しながら、今までの我（わが）愚かさを自ら異（あや）しむが如く、首ばかり竦（すく）めてゐた。心の中（うち）で、「これがソノ鐵（くろがね）の意志といふ奴なんだ……」
**其晩は**誠に寢苦しく明かして、**翌朝**（あくるあさ）は晏（おそ）く起出（おきいで）たが、**晩までは**何處へも出ずに、ひどく淋しがつてゐた。(Futabatei Shimei 1964b: 232)

[Then, (he) went out of the house, but he did not go to see anyone. He wandered about the town, and watched the sunset, and it was, supposedly, **about nine o'clock** when he returned home. Wearing a smile, he constantly shrugged his shoulders, as though marvelling at his own stupidity. In his mind, "this is what is called an iron will..."
**That night** he slept terribly badly, and **the next morning** got up late, then (he) stayed home **till evening** and felt awfully lonely.]

With several clear indications of time, the whole passage translated by Futabatei surely conveys the meaning of the past tense, with "-te ita" forms being used to translate past imperfective verbs. Although Futabatei made an error in translating one of the indications of time ("chasu v devyatom [some time after eight o'clock (literally at about the ninth hour)] is translated as "karekore kuji goro [at about nine o'clock]"), he was well aware that the exact indication of time was a significant feature of Turgenev's works. Thus, whenever the time is indicated in *Petushkov,* Futabatei translates the whole sentence or passage using "-te ita" forms carrying the meaning of the past tense. Although this "-te ita (no de aru)" form becomes the most prominent feature emphasizing the extraneous nature of the narrator, it creates a certain discordance with the graphic descriptions in which "-te iru" forms are used to translate past imperfective verbs.

In translating *Petushkov,* which has distinct Gogolian features in its plot, in its incoherent conversations and in its characters, Futabatei opted for the same approach as he had done in *The Portrait,* translating most past and present imperfective verbs as "-te iru" or "-(r)u" forms, and some past perfective verbs as "-ta" forms. In so doing, Futabatei once again succeeded in creating vivid, first-hand images for the reader. However, because of the clear indication of time in *Petushkov,* (a distinctive feature of Turgenev's works), Futabatei was compelled to alter his approach somewhat, translating some past imperfective verbs as "-te ita no de aru" form verbs in those sentences where time is clearly indicated. The result of combining "-te ita" forms with the ponderous tone of the specific ending "-no de aru" is to set the narrator most clearly outside the story. This meant that Futabatei was unable to interchange the viewpoint between the narrator and the protagonist Petushkov. The narrator's viewpoint, being set outside the story, does not slip into a revelation of Petushkov's inner thoughts, even in the climax of the story.

The Japanese Slavist Kimura Shōichi (1956: 41-49) has made some general observations regarding Futabatei's translation of eight works by Turgenev. Kimura suggests that Futabatei had completely established his style by the end of the second period of his translation activity, and that substantial change did not occur during the third period of his translation activity. Kimura values all of Futabatei's translations from Turgenev highly, noting his adherence to a meticulous and accurate 'word-for-word' translation method, and his refraining from free translation such as that undertaken by Mori Ōgai in *Sokkyō Shijin*, (a translation of Andersen's *Improvisatoren*). Kimura concludes that although he cannot judge whether Futabatei's style entirely suited Turgenev's style or not, Futabatei indeed developed a translation style which has a fine unity, and that this style had a great impact on contemporary writers.

If Kimura is right in maintaining that Futabatei followed a literal, 'word-for-word' translation method throughout his translation of Turgenev's works, we should expect a consistent approach to the translation of the verb forms of the original. If we limit our focus on Futabatei's style to the sentence endings, the style which Futabatei developed in his attempt to translate the verb forms of the original Russian must be that same original style which Kimura claims Futabatei developed in the process of translating Turgenev's works. This style incorporates graphic first-hand descriptions resulting from the use of "-te iru" and "-(r)u" forms to translate past imperfective verbs describing states and continuous and habitual actions. It incorporates the use of "-ta" forms to convey the aspectual meaning of completion of the original past perfective verbs.

However, the story for which this style is the most accurate reflection is *The Portrait,* the only story by Gogol which Futabatei translated during the first and second periods of his translation activity. In *The Portrait* Futabatei perfected an original style dominated entirely by the present tense, with the narrator inside the story. In translating Turgenev's works, Futabatei needed to alter his style (or his approach to dealing with verbs) and employed "-te ita" forms to translate some past imperfective verbs. In first-person narrative stories, these "-te ita" forms reveal the narrator-protagonist's retrospective point of view, and create two streams of time in each story. In third-person narrative stories translated from Turgenev's works, "-te ita" forms confirm the narrator's narrative position outside the story, by clearly indicating the past tense.

Our next task is to clarify whether Futabatei indeed created this style in the process of translation, and whether it differed significantly from the styles of other contemporary writers. Comparison will be made between the style Futabatei developed and the style of leading contemporaries such as Ozaki Kōyō and Hirotsu Ryūrō. This will help us to clarify whether Futabatei adopted a foreignizing or domesticating strategy during the second period of his translation activity.

# Chapter 6 — Futabatei's Translation Style and the Styles of Kōyō and Ryūrō

The year 1896 was not only the year in which Futabatei began the second period of his translation work with the publication of *One-sided Love, A Fortuitous Encounter* and the second version of *The Tryst.* It was also a remarkable year for the literary *genbun itchi* movement[1]. In February of that year Ozaki Kōyō, the leader of *Ken'yūsha* [The Society of Friends of the Inkstone], the first and most influential modern literary organization in Japan, which dominated literary circles at that time, started to serialize his first and last *genbun itchi* novel *Tajō takon [Passions and Griefs]* in the *Yomiuri shinbun.* (The final episode appeared in December of that year.) In the same year another *Ken'yūsha* member, Hirotsu Ryūrō, whose works are remembered as "grave" (*shinkoku*) or "tragic" (*hisan*) novels[2], published *Imado shinjū [Love Suicide at Imado]* (in July) and *Kawachi-ya [Shop Kawachi]* (in September), reaching the pinnacle of his literary career. All these stories were written in the *genbun itchi* style.

Yamamoto Masahide, who devoted his life to research into the *genbun itchi* movement, divided it into seven periods as follows (Yamamoto Masahide 1965: 33):

| | | |
|---|---|---|
| 1. | 1866-1883 | Dawn |
| 2. | 1884-1889 | First awareness |
| 3. | 1890-1894 | General lull |
| 4. | 1895-1899 | Second awareness |
| 5. | 1900-1909 | Establishment |
| 6. | 1910-1922 | Consolidation and completion I |
| 7. | 1923-1946 | Consolidation and completion II. |

The second period, the period of first awareness, ends in 1889, when Futabatei left his *genbun itchi* novel *Floating Clouds* unfinished, stopped translating literature, and left literary circles completely. The third period, the period of general lull, from 1890 to 1894, coincides roughly with Futabatei's absence from the literary scene. The fourth period (second awareness), from 1895 to 1899, corresponds roughly to Futabatei's second period of literary activity. This coincidence must be seen as accidental, as the leading writer in the *genbun itchi* movement was not Futabatei but Ozaki Kōyō. Kōyō's *Ninin bikuni iro zange [Two Nuns' Confession of Love],* a work which brought him instantly into prominence, was published in April 1889, and led to the revival of traditional styles and the disappearance for a time of *genbun itchi* novels. Kōyō was thus responsible both for a temporary set-back to the *genbun itchi* movement, and also for its revival, with the publication of *Passions and Griefs.* Before writing *Passions and Griefs,* Kōyō had experimented with the *genbun itchi* style in several

---

[1] The *genbun itchi* style implies a unity of speech and writing. The *genbun itchi* movement began as a stylistic revolution: a conscious departure from the classic style in which the spoken and written modes are completely separate.

[2] Hirotsu's works typically treat gloomy subjects, with his characters being either physically deformed or living in oppressive social conditions.

short stories, which were either original works or adaptations of Western stories. They included *Ninin nyōbō [Two Wives]* (written between August 1891 and December 1892), *Tonari no on'na [The Woman Next Door]* (August to October 1893), *Murasaki* (January to February 1894) and *Reinetsu [Cold Fever]* (May to July 1894), all written during the general lull in the *genbun itchi* movement. *The Woman Next Door* was adapted from Emile Zola's *Pour une nuit d'amour [For a Night of Love],* while *Cold Fever* was based on a tale from the *Decameron*. Following these attempts at writing in the *genbun itchi* style, Kōyō published a more refined *genbun itchi* work, *Aobudō [Green Grapes],* in 1895, which is considered by Yamamoto as the beginning of the fourth period of the *genbun itchi* movement. Finally, the novel *Passions and Griefs* appeared in 1896.

Thus Kōyō's works played a crucial role in the early days of the *genbun itchi* movement. It is rather astonishing that Kōyō was able to command the various styles according to the material he worked with. Yet because of his flexibility in employing various styles, rather than adhering to one principle, he is often criticized by scholars of the *genbun itchi* movement for lacking an understanding of the importance of *genbun itchi* (Yamamoto Masahide 1971: 183). He is also accused of a lack of artistic integrity in writing his novels, of merely pursuing interesting and novel plots, and decorating them in a variety of styles, rather than being moved by higher purpose (Kataoka Ryōichi 1965). It could equally be said that Kōyō was a born writer whose various styles emerged to match the material he was working with. Fukuda Kiyoto, who studied the complete works of all *Ken'yūsha* members, suggests that style and plot were the key elements of interest to Kōyō when he was writing. Fukuda adds that the writer with the greatest influence on Kōyō's early works was Ihara Saikaku (1642-1693), a poetic (*haikai*) and prose (*ukiyo zōshi*) writer during the Edo period. Fukuda writes:

> In Kōyō's case, [the influence of Saikaku] was not confined to the style itself, it extended to content. It defined not only the style but also the treatment of the subject matter. Consequently it determined the tendency of his early works. (Fukuda Kiyoto 1992: 129)

The influence of Saikaku over Kōyō's works is summarized by Fukuda as follows:

1. Particles such as "te", "ni", "o" and "wa" are often omitted. By the omission of these particles, the sentences become less prolix and more rhythmical and dynamic.
2. Incomplete sentences, noun endings and short phrases are distinguishing characteristics. The interchange of long and short phrases also contributes to the creation of rhythmical sentences.
3. Detailed explanatory descriptions of the features and clothes of the main characters, and short didactic phrases expressing worldly wisdom are often inserted.

However, when Kōyō wrote *Two Nuns' Confession of Love,* Saikaku's influence was not nearly as apparent as in later works such as *Kyara makura [Pillow of Aloes-wood Perfumery]* (1890) or *San'nin zuma [Three Wives]* (1892). Yoshida Sei'ichi (1954: 412) goes so far as to affirm that there is hardly any resemblance between Saikaku's style and that adopted by Kōyō in *Two Nuns' Confession of Love*. On the other hand, the writer and critic Itō Sei (1973: 10-11) suggests there are some similarities between the two styles, as well as some differences. He considers that Kōyō's style resembles Saikaku's in cutting phrases short with full stops and connecting these phrases in the same way as *renku* (linked verse), and also in inserting ideological (or subjective) words. It differs from Saikaku's style in separating conversational passages from the narrative. Itō Sei confirms the similarities which Fukuda summarized (points 2 and 3 above). Donald Keene (1984: 127) offers a further commentary on Kōyō's use of short phrases or noun endings:

> Like other writers of the period, he was troubled by what to do with the copula—whether the classical form 'nari' or one of the colloquial forms—which normally end Japanese sentences with monotonous regularity. His solution in *Confessions of Love* was to cut short the sentences often ending them with nouns, in the manner of Saikaku rather than of *gesaku* fiction. (Underline added)

Indeed, Kōyō employs the classical form "-nari" (the English equivalent is "to be" and its colloquial versions can be "-desu", "-da" and "-de aru") only five times throughout the narrative of *Two Nuns' Confession of Love.* What is more, two of these instances are contained in a description of the inner thoughts of the main characters. The following are the five instances of the use of "-nari" in *Two Nuns' Confession of Love:*

1. まだ爪紅の消え切らぬ指に。珠數つまぐる殊勝さ……過て哀れなり。
(Ozaki Kōyō 1965a: 5)

[How admirable she [is]... to use her prayer beads despite her youth. It is even pitiful to watch her at it.]

2. 當然の理に責められて。武重は—鎗を突き。鞍にもたれ—首を下げて無言なり。(Ozaki Kōyō 1965a: 12)

[Being persuaded by righteous reason, Takeshige—holds his spear and leans against a saddle—he is silent with his head down.]

3. 實に其鎗は守眞の亡父守道が双なき秘蔵の業物。遺物とてかれに譲れるなり。(Ozaki Kōyō 1965a: 14)

[Indeed that spear is the one which belonged to Morimichi, Morisane's deceased father; an unparalleled, treasured and fine spear. He inherited it as a keepsake.]

4. 鏡に花を翳して月の影とは見えず。此「自然」に逆らひて。泣くに笑ひ。怒るに喜ぶは。世なれし曲者の業なり。(Ozaki Kōyō 1965a: 17)

> [A mirror does not show the moon, when a flower is reflected. Being against this 'nature', to smile when one wants to cry, or to be joyful when one is angered are the deeds of a worldly man.]

> 5. 出陣の砌遺したる書置も。此心を籠しなり。(Ozaki Kōyō 1965a: 18)

> [This intention lies in my testament, which I left when I took to the battlefield.]

These classical "-nari" auxiliary verbs, which appear in the above-mentioned examples, clearly manifest the subject of each utterance. Instances 1 and 5 express the inner thoughts of main characters, whereas the other three instances indicate the presence of the narrator. Instance 4 expresses the narrator's worldly wisdom. Thus, when "-nari" is employed, the narrator's presence becomes apparent in the narrative. However, for most of the narrative of *Two Nuns' Confession of Love,* these "-nari" auxiliary verbs are omitted, by employing either noun endings or symbols such as "—" or "...". The following is the beginning of Chapter Two of *Two Nuns' Confession of Love,* which describes the battlefield.

> 高きは林か。低きは野か。唯一面に白く。なおチラチラ名殘をふらす曉の**空**。岡の片蔭に破れ硝子の薄氷に。縁を取せし小澤近く。古たる**梅樹**。下は幹を染分け—上は「紅蕋」を包む—**雪**。誰……此美亂し—此美を傷く……こは**何事**。低き梢に。切口から血汐を落す生首三ツ結ひつけて。鋸に柄や附けたる……こぼれ齒の長刃の。朱に染るを幹の二叉に寄掛け。諸膝組で雪を掬ぶ**若武者**—鎧は……**草摺**。(Ozaki Kōyō 1965a: 10)

> [Is that high part forest and the low part field? It is white all over. From **the sky**, in the dawn, white flakes are still falling. Shaded by the hill [there is] a small swamp, framed with thin ice like broken glass. **An old *ume* tree** stands near the swamp. The lower part of its trunk is covered in white stripes—the pink flowers of its upper part are covered with—**snow**. Who ---- disturbs this beauty? — harms this beauty ---- what is **the matter**. On the lower branch. Someone is tying three freshly severed heads, dripping blood. Is that a saw with a handle? ---- He leans his broken halberd stained with blood against the crotch of the tree. [He is] **a young warrior** who squats and scoops up the snow—His armour ----[is] **the colour of grass**.]

Thus, cutting phrases short by employing full stops,[3] and limiting the use of the auxiliary verb "-nari" by frequent use of noun endings, Kōyō created a new narrative style in *Two Nuns' Confession of Love.* He claimed as much in his author's remarks:

> With respect to style, I have mulled over the different possibilities, bored by the usual compromise between literary and colloquial, and irritated by the *genbun itchi* style,

---

[3] At that time, the full stop did not necessarily indicate the end of the sentence, as it does now.

> and I have in the end created a new and individual style. It is not for me to judge whether it is a phoenix or a barnyard fowl, a tiger or a cat. (Cited in Keen 1984: 129 - emphasis added)

In this new style the narrative became more poetic and rhythmical, reminiscent of *haiku*. However, at the same time it became anonymous. The narrator's presence is concealed by the limited use of "-nari". We may conclude that Kōyō created a new narrative style in *Two Nuns' Confession of Love* by attempting to eliminate auxiliary verbs, countering the *genbun itchi* style, and more precisely, Futabatei's "-da" and Bimyō's "-desu" styles.

It would appear that Kōyō was for quite some time satisfied with this anonymous narrative style created in *Two Nuns' Confession of Love.* The more he became familiar with Saikaku's style, the greater became its influence over his works. Kōyō no longer separated dialogue from narrative in his most "Saikakuesque" (Keene 1984: 131) works such as *Pillow of Aloes-wood Perfumery* and *Three Wives.* In these works Kōyō was not troubled by the problem of the narrator—who should narrate and in which style—since it was taken for granted that the narrator was the author. All description, including dialogue, is made in rather subjective Saikakuesque style. The author manipulates all the characters from his own fixed point of view. The following is a scene from *Three Wives,* in which Oen, who is to become Yogorō's third mistress, hurries to an arranged meeting with him:

> 折から人の見えざるに稍心落着き、男に座敷を問へば、二階の**奥**。それへと急ぎて階子を昇らむとすれば、夫婦奥より駈出で、これはといふに悚然としたれど、袋の鼠竄るゝ路無く、今朝程はと、まづ女房に挨拶すれば、想ひの外なる機嫌にて、諜々しく世辭いふ側より、亭主は無上に嬉しがり、ようこそを五つ六つもいうて、お二階へと夫婦揃うて愛想好き對遇に、難所一つ越えたりとおもへば、二階の奥に聞ゆる笑語の聲、之に胸は又塞りぬ。(Ozaki Kōyō 1965a: 69)

> [Calming down a little, as no-one is to be seen, [Oen] asks a servant to which room she is to go. It is **a rear upstairs room**. As she is rushing to go up the stairs, the [servant] couple run out and say: "Alas!" She is frightened of them, but there is no way of escaping, so she first greets the wife with "Thank you for this morning", and finds that the wife is in an unexpectedly good mood and flatters her a lot, and the husband is also extremely pleased [to see Oen] and welcomes her five or six times. As both the husband and wife receive her warmly and invite her upstairs, she thinks that she has cleared the first obstacle, but then she hears laughter from upstairs and becomes anxious again.]

This passage demonstrates how dialogue is incorporated into the narrative, and the subjective nature of the account. (For example: "fukuro no nezumi nogaruru michi naku [there is no way of escaping, as if a mouse in a trap]".) So, although noun endings are employed less frequently, and "-nari" is found more often in these "Saikakuesque" works, the style of the narrative no longer troubled Kōyō, as dialogue was absorbed into the narrative. It was only when Kōyō once again began to separate dialogue from narrative, in *Two Wives,* that the problem of the narrator emerged again. It was in this work that Kōyō first employed his "-de aru" *genbun itchi* style.

The reasons for Kōyō's suddenly abandoning the traditional *gazoku setchū*[4] "Saikakuesque" style and adopting a *genbun itchi* style have been disputed over the years. Nanette Twine (1975: 157-158) in her study of the *genbun itchi* movement, summarizes the various proposed reasons as follows:

1. Ozaki was influenced by the trend of the times towards Genbunitchi in both novels and general use; not wanting to be left out, he tried his hand at it. (Honma Hisao)
2. One of the most outstanding characteristics of Ozaki's work was his diversity of style. He tried to write in as many different styles as possible, and was publishing "gazoku setchū" style novels at the same time as Genbunitchi novels. (Seki Ryōichi)
3. His contact with foreign literature may have been a factor in his turning to colloquial writing. (Yamamoto Masahide)

All these reasons seem convincing, as Kōyō's *genbun itchi* novels were published alternately with *gazoku setchū* style novels, and Kōyō's interest in foreign literature is borne out by his many translations and adaptations of foreign works. It would appear, however, that the immediate stimulus for Kōyō's adoption of the *genbun itchi* style was the separation of dialogue from the narrative. Yamamoto Masahide (1971: 177-180), as well as pointing to Kōyō's interest in foreign literature as a reason for turning to a colloquial style, also suggests that the imbalance between the styles of the narrative and the dialogue in *Two Wives* led Kōyō to try out the *genbun itchi* style. Donald Keene supports this suggestion, and adds another cause: the temporal setting of *Two Wives*. Keene (1984: 133) states:

> ... since the story was set in the present time, and the proportion of dialogue to descriptive matter was unusually high, he gradually altered the style of his descriptions from the classical to the colloquial, in order to achieve a greater unity of effect.

However, once the styles of narrative and dialogue are brought together, inevitably the problem of the narrator—who is narrating and from which point of view—must emerge.

In relation to this, Suge Satoko (2000: 109-118) draws attention to the sentence endings in *Two Wives*. Suge (112) observes that Kōyō gradually replaces "-nari" expressing judgement with "-de aru", and "-keri" expressing past tense with "-ta". In some parts of the story the two forms even coexist. She suggests that Kōyō was not conscious of the difference in use between "-nari/keri" and "-de aru/ta", and merely replaced one with the other, not considering them essentially different. She further observes that the narrator's point of view is fixed within each presently unfolding scene, and the story is told in the historic present. Only when the narrator sums up the account and adds his own general comments, does he resort to predominant use of the forms "-nari", "-keri" and "-nu" (which expresses completion of action).

Thus, when Kōyō first tried out the *genbun itchi* style in *Two Wives,* the auxiliary verb

[4] *Gazoku setchū* is a flowery mixture of literary and colloquial language.

"-ta" was used not so much as a past tense marker (as it had been in Futabatei's translations of *The Rendezvous* and *Three Encounters*), but rather as an aspect marker showing completion. Moreover, the narrator's point of view seems to be divided into two: one is set inside the story, fixed within its present time (with both "-keri" and "-ta" being employed), the other is set outside the story, in order to be able to sum it up, or to comment on it (with only "-keri" being employed).

The process of evolution of Kōyō's *genbun itchi* style was completed in the novels *Green Grapes* (1895) and *Passions and Griefs* (1896). The former is a first-person narrative story and the latter is a third-person narrative. Mizuno Kiyoshi (1958) has investigated possible stylistic links between these works and works published by Futabatei. Mizuno studied the verb endings employed in *Floating Clouds, The Tryst* and *A Chance Encounter.* He regards the present tense forms used in the revised translations of *The Rendezvous* and *Three Encounters* as the historic present, and suggests that their frequent use in these works, published in 1896, may have resulted from the influence of works by Kōyō and Ryūrō. Mizuno conducts an examination of the sentence endings in sections of Kōyō's *Passions and Griefs* and Ryūrō's *Love Suicide at Imado.* He finds that the ratio of "present tense forms" to "past tense forms" in these works is four to one in *Passions and Griefs* and two to one in *Love Suicide at Imado.* He suggests that this finding proves the stylistic influence of these works on Futabatei, pointing out that Futabatei, at that time, showed particular affinity with Ryūrō as a writer who convincingly depicted human grief.

Mizuno's proposition seems rather convincing when comparison is made solely of the numbers of verb endings. However, further examination of "-(r)u" and "-ta" forms (which according to Mizuno express present and past tense) is needed to clarify any essential resemblance between Futabatei's style and the styles of Kōyō and Ryūrō. In particular, we should examine "-te iru" and "-te ita" form verbs, which were used to translate past imperfective verbs in Futabatei's translations. These forms played a crucial role when Futabatei wrote his second versions of *The Rendezvous* and *Three Encounters,* and also in his translations of Turgenev's first-person narrative stories. We should examine how "-te shimatta" forms are used, as these were employed by Futabatei exclusively to translate past perfective verbs in the second versions of *The Rendezvous* and *Three Encounters.* We should also examine "-no de aru" endings. Although Kōyō was not the first writer to employ "-no de aru" endings, he is widely regarded as the first to establish their use (Yamamoto Masahide 1971: 186-189), in his novel *Passions and Griefs*, and as being responsible for the spread of the "-de aru" style, which is nowadays the most common (Nakamura Mitsuo 1968: 59). To clarify the influence of Kōyō's "-de aru" style over Futabatei's translation style at that time, we should particularly examine "-no de aru" endings, whose use by each writer is optional, and manifests the subject of speech. Finally, in the case of "-ta" form endings, it is not their frequency so much as their distribution which should be examined. As we observed earlier, in the translations of Futabatei's second period he attempted to break the monotony in the use of this form, and successive instances of this form are rare. The "-ta" form tends to be used in isolation, to carry the aspectual meaning of completion, rather than the meaning of the past tense.

Let us start by examining the style of Kōyō's *Green Grapes,* which was published almost a year before Futabatei marked the beginning of the second period of his translation activity with the appearance of a collection under the title *One-sided Love*. *Green Grapes* was written as Kōyō's own private account of the night he kept vigil over his disciple Oguri Fūyō, who was seriously ill with symptoms of cholera. Kōyō did not publish this account as a novel, nor did his contemporaries consider it as such (Yoshida Sei'ichi 1954: 412). None the less, it is highly regarded, Ikari Akira (1961: 145) suggesting the story would have been even more well received if the"confessional novel" (*shi shōsetsu*) had already been an established genre. Its colloquial *genbun itchi* style was also praised by Masamune Hakuchō (1926: 388), one of the naturalist writers, as the most harmoniously presented of Kōyō's *genbun itchi* works. Because *Green Grapes* was based on Kōyō's real experience, many critics praised the naturalness of its style (Maruoka Akira 1967: 307). Some critics, however, suggested Kōyō lacked the imagination to create novels (Kataoka Ryōichi 1965: 390).

Unlike other works to be examined in this section, the number of "-ta" form verbs in *Green Grapes* is almost the same as the number of "-(r)u" form verbs. If "-ta no de aru" endings are excluded from the total, the number of "-ta" forms exceeds that of "-(r)u" forms. Generally speaking, "-(r)u" forms are employed to depict the author-narrator's (i.e. Kōyō's) inner thoughts. On the other hand, "-ta" forms are used to advance the action, to describe the incident in its process. In some chapters (five and twelve) the number of "-ta" forms simply exceeds that of non "-ta" forms, which include noun and "-no de" endings. In one moving scene from chapter five, the narrator-protagonist urges his quickly failing disciple to drink some wine which he has rushed out to buy for his nourishment:

「然し、おれが買つて來たのだから飲みな。」
と瓶を引寄せて栓抜(せんぬき)を刺した。
門生に對する自分の「おれが」と云ふ語は、最上權の嚴命で、渠等は先生の「おれが」の言下には、無理も道理も服さなければならぬことに躾けられたのである。果して**渠は**、
「飲むで見ます。」
と奪つて答えた。
「見ますでは可けない、飲むのだ。」
と例の皮肉を言つて逼つた。此間に口を開けて、玻璃盞(コツプ)に注(つ)いで、まづ自(みづから)嘗めて、
「うむ、是は佳い。」
と患者の前に出すと、
「とても恁(か)うは飲めません。」
なるほど多過ぎたから、又半分ばかり飲むで、餘を勸めた。
**渠は**一口飲むと、躊躇したので、
「ぐツと飲め、ぐツと飲め。」
と自分は頻(しきり)に逼つた。**渠は**ぐツと飲み、ぐツと飲むだ。 (Ozaki Kōyō 1954: 212)

[—But, because I [*ore*] bought it, you should drink it.
I drew the bottle towards me, and pushed the opener in it.
The word "*ore* [I]" to all my disciples carries the meaning of an absolute order. They were trained to obey under the word "*ore*" without question.
As I expected, **he** answered willingly.

—I shall try it.
—Try is not enough, you should drink it.
With the usual irony I urged him to drink it. In the meantime, I opened the bottle and poured some wine into the glass. I tried it first.
—Well, it's quite nice.
I pushed it towards the patient.
—It is too much for me to drink.
Indeed, it was too much, so I drank almost half, and asked him to drink the rest.
**He** had a sip, and then he hesitated.
—Drink it up, drink it up.
I eagerly urged him to drink it. **He** gulped it down once, and again.]

Kōyō's disciple Fūyō, thinly disguised as Shun'yō in *Green Grapes,* vomits all he has drunk. In this passage "-ta" forms are employed almost exclusively, and successively, to depict the unfolding action, revealing the firm retrospective point of view of the narrator-protagonist. The "-no de aru" form is the only non "-ta" form employed in this passage. In *Green Grapes* "-no de aru" endings are employed frequently, and often following "-ta" forms. (The number of "-ta no de aru" endings in *Green Grapes* is more than double that of "-(r)u no de aru" endings.) We may also note that "-ta no de aru" endings are used mainly to depict the actions and inner thoughts of the narrator-protagonist.

Furthermore, as Okumura Tsuneya (1954: 68-69) has pointed out, in *Green Grapes* Kōyō for the first time established the use of a third-person pronoun, "kare", which indicated others in classical Chinese. It is significant that Kōyō did this not in a third-person narrative, but in a first-person narrative. It was, presumably, more natural for Kōyō to use third-person pronouns in his first-person narrative story, which he did not consider so much a story as a personal account. The use of third-person pronouns, the frequent and successive use of "-ta" forms and the use of "-ta no de aru" emphasizing the narrator's presence, all contribute, in *Green Grapes*, to a narrative with a firm retrospective point of view, similar to the narratives of the naturalist school of writers, but quite different from the narratives of the first-person stories translated by Futabatei.

When we compare the narrative styles of *Green Grapes* and Futabatei's second version translations of *The Rendezvous* and *Three Encounters,* the differences are clear. Firstly, the number of "-(r)u" forms employed in Futabatei's translations is almost double that of "-ta" forms. Secondly, the successive use of "-ta" forms by Futabatei is rare. Thirdly, Futabatei rarely uses "-ta no de aru" endings: there are no instances in *The Tryst* and only three instances in *A Fortuitous Encounter.* In *A Fortuitous Encounter* they are used to explain the narrator-protagonist's feelings or thoughts, and are more obligatory than the "-ta no de aru" endings in *Green Grapes.*

Verbs of the form "-te iru", which Futabatei uses consistently to translate past imperfective verbs in the Russian originals, and which are a prominent feature of *The Tryst* and *A Fortuitous Encounter,* are in *Green Grapes* overshadowed by the use of "-te ita" forms. These "-te ita" form verbs, hardly employed in the two translations by Futabatei, are used twenty four times in *Green Grapes.* Later, in his translations of Turgenev's first-person narratives *Asya, The Dream* and *The Jew,* Futabatei was to refine his use of "-te iru" and "-te ita" forms to translate past imperfective verbs. In these later translations he employed "-te iru" forms to translate past imperfective verbs describing the actions of main characters other than the narrator-protagonist. Verbs describing the actions of the narrator-protagonist, on the other hand, were translated using "-te ita" forms. This resulted in the creation of two streams of time in the first-person narrative. In *Green Grapes,* however, there is no such difference in the use of "-te iru" and "-te ita" forms, both of which are equally employed to describe the background and the actions of the main characters, including the narrator himself. The only observable difference in their use is that, whereas "-te iru" forms are used to depict the narrator's inner thoughts, "-te ita" forms tend to be used to describe the narrator's actions. Kōyō is also more likely to use "-te iru" forms than "-te ita" forms in the description of the setting. However, such descriptions are far less prominent in *Green Grapes* than in Futabatei's translations of *The Rendezvous* and *Three Encounters.*

Finally there is a marked difference between Kōyō's and Futabatei's styles in the use of the "-te shimatta" form. In *The Tryst* and *A Fortuitous Encounter* this form was used specifically to translate verbs which were past perfective in the original, often expressing the narrator's feelings of regret. The "-te shimatta" is used by Futabatei to emphasize the aspectual meaning of the original Russian verbs. Kōyō hardly employed this form. There is only one instance in *Green Grapes,* and even in his full length novel *Passions and Griefs* this form appears a mere eighteen times.

To sum up our comparison between *Green Grapes* and *The Tryst* (second version) and *A Fortuitous Encounter,* it would appear that the stylistic resemblance is slight, the narrative of *Green Grapes* being more like those of the naturalist school of writers than like Futabatei's, particularly in its use of "-ta" forms. This would suggest that Futabatei's style was developed more through his translation than through imitation of Kōyō.

Let us now turn to a comparison of the narratives of Kōyō's *Passions and Griefs* and Futabatei's translations of third-person narrative stories by Gogol and Turgenev. In particular, it is worth comparing *Passions and Griefs,* published in December 1896, with *The Portrait,* which was published in January 1897. As well as being published one after the other, these two stories share the portrait theme. With *Passions and Griefs* (unlike *Green Grapes*), Kōyō was confident that he had produced an original work of fiction (*sōsaku*). An advertisement which appeared in the *Yomiuri shibun* declared:

> This is not a work of *haikai,* nor is it a miscellaneous sketch, nor an adaptation, nor a collaborative effort, but a truly great [original] new work in which the author has given free play to the genius of his brush. (Keene 1984: 137 - emphasis added)

However, *Passions and Griefs* came to be praised more for its stylistic achievement as a *genbun itchi* novel than for its thematic achievement in attempting to describe a human mind realistically. Stylistic and thematic comparisons are often made between *Passions and Griefs* and Futabatei's *Floating Clouds.* Concerning the style, Twine (1975: 157) writes:

> Ozaki had chosen the "de aru" style of Genbunitchi; in "Tajō takon [Passions and Griefs]" he perfected a colloquial style so polished as to make that of Yamada and Futabatei look crude by comparison.

Concerning the theme of *Passions and Griefs,* Kataoka (1965: 392) approves its detailed description of the human mind, and its simple structure, but accuses Kōyō of a lack of artistic integrity in writing the work:

> It was written by Kōyō as if he were prompted by circumstances and followed the literary trend of the time, .... In short, it lacked the serious real-life experience which the works of Futabatei or Ichiyō possessed.

Kōyō has thus been praised for his stylistic achievement in *Passions and Griefs,* while at the same time being criticized for having given too much attention to style at the expense of content. Moreover, although most emphasis has been laid on the style of the work, few attempts have been made to clarify how "modern" Kōyō's *genbun itchi* novel is. In fact in *Passions and Griefs* Kōyō employs non "-ta" forms (including noun endings, "-no de" endings and "-i" adjectival endings) four times as frequently as "-ta" forms. In the light of this figure, it does not seem appropriate to suggest that there is little difference between the style of *Passions and Griefs* and that of present day novels, in which "-ta" forms dominate and suggest an omniscient narrative point of view.

To clarify whether Kōyō's frequent use of "-(r)u" forms in *Passions and Griefs* can be regarded as a use of "the historic present" (as Mizuno has suggested), an attempt will now be made to compare Kōyō's use of "-(r)u" and "-ta" forms in *Passions and Griefs* with Futabatei's use of these forms in *The Portrait.* More precisely, we shall examine the employment of "-te iru", and "-te ita" forms, "-te shimatta" forms, "-no de aru" endings and the distribution of "-ta" forms.

*Passions and Griefs* is the story of a middle-aged professor of geology, Sumi Ryūnosuke, who suddenly loses his beloved wife Orui, and grieves for her. His grief is so intense that he fears he will go insane. The motif of the portrait appears as Ryūnosuke attempts to ease his grief by having his wife's likeness preserved in a painting. However, contrary to his expectations, the portrait intensifies his grief by constantly reminding him of his wife's death. In his battle to regain his zest for life, he gradually finds comfort in his friend's wife, Otane, when he stays at their home. The following is the well-known opening of the novel:

> 鷲見柳之介は其妻を亡つてはや二七日になる。去る者は日に疎しであるが、**彼は**此十四日をば未だ昨日のやうに想つてゐる、時としては、今朝のやうに唯の今のやうにも想ふ。余り思ひ窮めては、未だ生きてゐるやうにも想つてゐる。（中略）
>
> 柳之介は多く人を好かぬ、代には又多く人に好かれぬ性で、男では朋友の葉山誠哉、女では妻の類子、此二人の外には世界に柳之介の好いたものは無い。**彼は**多くの人を好く代に、唯此二人を好いたのであるから、その情の篤いことは夥しいもので、実に見苦しいほど其妻には惚れていた。
>
> 一も妻、二も妻、三も四も五も類で無くては、柳之介の夜は明けなかつた。**彼の**同僚は「妻が」先生と仇名を付けたほどで、妻は**彼の**命であつたものを、**彼は**今その妻に死なれたのである。（中略）
>
> 例の同僚は嗤つた、鷲見は全力を挙げて其妻に惚れてゐるのだと。其通り、「全力を挙げて」とは嘲弄でない、適評であつた、適評ではない、事実であつた。(Ozaki Kōyō 1965b:5)

> [Fourteen days have already passed since Sumi Ryūnosuke lost his wife. Far from eyes, far from heart, they say, but **he** thinks of the past fourteen days as if they were yesterday. Sometimes it seems to him as if it happened this morning, or even just now. When he broods over it too much, he even feels as if she were still alive. ...
> Ryūnosuke hardly likes people, for people often dislike him, and there is nobody he likes in this world except for his best friend Hayama Seiya amongst men, and his wife Ruiko amongst women. Because **he** liked these two instead of loving many people, his passion towards them was extreme, and in particular he was so infatuated with his wife that it even made others embarrassed.
> He relied on his wife for this and that, for virtually everything. Ryūnosuke couldn't live without Rui. **His** colleague even gave him the nickname professor "Sai ga [my wife]". Sai [his wife] was **his** life, but now **he** was deprived of that wife.
> That colleague mocked him saying Sumi was in love with his wife with all his might. Indeed the words "with all his might" were not a mockery, but an apt remark, and not even an apt remark, but a veritable fact.]

Commenting on this passage, Munakata Kazushige observes that the punctuation, sentence length, structure of paragraphs and sentence endings seem quite familiar to contemporary readers, and easy to read (Munakata 1995: 41). In particular, Munakata examines the various sentence endings: the "naru", "-iru" and "-ta" forms, the dictionary forms of adjectives "-i" and "-(r)u", and also "-no de aru" endings. These forms are employed harmoniously, and form a style from which the style commonly seen in modern novels originates. Munakata defines the narrator in *Passions and Griefs* as the one who "follows the golden mean", one who never deviates from the stance of a man with common sense. Unlike the narrator in *Floating Clouds,* he neither mocks nor criticizes his protagonist directly, but narrates the story moderately with some distance.

Indeed, the passage just quoted does contain diverse sentence endings such as "-(r)u" and "-ta" forms, "-te iru" and "-te ita" forms and "-no de aru" endings, as Munakata points out. However, attention must equally be paid to the positions of these endings. Kōyō begins the first paragraph of his novel by employing the "-(r)u" forms "naru" and "omou", then shifts to the "-te iru" forms "omotte iru" and "shinda ni kimatte iru [she must have died]", and finally employs the "-no de aru" ending "ikite iru no de aru [(she) is surely alive]". Judging by these verb forms, Kōyō apparently set the narrative point of view inside the story. However, the verb forms suddenly shift in the middle of the second paragraph. When the description turns to Ryūnosuke's "passion" for his deceased wife, Kōyō employs "-ta" forms exclusively: "hore te ita [was infatuated]", "(yo wa) akenakatta [couldn't live]", "(sai ni) shina re ta no de aru [(he) was deprived of (that wife)]", "omowanakatta [(she) did not adore him]", "shinjite ita no de aru [(he) surely conceived]", "waratta [mocked]", "(jijitsu) de atta". That is, once the description shifts to Ryūnosuke's past, the narrator employs a retrospective point of view. Although this description of Ryūnosuke's past temporarily shifts the narrative point of view to a retrospective one, it is as if Ryūnosuke is himself reviewing his past, and the narrator's point of view remains inside the story. Since, in the first chapter, the whole description of Ryūnosuke's 'present' is made using non "-ta" forms, those "-ta" forms which do occasionally appear in isolation carry the meaning not of past tense, but of complete aspect. The style of narrative observed in the first chapter of *Passions and Griefs* resembles quite closely the style of *The Portrait,* except for those passages where Ryūnosuke's past is described, with the successive use of "-ta" forms.

In general, Kōyō employs "-ta" forms in *Passions and Griefs* with a similarly low frequency to Futabatei in *The Portrait.* The number of non "-ta" forms is three to four times the number of "-ta" forms. However, in *Passions and Griefs* Kōyō uses "-ta" forms intensively and successively—in the first instance to depict Ryūnosuke's past. When we study the text of *Passions and Griefs* to see when Kōyō employs successive instances of "-ta" forms, the following picture emerges. In Part One Kōyō depicts past incidents which were experienced not only by Ryūnosuke, but also by other main characters. In Part Two there is a shift in the use of successive "-ta" forms. The following passage contains a description of Ryūnosuke's inner thoughts, quoted from Part Two of Chapter Four. After recalling the happiest moment of his marriage, when he looked after his heavily intoxicated friend Hayama with his wife Orui, his loss and grief is brought home all the more keenly.

> 大酔の葉山は其時前後も知らなかつたが、**自分は**今知過るほど何も彼も知つてゐる。大酔したやうに此悲がもつと劇しく、もつと急であつて、寧ろ前後を知らなかつたならば、此不愉快は覚えぬかも知れぬ。此悲がもつと劇しく、もつと急であつたらば、**自分は**甚麽になるのであらう！（**彼は**果して其を願ふのであらうか。此悲の大酔は発狂である、その酔覚の水は無論自殺でなければならぬ。**彼は**自殺を喜ぶ狂人ではなかつた、発狂に楽まむとするほどの変人でもなかつた。然し、**彼は**何を楽に生きてゐるのか、生きてさへ居たらば失つた楽が又得られるのか、と常に考へては迷つてゐたのである。）(Ozaki Kōyō 1965b:132)

> [Hayama, dead drunk, lost consciousness completely at that time, but **I** know everything too clearly. If this grief were far more deep and intense, so that I lost consciousness completely, I would not experience this discomfort. If this grief were far more deep and intense, what would become of **me**? (Does **he** really desire to be like this? To lose consciousness from grief means to become insane. But to take a cup of water to cool his coppers must mean to commit suicide. **He** was neither so mad as to commit suicide for joy, nor so queer as to enjoy being insane. However, **he** had been wondering what he was living for, and if he were to live, if he would ever regain the pleasure he had lost.)]

In this passage, albeit in parentheses, the narrator for the first time explicitly comments on Ryūnosuke's mental condition. The "-ta" forms employed here (in the specific forms "-nakatta" and "mayotte ita") express the meaning of the past tense. However, this past tense does not relate to Ryūnosuke's present in the way in which it did in Part One. This past tense is absolutely and tightly related to the narrator. For these past tense verbs to carry the absolute past meaning that they do, the narrative point of view must be set outside the story. Here, for the first time, Kōyō sets an omniscient narrative point of view in his *genbun itchi* novel *Passions and Griefs.* The third-person pronoun "kare [he]" and the "-ta no de aru" endings also facilitate the setting of an omniscient point of view in the novel.

In general, Kōyō employed "-ta" forms more frequently in Part Two than in Part One. In chapters IV-2, V-3, VI-2, VIII, VIII-2, VIII-3, IX-2 and X-2 the number of non "-ta" forms exceeds that of "-ta" forms by only 1.5 to 2.5 times. The third-person pronoun "kare [he]" is also used more frequently. As Okumura (1954: 69) points out, Kōyō firmly established the use of the third-person pronoun "kare [he]" in *Passions and Griefs,* although he used it to refer to female as well as male characters. We should add that the use of this pronoun is more pronounced in Part Two, where, together with the more frequent use of "-ta" forms, it accentuates the objectivity of the narrator's descriptions, and underlines his omniscient point of view. The following is a passage from chapter eight which illustrates these points. The narrative here bears close resemblance to that of modern novels.

> 多くの人を好かぬ代に好く人をば甚しく好くと云ふ**彼の**気質は、燃ゆる如くお類を愛して、葉山を信ずることは一図に凝固つてゐるのである。**彼は**此二人よりは無い友の別けて難換き一人を亡つた為には、他が両親妻子兄弟と一度に一家を挙げて亡つたほど力を落して、一時は殆ど此世に望をも絶つたのである。而して其人の亡い後も、一旦燃された**彼の**念は、なかなか急に消えては了はなかつた。猶其火は他に向つて費さるゝ所が無かつたので、竟には自己の心を焼れて、**彼は**如何ばかり苦まされたであらう？日毎夜毎の**彼の**涙も此胸苦き餤をば得鎮めぬのであつた。（中略）
>
> 薬を美味として服する病人は無いけれども、病は其が為に痊るのでなければならぬ。**彼の**葉山に同居したのは、而して自とお種に親くなつたのは、好しからぬ薬を飲されたも同じで、姑くは苦い思いをしてゐたのである。漸く其にも慣れて見れば、図らざりき、お種の優しい声と、柔かい手と、温い心とは**彼の**不愉快の苦痛を劬るのであつた。（中略）
>
> 葉山が男子としての友である如く、女子の友として**彼は**お種を愛するのであつた。(Ozaki Kōyō 1965b:155-156)

[**His** inclination, as one who did not love many people, but who adored the one whom he loved, led him to love Orui passionately and to believe in Hayama wholeheartedly. Because **he** lost the one who was most indispensable to him, he was deeply at a loss, as one who had lost his parents, partner, children, brothers and sisters all at once, and at one stage he completely lost hope in this world. Even after the loss of that special person, **his** passion towards her, which once had possessed him, did not go away so quickly. He could not, moreover, find any other person at whom to direct his passion, and ended up being consumed by its fire. We never knew how seriously **he** suffered from it. **His** tears, which poured, day after day, night after night, did not cure his malady.

There is no patient who enjoys having his medicine, yet an illness must be cured by it. For **him**, staying with Hayama, and getting close to Otane, seemed like being forced to take some undesirable medicine, and he had been suffering from it. Once he got used to it, to his surprise, Otane's gentle voice, her soft hands and her warm

heart <u>consoled</u> him in **his** anguish. ...
**He** <u>loved</u> Otane as a female friend, just as Hayama was a male friend.]

Kōyō begins this chapter using the third-person pronoun "kare [he]" in order to signal that the whole chapter will be devoted to the narrator's commentary on the protagonist. We may also note that "-no de at<u>ta</u>", the past tense form of the "-no de aru" ending, is employed three times in this chapter. This "-no de at<u>ta</u>" ending is employed nine times in Part Two, though it appears only once in Part One, and it reveals the narrator's omniscient point of view particularly clearly. We may thus conclude that in *Passions and Griefs* Kōyō succeeded in creating a "modern" objective narrative with an omniscient point of view, through the successive use of "-ta" forms, particularly the "-no de atta" form, and the conscious use of the third-person pronoun "kare [he]" to refer to the protagonist. This is a notable achievement by Kōyō in his *genbun itchi* novel. Neither the successive use of "-ta" forms, nor the use of the third-person pronoun "kare [he]" are observed in Futabatei's *The Portrait.*

Indeed, Kōyō's narrative in the above cited passages from *Passions and Griefs* may be more successful than Futabatei's *The Portrait* in establishing an omniscient point of view. At any rate, *Passions and Griefs* is more "modern" than *The Portrait,* in the sense that Kōyō's narrative is at times closer to the currently dominant style characterized by the successive use of "-ta" forms. However, these comments apply only to a small part of the narrative of *Passions and Griefs,* as for most of it the narrator is set inside the story, as shown by the frequent use of non "-ta" forms.

It should also be taken into account that in *The Portrait* Futabatei made a conscious decision to set the narrator inside the story. Futabatei created a narrative written in the present tense, by translating past imperfective Russian verbs as "-(r)u" forms. In particular, the use of "-te iru" forms to translate past imperfective verbs expressing states, continuous actions, repetitive and habitual actions is the most prominent feature of Futabatei's translation style in *The Portrait.* Interestingly, these "-te iru" forms are employed in *The Portrait* also to depict the protagonist's inner thoughts, allowing the narrator's point of view to merge instantly with the protagonist's point of view. This is different from the frequent use of the "-te iru" form by Kōyō in *Passions and Griefs.*

The "-te iru" forms employed in *Passions and Griefs* similarly express states, continuous actions and habitual actions. However, whereas in *The Portrait* the state of mind and the continuous actions of the protagonist are depicted impressionistically, especially in the successive dream scenes, in *Passions and Griefs* they are depicted more objectively, as if they are stage directions appended to the dialogue. The following are some examples of the use of the "-te iru" form, interpolated in the dialogue of *Passions and Griefs:*

1. 「さあ、もう好加減(いいかげん)にしないかよ。」
と肩先を軽く拊(たた)けば、やうやう挙げた顔は、洗つたやうに涙に浸(ひた)<u>されてゐる</u>。(Ozaki Kōyō 1965b:15)

[—Enough is enough, stop talking about her.
So saying, [Hayama] taps him on the shoulder; [Ryūnosuke] lifts his face, which <u>is drenched</u> with his tears.]

2. 「何と言つてゐた。」と葉山は起直(おきなほ)る。
言はなければ可(よ)かつた、と心を叱つてゞもゐるやうに、細君は慎重(まじく)なつて火鉢の縁を拭いてゐる。(Ozaki Kōyō 1965b:25)

[—What was she saying? asks Hayama, straightening himself up.
His wife is wiping the edge of a *hibachi* [a charcoal brazier] as if she is regretting what she has said.]

3. 「明日何だい、此間お話したものだなどゝ暗号電信を打つたりなにかして。」
と葉山はお種から聞いたのを忘れて了(しま)つてゐる。(Ozaki Kōyō 1965b:129)

[—What's going to happen tomorrow? You are talking in a secret code, hinting at the one you mentioned some time ago.
Hayama has forgotten what he heard from Otane.]

More than half the "-te iru" forms employed in *Passions and Griefs* appear interspersed with the dialogue, depicting the state of mind or continuous actions of the main characters. Though the "-te iru" forms employed in *Passions and Griefs* are highly descriptive, bringing to life the states of mind of the main characters, the present tense depicted by them is neither so clear, nor so significant as in *The Portrait.* We might say that the employment of the "-te iru" form by Kōyō in *Passions and Griefs* is more in the nature of a conventional method, inherited from his "Saikakuesque" stories. Moreover, when Kōyō began employing this form in *Passions and Griefs*, he may not have had a clear idea of his narrator and of the narrative point of view. In his previous stories, written in a pseudo-classical style, it was taken for granted that the author narrated, employing non "-ta" forms and noun endings. Then in *Two Nuns' Confession of Love* Kōyō attempted to eliminate the narrator in a "new" narrative style which employed noun endings.

However, in the process of writing his first *genbun itchi* novel, Kōyō may gradually have become conscious of the presence in it of a narrator, especially when comments were made on the mental state of the protagonist. Even in those sections where description is dominated by the use of "-(r)u" and "-te iru" verbs, Kōyō occasionally inserted "-ta no de aru" endings in order to clarify that the narrator was making the utterance. As for the use of "-no de aru" endings, whereas Kōyō tended to employ "-(r)u no de aru" endings for the direct description of the main characters' inner thoughts, "-ta no de aru" endings were employed for the actual narrative. The classical auxiliary verb "-nu", expressing the meaning of negation, frequently appears in conjunction with "-no de aru" endings, when the main characters' inner thoughts are depicted directly or indirectly. Typical examples of these classical expressions are: "suka nu no de aru [do not like]", "taera re nu no de aru [cannot bear]", "wasure nu no de aru [does not forget]", "(saiwai no hikari wa kono mi o) terasa nu no de aru [(the light of happiness) does not shine on me]". On the other hand, "-ta no de aru" or "-no de atta" endings are coupled with relatively modern expressions such as "shina re ta no de aru [(he) had (his wife) die]", "daini no inochi o ubawa re ta no de aru [(he) was deprived of his second life]", "mitome ta no de aru [(she) recognized]" , "fukaku shitsubōsuru no de atta [(he) was deeply disappointed]", "iken o sa re ta no de aru [(he) was advised]", "aisuru no de atta [(he) loved]". Thus, in *Passions and Griefs,* Kōyō gradually transformed his narrative into a modern and objective one, by employing "-ta" forms more frequently and more consistently, and by utilizing "-ta no de aru" and "-no de atta" endings. Whether this was done consciously or not is not clear, but it seems very likely that Kōyō's reading of Western novels would have influenced his writing. Clearly, however, the narrative styles in *Passions and Griefs* and *The Portrait* are very different, and even opposed to each other.

As for "-ta" forms, while those employed in *The Portrait* consistently convey the meaning of complete aspect, reflecting the meaning of Russian past perfective verbs, those in *Passions and Griefs* carry the meanings of both complete aspect and past tense. In Part One of *Passions and Griefs,* "-ta" forms carrying the meaning of past tense are seen when the main characters' past experiences are narrated. In Part Two, on the other hand, they are employed to set the narrator outside the story. As a result, the narrative point of view becomes omniscient.

To sum up, although the ratio of "-ta" forms to non "-ta" forms is similar in *Passions and Griefs* (1:4) and *The Portrait* (1:3), the specific use of these forms, particularly "-ta" and "-te iru", is significantly different. We may also observe that in *The Portrait* "-no de aru" endings are employed far less than in *Passions and Griefs.* In *Passions and Griefs* "-no de aru" endings, particularly "-ta no de aru" endings, facilitate the creation of an objective narrative. It would thus seem that Kōyō's narrative style in *Passions and Griefs* exerted little influence over Futabatei's narrative in *The Portrait.*

If we extend the comparison to Futabatei's translations of Turgenev's third-person narrative works, *Floating Weed* (April-October 1897) and *The Mismatch* (November 1898), we still find little resemblance between their narratives and that of *Passions and Griefs.* Firstly, the "-te iru" forms found in *Floating Weed* and *The Mismatch* are mainly translations of past imperfective verbs, expressing continuous and habitual actions and states. Secondly, the "-ta" forms which appear in *Floating Weed* and *The Mismatch* are mostly used to translate past perfective verbs. Consequently, these "-ta" forms carry the meaning of the perfective aspect. Yet because Turgenev clearly indicates the temporal setting of these works, Futabatei needed to change some of his translations of past imperfective verbs. When the time at which the action takes place is clearly specified in *Floating Weed,* Futabatei employs "-te ita" forms to translate past imperfective verbs referring to the continuous actions of the main characters. In so doing Futabatei places the narrative point of view outside the story. In the case of *The Mismatch,* Futabatei employs "-te ita no de aru" endings for some past imperfective verbs, creating a ponderous tone for the narrator, who is also placed outside the story. Some "-ta" form verbs do thus carry the meaning of the past tense. These "-te ita (no de aru)" forms are, however, tightly related to the main characters' actions. Therefore they do not indicate the narrator's absolute past as they did in Kōyō's *Passions and Griefs.* Thirdly, in both *Floating Weed* and *The Mismatch* Futabatei rarely employs the third-person pronoun "kare". In *Floating Weed* it is used in the same way that Kōyō uses it, but only once, in the sentence "**Kare** no namida wa riko no namida de atta [**His** tears were tears of self-love]". In this sentence the "-ta" form is employed to express the narrator's comment. Futabatei's translation closely reflects the wording and narrative posture of the original "... i slezy **ego** byli samolyubivye slezy [...and **his** tears were tears of self-love.]". In *Floating*

*Weed* and *The Mismatch* the narrator's comments about the main characters are generally made using "-(r)u" forms. Kōyō, on the other hand, creates an objective narrative with an omniscient point of view, using the third-person pronoun "kare" to refer to the protagonist Ryūnosuke, and "-no de atta" endings, for the narrator's direct comments on Ryūnosuke's mental state. It would thus appear that the overall influence of Kōyō's narrative style, as found in *Passions and Griefs,* over the narrative of Futabatei's third-person narrative translations, is at best slight.

As Mizuno Kiyoshi (1958: 64) has pointed out, Futabatei valued Hirotsu Ryūrō's works more than Kōyō's. In his talk "Sakka kushin dan [An Account of a Writer's Labours]", Futabatei refers to Ryūrō and another popular writer who is most probably Kōyō:

> Ryūrō's works are aiming to depict the poignant feelings of human beings. I might mention one other writer; at first it seemed to me that he was writing his works simply for amusement, but gradually he has been getting serious. His case is quite an interesting one. (Futabatei Shimei 1965a: 166)

Moreover, in 1896, when Futabatei published *One-sided Love,* it was Ryūrō who had just taken the literary world by storm with his "tragic novels" (*hisan shōsetsu*) *Love Suicide at Imado, Shop Kawachi* and *Asase no nami [The Tide in a Shoal].*

Following examination of the verb forms in *Love Suicide at Imado,* Mizuno Kiyoshi has come to the conclusion that Ryūrō exerted some influence over the narrative style of Futabatei's retranslations of *The Rendezvous* and *Three Encounters.* Although Mizuno points out that the number of present tense forms exceeds the number of past tense forms by two to one in some parts of *Love Suicide at Imado,* an examination of the verb forms in the whole story reveals that the number of non "-ta" forms exceeds the number of "-ta" forms in only two chapters (one and eight). Moreover, the predominance of non "-ta" forms in these two chapters is due to two passages: a description of the main character's features in chapter one, and of her inner thoughts in chapter eight. Overall, contrary to Mizuno's suggestion, the total number of "-ta" forms exceeds the number of non "-ta" forms. A count of the verb forms in *Shop Kawachi* and *The Tide in a Shoal* reveals that in these stories the number of non "-ta" forms does indeed exceed the number of "-ta" forms, by 1.2 times and 1.5 times respectively. Once again, however, in the chapters where non "-ta" forms are dominant, this is due to passages where either the external features or the inner thoughts of the main characters are described. When we extend our examination to Hirotsu's later stories, *Shichi-ki ochi [Seven Soldiers Escape]* (1897), *Murasaki hifu [A Woman with a Purple Overcoat]* (1899), and *Yawata no kyōjo [The Mad Woman of Yawata]* (1901), we find that the total number of "-ta" forms exceeds the number of non "-ta" forms by 1.7, 1.6 and 1.5 times respectively. There are thus only two out of six stories in which the use of non "-ta" forms (including "-i" adjectival endings, noun endings and "-no de" endings) slightly exceeds the use of "-ta" endings. It is also clear that most of the non "-ta" forms are used to describe the main characters' external features, or their internal thoughts (in the form of monologues).

If we analyze which non "-ta" forms are used by Ryūrō in the six works under discussion, several features emerge. Firstly, amongst non "-ta" forms, "-de aru" and "-te iru" forms predominate. The "-te iru" form, in particular, is extensively used in all six works. It is used to depict states rather than continuous actions. The following passages from *Love Suicide at Imado* and *Shop Kawachi* are typical:

1. 西宮は昵と小萬の顔を見た。吉里は西宮の後に垂頭いて居る。平田は廊下の洋燈を意味もなく見上げて居る。
『もう此儘出掛けやう。夜が明けても困る。』(Hirotsu Ryūrō 1965: 12)

[Nishimiya gazed into Koman’s face. Yoshizato [stood] behind Nishimiya, her head drooping. Hirata [stood] looking blankly at the corridor lamp.
—Let’s go now, straightaway. We shouldn’t wait for the dawn.]

2. 『嫂さん。』と、清二郎は涙に暮れて、何とも云へなくなつた。
お染は昵と清二郎を見ると、顔色が蒼白め、眼中血走り、右の手には血の塗いた白刃を取つて居る。
『まア、清さん。』と、お染は身動さへなるまじき體を、悶躁悶躁漸と起上つて、『清さん、まア、貴郎は。』と、睜つた眼は輝くが如くである。
(Hirotsu Ryūrō 1965: 114-115)

[—*Nēsan* [sister-in-law]—bathed in tears, Seijirō could not continue.
Osome gazes at him, and notices that his face is deathly pale, his eyes are bloodshot, and he is holding a bloodied sword in his right hand.
—O dear Sei-san—Osome barely raises her deadly weakened body with a great struggle. —Sei-san, my dear, you—[she says] with her wide open eyes sparkling.]

In the first passage the protagonist Yoshizato, the second highest ranked *oiran* [prostitute] in a brothel in the Yoshiwara district, is parting with her doting client, Hirata. In the second passage, two of the main characters, Osome and Seijirō, meet in the darkness, after Seijirō has attempted to murder his brother Jūkichi (Osome’s husband) and has succeeded in murdering his brother’s lover Oyumi. Seijirō and Osome are about to commit a love suicide. The “-te iru” forms are frequently employed, as they are here, to depict the state of mind of the main characters. They are often used in dialogue, as we observed to be the case in Kōyō’s novel *Passions and Griefs*. In Ryūrō’s works this use of “-te iru” forms to depict the state of mind of characters during dialogue becomes the most distinguishing feature. Ryūrō’s focus was on the dialogue rather than the narrative, and later he even attempted to eliminate the narrative. The present time indicated by these “-te iru” forms is thus far less significant than in Futabatei’s translations.

Secondly, regarding the “-te ita” forms which indicate the past tense, and are frequently found in Futabatei’s translations of first-person narrative stories, Ryūrō employs them in his third-person narrative works extensively, but less frequently than “-te iru” forms. This is especially so in *Love Suicide at Imado* and *The Mad Woman of Yawata.* These are the two works in which “-ta” forms predominate, and the following passages show their typical use:

1. 善吉が吉里の許(もと)に通初(かよひはじ)めたのは一年ばかり前、丁度平田が來初めた頃の事である。吉里は兎角善吉を冷遇し、終宵(いちや)全たく顔をみせない時が多かツた位だツた。其にも構はず善吉は毎晩の樣に通詰め通透(かよひとほ)して、此十月頃から別して足が繁くなり、今月になツてからは毎晩來て居たのである。死金(しにがね)ばかりは使はず、きれる處にはきれもするので、新造や店の者には何時(いつ)も笑顔で迎へられて居たのであつた。(Hirotsu Ryūrō 1965: 13)

[Zenkichi began frequenting [Yoshiwara] to see Yoshizato almost a year ago, just when Hirata started seeing her. Yoshizato was apt to give the cold shoulder to Zenkichi, and more often than not she did not show up all night. In spite of her treatment [of him], Zenkichi came and tried to see her nearly every night. His visits became particularly frequent from October, and this month he came every night. As Zenkichi used his money not only on his wasted visit, but lavished it elsewhere if necessary, he was always warmly welcomed by the *Oiran* maids and the other servants in the shop.]

2. お兼は突倒された時、打處でも惡かつたのか、俯伏(うつぶせ)に倒れた儘、少時(しばらく)は起上らなかつた。が、輿九郎の影が見えなくなつた時、半身(なかばみ)を起して、眼には溢るゝばかりの涙、彼野(かの)薔薇に掩はれた凹地(くぼみ)を眤(ぢつ)と凝視(みつ)めて居た。
(Hirotsu Ryūrō 1965: 326)

[Okane remained lying with her face down for a while, as though she had been terribly hurt when she was thrust down. But when Yokurō's figure had gone, she half raised her body, her eyes full of tears, and was staring at the depression covered by the wild rose.]

The first passage, from *Love Suicide at Imado,* describes Zenkichi, Yoshizato's ugly, importunate and unwelcome client, with whom she unexpectedly commits suicide. The second passage, from *The Mad Woman of Yawata,* describes Okane, the protagonist of the story, at the place where her father was murdered. Pretending to be insane, Okane finally takes vengeance on Yokurō, who murdered her father because of his passion for her mother Okita. The "-te ita" forms seen in both passages clearly express the meaning of the past tense, placing the omniscient narrator's point of view outside the story. The first passage shows the external narrator's presence by the successive use of "-de aru", "-no de aru" and "-no de atta" endings, employed together with "-te ita" forms. The second passage is from a kind of detective story. The narrator, who has prior knowledge of the unfolding story, depicts the protagonist Okane's inexplicable actions, swaying between insanity and sanity, using "-te ita" forms, hinting at her later vengeance. In this story the number of "-te ita" forms exceeds that of "-te iru" forms, and their use is concentrated on the description of Okane's actions. (Almost two thirds of all "-te ita" forms are devoted to this.) In *Love Suicide at Imado* and *The Mad Woman of Yawata* the external narrator's presence is thus indicated relatively strongly. In the other four stories, however, the number and significance of "-te ita" forms are less. In these four stories most of the "-te ita" forms simply indicate those actions of the main characters which continue for some time, or which are discovered by other characters.

Thirdly, concerning "-no de aru" endings, "-ta no de aru" endings are rarely employed in Ryūrō's stories. In general, Ryūrō employed "-ta no de aru" endings for explanations by the narrator, and "-(r)u no de aru" endings for direct descriptions of the main characters' inner thoughts. In the latter case, "-no da" endings, which are more personal, are also used. "-No de atta" endings, which explicitly indicate the external narrator's presence, are hardly found in Ryūrō's stories. Only *Love Suicide at Imado* and *The Mad Woman of Yawata* show instances which demonstrate the external narrator's presence or, indeed, the presence of any narrator. The following passage is from *Love Suicide at Imado:*

> 善吉は次の日も流連(いつづけ)をした。其次の日も去(かへ)らず、四日目の朝漸(やう)やく去(かへ)ツた。それは吉里が止めて置いたので、平田が別離(わかれ)に殘して置いた拾圓の金は、善吉の爲めに殘りなく費(つかひ)盡し、加上(そのうへ)一二枚の衣服(きもの)までお熊の目を忍んで典(あづ)けたのであつた。(Hirotsu Ryūrō 1965: 22)
>
> [Zenkichi stayed for another night. He didn't leave the following day either. It was only on the morning of the fourth day that he left. It was Yoshizato who asked Zenkichi to stay and for his sake she spent the whole ten yen which Hirata left at parting; she even deposited several of her kimonos secretly, avoiding Okuma's eyes.]

Yoshizato, abandoned by Hirata, soon discovers that Zenkichi has lost his wife and property because of his frequent and unrequited visits to Yoshiwara to see her. The narrator describes Yoshizato's sudden change of attitude towards Zenkichi from a clear retrospective and omniscient point of view. Together with the "-no de atta" ending, the regular use of "-ta" forms facilitates the emergence of a clear narrative point of view. However, the "-no de atta" ending is seen only once in *Love Suicide at Imado.* In *The Mad Woman of Yawata,* on the other hand, there are eight instances of this ending, strongly indicating the presence of a narrator who has prior knowledge of all the action unfolding in the story. In the other four stories "-no de atta" endings are hardly seen.

Finally we must comment on the use of "-ta" forms. As has been observed, the use of "-ta" forms in Ryūrō's works is much more frequent than in Futabatei's translations. In most stories the number of these "-ta" form exceeds that of non "-ta" forms. This is especially evident in the closing passages of *Love Suicide at Imado* and *The Mad Woman of Yawata,* where it clearly indicates the presence of the narrator. In general, Ryūrō employs consecutive sequences of "-ta" forms far more than Futabatei. Most of the main characters' actions are depicted using these "-ta" forms. On the other hand, the non "-ta" forms, such as "-te iru" and "-de aru", are inserted to portray the state of mind or appearance of the main characters. We also observe that most of the non "-ta" forms are either "-te iru" or "-de aru" form verbs, and that "-(r)u" forms are rarely found. Thus the strong visual effect produced by Futabatei's alternation between "-ta" and "-(r)u" forms is generally not found in Ryūrō's writing. It seems that Ryūrō rather mechanically appropriated "-ta" forms for the actions of the main characters and non "-ta" forms for states.

Yoshida Sei'ichi points out, in his commentaries on Ryūrō's selected works (Yoshida 1954: 415), that Ryūrō attempted to depict the mental states of the main characters mainly through their actions and their dialogue, and tried to eliminate explanations from the author. This attempt, however, led him to be criticized for the superficiality of his descriptions. Yoshida concludes that Ryūrō lays disproportionate emphasis on the dialogue, and neglects the narrative, relying too heavily on the plot itself to sustain interest. This aggravates his tendency to sensationalism, his penchant for abnormality and unusual circumstances. In fact, Ryūrō's narrative is concise; sentences are generally cut short, "-ta" forms are used for the main characters' actions, non "-ta" verbs for states, and the use of "-no de aru" endings is minimized. Ryūrō was aiming to achieve an objective narrative, but not in the fashion of either Kōyō or Futabatei. His own approach was to minimize the narrator's presence in the narrative.

To sum up, Futabatei, Kōyō and Ryūrō all aspired to a "modern" objective narrative in their third-person narrative stories, one free of the author's direct intervention. Futabatei achieved this in *The Portrait,* by intentionally placing the narrator inside the story. Kōyō, on the other hand, succeeded in creating an objective narrative in part of *Passions and Griefs,* by placing the narrator outside the story. Ryūrō, unlike the other two, attempted in his "tragic" stories to achieve an objective narrative by concealing the narrator. He even attempted, in *A Woman with a Purple Overcoat,* to compose a story of dialogue alone, deleting the narrative completely. Consequently, the use of "-ta", "-(r)u" and "-te iru" forms in the works of Kōyō and Ryūrō is different from that in Futabatei's translations. Futabatei often uses "-ta" forms in isolation, conveying the aspectual meaning of the original Russian perfective verbs. Kōyō and Ryūrō use "-ta" form verbs in succession. In Kōyō's case this successive use of "-ta" forms occurs when the narrator's presence is apparent. While "-te iru" forms are used by Futabatei to describe the continuous actions of the main characters, emphasizing the present time in which the action flows, such verbs are used by Kōyō and Ryūrō to describe the states which the characters experience. In Futabatei's translations, and especially in *The Portrait,* the alternation between "-ta" and "-(r)u" forms creates a particularly vivid narrative. Here the "-(r)u" forms fit the definition of the "historic present" proposed by Terence Wade (1992: 287):

> ....The use of the present tense with past meaning brings the action more graphically before the mind's eye of the reader or listener.

The use of "-te iru" forms by Kōyō and Ryūrō, on the other hand, does not produce such a graphic effect, since they portray only states, and do not indicate the flow of time in the narrative. The use of "-(r)u" forms by them cannot be called a use of the "historic present". It would thus seem that the influence of works by Kōyō and Ryūrō on Futabatei's translations was not significant.

# Chapter 7 — Futabatei's Third Period of Translation Activity and *In His Image*

The second period of Futabatei's literary activity ended with the publication of *The Mismatch* in November 1898. Despite his intention to write an original work, Futabatei produced only translations during this period (eight in all), including the second versions of Turgenev's *The Rendezvous* and *Three Encounters*. It was not until 1906, nearly twenty years after the publication of *Floating Clouds,* that Futabatei's long-awaited second novel, *Sono omokage [In His Image],* was serialized in the *Asahi shinbun.*

Futabatei's third period of translation activity caught the attention of the reading public in July 1904, with the publication of two war stories: Tolstoy's *Rubka lesa [The Woodfelling]* (under the title *Tsutsu o makura [A Rifle for a Pillow]*) and Garshin's *Chetyre dnya [Four Days]* (under the title *Yokka-kan [Four Days]*). In fact Futabatei had attempted several other translations since his return from China in July 1903, mainly because of financial pressures. A translation of Turgenev's *Dym [Smoke]* remained uncompleted, while a project to translate Tolstoy's *Voina i mir [War and Peace]* never got off the ground. Two other short translations were completed[1], but these were of stories by two minor writers (Elets and Potapenko) and attracted little attention. They do not merit our close examination.

The reason for the popularity of *A Rifle for a Pillow* and *Four Days* is not hard to find. In February of 1904 war had broken out between Japan and Russia. Shortly afterwards, in May, Futabatei was appointed Tokyo correspondent for the *Ōsaka Asahi shinbun,* and was thus given an opportunity to demonstrate his knowledge and expertise in Russian, not just in the literary sphere, but in the social sphere. Indeed, Futabatei hoped that his contribution in the social and political arena would be more significant than his contribution to literature, and would become his true mission in life. This is apparent from comments he made to friends in his literary circle, prior to his departure for Russia in 1908 as a foreign correspondent for the *Ōsaka Asahi shinbun:*

> Let me speak of my personal interpretation of literature. For me, literature is somehow trivial and of scant value. When I take up the pen and look down upon the paper, for some reason, I feel I can't fully commit myself to it. There is an element of play in it. I cannot get worked up about literature, nor give my life to it, nor lose myself in it. I have been troubled about this feeling for some time. ... However, in the case of international problems—and by "international problems" I mean, according to my personal interpretation, something different from so-called diplomatic relations and the like—I can get worked up about them, I can give my life to them, I can devote myself to them. I should die quite contentedly for the sake of such problems. I cannot feel that way about literature. I feel as though literature is not worth dying for. I do not consider it my mission.[2] (Futabatei Shimei 1965a: 275-276)

---

[1] *Kokuryū kohan no yūfu [A Courageous Woman of the Amur River Region]* and *Yonin kyōsan dan [Four Person Communist Group].*

[2] Apart from the first sentence, which I have added, the translation is one made by Dennis Washburn (1995: 112).

Futabatei's unexpected death the following year from an illness contracted during his posting to Russia gave added significance to this farewell speech, and his attitude to literature as expressed here began to be taken out of context. In consequence, Futabatei has been labelled as a writer who disliked being known as a writer. The statement often attributed to him, that "literature is not an enterprise to which a man can devote himself" is often emphasized by those who are critical of his later works *In His Image* and *Heibon [Mediocrity]* (1907). However, it should be noted that "literature", in the statement cited above, is not used in a general sense, but only in Futabatei's interpretation. Both "literature" and "international problems" are used subjectively, and should be understood in the sense in which Futabatei intended. Futabatei left further clues to his interpretation of literature in the same speech. Having emphasized again that he did not regard himself as a writer, Futabatei declined to represent Japanese literary circles in Russia. He then qualified this statement:

> However, I would at least like to do the following thing with respect to literature. That is, using my Russian language, which I have had the good fortune to have studied, ... I shall translate some works from Japanese literature [into Russian] and try to introduce Japanese literature [to the Russian people]. My personal literature is trivial, but I acknowledge the value of literature in a broad sense. Therefore I shall try to do this. ... I shall translate and introduce Japanese literature to deepen mutual understanding between Japanese and Russian people, so that we can avoid further conflict. (Futabatei Shimei 1965a: 276)

It would appear, then, that the translation of literature seemed of immense value for Futabatei, even though he could not find value in his personal "literature". Futabatei also seemed to believe that "literature" should be more serious, and should exert influence upon people, as, according to his understanding, Russian literature did.

It is ironical that Futabatei was unsuccessful in his work for the *Ōsaka Asahi shinbun,* to which he was prepared to devote his life. He was apparently incompetent in his attempts to address "international problems". His numerous articles on Russian affairs, while thoroughly researched, were so detailed that they were frequently rejected as unsuitable for a newspaper. His literary activity thrived, however, as his translations continued to enjoy popularity. Indeed, Futabatei nearly lost his job as a correspondent because he persisted in publishing translations in various journals.

Apart from Tolstoy's *The Woodfelling* and Garshin's *Four Days,* Futabatei translated Gorky's *Kain i Artem* (under the title *Jū no ukiyo [The Hard Life of a Jew],* February-March, 1905) and *Toska [Heartache]* (under the title *Fusagi no mushi [The Depression Bug],* January-March, 1906). He also translated Gogol's *Starosvetskie pomeshchiki [Old-fashioned Landowners]* (under the title *Mukashi no hito [Olden Day People],* May, 1906). Then, in October of 1906, Futabatei began publishing *In His Image,* his second original work, in the *Asahi shinbun,* as if to compensate for his succession of translations. In fact, Futabatei was persuaded to write *In His Image* by the chief editor of the *Tokyo Asahi shinbun,* Ikebe Sanzan, whose efforts were largely responsible for Futabatei retaining his post with the *Ōsaka Asahi shinbun.*

Among Futabatei's translation works, *The Depression Bug,* his translation of Gorky's *Heartache,* created a sensation in literary circles. Because of what many considered an excessive use of Japanese dialect in the translation of Russian, and the playful tone of

Futabatei's translation (reminiscent of Edo *gesaku* works), *The Depression Bug* became the focus of harsh criticism. Even Futabatei's rendition of the title as "Fusagi no mushi [The Depression Bug]" was criticized as frivolous and disrespectful to Gorky, who was regarded as a writer of the new era. One critic suggested as an alternative "Sekaiku [World Anguish]", from the title of a German translation (*Im Weltschmerz*), while another suggested title was "Raifu no omoi [Anxiety in One's Life]" (Futabatei Shimei 1964c: 386-387). The chief difference between these titles and Futabatei's lies in the word "mushi [a bug or worm]", which is widely used in Edo *gesaku* works, to denote the bugs which cause various emotions or ailments in people. Behind the controversy lies the central question regarding Futabatei's translations and translation in general: should the translation be strictly faithful to the original, and thus foreignizing, or can it be partially a creation of the translator, in the interests of domestication?

In discussing two translations from works by Gorky, *The Depression Bug* and *The Hard Life of a Jew,* the prominent Japanese Slavist and translator Yonekawa Masao observes regretfully that during this period Futabatei had established the so-called "Futabatei tone" in his translations, which is similar to the tone of Edo light literature. Futabatei changes the tone of the Russian original by making excessive use of Japanese idiom and proverbs. Consequently Futabatei is unfaithful to the tone of Gorky's originals, though the two translations do demonstrate his mastery as a writer (Yonekawa Masao 1963: 93). The Slavist Satō Seirō, on the other hand, regards the same two translations highly, as original creations produced in the process of translation. Satō cites the views of the discerning critic and naturalist writer Masamune Hakuchō:

> The translations of Gorky's stories *The Hard Life of a Jew* and *The Depression Bug* are strongly embellished by <u>the Futabatei tone</u>. Futabatei seemed so elated in these translations, and their style is so witty and vibrant, that we are left wondering whether Gorky's originals have the same elaborate style. Yet these translations are immensely interesting if you regard them as creations which use the material from Gorky's stories. (In Satō Seirō 1995: 448 —underline added)

Satō concludes that these are "creative translations" rather than adaptations. While Futabatei employed many expressions borrowed from *gesaku* literature, he made his translations on the basis of grammatical correctness. Satō considers Futabatei's translations superior to those of his critics, such as Nobori Shomu and Yonekawa Masao, who consciously made "anti-creative" translations, influenced by the style of the naturalist school of writers.

The focus of this argument would appear to be Futabatei's phraseology and vocabulary. Yet the style of these translations is often determined by the sentence endings, and once again that will be our focus in this chapter, as we examine four major translation works which preceded *In His Image,* and then the novel itself. We shall examine how Futabatei translated the Russian verb forms of the originals, and whether he followed the same practices that he had established during the second period of his translation activity. (We shall pass over *The Hard Life of a Jew*, in which Futabatei adopted a similar approach to that adopted in *The Depression Bug.*[3]) We shall consider whether Futabatei adopted a foreignizing or a

[3] The frequent use of third-person pronouns is the most prominent feature of *The Hard Life of a Jew.* A detailed analysis of the translation may be found in Cockerill (2003).

domesticating strategy during his third period of translation activity, and how his translation work impacted upon his original work. Attention will again be given to the position of the narrator in each work, particularly in the translations of the third-person narrative stories *The Depression Bug* and *Olden Day People.* We shall examine the translations in chronological order, beginning with *A Rifle for a Pillow.*

## *Tsutsu o makura [A Rifle for a Pillow]* (from Tolstoy's *Rubka lesa [The Woodfelling]*)

Tolstoy began writing *The Woodfelling* in 1853 in the Caucasus, where he was serving as an army cadet, and finished it the following year. Apparently Tolstoy was strongly influenced by Turgenev at the time. He wrote in his diary: "I read Turgenev's *A Sportsman's Sketches [Zapiski okhotnika],* and somehow it is difficult to write after that". The tentative titles of work in progress, which appear in Tolstoy's diary at the time, are reminiscent of Turgenev's title: "The Diary of an Officer of the Caucasus", "Memoirs of an Officer of the Caucasus [Zapiski Kavkazskogo ofitsera]", "Memoirs of a Bombardier" and "Memoirs of a Cadet". The eminent poet and editor of the journal *Sovremennik [The Contemporary]* N.A. Nekrasov welcomed Tolstoy's new story, in spite of the author's own reservations about it:

> My opinion of this work is as follows: its form certainly reminds us of Turgenev, but that is where the similarity ends: all that remains belongs to you, and could not have been written by anyone but you. In this sketch there are a multitude of wonderfully acute observations, and as a whole it is new, interesting and concise. Do not scorn such sketches: after all, until now our literature has had nothing to say about the soldier except banalities. You are only beginning, and in whatever form you tell what you know about this subject, it will all be highly interesting and useful. (Nekrasov 1898: 344, quoted in Tolstoy 1972: 309-310)

In the end, however, Tolstoy dedicated his story to Turgenev, because he found in it "much unwitting imitation of his stories". The similarity in form between Tolstoy's work and Turgenev's may have encouraged Futabatei to adopt a similar approach to translating it as he had done with his earlier translations from Turgenev. Once again we find that past imperfective verbs may be translated as either "-(r)u" or "-te iru" forms, or as "-ta" or "-te ita" forms, though the proportion of the former is much higher.

*The Woodfelling* is a story related by a narrator-protagonist, a young cadet. The plot centres on the death of an ordinary soldier, Valenchuk, who belongs to that category of soldiers referred to by Tolstoy as "pokornye khlopotlivye [bustling submissive]", but the plot is secondary to the depiction of the character of the Russian soldiers and officers on duty in the Caucasus. As one commentator has noted:

> In the stories *Nabeg [The Raid]* and *Rubka lesa [The Woodfelling]* the author strives to reveal the spiritual qualities of the simple Russian man, and the features of his behaviour in war time. He achieves this in many ways, first and foremost by direct juxtaposition of the spirit of the soldiers with the attitudes and temper of the aristocratic officers. (Shifman cited in Tolstoy 1960: 420)

Tolstoy finds many admirable qualities in the ordinary Russian soldier: courage, naturalness and simplicity, calm efficiency, disdain for loud boasting, and friendliness towards their fellows. Minamoto Takashi (1989c: 112-113) suggests that the "aristocratic" officers are more conscious of and sensitive to the war situation and the constant threat of death. Their meaningless conversation is a way of keeping at bay the fear of death. The narrator constantly relates his own sensations on the battle field.

Futabatei seems acutely aware of the retrospective point of view of the narrator-protagonist and of the way the narrator recalls his sensory impressions. The original Russian text is written almost entirely in the past tense. The present tense appears only when the narrator's retrospective viewpoint is emphasized by inserting phrases such as "ya govoryu [I say]", "ya pomnyu [I remember]", "ne znayu pochemu [I don't know why]" or "priznayus' [I confess]". Futabatei employs "-ta" form verbs in sentences where these insertions appear. Futabatei's translation of the following description of the soldier Zhdanov illustrates this use of the "-ta" form to indicate the narrator's retrospective point of view:

> По службе нельзя было желать лучше знающего дело, храбрее и исправнее солдата; но он был слишком смирен и невиден, чтобы быть произведенным в фейерверкеры, хотя уже был 15 лет бомбардиром. Одна радость и даже страсть Жданова были песни; особенно некоторые он очень любил и всегда собирал кружок песенников из молодых солдат и, хотя сам не умел петь, стоял с ними и, заложив руки в карманы полушубка и зажмурившись, движениями головы и скул выражал свое сочувствие. **Не знаю почему**, в этом равномерном движении скул под ушами, которое я замечал только у него одного, я почему-то находил чрезвычайно много выраженья. (Tolstoy 1972: 48)
>
> [One could not have wished for a soldier who knew his job in the service better, who was braver or more conscientious; but he was too meek and self-effacing to be promoted to gun-sergeant, although he had already been a bombardier for fifteen years. Zhdanov's sole joy, his passion even, was songs; especially some he particularly liked, and he was always organizing a choir from among the young soldiers and, although he couldn't sing himself, standing with them, putting his hands in the pockets of his sheepskin coat, and screwing up his eyes, expressing his involvement through the movement of his head and cheek-bones. **I don't know why**, but in that regular movement of his cheek-bones below the ears, which I observed in no-one else but him, I found something extraordinarily expressive.[4]]
>
> 職務に掛けては此ほど能く心得てゐる者はなくて、勇敢なことも嚴格なことも均(ひと)しく群を抜くのである。けれども餘り温當で風采が揚らんため、十五年も臼砲卒(きうはうそつ)を勤めてゐながら、まだ砲手長にも昇進しない。此(ここ)にこの男に一つの道樂がある。それは唱歌で、歌となると殆ど夢中になる。中にも

[4] In making translations from *The Woodfelling*, I have referred to Ronald Wilks' translation (Tolstoy 1993).

取分けて好きなのが幾什もあるが、いつも其心得のある若い兵を集めて、自分は歌へぬ癖に其中に立交じり、半外套の隱袋に兩手を入れ、眼を半眼に閉ぢ、頸を振り顋を動かして調子を取る。それが下顋を變化なく動かすので、餘り類のない所作であるが、それを見ると、**何故とは知らず**自分にはいろいろの意が讀まれるのであつた。(Futabatei Shimei 1964c: 12-13)

[As far as the service is concerned, no-one knows his job better than him, he distinguishes himself in bravery and sternness. However, he is too gentle and poor in appearance to be promoted to the position of head gunner, although he has been a bombardier for fifteen years. Well, this man has a source of joy. It is singing, he nearly loses himself in singing. There are some songs which he especially likes, he always collects young soldiers who are good at singing, although he can't sing himself, he stands with them, putting both hands in his coat pockets, half closing his eyes he beats time by shaking his head and moving his jaw-bones. He moves his jaw-bones evenly, in a unique way, when I saw it, **I don't know why**, I spontaneously read much expression in it.]

In the original Tolstoy uses only past imperfective verbs to describe Zhdanov and his habitual actions. Futabatei, on the other hand, uses mainly "-(r)u" form verbs. Yet, as soon as the narrator's retrospective viewpoint is introduced by the phrase "ne znayu pochemu [I don't know why]", Futabatei changes the verb forms from "-(r)u" to "-ta".

Generally speaking, Futabatei employs "-(r)u" and "-te iru" form verbs three to four times more frequently than "-ta" or "-te ita" forms when translating past imperfective verbs. In *A Rifle for a Pillow* these "-(r)u" and "-te iru" forms are used firstly to describe the main characters' features and habitual actions, as in the instance just cited. Secondly they are used to describe the setting. We note that Futabatei tends to employ expressions which are classical in their grammar and vocabulary, which seem in keeping with the background setting of the battlefield.

A third use of "-(r)u", and particularly "-te iru" forms, is to depict the continuous actions of the main characters, as observed by the narrator-protagonist. As noted in earlier translations from first-person narrative stories by Turgenev, in *A Rifle for a Pillow* Futabatei employs "-te iru" forms to describe the continuous actions of the main characters (soldiers) other than the narrator-protagonist. However, this usage is observed markedly less in *A Rifle for a Pillow* than in those earlier translations from Turgenev's first-person narratives. The simplicity of the plot in this story seems to contribute to this. More space is devoted to lengthy descriptions of conversations between the officers, than to descriptions of the battle field. The following is one of the rare descriptions of soldiers in danger of being fired upon:

Вот теперь, когда у каждого в душе должна была быть мысль о Валенчуке, и когда всякую секунду мог быть по нас залп подкравшихся татар, все слушали бойкий рассказ Чикина, и никто не упоминал ни о нынешнем деле, ни о предстоявшей опасности, но о раненом, как будто это было Бог знает как давно или вовсе никогда не было. Но **мне показалось только**, что лица их были несколько пасмурнее обыкновенного; они не слишком внимательно слушали рассказ Чикина, и даже Чикин чувствовал, что его не слушают, но говорил уж так себе. (Tolstoy 1972: 71)

[And now, when everyone's thoughts must have been of Valenchuk, and when at any second there could be a volley of shots from some Tartars who had stolen upon us, everyone was listening to Chikin's lively tale, and nobody mentioned today's action, or the impending danger, or the wounded soldier, as if it had all happened God knows how long ago, or had not happened at all. But **it appeared to me** that their faces were somewhat gloomier than usual; they were not listening to Chikin's tale very attentively, and even Chikin sensed that they were not listening to him, but spoke as if to himself.]

今も即ちそれで皆心はウェレンチウクの身の上に走せ、又今にも韃靼兵の忍び來て一齊射擊を浴せ懸けむことを憂慮つゝも、誰一人今日の戰鬪の事を語らず、今に降つて湧かうも知れぬ危險を餘所に、敢て手負の噂をもせずして、宛然とつくの昔其樣な事もあつたやうなといふよりは寧ろそんな事は一向知らぬといつたやうな面をして、皆チキンの壯な話を聽いてゐる。たゞ誰の顏色も平生よりは冴えずして、チキンの話に餘り氣を留めてはゐぬらしく、又チキンも其と知りながら獨りで饒舌てゐるといふ**氣味であつた**。(Futabatei Shimei 1964c: 39-40)

[And here is a typical example [of the attitude of Russian soldiers]. Everyone's thoughts are of Valenchuk, and everyone is worried that at any moment Tartars may steal up and fire a volley, but nobody mentions today's battle, or worries about the impending danger, or talks about the wounded comrade. Everyone seems to pretend it happened a long time ago, or did not happen at all, and is listening to Chikin's lively banter. But **it appeared [to me]** that their faces were gloomier than usual and did not pay much attention to Chikin's talk, and Chikin also felt that they were not listening and talked to himself.]

This description of the remarkable composure of the Russian soldiers in a situation fraught with danger is effectively realized through the use of past imperfective verbs in the original. Futabatei, on the other hand, opts for "-te iru" forms, which make the description more immediate and vivid. However, when the narrator's retrospective point of view is emphasized by the phrase "mne pokazalos', chto [it appeared to me that]", Futabatei opts for the "-ta" form.

Thus, in *A Rifle for a Pillow* objective and descriptive sections of the narrative are conducted with the use of "-(r)u" and "-te iru" forms, translating past imperfective verbs. For more subjective parts of the narrative, where the narrator retrospectively relates his own deeds or comments on the actions of other characters, Futabatei tends to employ "-ta" or "-te ita" forms, though these also correspond to past imperfective verbs in the original. The following paragraph is a striking example of a more subjective part of the narrative, revealing the narrator's inner thoughts:

> —Это *он*, братцы мои!—послышался в это время встревоженный голос одного из солдат,—и все глаза обратились на опушку дальнего леса.
> Вдали увеличивалось и, уносясь по ветру, поднималось голубоватое облако дыма. Когда я понял, что это был против нас выстрел неприятеля, всё, что было на моих глазах в эту минуту, всё вдруг приняло какой-то новый величественный характер. И козлы ружей, и дым костров, и голубое небо, и зеленые лафеты, и загорелое усатое лицо Николаева,— всё это **как будто говорило мне**, что ядро, которое вылетело уже из дула и летит в это мгновение в пространстве, может быть, направлено прямо в мою грудь. (Tolstoy 1972: 55-56)
>
> [—They're there, lads!—at that moment the excited voice of a soldier was heard, and all eyes turned to the edge of the distant forest.
> In the distance a bluish cloud of smoke was growing and rising, carried away on the wind. When I realized that it was the enemy firing at us, everything I saw at that moment somehow took on a new and majestic character. The stacks of rifles, the smoke of the campfires, the blue sky, the green gun-carriages, and Nikolaev's sunburnt, moustached face—everything **seemed to be saying to me**, that the cannon ball which had already left the barrel, and which was at that moment flying through space, could be directed straight at my chest.]
>
> 「ヤ敵が！」と一人の兵が周章(うろたへ)た聲で云つたので、皆振向いて遥か前方(むかふ)の森を佶(きつ)と見据ゑると、青い烟が遠方にパツと起(た)つて、擴(ひろが)つて、風に靡(なび)くのが見える。さては敵がと氣が附くと、忽然(こつぜん)として天地一新して眼中の物皆急に莊嚴(さうごん)の色を帯び、交叉した小銃、篝(かがり)の烟、蒼空(あをぞら)、青い砲車、ニコラーエフの日焦(ひやけ)のした髭面と、何を看(み)ても今烟を離れ空(くう)を截(き)つて飛び來る砲彈がまともに自分の胸に中(あた)る前兆であるやうに思はれた。(Futabatei Shimei 1964c: 21)
>
> [—There they are—as one of our soldiers gives the alarm in confusion, everyone turns their eyes and fixes them on the distant forest. Blue smoke, rising in the distance, is visible, it grows and drifts on the wind. When I realized that our enemy was firing, all of a sudden the universe changed its character; everything before me suddenly took on a majestic air: the stacks of rifles, the campfire smoke, the blue sky, the blue gun-carriages and Nikolaev's sunburnt, moustached face—everything **seemed** to be a portent that the ball which had just left the smoke and was flying through space would directly strike my chest.]

The original Russian text, describing the moment when the narrator first experiences the fear of death on the battle field, employs both perfective and imperfective past tense verbs. The narrator's initial impressions are described using past perfective verbs ("ponyal", "prinyalo"), whereas past imperfective verbs are used to express the narrator's later recognition of the meaning of those initial impressions. In particular, the language used to describe the recognition that he was in danger, the inserted phrase "vse eto kak budto govorilo mne [everything seemed to be saying to me]", indicates that the narrator is reflecting on the experience after some interval of time. Referring to this same paragraph, Minamoto (1989c: 111) suggests that here we may read the embarrassment of the intellectual who experiences a brush with death not through logic, but through the feelings brought about by a real situation. Futabatei clearly expresses the retrospective nature of the narrator-protagonist's recognition by employing the "-ta" form for the past imperfective verb "govorilo [was saying]".

Compared with Turgenev's *The Rendezvous* and *Three Encounters,* Tolstoy's *The Woodfelling* gives a significantly deeper portrayal of the inner world of the narrator. The narrator of *The Woodfelling* does not remain a mere observer of others, but also observes his own state of mind. It is thus not surprising that following *The Woodfelling,* Futabatei chose to translate Garshin's *Four Days,* which takes us even deeper inside the narrator's inner world, showing his stream of consciousness. Judging from the use of "-ta" and "-te ita" forms to translate past imperfective verbs in *The Woodfelling,* Futabatei was well aware of the reflective nature of the narrator in Tolstoy's story. In his forthcoming second original work, *In His Image,* Futabatei uses this reflective observation of mentality in the depiction of Tokiko, the wife of the protagonist Tetsuya:

> 何處迄も非は夫に在ると思ふから、捩合つた末は、惡かつた位言はせて仲直りして了ふ積であつたのに、思ひきや、可惜理詰の千言萬語も空に消えて、哲也は色一つ動かさず、冷然として藁木死灰の如くなるのを見ると、豫期するやうで豫期しなかつた、女の身には一大事の「離縁」といふものと、直と面を突合せたやうな心地がした。此時、不思議や、其處等の物が一時に燦然と異様の光を放つて、瞬く間に面目を改め、過去の怨みも、未來の不安も、何處やらへ消え失せて、見識も外聞も忘れて了ふと、もう嫉妬も瞋恚も無くなつて、只一筋に情ないといふ刹那の心になり、我を忘れて夫に縋り付き、「其ぢや、貴方、餘りだ、餘り酷いぢや有りませんか！」と其膝に泣伏した**時子**は、平生の**時子**の樣ではなくて、若し**時子**以上の**時子**が有つたら、此樣なものかと思はれたが、ー (Futabatei Shimei 1964c: 336-337)

> [She firmly believed the fault lay with her husband, and she expected that when she had fought with him, she could make him say sorry; they would then be reconciled with each other. To her astonishment, all her many arguments proved vain: Tetsuya did not even change the expression on his face. As she looked at him, cool and unmoved as a dry tree or dead ashes, Tokiko felt that she was confronted with the serious event for a woman of 'divorce', which she did not exactly anticipate, though she vaguely feared it. At this moment, strange to say, everything around her shed a bright but indescribable light and instantly changed in appearance. Her heartaches in the past and worries for the future passed away. She forgot her reason and her pride, and even jealousy and anger touched her not; a feeling of pure misery permeated her being. She clung to her husband, beside herself, "You are too — too cruel!". **Tokiko**

> fell in his lap weeping, quite unlike the usual **Tokiko**. If there existed a **Tokiko** more genuine than the usual **Tokiko**, she would have acted like this.][5]

This description of the feeling which seized Tokiko when she thought she was confronted with divorce (clearly indicated as a subjective impression) is first perceived by her as a change in the appearance of her surroundings. This description of a process of recognition is very similar to the narrator's description just cited from *A Rifle for a Pillow*. In *In His Image* Futabatei deliberately omits the subject "Tokiko", so the reader can perceive the impressions as being related by Tokiko herself. However, Futabatei does not let the cynical narrator remain silent, and allows him to comment on Tokiko's rare "genuine" state. Thus the reflective narrative device found in the first-person narrative of *The Woodfelling* is used in a modified form in the third-person narrative of *In His Image.* Consequently the description of Tokiko's mental state is given a rather satirical slant. It appears very likely, however, that Futabatei was struck by the distinctive perception of danger described in such distinctly Tolstoyan fashion by the narrator-protagonist in *The Woodfelling*, and could not help using it in his original work.

To conclude, in *A Rifle for a Pillow* Futabatei clearly follows the translation practices hitherto found in the translations of Turgenev's first-person narrative stories. He employs "-(r)u" or "-te iru" forms to translate past imperfective used to describe the actions of characters other than the narrator-protagonist, whereas "-ta" or "-te ita" forms are used to describe the narrator's own actions, his comments on others, and most uniquely his psychological analysis of his own mental states. However, unlike the translations of Turgenev's first-person narratives, in *A Rifle for a Pillow* this differentiation in the translation of past imperfective verbs does not create two streams of time, since the plot in *The Woodfelling* is considerably simpler than that of the translations from Turgenev, such as *One-sided Love* or *The Jew*. The most distinctive feature of *The Woodfelling* is not its first-person narrative structure, but the reflectiveness of the narrative, the narrator's thorough analysis of his own state of mind. Futabatei sensed this acutely and applied a similarly analytical description to Tokiko in *In His Image*.

As far as the verb forms are concerned, Futabatei once again accentuates the aspectual meaning of the original, bringing the description of the soldiers more vividly before the reader's eye. To this extent he is still adopting a foreignizing strategy. Yet the effect is less pronounced than in the translations from Turgenev's first-person narratives, because of more limited use of "-te iru" forms to describe the continuous actions of the characters.

## *Yokka-kan [Four Days]* (from Garshin's *Chetyre dnya [Four Days]*)

In July 1904 Futabatei translated another war story, Garshin's *Four Days*. He seemed to be continuing to explore the first-person narrative, but with a more complex spatial and temporal setting. *Four Days* is a monologue rather than a story, told by a young, intelligent

[5] In making translations from *In His Image* I have referred to the translation made by Buhachirō Mitsui and Gregg M. Sinclair (Futabatei Shimei 1919).

soldier, wounded in both legs, lying and waiting to die for four days. He gradually realizes his desperate plight. He is left alone in a dense thicket. Beside him lies the corpse of a Turkish soldier killed by him, rapidly decomposing in the midsummer heat. Ironically, the water left in the flask of the Turkish soldier saves his life, and in the end he is rescued, though one of his legs has to be amputated.

Garshin started writing this story while recovering in a military hospital from a wound to his own leg, though the story is based more closely on the experience of another Russian soldier who fought against the Turks and died of wounds to both legs. Peter Henry (1983: 51-52) suggests that Garshin's intention in transforming the narrator-protagonist's personality from a "brave, stoical Russian peasant-soldier" to a "sensitive Russian *intelligent*" was to transform "a simple tale of heroic endurance" into a "stream of consciousness record of moral anguish". Henry also suggests (1983: 44) that a sudden change of tense, indicating a shift from a "live" present record to a story related by the narrator after his rescue, and the use of mixed tense forms within the inner monologue itself, contribute to a pervasive sense of uncertainty and confusion. "His [the narrator's] bewilderment is conveyed by the frequently blurred and ambiguous narrative".

Futabatei was evidently aware of this shift in tense forms, which is found throughout *Four Days*. This is shown by the underlining of verbs in the original text from which Futabatei made his translation, held in the Futabatei Shimei archive at Waseda University library. Futabatei underlined four verbs in the following passages from the original. Futabatei's translations follow:

> 1. Я никогда не находился в таком странном положении. Я **лежу**, кажется, на животе и вижу перед собою только маленький кусочек земли. (Garshin 1897: 6)
>
> [I have never been in such a strange situation. I **am lying**, it seems, on my belly and can see before me nothing but a tiny patch of ground.][6]
>
> どうも變さな、何でも**伏臥**(うつぶし)**になつて居るらしい**のだがな、眼に遮ぎるものと云つては、唯掌大(しやうだい)の地面ばかり。(Futabatei Shimei 1964c: 46)
>
> [It's quite funny, **it seems as if I am lying on my belly**. What I can see before me is only a small patch of ground.]
>
> 2. Почему же меня не подобрали? Ведь здесь на поляне открытое место, все видно. Ведь наверно, не я один **лежу** здесь. Они стреляли так часто. Нужно повернуть голову и посмотреть. (Garshin 1897: 7-8)
>
> [Why haven't they picked me up? I mean, it's quite open here in the clearing, you can see everything. Besides, surely I **am** not the only one **lying** here. They shot so fiercely. I must turn my head and have a look.]

[6] In translating passages from Garshin's *Four Days* I have referred to the translation by Peter Henry (Garshin 1988).

それなら何故俺の始末をしなかつたらう？此處は明放しの濶とした處、見えぬことはない筈。それに此處でかうして**轉がつてゐる**のは俺ればかりでもあるまい。敵の射撃は彼の通り猛烈だつたからな。好し一つ頭を捻向けて四下の光景を視てやらう。(Futabatei Shimei 1964c: 47-48)

[Then why didn't our men look after me? It's a wide open space here, it couldn't be possible not to see me. Besides, surely I **am** not the only one **lying** here. The enemy's shooting was really fierce. Well I am going to turn my head and have a look around.]

3. В ту минуту, когда я собираюсь ложиться, широкая бледная полоса лунного света ясно озаряет место, где я **лежу**, и я вижу что-то темное и большое, лежащее шагах в пяти от меня. Кое-где на нем видны блики от лунного света. Это пуговицы или аммуниция. Это или труп, или раненый.
Все равно, я **лягу**. (Garshin 1897: 9)

[Just as I am about to lie down, a broad pale strip of moonlight clearly lights up the spot where I **am lying**, and I see something dark and big, lying about five paces from me. Specks of moonlight are visible on it here and there. It is either buttons or ammunition. It is either a corpse or a wounded man.
Any way, I **am going to lie down**.]

臥やうとすると、蒼白い月光が隈なく羅を敷たやうに假の寢所を照して、五歩ばかり先に何やら黒い大きなものが見える。月の光を浴びて身邊處々燦たる照返を見するのは釦紐か武具の光るのであらう。はてな、此奴死骸かな。それとも負傷者かな？
何方でも關はん。おれは臥る…… (Futabatei Shimei 1964c: 48-49)

[When I am going to lie down, the pale moonlight lights up my temporary bedchamber as if laying thin silk over it, and I can see something dark and big about five paces away from me. Bathed in moonlight, specks are visible on it here and there. They must be the reflections of buttons or ammunition. I wonder if it is a corpse or a wounded man. I don't care. I **am going to sleep**.]

All four verbs underlined by Futabatei depict the symbolic posture of the narrator: "lezhu [I am lying]" is underlined three times and "lyagu [I will lie down/go to sleep]" is underlined once. In the first passage cited the appearance of "lezhu [I am lying]" is quite significant, as it marks the first shift of tense from past to present. Up till that point, Garshin had employed mainly past tense verbs, which are further reinforced by repeated use of the present tense verb "pomnyu [I remember]", underlining the efforts of the narrator to reconstruct his recent past retrospectively:

Я помню, как мы бежали по лесу, как жужжали пули, как падали отрываемые

> ими ветки, как мы продирались сквозь кусты боярышника.
> (Garshin 1897: 5)
>
> [I remember how we were running through a forest, how bullets were buzzing overhead, how tree branches torn off by them were falling, how we forced our way through hawthorn bushes.]
>
> 忘れもせぬ、其時味方は森の中を走るのであつた。シュッシュッといふ彈丸(たま)の中を落來る小枝をかなぐりかなぐり、山査子(さんざし)の株を縫ふやうに進むのであつたが、一　(Futabatei Shimei 1964c: 46)
>
> [I do remember, we were running through a forest, we were forcing our way through hawthorn bushes, throwing away tree branches torn off by whizzing bullets.]

Futabatei opts for "-no de atta" endings for Garshin's frequent past imperfective verbs, depicting continuous past actions. Using "hashiru no de atta" and "susumu no de atta" to translate the verbs "bezhali [were running]" and "prodiralis' [forced our way through]", Futabatei emphasizes the narrator's efforts to recall the past. Similar endings appear throughout the first paragraph of Futabatei's translation when translating past imperfective verbs: "Ōkina kuraifutotta yatsu de atta [He was a huge, fat fellow]" for "On byl ogromnyi, tolstyi turok [He was a huge, fat Turk]"; "Tada naniyara mukō ga aoi to omotta no wa, ōkata sora de atta no darō [What I noticed was something blue over there, it should have been the sky]" for "a videl tol'ko chto-to sinee; dolzhno byt', eto bylo nebo [but I saw only something blue; it must have been the sky]".

Thus, in the first paragraph, most past imperfective verbs are translated using "-ta" forms, and leave us with a sense that the action described is firmly set in the past. The "-no de atta" forms clearly indicate that the first paragraph is the conscious account of a narrator with a retrospective point of view. In the second paragraph, however, the narrator's present time turns out to be not the time when he is rescued or has recovered, but the time when he regains his senses and finds himself lying wounded on the battlefield. At this point Garshin shifts from past tense to present, and most of the story is narrated as occurring in the present. Only occasionally past imperfective verbs continue to be inserted in a predominantly present tense narrative, as the narrator's agonizing present is interrupted by memories of the past.

Although the second paragraph (in which Futabatei underlined the verb "lezhu [I am lying]") is not translated as literally as the first, Futabatei selects the "-te iru" form to translate the underlined present imperfective: "Dōmo hensa na, nandemo utsubushini natte iru rashī no da ga na [It is quite funny, it seems as if I am lying on my belly]". In the first passage cited above the colloquial tone and even the comic effect imparted by the particle "na", skillfully imply that the narrator's monologue is now set in the present. As the translation of this section progresses, "-(r)u" becomes the dominant verb form. In the second passage the original is written with mixed tense forms. The past perfective verb "ne podobrali [they haven't picked me up]", the present imperfective "lezhu [I am lying]", the past imperfective "strelyali [they were shooting]" and even the perfective infinitive "povernut' [to roll over]" combined with the modal word "nuzhno [it is necessary]" are all translated in a way that reproduces as accurately as possible tense forms. Worth particular note is the translation of the past imperfective "strelyali [they were shooting]" as "Teki no shageki wa ano tōri mōretsu datta kara na [The enemy's shooting was really fierce]". The use of the past tense form shows that Futabatei was well aware of Garshin's use of past imperfective verbs to insert flashbacks into the present tense narrative. The third passage also shows Futabatei's attempt to reproduce the tense forms of the original verbs, using "-(r)u" forms to translate the predominantly present imperfective verbs. The verb "neru [(I am) going to lie down]" is adequate to convey the meaning of the future perfective verb "lyagu [I will lie down]". What we observe in the three short passages cited above, then, is a heightened attention to Garshin's specific use of verb forms and the frequent shifts in tense. We may also note Futabatei's keen, intuitive sense as a translator, in underlining the crucial word "lezhat' [to lie]", which is repeatedly used by Garshin to depict the narrator's desperate posture and also the posture of the utterly motionless corpse which suggests the narrator's likely future. Closer examination of Futabatei's translation of various forms of "lezhat' [to lie]" makes even more apparent his attention to the tense form of the original verbs:

> 1. Передо мною лежит убитый мною человек. За что я его убил?
> Он лежит здесь мертвый, окровавленный.
> (Garshin 1897: 11)
>
> [Before me lies the man whom I killed. Why did I kill him?
> He lies here dead, covered in blood.]
>
> **現在**俺の手に掛けた男が眼の前に踏反(ふんぞ)ツてゐるのだ。何の恨(うらみ)が有つておれは此男を手に掛けたらう？
> たゞもう血塗(ちみどろ)になつてシヤチコばつてゐるのであるが、一 (Futabatei Shimei 1964c: 50)
>
> [**Now** the man whom I killed is lying on his back with his legs stretched before me.
> I wonder why I killed him.
> He is lying stiff and covered in blood.]
>
> 2. Совсем разбитый, одурманенный, я лежал почти в безпамятстве. (Garshin 1897: 18)
>
> [Completely broken, stupefied, I lay almost unconscious.]
>
> 全く敗亡(まゐつ)て、ホウとなつて、殆ど人心地(ひとここち)なく臥(ね)て居(をつ)た。(Futabatei Shimei 1964c: 55)
>
> [Utterly broken and stupefied, I lay almost unconscious.]
>
> 3. Могу ли я припомнить то оцепенение, которое овладело мною после этого ужасного случая? Я лежал неподвижно, с полузакрытыми глазами. (Garshin 1897: 19-20)

[How can I recall the numbed feeling that overcame me after that terrible incident? I lay motionless, with eyes half-shut.]

この情ない目を見てからのおれの失望落膽と云つたらお話にならぬ。眼を半眼に閉ぢて死んだやうになつてをつた。(Futabatei Shimei 1964c: 57)

[I cannot describe my despair and disappointment after I experienced this miserable incident. I lay deadly still with my eyes half-closed.]

Generally speaking, Futabatei rarely employs "-te iru" forms in *Four Days,* although the imperfective verb "lezhat' [to lie]" is used thirteen times in the original: "lezhu [I am lying]" appearing nine times and "lezhit [he/it is lying]" four times. In the first example above we see one of the rare instances where Futabatei uses a "-te iru" form. Together with the adverb "genzai [now]" and the "-no de aru" ending the "-te iru" form serves to reinforce the expression of the narrator's deep shock at recognizing the man whom he killed. Futabatei repeats this same "-te iru no de aru" form to translate "lezhit [he/it is lying]", in order to express the sense of guilt which overcomes the narrator. Whereas "-te iru" forms are used to indicate the narrator's recognition of the state of the nearby corpse, they are not often used to describe the narrator's own state, and even appear to be avoided. Futabatei may have consciously avoided the use of "-te iru" forms to translate "lezhu [I am lying]", in order to express the narrator's reluctance to recognize his own desperate state.

Finally, however, the narrator interprets his situation correctly. The second and third examples show Futabatei's sensitive renditions of the past imperfective "lezhal [I was lying]", using the "te otta" form, a variant of "-te ita". "Nete otta [I was lying]" and "shinda yōni natte otta [I was lying still like a dead (man)]" sound slightly pompous, yet they fully express the narrator's acknowledgement of his desperate plight, coming as they do before and after the incident when he fails to attract the attention of Russian soldiers who might have rescued him. We may also note that the narrator's recognition of his situation is only possible from a retrospective point of view, as indicated in the original, so these past imperfective verbs have to be translated in the same tense in which they appear in the original, using the "te otta" form.

A striking feature of *Four Days*, then, is the strictness with which Futabatei adhered to the tense of the original verbs, rather than to their aspectual form, as he had done during his second translation period. However, he does not adhere to the tense of the original quite so closely as he had done in his very first translations from Turgenev. He occasionally translates past imperfective verbs as "-(r)u" forms: when describing the corpse, some scenery, and particularly the image of the little white dog run over by a horse-drawn tram, which haunts him as he lies alone on the battlefield:

Целая картина ясно вспыхивает в моем воображении. Это было давно; впрочем, все, вся моя жизнь, *та* жизнь, когда я не лежал еще здесь с перебитыми ногами, была так давно... Я шел по улице, кучка народа остановила меня. Толпа стояла и, молча, глядела на что-то беленькое, окровавленное, жалобно визжавшее. Это была маленькая хорошенькая собачка: вагон конно-железной дороги переехал ее. Она умирала, вот как теперь я. Какой-то дворник растолкал толпу, взял собачку за шиворот и унес. Толпа разошлась. (Garshin 1897: 10-11)

[A whole scene is clearly illuminated in my imagination. It was a long time ago; but then, everything, my whole life, the life [I knew] before lying here with shot up legs, was so long ago... I was walking along the street, a crowd of people stopped me. They were standing and looking, silently, at something white, covered in blood, pitifully yelping. It was a nice little dog: a horse-drawn tram had run over it. It was dying, just as I am now. Some caretaker pushed through the crowd, grabbed the little dog by the scruff of the neck and carried it away. The crowd dispersed.]

在りし昔が顯然(ありあり)と目前に浮ぶ。これはズツと昔の**事**、尤もな、昔の事と思はれるのは是ばかりでない、おれが一生の事、足を撃れて此處に倒れる迄の事は何も彼(か)もズツと昔の事のやうに思はれるのだが……或日町を通ると、人だかりがある。思はずも足を駐(とど)めて視ると、何か哀れな悲鳴を揚げてゐる血塗(ちみどろ)の白い物を皆佇立(たちどまつ)てまじりまじり視てゐる**光景**(やうす)。何かと思へば、それは可愛らしい小犬で、鐵道馬車に敷かれて、今の俺の身で死にかゝつてゐるのだ。すると、何處からか番人が出て來て、見物を押分け、犬の衿上(えりがみ)をむづと掴んで何處(どこ)へか持つて去(い)く、そこで見物も**ちりぢり**。
(Futabatei Shimei 1964c: 50)

[A whole scene from the past is clearly illuminated in my head. It **happened** long ago, though this is not the only scene which seems to be a long time ago, everything which had happened before I fell [and found myself] lying here with shot up legs seems to be a long time ago... One day when I am walking along the street, I find a large crowd. I stop involuntarily and look at it. People **are standing and staring** at something white and covered in blood that was screaming pitifully. It turns out to be a cute little dog, it has been run over and is dying, just like me. Then a guard comes out and pushes through the crowd. He grabs the dog by the scruff of the neck and carries it away. Then the crowd **disperses**.]

This scene which haunts the narrator-protagonist is described using past tense verbs in the original, indicating that this is the recollection of the narrator from a retrospective point of view. Futabatei, however, uses only "-(r)u" forms, combined with noun-endings (shown in bold). This is more like the translation style found during his second period of literary activity, when he emphasized the aspectual meaning of the verbs in the original. The use of "-te iru" forms to translate past imperfective verbs often helps to create a vivid description in both first-person and third-person narratives. This device is used later in the third period of his literary activity in *Mediocrity* (1907), his third novel, where he describes the haunting memory of the death of a beloved dog at the hands of a merciless dog catcher. Futabatei once again employs "-te iru" forms in a first-person narrative, though the effect is somewhat different, and not restricted to creating a vivid narrative, as we shall see when we discuss *Mediocrity* in the next chapter. For now we shall merely note that there is some stylistic resemblance between the scene in *Four Days* and that in *Mediocrity.* Both incidents are introduced as having happened in the past. In *Four Days* the scene is introduced with the words "Kore wa zutto mukashi no koto [It happened a long time ago]", while in *Mediocrity* the following sentence is used: "Wasure mo se nu, sobo no nakunatta yokuyokutoshi no harusame no shitoshitoto furu usurasamui aru yoru no koto de atta [I clearly remember it happened two years after my grandmother's death, (it was) a chilly night when spring rain was drizzling]".

In *Four Days,* then, Futabatei extended his methodology for translating first-person narratives and made a translation that, for the most part, adheres to the tense forms of the original verbs. As a result, he created a fresh translation style which conveys a more immediate and unedited stream of consciousness. The limited use of "-te iru" forms contributes to the description of the narrator's confusion. The insertion of "-ta" and "-te ita" forms in the midst of a narrative dominated by "-(r)u" forms effectively conveys the fragmented recollection of the narrator. We may thus conclude that in *Four Days* Futabatei continued to apply a foreignizing strategy.

## *Fusagi no mushi [The Depression Bug]* (from Gorky's *Toska [Heartache]*)

Gorky was almost the same age as Futabatei, and the writer most often translated by him after Turgenev. Futabatei translated five of Gorky's early works. A thorough chronological examination of these five translations has been carried out by Komatsu Katsusuke (1971). Futabatei made the five translations almost in the reverse order of their publication dates, with the exception of *Hai'iro bito [Person in Grey],* the translation of *O serom [About the Colour Grey]* (1906).[7] This short allegory was translated only a year after its publication in Russian. This is clear evidence of Futabatei's preference for Gorky's early works, ahead of later works such as *Mat' [Mother]* (1907-1908). Further evidence of this preference for Gorky's early works is found in a lecture he gave entitled "Gōrikī to Andorēefu no kingyō [On Recent Works by Gorky and Andreyev]" (1907). Futabatei clearly values Gorky's early story *Chelkash,* which was published to acclaim in 1896, more highly than *Mother*:

> *Haha [Mother]* took its subject matter from current revolutionary movements. ... Judging from the parts which have already been published, it is to be classified not so much as a story, as Gorky's socialist ideas clothed in the form of a story. Its [method and material] are quite different from those of *Chelkash*... (Futabatei Shimei 1965a: 220)

Futabatei's translation *The Depression Bug* was serialized in the journal *Shin-shōsetsu [New Novel]* from January to March 1906. The year 1906 was a very productive one for Futabatei. During this year Futabatei was to publish *Nenashi-gusa [Rootless Grass]* (from

---

[7] The following is a list of the publication dates of Gorky's originals and Futabatei's translations:

1. *Ded Arkhip i Len'ka* (1894) → *Kojiki [Beggars]* (1907)
2. *Oshibka [A Mistake]* (1895) → *Ni kyōjin [Two Madmen]* (1907)
3. *Toska [Heartache]* (1896) → *Fusagi no mushi [The Depression Bug]* (1906)
4. *Kain i Artem* (1899) → *Jū no ukiyo [The Hard Life of a Jew]* (1905)
5. *O serom [About the Colour Grey]* (1905) → *Hai iro bito [Person in Grey]* (1906)

Garshin's short story *To, chego ne bylo [That Which Was Not]*), *Person in Grey* (from Gorky's *About the Colour Grey*), *Olden Day People* (from Gogol's *Old-fashioned Landowners*), and his second original work, the novel *In His Image.*

While in retrospect 1906 turned out to be a most productive and revolutionary year for Japanese literature,[8] at the beginning of the year, when Futabatei was serializing *The Depression Bug,* the Japanese literary world appeared stagnant. Responding to the publication of *The Depression Bug,* a critic writing in *Waseda bungaku [Waseda Literature]* complained about the dominance of established writers of the Ken'yūsha group such as Hirotsu Ryūrō and Izumi Kyōka, and about the tendency for many young writers to attempt translations rather than original works. In this context, he appreciated Futabatei's translations, and valued them more highly than many conventional original works (Futabatei Shimei 1964c: 385). He defended Futabatei's translation, suggesting that a comical vein is necessary to reveal the theme of Gorky's *Heartache:*

> In general, many of Gorky's protagonists are uneducated, and they are overcome with anguish concerning life's problems. This story also depicts these people. Life's problems are themselves, of course, significant, and they should not be treated frivolously. However, a miller—an ordinary uneducated worker operating a flour mill, being unenlightened by letters, almost unconsciously starts thinking over his life, and his feelings undergo a sudden change. This state of mind (of a miller) must be comical. To add a comical vein to the depiction of life's problems is a kind of ironical way for its depiction. It rather deepens the depiction of the life's problems of uneducated people. (Futabatei Shimei 1964c: 387-388)

Clearly the author of these comments is sympathetic to Futabatei's work, and supports the translation method developed in *The Depression Bug,* despite its being widely criticized as "frivolous". He does concede, however, that Futabatei's decision to use dialect for the speech of the main characters is open to question.

As noted earlier in this chapter, the response to *The Depression Bug* was heated. It appears that Futabatei's "frivolous" translation method, as evidenced in his first two translations from Gorky, was the chief target of criticism. It appears, though, that criticism did not go beyond complaining about the title and the use of dialect.

Gorky's *Heartache* was published in the journal *Novoe slovo [New Word]* in 1896. The story was written before the publication of the two volumes of *Ocherki i rasskazy [Sketches and Stories]* in 1898, which established Gorky's reputation, and were reissued in 1899. Posse, who "discovered" Gorky's talent and organized the publication of these volumes, greatly admired *Heartache*, as well as the earlier story *Chelkash*, which was published in 1895 (Kaun 1968: 144). In preparing *Heartache* for publication in *Sketches and Stories* Gorky undertook some revision of the text, polishing the style and eliminating some foreign words. When these books were republished by *Znanie* in 1903, Gorky further revised the style, and cut out several paragraphs, including some dialogue which he judged to be too philosophically sophisticated for the tramp Bezrukii [Armless]. A detailed comparison of Futabatei's

---

[8] In March 1906 Shimazaki Tōson published *Hakai [The Broken Commandment],* which launched the Japanese Naturalist movement. In the same year Natsume Sōseki finished serializing his novel *Wagahai wa neko de aru [I Am a Cat]* and rose to a position of literary prominence.

translation with the various versions cited in the *Nauka* edition of Gorky's complete works reveals that the original translated by Futabatei is almost certainly the very first edition published in the journal *Novoe slovo* in 1896.

*Heartache* is the story of a miller named Tikhon, who by chance joins the funeral procession of a poor writer, and is led to an anguished reappraisal of his own life. He is also struck by the contrast between himself and his free-spirited employee, Kuz'ma, and becomes deeply depressed. He then decides to confront a teacher who has exposed his unfair dealings with a neighbour, and the confrontation leaves him even more depressed. Tikhon ends up going on a binge for four days with a prostitute named Anna and her vagabond friends. One of these is a tramp named Mishka, nick-named "Bezrukii [armless]", whose philosophy of life would appear to be an expression of Gorky's own point of view. Returning home after his brief odyssey, Tikhon reflects:

> —Жизнь...Колебание одно только...рябь.
> (Gorky 1908: 255-256)
>
> [—Life... is just an oscillation...ripples [on a surface].]
>
> 人(ふと)の一生は是(これ)だ、漣(さざなみ)だア……たんだ上面(うはツつら)が動(うご)くばかしの事(こん)だ。
> (Futabatei Shimei 1964c: 166)
>
> [Human life is... these ripples... only the surface of them is moving.]

This final message is simple, even banal, but when Futabatei translates it employing the Katsushika dialect, he fully captures the comical, yet melancholy, mood of the protagonist. Let us, however, begin our examination of the story with the opening passage:

> ...Помолившись Богу, **Тихон Павлович** медленно разделся и, почесывая спину, подошел **к кровати, наглухо закрытой пестрым ситцевым пологом**.
> —**Господи, благослови**!—прошептал он, затем широко зевнул, перекрестив рот, отдернул полог и стал смотреть на мощную, покрытую мягкими складками простыни, фигуру **своей** жены.
> Сосредоточенно и подробно рассмотрев эту неподвижную, задавленную сном кучу жирного тела, Тихон Павлович сурово нахмурил брови и вполголоса сказал:
> —**Машина!**...
> ...Доносился **серебристый** мягкий звук падения капель воды с мельничного колеса; в роще, за плотиной, гукала выпь; мрачный, стонущий звук тихо плавал в воздухе; когда он пропадал—листва деревьев шумела сильнее, точно испуганная им, и откуда-то доносилась **звонко-унылая** песнь комара. (Gorky 1908: 306)[9]
>
> [Having said his prayers, **Tikhon Pavlovich** slowly undressed and, scratching his back, walked over **to the bed, which was completely enclosed with a many-coloured chintz bed-curtain**.

[9] With variations added from Gorky (1970: 172)

—**God bless us!**—he whispered, then yawned widely, crossing himself in front of his mouth, drew back the bed-curtain, and looked at the powerful figure of his wife, covered in the soft folds of the sheet.
Having examined in detail and with concentration this motionless mass of fat body, overcome with sleep, Tikhon Pavlovich frowned sternly and softly said:
—**[What an impressive] machine!**...
... The **silvery** soft sound of water dripping from the mill-wheel carried to them; in the grove beyond the dam a bittern called; the gloomy groaning sound floated in the air; when it faded the rustling of the leaves grew louder, as if frightened by it, and from somewhere there carried the **melancholy, ringing** song of a mosquito.]

夜祈祷(よぎたう)を濟(すま)してから、**粉屋のチホン**はやつとこなと上衣(うはぎ)を脱いで下衣(したぎ)一枚になり、背中ぢゆうをぼりぼり掻きつゝ寢臺(ねだい)の側へ來た。で、口の中で**なむまみだぶなむまみだぶ**といふのが、頓(やが)て大きな欠(あく)びになつたところへ、透(すか)さず十字を切掛(きりか)けて、颯(サツ)と**形附更紗(かたつきさらさ)の帷(カーテン)**を引くと、其處に古女房(ふるにようばう)の大柄なやつが鹽梅(あんばい)よく夜着に包(くる)まつて臥(ね)てゐる。眠(ね)くさつて死人のやうになつた肥胖(でぶでぶ)のその寢姿をチホンは熟々(しげしげ)眺めて、**宛(まる)で吹韛(ふいご)の向面(むかふづら)**だア、これ、と呟くやうに言つて、（中略）　水車を水の滴(したた)る音は徐(しづ)かに**銀鈴を鳴す如く**傳へ來て、土手向(どてむかふ)の森に啼く青荘(あをさぎ)の聲は、唸(うな)るのかと思はれて物凄く、之が次第に消行(きえゆ)いた後は、此聲(これ)に脅(おびや)かされた如くに木の葉が一段とさわ立ち、何處やらに**ブーンと心細い**蚊の聲が聞える。(Futabatei Shimei 1964c: 104)

[Finishing his prayers, **Tikhon, a miller**, slowly strips to his shirt and has come up to the bed, while scratching his back. **Namumamidabu, namumamidabu [Save us, merciful Buddha!]**, his whispering soon becomes a big yawn, but he quickly crosses himself (on his mouth), and he flings aside **the printed cotton bed-curtain**. There he finds the large figure of his wife, sleeping comfortably, covered by the sheet. Chikhon stares hard at the fat body of his wife, sleeping like the dead, and says in an undertone that **her face looks like someone blowing bellows**....
...The sound of water dripping from the mill-wheel drifts quietly over, **as if ringing a silver bell**, the voices of herons in the forest beyond the bank sound like someone moaning. When the sound has faded, tree leaves make a louder noise, as if they are threatened by it, and the **ringing but melancholy** sound of mosquitoes is heard from somewhere.]

In October 1906 Futabatei's well-known lecture about his translations "Yo ga hon'yaku no hyōjun [My Standard in Translation]" appeared in the journal *Seikō [Success]*. In it Futabatei explains the methodology he adopted in the past, as he endeavoured to reproduce the tone of the original, even using the same number of full stops and commas. He then adds: "However, this applies [only] to the translations made when I was seriously engaged in translation work. The recent ones are not worth talking about" (Futabatei Shimei 1965a: 177).

The opening paragraph of *The Depression Bug* is an example of the "free" translation method adopted in his later work, which contrasts so markedly with the rigorous method adopted in the early translations. Here Futabatei has changed not only the number of full stops and commas, but also a portion of the narrative. While in the original Gorky gives Tikhon's utterances in the form of direct speech, Futabatei presents them as indirect speech incorporated into the narrative. In some cases Futabatei includes additional information (e.g. that Tikhon is a miller), in other cases he withholds information till later in the narrative (e.g. that the bed is enclosed by a curtain). Even more significantly, Futabatei uses many words specific to the Japanese cultural context, clearly introducing elements foreign to the original. Tikhon's prayer "Gospodi, blagoslovi! [God bless us!]" is rendered as "Namumamidabu! [Save us merciful Buddha!]", which misrepresents Tikhon's religious background, and sits awkwardly with his gesture of the cross. Tikhon's second utterance is a single word, "Mashina! [[What an impressive] machine!]". In Futabatei's interpretation this becomes "marude fuigo no mukōzura dā [her face looks like someone blowing bellows]", an idiomatic exclamation often found in works from the Edo period. In *The Depression Bug* Futabatei appears to have adopted a domesticating strategy.

When we compare the verb forms used in *The Depression Bug* with those used in the original, however, it becomes equally apparent that Futabatei is continuing the same practices which he developed in *The Portrait.* He continues to employ "-ta" forms to translate most past perfective verbs, and to use "-(r)u" or "-te iru" forms to translate most past imperfective verbs. In the first half of the above passage a "-ta" form is used to translate a perfective verb. In the second half of the passage, as soon as Gorky introduces imperfective verbs, Futabatei uses a "-(r)u" form verb, to describe the melancholy setting, establishing the mood for Tikhon's descent into depression.

Tikhon is unable to fall asleep, and Gorky introduces the historic present to bring his suffering more vividly before the reader's eye:

> Было жутко. Сквозь цветы на подоконнике и ветви клена перед окном проникли в комнату лучи луны и нарисовали на полу теневой дрожащий узор. Одно из пятен, в центре узора, очень походило на голову хозяйки кресла. Как и тогда, при торге, эта голова, в темном, мохнатом чепце, укоризненно качается; и старческие губы шамкают **ему, мельнику**:.. (Gorky 1908: 258)
>
> [It was terrifying. Through the flowers on the window-sill and the branches of the maple tree in front of the window, rays of moonlight penetrated into the room and traced on the floor a shimmering pattern of shadows. One of the patches in the middle of the pattern looked very much like the head of the arm-chair's owner. Just like that time when she was bargaining, in a dark, shaggy bonnet, that head is shaking reproachfully, and the old-woman's lips are mumbling **to him, the miller**:..]

何となく薄氣味(うすツきみ)がわるい。月は窓外の楓(かへで)の枝を潜り、窓の植木の花越しに射込(さしこ)んで、床(ゆか)に朦朧(もうろう)たる花木(くわぼく)の影を印(いん)してゐたが、それが折節(をりふし)の風に婆娑(ばさ)とゆらめく。尚ほ其影の心(しん)になる一つの影を見れば其形髣髴(はうふつ)として椅子の舊(もと)の持主の婆樣(ばアさま)の頭(つむり)を憶出(おもひだ)させる。競賣(けいばい)の時見たと變らず今もぼやけたやうな黒い帽(ばう)ごと、恨めしさうに首を振り振り、老(おい)の口元をむぐむぐ

させて、(Futabatei Shimei 1964c: 106)

> [It is somehow terrifying. The moonlight penetrates through the branches of the maple tree in front of the window and the flowers on the window-sill, it traces their obscure patterns on the floor. They shimmer rapidly with the occasional [gusts of] wind. When **one** looks at the shadow forming the centre, it vividly reminds **one** of the head of the old lady who owns the arm-chair. As, when bargaining, she shakes her head reproachfully in her shaggy black hair-cap, and mumbles with her senile lips...]

The description shifts from the dismal, frightening garden to the unstable mental condition of the protagonist. In the original this change from objective description to subjective is facilitated by a shift in verb forms. At the same time there is a change in the narrative point of view, which merges with that of the protagonist, in a similar way to that found in *The Portrait.* Unlike Gogol in *The Portrait,* however, Gorky cannot help inserting the word "mel'nik [miller]", which helps to sustain the narrator's separate point of view. It is worth noting that this is the first time Gorky has used the word "miller". Futabatei had introduced it earlier, but omits it here. In *The Depression Bug* this whole passage is rendered using "-(r)u" forms, uttered by a narrator who is set inside the story, and whose viewpoint merges with that of the protagonist, due to the omission of the word "konaya [a miller]". The description of the garden is even more subjective in *The Depression Bug* than in the original, and closely resembles the following description of a garden from *Floating Clouds*:

> 既にして日はパツタリ暮れる、四邊はほの暗くなる。仰向て瞻る蒼空には、餘殘の色も何時しか消え失せて、今は一面の青海原、星さへ所斑に燦き出でゝ殆んと交睫をするやうな眞似をしてゐる。今しがたまで見えた隣家の前栽も、蒼然たる夜色に偸まれて、そよ吹く小夜嵐に立樹の所在を知るほどの闇さ。デモ土蔵の白壁は流石に白丈に、見透かせば見透かされる……サツと軒端近くに羽音がする、回首ツて觀る……何も眼に遮るものとてはなく、唯最う薄闇い而巳。(Futabatei Shimei 1964a: 25)

> [Suddenly the day has ended. Darkness is gradually gathering on all sides. The last trace of colour has disappeared from the sky above, in the great ocean of heaven stars are already glittering and twinkling here and there. The garden of the neighbouring house, which could be seen until just a moment earlier, has been completely covered by the darkness of the night. It is so dark that **one** can place the trees only by the gentle wind which blows. Yet **one** can just trace the shape of the white walls of the storehouse, because of its whiteness. **I** hear wings flutter close by under the eaves. **I** turn my head and look about... **I** can distinguish nothing but darkness.][10]

The similar motif found in *The Depression Bug* and *Floating Clouds,* the anxious

[10] I have referred here to the translation made by M.G. Ryan (1967: 223-224), but have modified the verb forms and the subjects of some sentences.

protagonist surveying the garden, and the use of "-(r)u" or "-te iru" forms contribute to the resemblance between these two passages. In both passages the protagonists' unsettled minds are revealed by showing how easily they are disturbed by slight sounds from the garden. Then, in each case, the narrator's point of view merges with that of the protagonist, as each views the scene, the only difference being that in *Floating Clouds* the narrator is embodied. The narrator in *Floating Clouds* not only relates the story, but also greets the reader directly and even acts in the story. It is thus difficult for the reader to accept the shift of narrative point of view from the narrator to the protagonist Bunzō, even though that shift is credibly traced in the text, as there is no clear indication of the subject in the last four sentences. Nonetheless, the similarity between these two passages shows how closely Gogol's, Gorky's and Futabatei's narrators resemble each other. Once again we are convinced that had Futabatei disembodied the narrator, while still maintaining his point of view inside the story, *Floating Clouds* might have been a truly "modern" story, similar in narrative structure to Gogol's.

A further similarity may be observed in the descriptions of hallucination found in *The Depression Bug* and *Floating Clouds*. In *Heartache* Tikhon is imagining the head of the previous owner of the chair in which he is sitting, visible in the shadows cast on the floor by the moon:

> И покойник Федор Петрович тут же, на полу: вот его большая кудлатая голова с густыми хохлацкими усами. (Gorky 1908: 258)
>
> [And the deceased Fedor Petrovich is here as well, on the floor: there is his big, shaggy head with its thick Ukrainian moustache.]
>
> 一、髪を蓬と振亂した、死んだ爺様の大頭が、ツイソレ其處の床の上に、アレもぢやもぢや髯が……。 (Futabatei Shimei 1964c: 107)
>
> [And now, indeed, the big head of the deceased old man with dishevelled hair is there on the floor, and his bushy moustache (is also)...]

Compare this with the following passage from *Floating Clouds*:

> 「寧そ今夜は此儘で」トおもふ頃に漸く眼がしよぼついて來て額が亂れだして、今まで眼前に隱見てゐた母親の白髪首に斑な黒髯が生えて……課長の首になる、そのまた恐らしい髯首が暫らくの間眼まぐろしく水車の如くに廻轉てゐる内に次第次第に小ひさく成ツて……軈て相恰が變ツて……何時の間にか薔薇の花搔頭を挿して……お勢の……首……に……な…… (Futabatei Shimei 1964a: 34)
>
> [—I would rather not sleep tonight—having just decided this, his eyes begin growing heavy and his thoughts become jumbled. The image of his white-haired mother, which has been flickering before his eyes, grows a speckled black beard and becomes

> the head of his chief. While that terrifying head is swirling around and around like a water wheel, it gradually grows smaller and smaller... its features soon change... gradually into a head with a rose-shaped hair pin... Osei's head.] (Adapted from Ryan 1967: 233)

This passage appears in the same chapter as the other passage from *Floating Clouds* just cited. After a brief conversation with Osei and Omasa, Bunzō is still pondering whether to confess to them that he has lost his job. His anxiety at losing his fiancée's love and respect keeps him from sleeping, and results in the hallucinations described above. Similarly anxious and sleepless, in the grip of an inexplicable anguish, Tikhon also hallucinates and his unsettled, guilt-ridden mind perceives the heads of his neighbours, whose property he has acquired at an unfair price.

Both descriptions are apparently made using "-(r)u" forms, though this is not perfectly clear, as the sentences are clipped, omitting the verbal endings. It is clear, however, that the descriptions are made from the protagonists' point of view. Even in the original, Gorky consistently employs the historic present to emphasize the description of Tikhon's inner thoughts. Gorky's use of the historic present in *Heartache* is similar to Gogol's in *The Portrait,* where the protagonist's inner thoughts are portrayed by merging the narrator's point of view with that of the protagonist. In each case, Futabatei's translations, using "-(r)u" or "-te iru" forms (or clipped sentences as seen above), closely resemble the description of Bunzō's unstable state of mind in Part One of *Floating Clouds,* with the exception of the embodiment of the narrator.

Gorky extends the use of the historic present to the scenes from the funeral procession of a poor writer, which trigger Tikhon's "heartache", and to the dispute with a sick and poverty-stricken teacher who has written a letter to the newspaper about Tikhon's treatment of his neighbours. While the funeral procession is depicted as Tikhon's mental recollection, the dispute with the teacher is described as a currently unfolding incident, seen from the narrator's point of view. Interestingly, in later editions Gorky reduced the use of the historic present in this latter scene. The following are illustrative passages from each of the two scenes:

> 1. По пыльной, залитой знойными лучами солнца, улице тихо движется похоронная процессия. Ризы священника и дьякона слепят глаза своим блеском; в руках дьякона позвякивает кадило, маленькие клубы голубого дыма тают в воздухе.
> —Свя-я...—тоненьким тенором выводит маленький, седенький священник.
> —Тый!—гробовым басом гудит дьякон, **высокий, черный мужчина, в густой шапке черных волос и с большими глазами, добрыми, то и дело улыбающимися**. (Gorky 1908: 259)[11]
>
> [Along the dusty street, flooded with the scorching rays of the sun, a funeral procession is quietly moving. The chasubles of the priest and deacon blind the eyes with their brilliance; the censer tinkles in the hands of the deacon, little clouds of light blue smoke melt away in the air.

[11] With variations added from Gorky (1970: 173)

—Ho-o..—the small grey-haired priest leads in a thin tenor voice.
—Ly!—booms, in a thunderous bass, the deacon, **a tall, dark-haired man with a cap of thick black hair and with big, gentle, continually smiling eyes**.]

まづ、夏の日の一杯に射した町中を、埃を蹴立てゝ葬式の行列がしづしづと練つて行く。導師の法衣は爛として見るに眩ゆく、伴僧の掌げた香爐の蓋は、歩みを移すごとにことことと鳴つて、蒼煙一道裊として空に消行く。
導師は小作の老僧で、細い聲で、
「かしイ……」
と唱ひ出すを、背の高い黒衣の伴僧が、太い破鐘のやうな聲で、
「こヲきイ……」
と引取る。**これは髪の毛の濃く黒い、大きいけれど毒の無い目付の坊様で、その眼に又しても又しても莞爾と笑を含む**。(Futabatei Shimei 1964c: 107)

[In the town flooded with the summer sun, a funeral procession is quietly moving on, stirring up the dust. The priest's chasuble blinds the eyes with its brilliance, the lid of the censer held by the deacon makes a rattling sound with each pace he takes and a small puff of blue smoke is drifting softly and vanishing away in the air.
The priest is a small, old man, and leads with a thin tenor:
—Ho...—
And the tall deacon in his black clothes with his with his thunderous voice booms:
—Ly!...—
**He has thick black hair with big but gentle eyes, and they smile time and again**.]

2. Тот тоже молчит, хмуря брови и уставившись лбом в пол. И снова это молчание длится долго и злит их обоих...
—Ну-сь, так вот...—говорит учитель, потирая левый бок.—Вы, значит, хотите говорить со мной...
—Это самое...—**соглашается** мельник, кивая головой.
—Хорошо...Я догадываюсь, о чем именно...
—Ну? —подымая брови, **спрашивает** Тихон Павлович и недоверчиво **улыбается**.
—Конечно, о том, что я написал про вас в газете,—сдвигая брови, говорит учитель и зачем-то озабоченно отдувает щеки и еще суровее хмурит лоб. (Gorky 1908: 278)

[The other man is also silent, frowning and staring at the floor. And again this silence continues for a long time and fills them both with malice. ....
—Well, then...—says the teacher, stroking his left side—So you want to talk to me...
—That's right...—the miller **agrees**, nodding his head.
—Very well...I can guess what it is about...

—You can? —raising his eyebrows, **asks** Tikhon Pavlovich and **smiles** mistrustfully.
—Of course about the fact that I wrote about you in the newspaper,—says the teacher, knitting his brows, and for some reason puffs his cheeks out anxiously and frowns even more sternly.]

先生も黙つて、眉を寄せて、直と板の間を**諦視てゐらるゝ**。又無言の行が始まつて、いつ果つべくも見えぬので、客も主人も共に焦ち心になる。
（中略）
一、先づ先生が横腹を摩り摩り、
「ぢや、何かソノ……私に話が有ンなさるンだね？」
「でがンすよ」、と粉屋は首肯く。
「よろしい！私には何の話だか分つてる……」
「だら、當てゝみなさろ」、と粉屋は眉を釣上げて、胡亂さうに微笑とする。
「無論私が貴公の事を新聞に投書した一件だらう？」
と先生は眉を寄せた上に、何故か故意ムツと頬を膨らませて、眼も口も一つになれと**澁面を作らるゝ**。(Futabatei Shimei 1964c: 131)

[The teacher also remains silent and frowns, then **fixes** his gaze upon the floor. Again the non-talking penance begins and seems to go on forever. So both guest and master become irritated...
The teacher is the first to open his mouth, stroking his side:
—So, well then...you want to talk to me I see...
—That's right,—the miller agrees.
—Very well! I suppose I know what you wish to discuss...
—Oh yes, what?—lifting his eyebrows, the miller smiles mistrustfully.
—Of course it's about the fact that I wrote a letter about you to the newspaper editor, isn't it?
The teacher knits his brows and for some reason deliberately puffs out his cheeks, then **frowns** severely till his eyes and mouth seem to join.]

The immediate impression gained from these passages is of Futabatei's attempt to reproduce the original in all respects. Without exception present imperfective verbs are translated as "-(r)u" forms, the continuous aspect being emphasized by the use of the "-te iku" form in the first passage. From a lexical point of view, Futabatei seems to search for words that are as close as possible in meaning to those employed in the original. Although ecclesiastical terms such as "svyashchennik [priest]", "d'yakon [deacon]", "riza [chasuble]" and "kadilo [censer]" are translated as "dōshi [officiating priest]", "bansō [assistant priest]", "hōe [vestment]" and "kōro [censer]", which retain a slight Buddhist nuance, the words of prayer of priest and deacon are translated as accurately as possible, even down to the punctuation marks. "Svya-a..tyi [Ho-o...ly]" is deftly translated as "kashi-i...ko-oki-i...

[majestic, holy]". The tactful use of katakana vowels explicitly reproduces the vowels "ya" and "yi" from the original "svyatyi [holy]".

It would seem, then, that Futabatei has made every effort to be culturally faithful to the original in this passage. This contrasts with the opening of the story, where Futabatei adopted a domesticating strategy to such an extent that Tikhon's religious background was misrepresented. In the crucial scene of the funeral procession, which acts as a catalyst for the expression of Tikhon's heartache (*toska*), Futabatei moves to a foreignizing strategy.

In the second passage cited above, which Gorky edited significantly in later editions, Futabatei again employs "-(r)u forms for all present imperfective, though the translation contains some significant innovation. In subsequent editions Gorky changed some verb forms, and cut out a small episode in which a pipe is dropped, prompting the two men to relax sufficiently to begin talking to each other. Gorky changed some verbs (shown in bold) from present imperfective to past perfective. These are "soglashaetsya [agrees]", "sprashivaet [asks]" and "ulybaetsya [smiles]". Interestingly, the subject of each of these verbs is Tikhon. The verbs left in the historic present are those which refer to the teacher's nervous actions. Whether by coincidence or not, Futabatei's translation also emphasizes the teacher's actions. Present imperfective verbs describing Tikhon's actions are translated simply into "-(r)u" forms, while those describing the teacher's actions are translated using the auxiliary verb "-(ra)ru", which expresses respect. "Mitsumete i raruru [fixes his gaze]" and "jūmen o tsukura ruru [frowns]" are renditions of the Russian verb forms "ustavivshis' [having fixed]" and "khmurit [frowns]". This honorific form of expression is observed in Futabatei's translation throughout the exchange between Tikhon and the teacher. "Do, domora ruru [stammers]", "wameka ruru [screams]" and "osoroshī gōsō o arawashite i raruru [displays a terribly sinful expression]" are further examples of this honorific style, and are used to translate "stal zaikat'sya [began to stammer]", "vykriknul [cried out]" and "litso u nego bylo strashnoe [his face was dreadful]", all of which describe the teacher's actions and his emotional state. Whose respect is expressed by these honorifics? If this scene were visualized by Tikhon, and the description conducted from his point of view, it might express Tikhon's cynical respect. However, the scene is unfolding before the reader as if in the present, and is related by the narrator, who is set within the story. Hence these honorifics are directed by the narrator himself towards the teacher. Although respect is paid to the teacher's social status, in this dispute it becomes ironic and produces a comic and cynical tone.

The whole description of the dispute between Tikhon and the teacher is translated with a predominant use of "-(r)u" forms as renditions of present and past imperfective verbs, together with some "-ta" forms for past perfective verbs. Consequently "-ta" forms carry the meaning of complete aspect rather than past tense. The narrator is thus clearly set inside the story and his mockery of the teacher is an integral part of the narrative of *The Depression Bug.* The narrator's mocking description of the main characters is also a common feature of Futabatei's writing in *Floating Clouds,* and of his translation *The Portrait.* It would appear that this cynical tone was what came most naturally to Futabatei, and that this helped him to translate Gogolian stories with a suitably comic tone. Such a tone is used to great effect in *The Depression Bug.* Consider the following passage:

> Лицо у него было красно и все в слезах, борода, смоченная ими, скомкалась,

> и в глазах, широко открытых, испуганных, полных болезненного напряжения, сверкало что-то дикое и восторженное, жалкое и горячее. (Gorky 1908: 302-303)

> [His face was red and all in tears, his beard, drenched in them, was dishevelled, and in his eyes, wide open, frightened, full of painful tension, shone something wild and exultant, pathetic and fervent.]

This is the description of Tikhon after he has listened to a soulful song from three tramps in a cheap eating-house, towards the end of the story. The description is conducted mainly with the use of past imperfective verbs. Futabatei's translation is as follows:

> 顔は面熱（おもぼて）りして紅（あか）く、ほろほろと落つる泪は髯を浸して、其處此處に濕毛（ぬれけ）の塊（かたま）りを拵（こし）らへ、心は悸（をのの）き**氣も張弓（はりゆみ）の**、一杯に睜（みひら）いた眼の中（うち）には、感極（かんきはま）つて**たつみあがりの、猛然たる意氣**は含みながら、何處（どこ）やらに又見るも傷（いた）ましい色をも浮べてゐる。(Futabatei Shimei 1964c: 161)

> [His face is flushed red, and his falling tears wet his beard until it is dishevelled. Frightened and tense, he opens his eyes wide, and in them gleams something fierce and keen, but somewhat painful.]

The narrator of *The Depression Bug* clearly manifests his presence in the story through the eloquence of his narration and the use of such expressions as "ki mo **hari**yumi no [(being) tense]" and "**tatsumiagari no** mōzentaru [fierce]". The former is *kakekotoba* [paronomasia or play on words[12]] and the latter is a fixed expression used to express a fierce state and often encountered in *gesaku* literature. The use of such ornamental language together with the "-te iru" form makes the narrator's presence more prominent and sets him inside the story. At the same time the use of language so specific to *gesaku* literature has the drawback of introducing an overly strong element of Edo Japanese culture into the translation.

Futabatei employs "-(r)u" forms for most past imperfective verbs, while using "-ta" forms mostly for past perfective verbs. When "-ta" forms are compared with the original Russian verbs, we find fifty-three instances of their use to translate past perfective verbs. There are only twelve instances of their use to translate past imperfective verbs. These latter appear as "-te ita", "-(r)u or -ta no de atta" or "-de or -ga atta" forms, and are used when there is a transition from one scene to another. The most common form used to translate past imperfective verbs is "-te iru" (fifteen instances). In the process of translating *The Depression Bug* Futabatei began observing the word order and syntax of the original more closely. Five

[12] Turney explains *kakekotoba* as follows: "These are normally termed pivot words, since they contain two connotations and thus help the sentence to 'swing' from one meaning to another" (Turney 1985: 285). He then cites an example contrived by Aston (1899): "The sun went down, and the welcome, the thrice-wished for, the best beloved knight/night sought a well-earned repose. On the morrow he rose from his couch donn/dawn ed his armour and sallied forth in quest of fresh adventuresome as was his bold spirit, his courage was now to be put to a testy old fool/full of meat as an egg-shaped domes, slender minarets, …".

instances of "-te iru" forms are found as translations of participles or gerunds of imperfective verbs, such as "spavshego [who was sleeping]" or "nablyudaya [observing]". Only three instances are found where "-te iru" forms are used to translate past perfective verbs.

When Futabatei employed "-te iru" forms to translate past imperfective verbs (which dominate Gorky's original) he was attempting to convey the aspectual forms of the original. In this sense we may say that Futabatei was still adopting a foreignizing strategy. However, in respect of the narrator's voice, and his use of devices from *gesaku* literature, we have to conclude that Futabatei adopted a domesticating strategy. The use of honorifics and *kakeko-toba* is specifically Japanese, though the use of honorifics in the description of the teacher's actions corresponds to Gorky's intention (evident in his later revisions) to emphasize the actions of the teacher.

Most significantly, the narrator in *The Depression Bug* shows his presence in the story far more clearly than the narrator of *Heartache.* Unlike the narrator in *The Portrait,* the narrator in *Heartache* never clearly shows his presence in the story. In *The Portrait,* the narrator describes the crowd gathered in front of the art shop with mockery. Not only the use of the present tense, but also the use of modal words such as "verno [probably]", "bez somneniya [without doubt]" and "kak budto [as if]", emphasize the narrator's presence at the scene of the action. In *The Portrait* the narrator's voice is also characterized by a garrulous eloquence, featuring excessive use of words such as "kazalos' [it seemed]", "togda, kogda [at the time when]" and "inogda [sometimes]". Although Gorky shares with Gogol the use of the historic present to show the protagonist's inner thoughts, for the most part his use of the historic present shows no signs of individuality. It is used simply to emphasize certain actions of the main characters. Gorky's narrator does not emphasize his own presence in the story through wordiness.

Thus, when Futabatei clearly set the narrator within the story, and bestowed on him an eloquence which reminds us of the narrators in *Floating Clouds, The Portrait* and even *The Mismatch*, he produced a translation of a different character from that of the original. Some critics have gone so far as to suggest that Futabatei's translation is more interesting and shows a more refined use of language than Gorky's original (Satō Seirō 1995: 448). Futabatei did have some reason, however, to choose to translate *Heartache* in a Gogolian way. In *Heartache* he would have found many motifs and characteristics which align it more closely with Gogol's works than with Turgenev's. The despair of the protagonist towards the end of the story, the physical description of the characters, the comical vein (especially in the dialogue), and the middle class, non-intellectual setting, would all have reminded Futabatei of Gogol's fiction. Interestingly, Futabatei also would have found a motif familiar from Turgenev's *The Rendezvous*—the protagonist's eavesdropping on a rendezvous between a young couple. While in *The Rendezvous* the narrator eavesdrops on a rendezvous between a conceited servant and a pretty peasant girl, in *Heartache* Tikhon eavesdrops on an encounter between his free-spirited employee Kuz'ma and a young girl whose character is not developed in the narrative. Both girls are abandoned by the young men. In *The Rendezvous* the narrator-protagonist deeply sympathizes with the young peasant girl, but in *Heartache* Tikhon shows no sympathy for the girl, yearning rather for the free spirit of his young employee. This different treatment of the same motif may have seemed to enhance the Gogolian character of Gorky's narrative.

We may conclude, then, that the presence of many Gogolian motifs in Gorky's story led

Futabatei to translate it in the same way in which he had translated other Gogolian stories. The narrative style adopted by Futabatei is similar to that found in *Floating Clouds* and *The Portrait,* leading to a resemblance between some scenes from those stories and scenes in *The Depression Bug.* This narrative style does not accurately reflect the narrative style of *Heartache,* as it gives more prominence to the narrator. In *The Depression Bug* Futabatei may have adopted a foreignizing strategy in his approach to translating verb forms. However, the prominence given to his narrator and the heavy use of *gesaku* language force us to conclude that his dominant strategy was a domesticating one.

## *Mukashi no hito [Olden Day People]* (from Gogol's *Starosvetskie pomeshchiki [Old-fashioned Landowners]*)

Futabatei's next translated story, *Olden Day People*, appeared in May 1906, two months after the completion of *The Depression Bug* and five months before Futabatei began serializing his second original work, *Sono omokage [In His Image],* in the *Asahi shinbun.* The choice is further evidence of the appeal of Gogol's style of narrative to Futabatei, and provides additional grounds for considering that he had approached his two previous translations of Gorky's stories in a Gogolian way.

Gogol's *Old-fashioned Landowners* is notable for its dramatized narrator, whose presence is indicated even more clearly than that of the similar narrator in *The Portrait* (which was translated by Futabatei ten years earlier). The following passage is taken from the beginning of the story:

> **Я очень любю** скромную жизнь тех уединенных владетелей отдаленных деревень, которых в Малороссии обыкновенно называют «старосветскими», и которые, как дряхлые живописные домики, хороши своею простотою и совершенною противоположностью с новым гладеньким строением, которого стен не промыл еще дождь, крыши не покрыла зеленая плесень, и лишенное штукатурки крыльцо не выказывает своих красных кирпичей. **Я иногда люблю** сойти на минуту в сферу этой необыкновенно уединенной жизни,... (Gogol 1874a: 1)

> [**I really love** the modest life of those solitary owners of remote villages, who in the Ukraine are usually called "old-fashioned", and who, like picturesque ramshackle houses, are attractive in their simplicity and their complete contrast to a smooth new structure, whose walls are yet to be washed by the rain, whose roof is not yet covered by green mould, and whose porch, having shed its plaster, does not [yet] display its red bricks. **I sometimes like** to go down for a moment into the sphere of this unusually solitary life, ...]

> 小露西亜の片田舎に、浮世を餘所(よそ)に身を埋もれて、地方(ところ)の人に昔氣質(むかしかたぎ)の地主様と呼ばれる人々の生涯ほど、質素で好ましいのも澤山(たんと)**はあるまい**。其の人も素朴なら、其家も古雅で、觸ればツルリと滑る新築の家の、壁は雨

に曝(さらさ)れず、家根(やね)は青苔を吹かず、上(あが)り段の漆喰も處剥(ところは)げして生地の赤煉瓦を露はすに至らぬ類(たぐひ)と、同日に談ずべからざるところが身上(しんしやう)。世離れたと云つても是程なは**滅多にない**。斯うした境涯をも偶(たま)には一寸(ちよいと)覗いて見るのも**興のあるもので**、— (Futabatei Shimei 1964c: 188)

**Nobody lives** so modestly and in such favourable circumstances as those who live solitarily in remote villages of Little Russia, and (who) are normally called old-fashioned landowners by the locals. They are modest, like their houses, and they should not be compared with new houses, which are very smooth and even slippery, whose walls are unwashed by the rain, whose roof is not covered by green mould, and whose front steps have not yet lost its plaster to show its own red bricks. **There are not many** other-worldly houses like those. **It is quite interesting** to pay a short visit occasionally to the sphere of this unusual life...]

Let us recall the observation made by Gerard Genette (1980: 244) concerning the difference between "first-person" and "third-person" narratives: "The novelist's choice, unlike the narrator's, is not between two grammatical forms, but between narrative postures: to have the story told by one of its characters or to have it told by a narrator outside the story". From this point of view, *Old-fashioned Landowners* seems to belong among those stories which are told by one of its characters. The narrator-protagonist appears to be speaking from within the story: "Ya ochen' lyublyu skromnuyu zhizn'... [I really love the modest life...]", "Ya inogda lyublyu soiti… [I sometimes like to go down...]". The narrator first reveals his nostalgic view of the life of the old-fashioned landowners; then the reader is informed that the narrator is paying a visit to them. The narrator's carriage arrives in the village, his coachman clambers down from the box and fills his pipe, and the old dogs bark from the house where the old-fashioned landowners live. There are detailed descriptions of the narrator's visit until the narrator himself appears, but the reader is told nothing about his physical appearance and he lacks any features of his own. Although we constantly hear him voicing his opinions, observations and judgements, his utterances appear only in the narrative, and not in dialogue with other characters, unlike the narrator-protagonists in Turgenev's stories. In *The Rendezvous,* for example, the "sportsman" waits patiently behind a bush throughout the story, but finally emerges to comfort the grief-stricken peasant girl, only to frighten her. His physical presence is shown unambiguously in the text.

If the conditions required to qualify as a character in the story are a physical presence and verbal exchanges with other characters, the narrator of *Old-fashioned Landowners* does not fulfil these conditions. This story, then, is told neither by "one of the characters", nor by "a narrator outside the story". The narrator does exist inside the story, yet his existence is shown only by his narration. *Old-fashioned Landowners* thus does not fit any of the paradigms suggested by Genette (1980: 248). If we were to attempt to classify it within Genette's framework, we would have to place it somewhere between the intradiegetic-heterodiegetic paradigm (a narrator in the second degree who tells stories from which he is, on the whole, absent) and the intradiegetic-homodiegetic paradigm (a narrator in the second degree who tells his own story). The narrator in *Old-fashioned Landowners* seems to exist in the story, yet his practical role is very similar to that of a narrator outside the story. Perhaps

*Old-fashioned Landowners* demonstrates the role of the narrator in Gogol's narratives even more explicitly than *The Portrait*.

As we observed in *The Portrait,* Gogol indicates the narrator's presence by employing present imperfective verbs and modal words such as "verno [probably]", "kak budto [as if]" and "kazalos' (mne) [it seemed (to me)]". In *Old-fashioned Landowners* the use of present imperfective verbs and modal words is more extensive. The first-person pronouns "ya [I]", "mne [to me]" and "menya [me]" are now employed frequently, explicitly reminding the reader of the narrator's presence in the story.

It is significant that Futabatei's translations of the opening sentences of these two stories are similar in their narrative structure. Futabatei translates both of them in the form of a "third-person" narrative, as clearly shown in the following examples:

1. **Нигде не останавливалось столько народа**, как перед картинною лавочкою на Щукином дворе. (Gogol 1973b: 79)

[**Nowhere were so many people stopping** as in front of the picture shop in Shchukin court.]

何處と云つて、シチウキン長屋の繪屋(ゑや)の前ほど、**人の群聚(たか)る處は有るまい**。
(Futabatei Shimei 1964a: 316)

[**Nowhere are so many people crowding** as in front of the picture shop in Shchukin tenement house.]

2. **Я очень люблю** скромную жизнь тех уединенных владетелей отдаленных деревень, которых в Малороссии обыкновенно называют «старосветскими»,.. (Gogol 1874a: 1)

[**I really love** the modest life of those solitary owners of remote villages, who in the Ukraine are commonly called "old-fashioned", ...]

小露西亞の片田舎に、浮世を餘所(よそ)に身を埋もれて、地方(ところ)の人に昔氣質(むかしかたぎ)の地主樣と呼ばれる人々の生涯ほど、**質素で好ましいのも澤山(たんと)はあるまい**。
(Futabatei Shimei 1964c: 188)

[**Nobody lives so modestly and favourably** as those people who live solitarily in remote villages of Little Russia, and who are commonly called old-fashioned landowners by the locals.]

The opening sentences of *The Portrait* and *Old-fashioned Landowners* make use of different verb forms: past imperfective in the former and present imperfective in the latter. In both translations Futabatei the present tense form "aru mai [(nowhere) are/(nobody) lives]". In his translation of *The Portrait* he shifts the tense from past to present in order to show the narrator's presence in the story. In *Olden Day People*, on the other hand, he sacrifices the first-person pronoun "ya [I]" and eliminates the physical presence of the narrator. Stylistically the result is very similar. It would appear that Futabatei was well aware of the particular function of Gogol's narrators. In Gogol's stories the narrator is positioned within the story, yet his physical existence is not specifically indicated, so he functions in the same way as a narrator outside the story. Thus in *Olden Day People* the first-person pronoun "watashi [I]" is employed far less frequently than in the original, at least at the beginning of the story.

Komori Yōichi (1988: 107-108) has noted this elimination of first-person pronouns in *Olden Day People*. He suggests that Gogol's narrator merely expresses the author's point of view and is not developed as a character, so that nothing is lost in eliminating the first-person pronoun. He also suggests that the narrator in *Old-fashioned Landowners* serves a similar function to the narrator in *Floating Clouds*. Komori's observations seem apt, though upon closer examination we find that Futabatei did not entirely eliminate the first-person pronoun from the narrative of *Olden Day People*. Moreover, the use of the first-person pronoun "watashi [I]" is associated with a sudden increase in the use of "-ta" forms expressing the past tense, making the narrative retrospective.

*Old-fashioned Landowners* is a description of the "quiet" way of life of an old couple, Afanasii Ivanovich and Pul'kheriya Ivanovna, who live in a village in the Ukraine. In the first half of the story this way of life is described warmly and nostalgically by the narrator, who appears to be an intellectual from the city. In this description there is an implied criticism of city life. However, a note of irony creeps into the narrative when we are told of the prominent role that eating plays in the lives of Afanasii Ivanovich and Pul'kheriya Ivanovna:

> Оба старичка, по старинному обычаю старосветских помещиков, очень любили покушать. Как только занималась заря (они всегда вставали рано) и как только двери заводили свой разноголосный концерт, они уже сидели за столиком и пили кофе...
> После этого **Афанасий Иванович** возвращался в покои и говорил, приблизившись к **Пульхерии Ивановне**:—А что, **Пульхерия Ивановна**? может быть, пора закусить чего-нибудь?
> —Чего же бы теперь, **Афанасий Иванович**, закусить? разве коржиков с салом или пирожков с маком, или, может быть, рыжиков соленых?
> —Пожалуй, хоть и рыжиков или пирожков, отвечал **Афанасий Иванович**;—и на столе вдруг являлась скатерть с пирожками и рыжиками.
> За час до обеда **Афанасий Иванович** закусывал снова, ... Обедать садились в двенадцать часов.
> ... Пред ужином **Афанасий Иванович** еще кое-чего закушивал. В половине десятого садились ужинать. (Gogol 1874a: 12-15)
>
> [Both the old people liked to eat very much, as was the ancient custom with old-time landowners. As soon as dawn broke (they always rose early) and as soon as the doors started their many-voiced concert, they were already sitting at a little table and drinking coffee...
> After this, **Afanasii Ivanovich** would go back inside and, coming up to **Pul'kheriya Ivanovna**, would say:—What do you think, **Pul'kheriya Ivanovna**? Perhaps it's time to have a bite to eat?
> —And what would you like to eat, **Afanasii Ivanovich**? How about lardy cakes or

poppy-seed pies, or perhaps salted mushrooms?
—Perhaps mushrooms or pies would be nice, **Afanasii Ivanovich** would answer—and on the table would suddenly appear a tablecloth with pies and mushrooms.
An hour before dinner **Afanasii Ivanovich** would have a bite to eat again,... They sat down to dinner at twelve o'clock.
... Before supper **Afanasii Ivanovich** would have something else to eat. At half past nine they sat down to have supper.]

夫婦共昔の人の癖で、ひどく口を可愛がる。早起なので、夜が明け離るゝや否や、戸が聲々に歌ひ出すや否や、もう二人は食卓(テーブル)について珈琲(コーヒー)を啜る。
（中略）
話がすむと、**お爺(ぢい)さん**は内へ這入つて、**お婆さん**の許(ところ)へ行き、こんなことを言ふ。
「**婆さん**や、もう何か喰べる時分ぢやなからうかの？」
「さうさね。何を召(あが)りますえ？フェットで揚げたお煎(せん)か、胡麻入りのパイか、それとも鹽茸(しほたけ)を召(あが)りますか？」
「さあの、鹽茸も好いが、パイも悪くないの。」
そこで忽ち食卓(テーブル)へナプキンが出る、鹽茸が出る、パイが出る。
晝食(ひるめし)の一時間前に又一寸口を動かす。（中略）さて十二時に晝の御飯。
（中略）
夜食前に何かしら喰べて、九時半に夜食の卓(テーブル)に向ふ。(Futabatei Shimei 1964c: 195-197)

[Both the old people like to eat, as is the habit of old people. As they get up early, as soon as the sun has risen, and as soon as the doors begin singing in various tones, they sit down at table and drink coffee...
After finishing their conversation, **grandpa** goes inside, comes up to **grandma** and says:
—**Grandma**, isn't it time to eat something?
—Well, what would you like to eat? Would you like lardy cracknels or sesame-seed pies, or pickled mushrooms?
—Well, it would be nice to have pickled mushrooms and perhaps pies as well.
Then at once the napkins are laid on the table and pies and pickled mushrooms follow.
An hour before dinner they eat something else... At twelve o'clock they have dinner...
Before supper they eat something else, and at half past nine they sit down to have supper.]

It appears that these two old people, and particularly the husband, eat constantly, almost all day long. Even when Afanasii Ivanovich is awakened from sleep by a stomach ache he is offered food by Pul'kheriya Ivanovna. In regard to this Richard Peace (1981: 35) makes the following observations:

> The narrator clearly tells us it is powerful heat: *sil'nyi zhar* (*zhar* might even be taken in the metaphorical sense of '*passion*') which made Afanasii Ivanovich get up. ... Nevertheless his wife thinks (apparently with justification) that the whole thing can be cured by the eternal solace of *food*.

Thus behind this couple's "idyll" there is perhaps a subliminal conflict between passion and food. Afanasii Ivanovich's passion is certainly tamed by Pul'kheriya Ivanovna's food. Yet Futabatei's translation gives us no hint of this concealed issue. First Futabatei substitutes the more general terms "ojīsan [grandpa]" and "obāsan [grandma]" for the old couple's names. Hatano Kazuhiro (1994: 73-75) has examined this substitution closely, and has found that it is consistent throughout the story. He has counted sixty-nine instances of "Afanasii Ivanovich" and seventy-seven instances of "Pul'kheriya Ivanovna" in the original, while in Futabatei's translation we find fifty-three instances of "ojīsan [grandpa]", and sixty-eight instances of "obāsan [grandma]". Hatano reasons that Futabatei made this substitution in order to capture the nostalgic mood of the original. "Ojīsan [grandpa]" and "obāsan [grandma]" are widely employed in Japanese folk tales, and the use of these words creates a mood of nostalgia for old Japan. Isahaya Yūichi (1982: 56-58) also suggests that in using these terms Futabatei was emphasizing nostalgia for the old couple's pastoral way of life.

However, when we carefully compare Futabatei's translation with the original it becomes apparent that Futabatei has done more than make a simple substitution for the couple's names. Through omission of the husband's name, he fails to provide the vital information that it is Afanasii Ivanovich, rather than his wife, who is doing most of the eating. In the extract cited above the name "Afanasii Ivanovich" appears five times, but the "nostalgic" term "ojīsan [grandpa]" appears only once. Therefore the domestication of the main characters' names, which we have observed in earlier translations such as *The Jew*, is again unsuccessful in *Olden Day People,* as it conceals the possibility of critical interpretation.

When we examine the verb forms in the above passage, it is clear that Futabatei is still following the same method which we observed in *The Portrait*. While in the original the habitual actions of the old couple are described using past imperfective verbs, in *Olden Day People* Futabatei uses "-(r)u" forms throughout. The first half of the story consists of a description of the old couple's "quiet" life, using past imperfective verbs which, for the most part, express habitual actions. In the corresponding passages of *Olden Day People* Futabatei uses mainly "-(r)u" forms. When the description becomes more stationary, Futabatei employs "-te iru" forms. We first find "-ta" forms used for the description of a past incident which occurred only once: the inspection of the forest by Pul'kheriya Ivanovna. They are subsequently observed when the narrator's retrospective point of view becomes evident, due to the faithful reproduction of the first-person pronoun "ya [I]" as "watashi [I]". The following is an example of the latter:

> Вообще Пульхерия Ивановна была чрезвычайно в духе, когда бывали у них гости. Добрая старушка! она вся принадлежала гостям. **Я** любил бывать у них, и хотя объедался страшным образом, как и все, гостившие у них, хотя **мне** это было очень вредно, однакож **я** всегда бывал рад к ним ехать. Впрочем, **я** думаю, что не имеет ли самый воздух в Малороссии какого-то особенного свойства, помогающего пищеварению, потому что еслибы здесь вздумал кто-нибудь таким образом накушаться, то, **без сомнения**, вместо постели, очутился бы лежащим

на столе.
Добрые старички!... Но повествование **мое** приближается к весьма печальному событию, изменившему навсегда жизнь этого мирного уголка. (Gogol 1874a: 21-22)

[Pul'kheriya Ivanovna was always in the best of spirits when they had guests. Dear old woman! She devoted herself entirely to her guests. **I** liked staying with them, and although I overate dreadfully, like everyone who stayed with them, although that was very bad for **me**, **I** was still always glad to visit them. Though **I** wonder whether the very air in the Ukraine has some special property that assists digestion, because if anyone took it into their head to overeat like that here, they would **without doubt** find themselves laid out on a board instead of in bed.
Good old people!... But **my** account is drawing towards a most unhappy event, which changed forever the life of this peaceful nook.]

總じて客の有る時は、お婆さんの機嫌が頗る好い。好いお婆さんだ。全(まる)で客の持物に成つて了ふ。**私(わたし)も**其の客となるのがすきであつた。訪ねさへすれば誰でもしたゝか喰(た)べさせられる。健康には甚だ宜しくないけれど、**私は**何時も其の客となるのを愉快に思はぬ事はなかつた。尤も彼地(あちら)の空氣は一種特別で、消化を助ける効(かう)が有るかも知れぬ。此所(ここ)らであんな大食(おほぐひ)をしようものなら、褥(とこ)に就くは扨置いて、屹度解剖臺へ臥(ね)かされるに違ひない。
好い人達だ……が、物語はいよいよ悲しい事件の上に移る。此事件の爲に此平和の境(さかひ)の調子が狂はせられて、取返しの附かぬ事に成つて了つたのであるが、ー (Futabatei Shimei 1964c: 201)

[Grandma is always in extraordinarily good spirits when she has guests. Dear grandma! She is entirely devoted to her guests. **I** liked staying with them too. Once you visit them, you are forced to eat a lot. Although it was harmful for me to overeat, there was not a single occasion when **I** did not feel glad to stay with them. But the air in that place is something so special that I find myself wondering whether it has the effect of promoting digestion. If you ever attempted to overeat in that way here, you would find yourself on the dissecting table, rather than in your own bed.
Good people... but my account is approaching a sad event. Because of this incident, this peaceful nook has been completely changed and will never be the same as it was...]

The past imperfective verbs in this passage are initially employed to describe Pul'kheriya Ivanovna's character. Futabatei shifts the tense from past to present only for the first two verbs, since these two verbs in the original express a state of being, and relate to Pul'kheriya Ivanovna's character. Here Futabatei is once again applying the practices he developed in *The Portrait.* Then the narrator refers to his own experiences from a clearly retrospective point of view, employing the verbs "**ya** lyubil [**I** liked]" and "**ya** vsegda byval rad [**I** was always glad]". The "-ta" forms employed in Futabatei's translation, in combination with the faithful reproduction of first-person pronouns, carry solely the meaning of the past tense, as clearly shown in "**Watashi mo**...suki de atta [**I** liked ~ too]" and "**Watashi wa**...yukaini omowa nu koto wa nakatta [there was not a single occasion when **I** did not feel glad]".

This passage marks the transition from the first half of the story to the second. The second half of the story is devoted to the incident which changes the old couple's "pastoral" life forever. This is Pul'kheriya Ivanovna's death, which is brought on by a most insignificant cause—the disappearance of her "tamed" cat. Like the narrator in *The Portrait,* the narrator of *Old-fashioned Landowners* sprinkles the narrative with fulsome commentary, and points out how insignificant causes may lead to significant consequences. In the original the narrator's intrusiveness is highlighted by the use of present imperfective verbs. Futabatei's use of "-(r)u" forms reflects the use of the present tense in the original. In the second half of the story Futabatei is quite rigorous in his rendition of the tense of verb forms. The second half of the story begins as follows:

> У Пульхерии Ивановны была серенькая кошечка, которая всегда почти лежала, свернувшись клубком, у ее ног. Пульхерия Ивановна иногда ее гладила и щекотала пальцем по ее шейке, которую балованная кошечка вытягивала, как можно выше. Нельзя сказать, чтобы Пульхерия Ивановна слишком любила ее, но просто привязалась к ней, привыкши ее всегда видеть. Афанасий Иванович, однакож, часто подшучивал над такою привязанностью. (Gogol 1874a: 22)
>
> [Pul'kheriya Ivanovna had a little grey cat, which nearly always lay, curled up in a ball, at her feet. Pul'kheriya Ivanovna sometimes stroked her and with one finger tickled her neck, which the spoiled cat stretched as high as she could. One could not say that Pul'kheriya Ivanovna loved her excessively, she was simply attached to her, having become accustomed to seeing her all the time. Afanasii Ivanovich, however, often teased her about this attachment.]
>
> さてお婆さんの手飼(てがひ)に小さな灰色の猫があつた。いつもお婆さんの足下に圓くなつて臥(ね)てゐるのであるが、お婆さんが折に觸れて頭を撫でたり、頤(あご)の下を摩(こす)つたりすれば、猫は甘(あまつ)たれて思ふさま首を延さうといふもので、大して愛してゐるのではなかつたが、年來(としごろ)目にみなれたので馴染(なじみ)が深いのであつた。お老爺(ぢい)さんは之を種に、能くお婆さんに調戯(からか)ふ。(Futabatei Shimei 1964c: 202)
>
> [Well, grandma had a little grey cat. She was always lying down, curled up at grandma's feet. Whenever grandma patted her on the head or stroked her under the chin, the spoiled cat stretched her neck as long as she could. Grandma was not very fond of her, but was attached to her, because grandma had got used to seeing her around for some years. Grandpa often teases her about her attachment to it.]

Soon we are informed that the cat appears to be tamed by Pul'kheriya Ivanovna giving her food rather than by affection. Moreover, the initial disappearance of the cat does not cause Pul'kheriya Ivanovna any great anxiety. It is the second disappearance of the cat, immediately after being fed by Pul'kheriya Ivanovna that leads to the old lady's death. The first disappearance simply tells us that the cat is lured away by a wild tomcat. The second disappearance signifies that the desire for food is overwhelmed by passion. It also suggests that Pul'kheriya Ivanovna, who has constantly offered her food, is openly rejected for the first time. She sees in this rejection a foretelling of her death.

The translation of past imperfective verbs as "-ta" forms, and particularly as "-atta", "-(no)de atta", "-te ita" and "-te iru no de atta" form verbs, carrying the meaning of the past tense, becomes the norm in the second half of the story. Only where the habitual actions of the protagonists are described, as, in the above passage, where Afanasii Ivanovich's teasing is described, does Futabatei employ "-(r)u" forms. Amongst the "-ta" forms, those of the form "-te ita" are particularly observed when continuous actions are described:

> Покойницу положили на стол, одели в то самое платье, которое она сама назначила, сложили ей руки крестом; дали в руки восковую свечу; он на все это глядел бесчувственно. Множество народа всякого звания наполнило двор; множество гостей приехало на похороны; длинные столы расставлены были по двору; кутья, наливка, пироги покрывали их кучами, гости говорили, плакали, глядели на покойницу, рассуждали о ее качествах, смотрели на нее; но он сам на все это глядел странно. (Gogol 1874a: 28)
>
> [They laid the deceased old lady on the table, dressed her in the frock which she herself had nominated, crossed her arms; they placed a wax candle in her hands; he was looking at all this numbly. Many people of all ranks filled the courtyard; many guests came to the funeral; the long tables were arranged in the courtyard; they were covered with masses of funeral wheat gruel, fruit liqueur and pies, the guests talked, cried, looked at the deceased lady, discussed her qualities, looked at her; but he himself was looking at all this strangely.]
>
> 亡き人を卓（テーブル）の上に安置し、遺言（ゆゐごん）通りの着物を着せ、手を十字に組ませて、蝋燭を持たせたのを、お老爺さんは放心（ぽかん）と見てゐた。貴き賤（いやし）き数多（あまた）の人が邸内を埋めて、訪問の客は、引きも切らず、庭前（ていぜん）に並べた細長がい食卓（テーブル）に、小麥の蜜煮に、林檎酒に、パイを堆高（うづたか）く積重ねた傍で、會葬者が語りつ、泣きつ、亡（な）き人の噂さをしては、お爺さんの樣子に目をつけたりなどするを、お爺さんは不思議の顔して見て居た。(Futabatei Shimei 1964c: 206)
>
> [They laid the deceased person on the table, dressed her in the clothes which she had requested as her dying wish, crossed her arms and placed a wax candle in her hands; grandpa was looking at all this blankly. Many people of high and low rank filled the courtyard, the guests arrived continually. Long tables placed in the courtyard were covered with masses of honey wheat, apple wine and pies; the guests talked and cried, they talked about the deceased and checked on grandpa; but he was looking at all this with a vague face.]

In contrast to the methods adopted in *The Portrait,* in *Olden Day People* Futabatei translates past imperfective verbs expressing continuous actions as "-te ita" forms, sometimes in the form "-te iru no de atta". At the same time he employs "-(r)u" or "-te iru" forms for past imperfective verbs describing states of being or habitual actions. In *The Portrait,* the use of "-te iru" forms to translate past imperfective verbs describing continuous actions facilitates the production of graphic images, particularly in the hallucination scenes. (The verb "glyadel [was gazing]", used to describe the fierce gaze of the moneylender, is translated as "mite iru [is looking]".) However, in the climax of *Olden Day People,* at Pul'kheriya Ivanovna's funeral, where the same verb "glyadel [was gazing]" is used to described Afanasii Ivanovich's numbed gaze, it is twice translated as "mite ita [was looking]". The choice of past tense verbs is closely related to the narrator's retrospective point of view. It is no coincidence that Futabatei also translated the first-person pronoun more frequently in the second half of the story. As observed previously, in *Olden Day People* "-ta" forms expressing the meaning of the past tense tend to be employed more frequently when the first-person pronoun "watashi [I]" indicating the narrator himself appears as a translation of the Russian first-person pronoun "ya [I]". That is, when a retrospective narrative point of view is emphasized by the use of the first-person pronoun, the predominant verb form in Futabatei's translation becomes "-ta". *Olden Day People* is the first translation since Futabatei's retranslations of *The Rendezvous* and *Three Encounters* in which the number of "-ta" forms carrying the meaning of the past tense exceeds the number of "-ta" forms carrying the meaning of the perfective aspect. More precisely, it is the first time that the number of "-ta" forms used to translate past imperfective verbs exceeds the number used to translate past perfective verbs (the ratio being 34:17, or twice as many).

In summary, Futabatei initially endeavoured to translate *Old-fashioned Landowners* in the same narrative style as he had developed in *The Portrait.* The first half of *Olden Day People* shows the predominant use of "-(r)u" and "-te iru" forms, the first-person being avoided as far as sentence structures will allow. Because of the descriptive nature of the first half of the story, where we are given an account of the old couple's seemingly idyllic pastoral lifestyle, it was possible for Futabatei to adopt the same narrative style as in *The Portrait.* However, once the plot of the story begins to unfold with the account of Pul'kheriya Ivanovna's death, Futabatei can no longer maintain the same narrative style. The more clearly the narrator's presence is manifested by the use of the first-person pronoun, the more frequently Futabatei needed to employ "-ta" forms carrying the meaning of the past tense.

In conclusion, it would appear that Futabatei, who initially followed the translation method developed in *The Portrait,* has rather accidentally modified that method, because of the clear indication of the first-person pronouns in the original. The ambiguous narrative style of the original, in which a first-person narrative is made to function as a third-person narrative, led to Futabatei's translation being inconsistent in style. At the same time the ambiguity of the content is removed by the use of general terms to name the main characters. As Futabatei attempts to reproduce the original verb forms, we may conclude that in this respect he adopts a foreignizing strategy. However in replacing the main characters' names with the nostalgic Japanese words "ojīsan [grandpa]" and "obāsan [grandma]", and in simplifying the content somewhat, he adopted a domesticating strategy. Since much of the ambiguity of the original is lost, we must conclude that this domesticating strategy is unsuccessful. The foreignizing strategy with regard to the translation of verbs is not really successful either, as the inconsistency between the first and second halves of the story results in some confusion.

This inconsistency in the narrative style of *Olden Day People* may have contributed to a similar inconsistency of style in his next original work, *In His Image,* to which we shall now turn.

## *Sono omokage [In His Image]* (Futabatei's Second Original Work)

In October 1906 Futabatei began serializing *In His Image* in the *Asahi shinbun* with the enthusiastic support of Ikebe Sanzan, the editor-in-chief of the *Tokyo Asahi shinbun*, who had retained Futabatei as a writer rather than as a correspondent. Ikebe was also planning to invite Natsume Sōseki to *Asahi*. In 1907 Sōseki and Futabatei serialized their works in turn in the *Asahi shinbun* as Ikebe had planned. These works were *Heibon [Mediocrity]* and *Gubijinsō [The Poppy]*. However, Ikebe's plan to feature the two writers was cut short by Futabatei's departure for Russia and his subsequent death.

When asked to contribute a novel for the *Asahi shinbun* Futabatei was already planning to write a novel about the problems facing war widows. Futabatei (1965a: 199) firmly believed that widows should remarry, no matter what their social status. Initially he began to work on a novel entitled *Chasengami [Tea-whisk Hair],* referring to a hairstyle worn by war widows, in which the hair was drawn up into a short ponytail that resembled a tea whisk (Washburn 1995: 114). However, he abandoned this first attempt and began afresh with the new title *In His Image.* Nakamura Mitsuo offers the following explanation for this change of tack. While Futabatei was writing *Tea-whisk Hair*, his centre of interest shifted from the main character Yukie, a war widow, to the secondary character Professor Shinjō, a friend of Yukie's late husband, who acts as her adviser. The problem facing Yukie is of a social nature, and is soluble. Although she is oppressed, she remains spiritually healthy. When Professor Shinjō falls in love with Yukie, he is racked by inner conflict of a kind which he has never faced before (Nakamura Mitsuo 1958: 290-291). His problem is of a spiritual nature, more akin to the problems facing Futabatei himself, and more difficult to solve. In order to bring the focus of attention more clearly on Professor Shinjō, Futabatei took away Yukie's social status as a war widow. At the same time he gave Professor Shinjō a more unstable social status to reflect the inner conflict he experiences.

In *In His Image* the main character is Ono Tetsuya. He retains Professor Shinjō's position as a university lecturer, but is an "adopted husband", morally forced to marry into the family of his bride Tokiko, because her father has financed his passage through college. Tetsuya falls in love with Sayoko, who, like Yukie, is a young widow. She is Tokiko's half sister, and lives with the family, which includes Tetsuya, Tokiko and Tokiko's mother Takiko. Futabatei makes the relationship between the main characters extremely close and complex, so that love between Tetsuya and Sayoko inevitably destroys the balance of the family and places Tetsuya in a moral dilemma. Should he remain loyal to Tokiko and her family, or should he honestly express his love for Sayoko? Nakamura observes that *In His Image* is a rarity amongst the numerous novels written during the Meiji period, because it deals with a middle-aged man's love and its tragic consequences. Despite its general unpopularity and the unfavourable criticism it has attracted, even from Futabatei himself, Nakamura (1958: 279-280) evaluates the novel highly and finds the description of each character believable.

*In His Image* probably owes much of this rare quality to models provided by

Russian naturalism, and in particular by Gogol. In characterizing Russian naturalism, Araya Keizaburō (1967: 64) suggests that "the plot typically involves a middle-aged and isolated man falling in love with a young girl and despairing when his love is not reciprocated".[13] Although Tetsuya's love for Sayoko is briefly reciprocated, their relationship is soon terminated by her. Rejected and disgraced, Tetsuya finally ends up living the life of a drunken tramp in China. The novel ends with Tetsuya's confession to his old friend Hamura, who comes searching for him. This confession can be seen as a variation of the "tragic monologue from the main character with which the story ends", which, according to Araya, is typical of Russian naturalist works.

Although thematically *In His Image* appears to be akin to Russian naturalist stories, it does not appear to have the other two characteristics which, according to Araya, define the method. One of these is that the dialogue "is frequently incoherent and absurd". The other refers to the physical descriptions of the main characters, "which frequently portray comical and trivial features". Much of the indispensable humour in Gogolian stories comes from these features, which are lacking in *In His Image*. While Futabatei succeeded in portraying a minor character like Kyūbei with distinctively Gogolian humour, he could not apply the same humorous touch to the main characters. The following passage shows the comparative lack of humour in his treatment of the main characters:

> 時子も平生は我儘に掩はれて然うとは見えぬけれど、哲也を便りに世を送るといふに僞もあるまいに、今更振棄てたら嘸心細からう**と思ふと**、何となく哀になり、其恥を忘れて取亂した姿も、勝氣な者だけに傷らしく、之を棄てゝ家を出ようとする我は成程鬼か**と思うと**、何も角も忘れて、乃公が惡かつたと、**ツイ言ひたいやうな氣になつた**が、此時時子は言ふ事を言盡しても、泣盡しても、哲也が矢張黙つてゐるので、持前の肝癪が勃然と發り、「是程事を分けて言つたら、貴方も其様に黙りこくツて居ないで、何とか言つて下すつたつて好いぢや有りませんか！」と噛付くやうに言つたので、哲也も一寸躊躇つてゐると、「ぢや、好うござんす、私も最う覺悟を極めました。其代り何ですよ、私の目の黒い中は、貴方が幾ら小夜と一所に成らうたつて、飽迄邪魔をして一所には爲せませんからね、然う思つてらツしやい」、とぷいと起つた。かうなると哲也も翻然と氣が變つて、續いて起上り、時子が出た後を礑と閉切つた時には、もう誰やらの詩を低誦しながら帯を解いてゐたが、軈て寢衣に着替て、床へ入つて、最う十分も經つたから寢たのか**と思へば、然うではなくて、**欷歔げてゐるのであつた。（五十六）(Futabatei Shimei 1964c: 338)[14]

---

[13] Note that Tayama Katai's *Futon [The Quilt]* (1907), parodied by Futabatei in *Heibon [Mediocrity],* places its protagonist Tokio in just such a situation.

[14] This scene is very similar to the final scene in *Futon,* where Tokio sobs into the quilt left by his young disciple Yoshiko.

> ["Tokiko has always been self-centred, but now she does not look that way, and probably it is not an idle statement that she depends totally upon him. How lonely she will be if I desert her." **When he thought about it**, he became sorry for her. The figure of Tokiko, who had forgotten her pride and thrown herself down before him moved him so deeply that **he thought**: "I should be a devil as she says. I am about to desert her and leave home". At that moment he forgot everything and was ready to accept the blame. He felt like telling her so. At exactly the same moment Tokiko, having said everything she wanted to say, and having poured out all the tears she could, suddenly lost her temper as usual at Tetsuya's persistent silence. "As I have been telling you my sincere feelings, you must say something. You shouldn't remain silent", she scolded sharply, and Tetsuya hesitated a moment. "Very well, then, [she said] I've made up my mind. Remember, as long as I live, I shall never allow you to live with Sayo. No matter how hard you try, I shall hinder you from living with Sayo". She <u>rose</u> abruptly. Now Tetsuya also changed his mind completely and stood up.
> When he shut the *shōji* screen loudly behind her, he was already reciting a Chinese poem in a low voice, and he began unfastening his Japanese belt. He soon changed into his night clothes and went to bed. Ten minutes passed, and **I thought** he must have gone to sleep... **but, contrary to my expectation**, he was still awake and he <u>was sobbing</u> away.]

The final quarrel between Tetsuya and Tokiko, which determines whether he deserts her to live with Sayoko, proceeds rather strangely. Tokiko's reaction to his silence decides his future. Until Tokiko questioned his intentions, Tetsuya had never seriously considered leaving her or divorcing her. After the dispute we find Tetsuya sobbing away, as he regrets not his indecision, but his silence, which has determined his future. Although the description of Tokiko's anger is fairly straightforward, Tetsuya's effeminate reaction to her anger is depicted not so much with humour, as with an irony which comes from the narrator. Here the narrator's presence is clearly indicated by "to omoe ba, sō de wa nakute [I thought..., but contrary to my expectation...]".

In chapters fifty-five and fifty-six, where the description of this dispute is found, Futabatei's use of "-ta" forms becomes noticeable in both number and meaning. Up to this point the predominant verb form in *In His Image* has been "-(r)u", and "-ta" forms have been mainly employed to express the meaning of complete aspect. "-Te shimatta" form verbs have often been used to emphasize the meaning of complete aspect. Some "-no de atta/de atta", "-atta" or "-nakatta" forms carrying the meaning of the past tense have also been observed, but their number has been too small to influence the overall narrative point of view, which has remained inside the story. However, in chapters fifty-five and fifty-six the number of "-ta" forms exceeds that of "-(r)u" forms. Particularly common are "-ta no de aru", "-(r)u no de atta" and "-no de wa nakatta" forms, which indicate the narrator's position outside the story. It is from outside the story that the narrator clearly explains Tetsuya and Tokiko's inner thoughts. Thus in the closing sentences of the above passage Tetsuya's sobbing is monitored closely by a narrator outside the story, who can, however, mock Tetsuya, as might a Gogolian narrator.

To clarify the narrator's position and role in *In His Image* it is worth comparing its narrator with that of *Floating Clouds*. Many critics have pointed out the similarity between these two novels, among them Futabatei's mentor Shōyō and Masamune Hakuchō, a perceptive critic from the circle of Japanese naturalist writers. Searching for something to say in favour of *In His Image,* Shōyō ventured that it was "more polished than *Floating Clouds*", but his faint praise clearly disappointed Futabatei. Hakuchō was more direct in his criticism of *In His Image*, suggesting that its opening was identical to that of *Floating Clouds*, and revealed a weakness in Futabatei's creativity as a writer (cited in Nakamura Mitsuo 1958: 278). Futabatei's closest friend, Uchida Roan (1980: 333), wrote in his recollections that *In His Image* adds nothing to *Floating Clouds* in its content, and that the descriptions in it lack vitality, however abundant they are in fine sentiment. All critics appear to agree that *In His Image* is more polished, but lacking vitality in style and freshness of content. The following passage is the much criticized opening of *In His Image:*

> 弱々とした秋の日は早や沈んで、夕榮ばかり赤々と西の空を染めた或夕ぐれ、九段坂を漫々登つて行く洋服出立の**二人連れがある**。一人は細長く、一人は横太りの、反對は格構ばかりでなく、**細長いのは**薄汚れた霜降の背廣の、洋袴の膝も疾に摺切れて毛が無いのに、黒とは名のみで、日向へは些と憚りある鍔廣の帽子で、是ばかりは不釣合な金縁眼鏡を掛た、面長で頰の削けた、眉の濃い割に髭の薄い、何處となく貧相な、一見して老書生といふ風采の男で、何やら痛か詰込んだ、手摺れて垢光のする、揉皮のポートフオリオを小脇に抱へてゐたが、**横太りの方は**（中略）、身に着いたもの何一つ新調ならぬはない。是は寒竹やら何やら細い洒落たステツキを杖てゐる。
> **熟々視ると**、其細長い方は、毎も秋になると、此服装で此ポートフオリオを抱へて、毎日午前八時ごろ、神田の某私立大學の赤煉瓦の門を、俯向加減に躡踵と這入つて行く彼人で、**聞けば**其處の講師で、一（一）
> (Futabatei Shimei 1964c: 222)

[One evening, the weak autumn sun has already set, and the afterglow has painted crimson the western sky, **there are two men** in western clothes walking slowly up the incline of Kudan. One of them is slender, the other stout; and they are opposite in many other ways. **The slender man** wears a smeary pepper-and-salt sack coat, trousers threadbare at the knees, and a broad-brimmed hat which once was black, but now is so worn that one would be ashamed to wear it in daylight. His gold-rimmed spectacles alone seem to belie his humble appearance. His face is long, his cheeks are sunken, and his moustache is disproportionately thin compared with his thick eyebrows. His meagre appearance might cause one at first glance to take him for a poor elderly student. He carries a heavily bulging leather portfolio, glistening with grime, under his arm. **The stout man** ... everything he wears is vulgarly new. He carries a thin, stylish bamboo cane, perhaps made of *kanchiku* [the non-hollow bamboo].
**When I look at him carefully, I notice that** the slender man is the man who, every autumn in the same suit, and carrying the same portfolio, walks, with eyes downcast, through the red brick gateway of a certain private university in Kanda at about eight

o'clock in the morning. **I have heard** that he is a lecturer at this university.]

There does indeed appear to be a close similarity with the opening of *Floating Clouds*. The description of two characters who are opposite in their features and dress is almost identical with that in *Floating Clouds,* where, instead of a slender man [hosonagai no] and stout man [yokobutori no], we have a tall man [takai otoko] and a man of average height [chūzei no otoko]. The slender man and the tall man even wear the same "pepper-and-salt" suit; the stout man and the man of average height carry the same "thin cane". Small wonder that Hakuchō doubted Futabatei's creative power as a writer. However, the apparently identical nature of these two openings, written at an interval of nearly twenty years, needs to be examined more closely. We must consider that during this interval of twenty years Futabatei had been constantly translating Russian literature, although he had been unable to write any original work. Secondly, we must consider that just before commencing work on *In His Image* Futabatei had been translating stories by Gogol and Gorky, for which he had adopted a method developed while translating Gogol's *The Portrait.*

Although there is a close similarity between the descriptions of the main characters in each of the two openings, the two narrators are not identical. The narrator in *Floating Clouds* is reminiscent of the raconteurs who act as narrators in Edo *gesaku* writing. He addresses the reader directly, and the reader feels his physical presence. The narrator in *In His Image* is more sophisticated, as the direct addressing of the reader and the sense of his physical presence are eliminated. Yet the narrator's position in relation to the story seems identical. In both novels, in the early chapters at least, the predominant verb form is "-(r)u", which sets the narrator inside the story. In the passage cited above the words "yokuyoku miru to [when I look at him carefully]" and "kike ba [I have heard]" clearly manifest the presence of the narrator inside the story. The narrator's position within the story is simply established with a greater degree of sophistication than in *Floating Clouds.* This may be what Shōyō was referring to when he suggested that *In His Image* is more polished than *Floating Clouds*.

Although the narrative is modernized by eliminating the physical presence of the narrator, the practical function of the narrator remains the same: to add humour by mocking the main characters. The following is a description of Tetsuya, when he can find no alternative to sending Sayoko to live as a governess with the rich Shibuya:

> ……あゝ、如何したもんかなあ……」といふ頃には、今迄蒼褪めて光澤氣のなかつた面にクワツと朱を濺ぎ、目に怪しき光を湛へて、容易ならぬ顔になつて居ながら、薄氣味わるくニタニタと笑つて、「僕あ何だか頭が混亂して、無茶苦茶になつて來た……」（八）(Futabatei Shimei 1964c: 235)

> ["...Oh what should I do?" By this time his face, which has been pale and lustreless, is flushed red, his eyes shine strangely, and his facial expression becomes extremely serious, but then all of a sudden he grins mysteriously. "My head has become too confused to think of anything... Everything seems out of order..."]

The wordy but "prudent" narrator shows us only those features and thoughts which are evident to an external observer, not those inner thoughts which are inaccessible to a narrator positioned within the story. In this he resembles the narrators of Gogolian stories. The sudden change in Tetsuya's facial expression produces enough comical effect to objectify Tetsuya's "serious" love for Sayoko and make a caricature of it. The narrator's wordiness and his position within the story is further evident in the scene where Tetsuya is forestalled by his friend Hamura, when it is arranged for Sayoko to go to live with Shibuya without Tetsuya's consent. Tetsuya has been trying to phone Hamura in order to stop him negotiating directly with Tokiko and her mother, who will have no hesitation in sending Sayoko away.

> 一、斯うして戸外へ出たに何の目的が有るでもなかつた。**唯焦燥さの棄場に困つて安坐して居られぬ爲であつた**が、一旦出ては最う引ツ返しもならず、いらいらしながらも、何やら見えぬ力に牽れるやうに、家路を辿ること四五町にして、偶と四角の自働電話に目を注けて立止まつた。暫く凝然と考へてゐる中に、稍蘇生つたやうな面になつて、衝と其箱の中に姿を隠したかとすれば、**軈て外へ漏れる其聲を聞けば**、又しても懲りずまに葉村を呼出すのであつたが、（中略）
>
> もう是で大丈夫、外の防ぎは付いたと思ふにつけ、今更氣掛りなは我家の光景、小夜さんが留守に責られて困つては居ぬかと、其を思へば、**閑な身も氣忙しくて、**俥 を呼んで壹岐坂下まで駈付け、**飛降りるなり、坂を走り上るなり、我家の門口迄息急きつて來て見ると、**（中略）待草臥た黒鴨仕立の車夫が蹴込に腰を掛けて生體なく寐込んでゐる。
>
> **けれども哲也はまだ其とは氣が附かず、誰が來てゐるのか知らと暢氣な事を思ひながら**、まづ内へ這入つて、**歩きもせぬに草臥れた腰**をどツかり玄關に卸す其音を聞付けて、一（十二） (Futabatei Shimei 1964c: 242-243)

[... he has come out in this manner with no particular purpose. **He did not know what to do with his excessive vexation. He could not sit quietly and came out**. Once he comes out, he cannot go back. Although he is still irritated, he walks for four or five blocks towards home as if seized by some invisible force. Then he happens to notice an automatic telephone on the corner. He has stopped. While he is sunk in deep thought for a while, his face suddenly brightens up and his figure slips into the booth. **When I hear a voice coming from the booth**, it is Tetsuya asking Hamura importunately...

"Now it is all right, I have made a good outer defence". When he has relieved himself of Hamura's visit he begins to worry about Sayoko, who may have been accused by her family members. When he thinks of Sayoko, he suddenly **feels an unnecessary urge to rush home**, so he hires a rickshaw, which quickly carries him to the bottom of the Iki slope. **He quickly jumps out, runs up the incline, and arrives panting at the gate of his house**. ... A rickshaw driver in a black uniform, who is evidently tired of waiting, is fast asleep, sitting on the footboard of his rickshaw.

**Yet Tetsuya has not become aware of the visit and is wondering insouciantly who**

> **is visiting**. He enters the yard and sits down with a thump, as if exhausted, **although he hasn't walked far**. As soon as the sound is heard...]

The narrator's position within the story is clearly shown by the phrase "yagate soto e moreru sono koe o kike ba [when I hear a voice coming from the booth]". His mocking tone is apparent in the frequent sarcastic evaluation of Tetsuya's behaviour: "modokashisa no suteba ni komatte [(he) did not know what to do with his excessive vexation]", "himana mi mo kizewashikute [(he) feels an unnecessary urge to rush]", "aruki mo se nu ni kutabireta koshi (o orosu) [He sits down as if he is tired, although he hasn't walked far]". The narrator's attitude towards Tetsuya in *In His Image* is identical to that of the narrator in *Floating Clouds* towards Bunzō, and both seem to have their antecedents in Gogol's stories. Adopting a similar wordy manner to the narrator of Gogol's *The Portrait,* the narrator of *In His Image* describes Tetsuya's physical appearance rather comically by repeatedly employing verbs and nouns of similar meaning or form: "tobioriru <u>nari</u>, saka o hashiriagaru <u>nari</u>, [(he) quickly jumps out and runs up the incline]". When Tetsuya realizes the visitor at his home is Hamura, his reaction is described as follows: "<u>odoroki</u>, <u>kaikon</u>, <u>shitsubō</u>, <u>tōwaku</u> sorera ga ichidoni kuwatto kao ni arawarete [a mixed expression of astonishment, regret, disappointment and embarrassment appears on his face all at once]". If we recall that Futabatei's first literary venture was a translation of a work by Gogol (unfortunately now lost), it is not unreasonable to suggest that Futabatei's original writing was influenced in part by Gogol's work.

An interesting article about *In His Image* appeared in 1907 in *Teikoku bungaku.* Its author, who wrote under the pen name "Reishū", appears to have had considerable knowledge of Russian literature. He expresses disappointment that Futabatei merely produced another work of Japanese naturalism, rather than one modeled on Russian naturalism as he had expected Futabatei to write a more Gogolian story. His understanding of Gogol's work is as follows:

> Gogol's comedy, or stories of this kind, make the reader laugh himself into convulsions, yet the reader then realizes there are many tears behind the laughter. These tears are neither destructive nor despairing, but show that the author always retains a deep sympathy for his protagonists. The laughable ignorance, the pitiful servility or hateful crime of the protagonists conceals something with which the reader cannot help sympathizing... (Futabatei Shimei 1964c: 396)

It is this sympathy for the protagonists that Reishū judges to be lacking from *In His Image,* and this is why he judges it to be no more than another work of Japanese naturalism. Yet Reishū does have praise for the first part of the novel up to chapter forty. Up to this point it unfolds smoothly, and he writes: "It may be my imagination, but I feel I am reading one of Gogol's stories" (Futabatei Shimei 1964c: 398). Indeed, as the passages cited above have shown, the way in which Futabatei positions the narrator inside the story, and his mocking attitude towards Tetsuya produce a similar effect to that found in Gogol's stories. This narrative stance is maintained up until chapter thirty-nine, when he makes the mistake of describing Sayoko's inner thoughts, which theoretically would not have been accessible to a narrator positioned within the story. Futabatei's failure in *In His Image* results neither from the similarity of its protagonists to those in *Floating Clouds*, as many critics have suggested, nor from lack of sympathy for the protagonist. It results from inconsistency in the narrator's position or viewpoint, as this is what determines how the author's sympathy is directed towards the protagonist.

The following passages come from chapters thirty-eight and thirty-nine. They show piteous Sayoko leaving her parents' home after a serious quarrel with her sister Tokiko over her rendezvous with Tetsuya.

> 一、此處で又改めて告別の挨拶をする時、隱居は言ふに及ばず、小夜子も思ひの外平氣で、泪一滴零すでもなかつた。が、門口へ出て、待せた車に鞄と合乘をして、車夫が彌轅棒を擧ると、福が挨拶に戸惑ひして、では行つてらツしやいましといふのを聞くと、如何した機か、急に胸が逼つて衝と涙が迸り懸たので、周章て手巾を面に當たまゝ、**あゝ**、哲也も歸らぬ中に、小夜子は遂に弓町の家を離れた**のである**。（三十八）
> ～、生れた家はありながら、夫にさへ住附かれず、かうして獨り淋しくも浮世に流離ふ此身の果は何となる事かと、小夜子は沁々我運命の拙きを嘆く**のであつた**。
> 僂ふれば、今は半年餘りの昔、便る夫に死別れて、悲ない身になつて家へ歸つて來れば、（中略）、慈悲深かつた亡父が坐ろに慕はれて、時々は其筐の寫眞に物を言ふことさへあつた。（三十九） (Futabatei Shimei 1964c: 300-301)

> [... Once again Sayoko said her parting words. Sayoko was unusually calm, her mother-in-law even more so, and neither of them shed a tear. But when she walked to the gate, got into the waiting rickshaw together with her bag, and the driver lifted the shafts ready to start pulling, Fuku, not knowing what to say, stammered out the usual parting words: "Itterasshaimashi!" When Sayoko heard this, somehow she felt her heart suddenly swell, and she felt herself about to burst into tears. She quickly covered her face with her handkerchief. **Alas**, she had left the house in Yumi-chō forever, before Tetsuya had returned home.
> ... Although she had her parents' home, she could not stay there. What would become of her, after wandering alone in this miserable world. When she contemplated her future, Sayoko felt deeply sorry for her own misfortune: "If I count my days back, it was about half a year ago, when I was parted from my husband, upon whom I depended solely, and I returned home as a piteous widow, ... I deeply missed my father, who had been tender, sometimes I would even speak to his photograph.]

The striking feature of these passages is that all the verbs appear in the "-ta" form. Moreover, variations of "-no de aru"—"-ta no de aru" and "-no de atta"—are also found in this passage. These forms, which originated in Kōyō's works, clearly indicate that the narrator is positioned outside the story. The narrator has become omnipresent, and his viewpoint omniscient. Although some of the narrator's humour is retained in the description of Sayoko riding with her heavy bag [kaban to ainori o shite] or in the mistimed and tactless parting words from Sayoko's maid [itterasshaimashi], on the whole the description becomes, in the words of Donald Keene (1984: 114), "dreary, suggesting the worst of the Naturalist school". To the extent that Futabatei shifts the narrator's position from inside to outside the story, the narrator's humour loses the effect of objectifying the main characters and their actions. Instead the narrator subjectifies them, and, with the loss of the narrator's sharp criticism, the whole narrative becomes melodramatic. From chapter thirty-nine on, the narrator's direct comments increase. The following are some typical examples:

1. 一、**あゝ**、哲也も歸らぬ中に、小夜子は遂に弓町（ゆみちやう）の家を離れたのである。（三十八）(Futabatei Shimei 1964c: 300)

[.**Alas**, she had left the house in Yumi-chō forever, before Tetsuya had returned home.]

2. 一、かうして考へてみると、權利は主張するよりも、寧ろ放棄した方が趣味がある。（中略）、しかし考へて見ると、主張は採用せられるよりも、寧ろ排斥せられた方が趣味がある。（中略）、しかし二人して所帶道具を買つて歸るといふ其處に、所帶道具だけに、**非常にソノ**趣味があるのであつた。（四十九）　(Futabatei Shimei 1964c: 323-324)

[...when he thinks about rights, it is much more interesting when one gives them up than when one claims them... when he thinks about advice, it is much more interesting when it is rejected than when it is accepted. .... but they were going home with household articles, **well indeed**, it was interesting because they bought articles for home-making.]

3. 一、と将來は如何にも光明（くわうめい）で多望で天下の幸福を二人で背負（しよ）つて立つやうな空想の夢話をも交へて、我から氣負つて、目を輝かし、拳（こぶし）を揮（ふ）つて、熱心に説くのであつた。（六十四）(Futabatei Shimei 1964c: 353)

[Introducing even his day dreams into his speech, as if their future were very bright and full of hope and all the happiness in the world were theirs, he talked eagerly and enthusiastically while his eyes flashed and his fist gesticulated.]

When all the "-ta no de aru" (six instances) and "-no de atta" forms (twenty-two instances) are examined, it becomes clear that they are employed mainly to describe Tetsuya's (thirteen instances) or Sayoko's (six instances) inner thoughts. The narrator's position outside the story becomes increasingly clear following the quarrel between Tokiko and Sayoko. Before this quarrel the narrator manages to position himself inside the story fairly consistently, and occasional lapses, when he recounts Tetsuya's past or describes his inner thoughts, are not sufficient to disturb the sense that the narrator remains inside the story. This sense is sustained by the predominant use of "-(r)u" forms. Following the quarrel, however, the use of "-ta" forms increases, especially of those expressing the past tense ("-atta", "-no de atta", -ta no de aru" and "-te ita").

Not only the frequency but also the usage of "-no de atta" forms changes. As demonstrated in the first and second passages cited above, "-no de atta" forms at first indicate only a shift in the narrator's position. The narrator retains the garrulous quality inherited from *Floating Clouds* and from Gogolian stories translated by Futabatei. Colloquial expressions such as "ā [alas]", "hijōni sono [well, indeed]" or the deliberately repeated phrase "shumi ga aru (no de atta) [it was interesting]", are examples of this inherited quality. In the third passage, however, the narrator has lost this garrulous quality. The reader no longer hears the narrator's direct utterances and the narrator seems to stop commenting directly on the actions of the main characters. Descriptions become impersonal and objective. The description of Tetsuya, eagerly speaking of their bright future, is very much like the description of Rudin in *Floating Weed*. The resemblance is found not only in what Rudin and Tetsuya are saying and how they are saying it, but also in the way the narrator describes them:

> Все мысли Рудина казались обращенными в будущее; это придавало им что-то стремительное и молодое... Стоя у окна, не глядя ни на кого в особенности, он говорил—... Рудин говорил о том, что придает вечное значение временной жизни человека. (Turgenev 1963c: 269)
>
> [It seemed that all Rudin's thoughts were directed towards the future; this lent him an impetuous and youthful quality... Standing by the window, not looking at anyone in particular, he spoke—and, ... Rudin spoke about what lends eternal significance to man's fleeting life.]
>
> ルーヂンの心は總(すべ)て未來に向つて働く、それ故に何となく勢(いきおひ)が善くて若々としてゐる。窓際に立つたまゝ、誰の顏を見るでもなくて話してゐたが、（中略）……ルーヂンは人の露の命が如何(どう)して不滅のものになるのか、其理由を説いてゐたのである。(Futabatei Shimei 1964b: 38)
>
> [All Rudin's heart longs for the future, so he looks somehow impetuous and youthful. Standing at the window, and looking at nobody in particular, he was talking, ... Rudin was talking about the reason why and how the fleeting life of man becomes eternal.]

Futabatei's translation of the past imperfective verb "govoril [spoke]" as "toite ita no de aru [was talking]" specifically shows that the narrator is positioned outside the story, as he is in the third passage from *In His Image* cited above. The impersonal manner of the description is also a common feature between *Floating Weed* and *In His Image*.

The similarities between *In His Image* and *Floating Weed* have been noted by others, though not as frequently as the similarities with *Floating Clouds*. It has been suggested that the figure of Sayoko owes much to the figure of Natal'ya in *Rudin*. Sayoko's laudable sentiments in asking Tetsuya to work for the socially oppressed remind us of Natal'ya's request to Rudin to work for the sake of others. Shimizu Shigeru (1958: 271) suggests that the creation of Sayoko as one of the main characters sets *In His Image* radically apart from *Floating Clouds* in its characterization and thematic development. Although Shimizu does not point out the direct resemblance between Sayoko's speech and Natal'ya's, he values her words as a positive element in *In His Image,* since they demonstrate Sayoko's wish to transform their self-centred relationship into a more meaningful one. Shimizu notes that the parting letter left by Sayoko for Tetsuya resembles the note left by Asya for the narrator-protagonist in *Asya.* Both notes accuse their recipients of faithlessness in love. Yanagi Tomiko (1971: 54) recognizes a direct influence on the creation of Sayoko's image of female figures from works by Turgenev such as *The Rendezvous, Three Encounters, Asya* and *Rudin.* All the women portrayed in these stories love wholeheartedly and devotedly. They are very unlike Osei in *Floating Clouds,* who spurns Bunzō's devoted love.

Yet the main resemblance between *In His Image* and *Floating Weed* lies in the images of the protagonists, Tetsuya and Rudin. A number of scholars have noted this similarity, and also a similarity in the endings of the two novels (Yoshida Sei'ichi 1965: 141; Odagiri Hideo 1970: 173). Whereas these observations are little more than impressions, Yanagi's analysis goes further, looking at similarities and differences. Yanagi argues that Futabatei created Tetsuya's character on the basis of Rudin, a "superfluous man" who lacks the will and the practical ability to act effectively in the real world. Like Rudin, Tetsuya is unable to act decisively at the most crucial moment, despite his talent and ability. The difference between the two novels is in the relationship between the characters, which is closer and more complex in *In His Image* than in *Rudin*. Yanagi (1971: 62-67) considers it a weakness of *Rudin* that the central character is able to escape so easily and completely from his relationships. Tetsuya cannot escape so easily from his relationships with Tokiko and Sayoko, with whom he is so closely tied by the family system.

Yanagi's argument seems plausible. There are indeed many similarities between *In His Image* and *Rudin,* including the resemblance between the central characters. But is Tetsuya really a "superfluous man"? Even if we accept that he is, did Futabatei portray him in the same way as Turgenev did his protagonist? Tetsuya is no Rudin. He completely lacks the lofty ideals and the impulse to sacrifice himself for the public good, which are the hallmarks of Rudin's character. The similarity of the two novels lies not so much in the portrayal of their protagonists as in their narrative structures.

Togawa Shinsuke (1971: 224) informs us of a letter from Futabatei to his friends Uchida Roan and Nishimoto Sui'in, dated 22 November 1906, in which he confesses he has suddenly lost enthusiasm for writing *In His Image.* Togawa estimates that this would have been before he commenced work on chapter forty. Nakamura Mitsuo (1958: 297) comments that in the second half of *In His Image* the author appears to manipulate the characters as freely as puppets, and consequently the tension of the story is lost.

In the second half of the novel Futabatei often inserts the narrator's direct comments on Tetsuya's words or actions:

> 1. と凝然と小夜子の面を視た目には、成程哲也の所謂或物の影が閃めくやうであつたが、**なに、能く見たら、其は矢張り尋常の戀愛の焔であつたかも知れぬ。**（四十四）(Futabatei Shimei 1964c: 311)

[In the eyes upon which Tetsuya fixed his gaze in Sayoko's face, indeed, there seemed to flicker the 'something' of which he had just spoken, **but if you look at it carefully,**

**it may have been simply the flame of ordinary love**. ]

2. 一句極めて散文的であつたので、哲也は何となく侮辱せられたやうな厭な氣持がして抑へた裾を放したが、**考へて見ると、哲也も氣の毒だ、今日程不出來なことは滅多にない**。（六十五）(Futabatei Shimei 1964c: 357)

[As her words were curt and prosaic, Tetsuya somehow felt bad, as if he had been insulted, and he let go of the bottom of her *kimono*. **Poor Tetsuya, when I look back, he has never failed as badly as he did today**. ]

These comments from a narrator who positions himself outside the story are remarkably similar to comments made by the narrator of *Floating Weed* about the protagonist Rudin:

Зачем же, не прикидываясь даже Ловласом,—эту справедливость отдать ему следует,—сбил он с толку бедную девушку? Отчего ожидал ее с тайным трепетом? **На это один ответ: никто так легко не увлекается как бесстрастные люди**. (Turgenev 1963c: 321)

[Why then, not even pretending to be a Lovelace—one must do him this justice—had he confused the poor girl? Why was he waiting for her with a secret tremor? **There is only one answer: nobody becomes so easily infatuated as those who are without passion.** ]

ルーヂンだと云つて、正可ロウラーイを氣取つてゐるのではない—それは慥に其様なことはないが、それなら何故、氣の毒らしいナターリヤなぞを迷はしたのだか、其理由が解らない。ナターリヤに遭ふのを窃に怕れてゐるのも怪しい。**けれども、情の薄いものに限つて惚れつぽいといふこともあるから、或はそんなことかも知れん**。(Futabatei Shimei 1964b: 97)

[It is hardly likely that Rudin would pretend to be a Lovelace. I am sure he does not. Why then, has he confused poor Natal'ya? I cannot understand this. It is also strange that he is waiting for her with a secret tremor. **Yet they say that nobody is so easily carried away as those who are less passionate. This applies to Rudin**. ]

Unlike the narrators seen hitherto in Gogolian stories, who are cynical but restrained in their description of the main characters' inner thoughts, the narrators in *Rudin* and the second half of *In His Image* freely perceive, explain and comment on these inner thoughts. The omniscient narrator sets himself comfortably outside the story. This leads to a loss of tension between the narrator and main characters and between the main characters themselves. Although the narrator's comments remain cynical, without this tension the cynicism loses its sharpness, and, as in many of Turgenev's stories, we begin to hear the author's voice emerging from behind the narrator's comments.

In *In His Image* Futabatei endeavoured to create convincing characters, as evidenced in his own words: "In writing *In His Image* I set myself the target of creating lifelike puppets. ... Consequently I put an emphasis on the depiction of their characters" (Futabatei Shimei 1965a: 230). These comments, made in February 1908, when the Japanese naturalist writers were in their heyday, show his resistance to their tendency to write confessional works about their own experience. Futabatei at first succeeded in creating realistic characters, though he clearly manipulated them towards the end of the novel. That is why Futabatei abruptly shifted the narrative position from inside to outside the story, which in turn led to his novel becoming merely another work of Japanese naturalism.

When Futabatei attempted to restore the original inside position of the narrator at the end of the novel, with his report on Hamura's prosperity, it was far too late. It only resulted in further incongruity, and the ending has been regarded as a "vestigial trace of *gesaku*" (Washburn 1995: 118), rather than as a Gogolian ending. Let us compare the ending of *In His Image* with that of *Olden Day People,* written just before it:

> Он до сих пор ездит по всем ярмаркам в Малороссии, тщательно осведомляется о ценах на разные большие произведения, продающиеся оптом, **как-то**: муку, пеньку, мед и прочее, но покупает только небольшие безделушки, **как-то**: кремешки, гвоздь прочищать трубку, и вообще все то, что не превышает всем оптом своим цены одного рубля. (Gogol 1874a: 36)
>
> [He still drives about all the markets in the Ukraine, thoroughly enquires about the prices of all sorts of major produce sold wholesale, such as flour, hemp, honey and so on, but purchases only small knick-knacks, such as flints, a nail to clean out his pipe, and generally anything which does not exceed at the most a rouble wholesale.]
>
> 今も此人は小露西亜の市から市と經廻つて、麥粉、麻、蜜**なんど**、大物の卸値を綿密に問合せては、燧石**だの**、烟管掃除の針金の棒**だの**と、卸値にしてから一ルーブル外へは出ぬ、くだらぬ物ばかりを**買歩くさうである**。(Futabatei Shimei 1964c: 211)
>
> **I hear that** this person still goes around all the fairs in Little Russia and thoroughly enquires about the wholesale price of all the major produce **such as** flour, hemp and honey, but he only buys trivial things **such as** flints and a piece of wire to clean his pipe, things which do not exceed at the most a rouble wholesale.]
>
> 時子は母と倶に水戸へ引込んだぎり、是も消息が絶えたが、獨り葉村ばかりは益盛んで、近頃では何會社専務取締役**だの**、何會社相談役**だの**といふ肩書が四ツも五ツも出來て、麹町平河町の天神様の側で立派な門構の家に住つてゐる。相場で儲けたといふ事で、當人は四十迄には屹度馬車に乗つて見せると力**むでゐるさうだ**。兎に角えらい勢である。(Futabatei Shimei 1964c: 381)
>
> [Tokiko has retired to Mito with her mother and we have not heard anything about her

> since then. Hamura alone grows more and more prosperous, and now has four or five titles, **such as** "Director of Such and Such a Company", "Advisor to Such and Such a Company", **and so on**; he lives in a superb house with a gate beside Tenjin Shrine at Hirakawa-chō, Kōji-machi. **I hear that** he has made much money in speculation, and that he is boasting that he is going to have a carriage of his own by the time he is forty years of age. Anyway, he is certainly prospering.]

The inside position of the narrator, shown by the use of "-(r)u" forms, and his garrulousness, demonstrated by the detailed description of insignificant characters (the inheritor in *Olden Day People* and Hamura in *In His Image*), undoubtedly resemble each other.

In summary, when Futabatei began writing *In His Image*, setting the narrator inside the story, he intended to portray the protagonist Tetsuya and his love for Sayoko as objectively as possible. In the Gogolian model, the reader is led, by a narrator set within the story, to feel deep sympathy for the protagonist (in spite of laughing at him). However, Futabatei was not able to sustain the narrator's position inside the story, and shifted it abruptly, in order that the narrator might omnisciently view the inner thoughts of the protagonists. As a result, the narrative point of view in the second half of the novel is extremely close to that found in Turgenev's third-person narrative, *Rudin.* In it the narrator's voice, outside the story, is close to the author's voice. The reader feels the author's direct manipulation of his "puppets". This shift in the narrative viewpoint may have been due to Futabatei's lack of experience in translating Gogolian novels, which would have involved dealing with multiple main characters. Or it may be explained by the fact that the last translation Futabatei made before commencing work on *In His Image* was *Olden Day People*, a complex third-person narrative in which "-ta" forms were used with increasing frequency, due to the clear presence of a narrator who holds a retrospective viewpoint within the story.

# Chapter 8 — 1907: Futabatei's Final Year of Literary Activity

After completing the serialization of his second novel *In His Image* in the *Asahi shinbun,* Futabatei worked continuously on the translation of stories by Gorky and Gogol for journals such as *Shin shōsetsu [New Novel]* and *Shumi [Hobby].* In March 1907 he translated Gorky's *Oshibka [A Mistake]* under the title *Ni kyōjin [Two Madmen].* From March to May of that year he translated Gogol's *Zapiski sumasshedshego [Notes of a Madman]* under the title *Kyōjin nikki [A Madman's Diary].* In July he translated Gorky's *Ded Arkhip i Len'ka [Grandpa Arkhip and Lenka]* under the title *Kojiki [Beggars].* It appears that Futabatei also worked on his translation of Andreyev's *Krasnyi smekh [Red Laughter]* during the summer of 1907 (Minamoto 1989b: 5), and had prepared its manuscript before he began serializing his final novel *Heibon [Mediocrity]* in the *Asahi shinbun* from October to December. His translation of *Red Laughter* appeared the following year under the title *Kesshōki [An Account of Bloodied Laughter],* and was the very last of his literary publications. In June of 1908 Futabatei departed for Russia as a foreign correspondent of the *Asahi shinbun*. He contracted tuberculosis in St. Petersburg and died on the return voyage to Japan in May 1909.

Because Futabatei's selection of stories for translation shows an inclination to treat the themes of death and madness, some scholars have sought to find thematic links between these stories and *Mediocrity.* It would appear, however, that such thematic links are slight, and that Futabatei's interest in translating these stories lay more in their narrative style. Unlike Futabatei's two earlier novels, *Mediocrity* is told in the first-person. More importantly, it is satirical in style. Futabatei himself commented on it as follows:

> About *Mediocrity*, I made a big mistake in writing it. At first I was not intending to make a satire, but because of the material it dealt with I ended up writing a satirical work. I was going to argue my case directly, but once I began writing, somehow it became sarcastic. I tried quite hard to be serious, but I failed. I could not change its sarcastic tone even at the end. In this sense *Mediocrity* is a complete failure. (Futabatei 1965a: 244)

Although Futabatei defines *Mediocrity* as a satire, he might more accurately have called it a parody of the style employed by the naturalist school of writers.[1] *Mediocrity's* style is commented on by none other than the narrator-protagonist himself:

> Next there is the style, but I need not worry about it. They say that of late the fashionable thing is a way of writing naturalism or something, in which the writer sets down all his experiences, no matter how ridiculous, without the least application of art, just as they happened, drop by drop like the drivel of a cow. A good thing it has become fashionable. I, too, shall fall in line. (Futabatei Shimei 1927: 7)

---

[1] According to Cuddon's *Dictionary of Literary Terms and Literary Theory,* "The satirist is a man who takes it upon himself to correct, censure, and ridicule the follies and vices of society" (pp. 827-828). A satire targets society, but *Heibon* targets only the small circle of writers of the naturalist school and their works.

Thus in *Mediocrity* the first-person narrative style is intentionally employed to caricature the works of the Japanese naturalist writers, which are generally written in a third-person narrative style. In this way he exposes the essential nature of their works.

Before Futabatei embarked on writing his own first-person narrative, he translated Gogol's *Notes of a Madman* and Andreyev's *Red Laughter,* which are themselves written in the first-person. By the time Futabatei completed the manuscript of *An Account of Bloodied Laughter* he had experimented with several models of first-person narrative in the course of his translation career. He had begun with *The Tryst* and *A Chance Encounter,* his early translations of Turgenev's *The Rendezvous* and *Three Encounters.* A significant feature of the style of these first translations was the use of "-ta" form verbs to translate verbs of the past tense.

During his second period Futabatei continued to translate first-person narrative stories by Turgenev, but with fundamental modifications to his translation style. In *One-Sided Love* and *The Jew* Futabatei created two streams of time, in a modified style in which the use of "-ta" forms was significantly reduced. In these works Futabatei employed "-(r)u" or "-te iru" form verbs to translate past imperfective verbs used to describe the actions of characters other than the narrator-protagonist, at the same time using "-ta" or "-te ita" form verbs to describe the narrator's own actions.

During the early part of the third period Futabatei extended his translation of first-person narratives to stories by Tolstoy and Garshin. In *A Rifle for a Pillow*, Futabatei adopted the same methods as he had during the second period. However, because of the simplicity of the plot the differentiation in the translation of past imperfective verbs does not result in the creation of two streams of time. The narrator-protagonist's reflections on his own mental state are the most distinctive feature. The focus shifts from the narrated events to the narrator himself.

In *Four Days* the narrative describes a stream of consciousness, displaying the ultimate degree of the narrator's self-absorption. Here Futabatei adheres to the tense of the original verbs, rather than to their aspectual form.

In this chapter we shall focus on Futabatei's further experimentation with first-person narrative style in his translation of Gogol's *Notes of a Madman.*[2] We shall then attempt to trace any stylistic influences from the various first-person narrative translations upon the style of his novel *Mediocrity.* We shall also compare the style of *Mediocrity* with that of Katai's *Futon [The Quilt],* which it parodies. Finally, a brief comparison will be made between Futabatei's style and that developed in Sōseki's *Kōfu [The Miner]* and Tōson's *Haru [Spring].*

Before discussing the first-person narrative of *A Madman's Diary*, we shall briefly examine the third-person narrative style of *Two Madmen*, Futabatei's translation of Gorky's *A Mistake.* In it Futabatei attempts to convert the narrative from third-person to first-person.

---

[2] In order to keep this monograph within acceptable limits, we shall not comment on Futabatei's translations of Andreyev's *Red Laughter* and Gorky's *Grandpa Arkhip and Len'ka.* These are both serious translations, with a relatively high use of "-ta" forms. While their content is worthy of study, a stylistic analysis yields little that is new or conclusive, compared with the analyses already undertaken so far in this study. Readers interested in an analysis of these works should see my doctoral dissertation (Cockerill 2003).

## *Ni kyōjin [Two Madmen]* (from Gorky's *Oshibka [A Mistake]*)

Gorky's *A Mistake* was written in 1894 and published the following year in the Moscow monthly *Russkaya Mysl' [Russian Thought]*, having been first rejected by *Russkoe Bogatstvo [Russian Riches]*, which had published his earlier success *Chelkash.* At the time the chief editor at *Russian Riches* was Nikolai Mikhailovsky, while Vladimir Korolenko was a co-editor. Korolenko, who saw value in the story, explained the reasons for Mikhailovsky's rejection of the story in a letter to Gorky:

> The story seems to him to be aimless, the psychology of the two madmen arbitrary... "The author is undoubtedly talented", writes Mikhailovsky, "He has strength, but there is no sense in waving his arms in empty space, even if they are strong". He expresses the desire that you should rid yourself of a certain artificiality, prolixity and "signs of decadence" (as in *The Sea* and *A Mistake).* (Letter of 23 April 1895, cited in Gorky 1968: 534)

In responding to Mikhailovsky's criticism, however, Gorky did not change his description of the two madmen, but limited the sphere of their actions by cutting out extensive description of their associates. In so doing, Gorky attempted to lay greater emphasis on the clash of wills between the two main characters.

*A Mistake* is the story of an intellectual who takes on the care of a "madman". Due to his close association with the madman for whom he is caring he becomes affected by his insane talk and in his turn loses his sanity. The story is based on Gorky's own experience of caring for a mentally unstable acquaintance named Gol Chitandze, in Tiflis. Chitandze was an intellectual peasant and his features are recognizable in Gorky's creation of the madman Kravtsov. The other character, Yaroslavtsev, possesses features common to intellectuals of the time, who sought new values, but vacillated between old and new.

In *Two Madmen* Futabatei adopts the translation practices found in two earlier translations from Gorky. He consistently employs "-(r)u" forms, particularly "-te iru" forms, to translate past imperfective verbs. He uses mainly "-ta" and "-te shimatta" forms to translate past perfective verbs. The story opens with the retired village teacher Yaroslavtsev staring at a sheet of paper on which appears a statistical table. The narrative is in the third-person. We learn that of late Yaroslavtsev finds it difficult to make sense of the figures on the sheet, and that he is often seized by an incomprehensible anxiety, his imagination conjuring up a phantom who might at any moment visit him:

> Представляя себе такую картину, **Кирилл Иванович** вздрагивал и жалобно смотрел на дверь.
> Дверь была тоненькая и хлибкая, а крючок проволочный. От посещения этого всезнающего существа она не оградит и ничего не оградит от его посещения. **Кириллу Ивановичу** казалось, что оно проникло бы и сквозь каменные стены. И в ожидании его **он** страдал, вздрагивая при каждом шуме и подозрительно присматриваясь к каждому незнакомому человеку,— страдал и чувствовал, что эта тоскливая боязнь с каждым своим возрождением становится все сильнее и охватывает **его** все крепче, и вот-вот она возрастет, поглотит **его**... и тут уж

воображение останавливалось перед чем-то темным и полным леденящего душу ужаса. (Gorky 1908: 147)

[Imagining such a picture, **Kirill Ivanovich** shuddered and plaintively looked at the door.

The door was thin and fragile, and the hook was made of wire. It will not protect him from the visit of that omniscient being and nothing will protect him from its visit. It seemed to **Kirill Ivanovich** that it would even penetrate stone walls. And in expectation **he** suffered, shuddering at every noise and suspiciously examining every stranger—he suffered and felt that each time it returned this melancholy fear grew stronger and gripped **him** more firmly in its embrace and that at any moment it would rise up and swallow **him**... and then his imagination stopped before something dark and full of a terror which froze his soul.]

こんな事を想像しながら、縮み上つて、情なさゝうに入口を視返へる。入口の戸は薄ペラな脆弱い出來で、加之も掛金は針金だ。者奴は萬事見徹しだといふに、そのお見舞ひを此様な物では防げぬ、いや、如何な物でも防げる筈がない、譬へば煉瓦の壁なりとも、スツと其中を抜けて來る奴だ。であるから、之を待つ身になつては、ゴトリといふにも悔として、知らぬ人さへ見れば、胡散さうに其擧動に注意してハラハラする。けれども辛氣な物思は度重なれば益々募つて愈々身に附纏ふ。今一息で之に頭から丸呑にされるかも知れぬ……**と思うと**、何やら眞黒けな慄然とする程凄い物に行當つたやうな心持がして、と胸を突く。(Futabatei Shimei 1964d: 6)

[While imagining these things, (he) shudders and plaintively looks at the door.

The entrance door is thin and fragile, moreover the hook is wire. That fellow is omniscient, how can I guard myself against his visit with such things. Nothing can protect me against him. He is a fellow who could penetrate even through brick walls. So a person like me who is anticipating his visit shudders at a little noise and cautiously examines any stranger and his movements. With each visit the melancholy fear grows stronger and takes a firmer hold on me. Soon it will swallow me up. **With this thought** [he] feels as if he encounters something dark and dreadful which freezes his heart, and [he] is startled.]

In the original, the whole opening scene, describing Kirill Ivanovich's incomprehensible fear, is written mainly using past imperfective verbs. Futabatei, on the other hand, uses mostly "-(r)u" and "-te iru" forms. Kirill Ivanovich's fearful state, and the actions which flow from that fear, are effectively conveyed with the use of these "-(r)u" and "-te iru" forms.

Minamoto Takashi (1997) has written an article tracing Futabatei's influence on Tanizaki Jun'ichirō. He points out that Tanizaki confused *Two Madmen* with *The Depression Bug*. In *Seishun monogatari [Reminiscences of My Youth]* Tanizaki recalls an incomprehensible fear which he and his friends shared. He remembers how deeply their nerves were affected by *The Depression Bug* and *An Account of Bloodied Laughter*. However, from Tanizaki's discussion of the content of the stories, it is clear that he is really referring to *Two Madmen* rather than *The Depression Bug.* His confusion of the two titles points to a significant resemblance between the two stories. There is a striking similarity between the opening scene of *Two Madmen* and that of *The Depression Bug.* Just as the miller Tikhon is seized by an inexplicable melancholy, the teacher Yaroslavtsev is overcome by a melancholic fear. In each opening scene Futabatei's use of verb forms creates similar visual imagery. The main difference is that Yaroslavtsev's fear is more acute, and consequently *Two Madmen* is a less comical story.

When we examine the above passage from *Two Madmen* more closely, we notice another, more subtle, difference, in the treatment of personal nouns and third-person pronouns. Whereas Tikhon's name is mentioned many times in the first four pages of *The Depression Bug,* appearing as "Chihon [Tikhon]" or "konaya no Chihon [the miller Tikhon]", Yaroslavtsev's name appears only twice in the first four pages of *Two Madmen.* Futabatei initially introduces him as "shoku ni hanareta inaka kyōshi no Kirīru Iwānowichi Yarosurāfutsefu [the retired village teacher Kirill Ivanovich Yaroslavtsev]" and subsequently refers to him as "shujin no Yarosurāfutsefu [the master Yaroslavtsev]" when he receives an unexpected visit from his friend. The third-person pronoun is used to refer to Tikhon twice in the first four pages of *The Depression Bug,* but is not used at all in the opening of *Two Madmen.* In fact the third-person pronoun appears only once in the whole story.

As a result of his avoidance of personal nouns and of the third-person pronoun, the narrative of *Two Madmen* at times takes on the appearance of a monologue. This effect is heightened by the use of the "-da" ending, which we observe in the passage already cited from the opening of the story. The ending "-da" expresses the speaker's judgement or affirmation, making the sentence more personal, and giving the appearance of a first-person narrative. The following passage, in which Yaroslavtsev is terrified by his own reflection in a mirror, is another example of this transformation of the narrative in Futabatei's translation:

> **Он** <u>дрогнул</u>, быстро <u>взглянул</u> перед собой и <u>вздохнул</u> свободно и легко: **он** <u>был</u> тут в комнате Кравцова, и под ногами **у него** <u>был</u> пол, твердый пол, в чем **Кирилл Иванович** и <u>убедился</u> сильно надавив его ногой. Тогда **ему** снова страстно <u>захотелось</u> еще раз взглянуть туда, на стену... Осторожно приподнимаясь со стула и в то же время поворачиваясь назад, **он** <u>увидал</u> его, это лицо; но теперь оно <u>было</u> только жалко и, выражая напряженное и боязливое ожидание чего-то, <u>замерло</u> в этой мине. Тут **он** <u>узнал</u> себя, ибо это **он** <u>был</u> весь исполнен ожидания и боязни. (Gorky 1908: 159)
>
> [**He** <u>shuddered</u>, quickly <u>looked</u> in front of him, and <u>sighed</u> freely and easily: **he** <u>was</u> here in Kravtsov's room, and the floor <u>was</u> under **his** feet, the firm floor, of which **Kirill Ivanovich** <u>convinced himself</u> further by pressing firmly on it with his foot. Then **he** again <u>felt</u> a passionate urge to look over there, at the wall... Carefully raising himself from the chair, and at the same time looking over his shoulder, **he** <u>caught sight</u> of it, that face; but now it <u>was</u> only pitiful, and, expressing tense and fearful expectation of something, <u>had frozen</u> in that expression. And now **he** <u>recognized</u> himself, because it was **he** who <u>was</u> completely filled with expectation and fear.]

> 身震ひして、急いで眼を開いて見て、咈と息をした。此處はクラフツォフの部屋で、足の下は床だ、丈夫な床だ。足に力を入れてウンと踏むで見て、それは確かに分つた。かうなると、もう一遍背後の壁が見たい、堪らなく見たい……そつと腰を浮かせながら、振反つて見た。が、此時は壁の顔は唯哀れで、惘々しながら一心に何かを待つ色が眉宇の間に現はれて、其儘其處に居ずくまつて了つた相好だ。尚ほ能く視ると、や、これは**自分**だ、**自分の**取越苦労をした心配面だ！(Futabatei Shimei 1964d: 17-18)

> [[He] shudders and quickly opens [his eyes] and has taken a light breath. This is Kravtsov's room, and there is a floor under [my] feet, a hard floor. [He] has convinced himself of it by pressing firmly with [his] foot. Then [he] wants to look over there at the wall behind [him] once again, [he] awfully wants to do so... Raising [himself] slightly from the chair, [he] has looked over his shoulder. Yet this time the face on the wall is simply pitiful, and an expression of anticipation of something appears in an absorbed and cowardly fashion on his face and freezes there. Looking at it more carefully, oh, this is **me**, [it is] **my** anxious face full of needless worries.]

The original is written in the past tense, with mixed aspectual forms. While the perfective past tense is used to describe Yaroslavtsev's successive actions, the imperfective past tense (principally of "byt' [to be]") is used to describe his perceptions or convictions. Futabatei translates the past perfective verbs as "-ta" forms expressing complete aspect. Past imperfective verbs are translated with the use of "-da" endings, which express Yaroslavtsev's strong conviction or unexpected recognition. By completely eliminating the use of personal nouns and third-person pronouns, and with the use of "-da" endings, Futabatei converts the whole passage into Yaroslavtsev's monologue. In particular, the use of "jibun [I]" in the last sentence completes transformation of a third-person narrative into the protagonist's first-person internal monologue.

In *Two Madmen* there are twenty-two instances of "-da" endings and up to eighteen instances are employed in the transformation of third-person narratives to first-person monologues. Although Futabatei gave his translation the title *Two Madmen,* it would appear Yaroslavtsev is the main protagonist. In converting part of the narrative to Yaroslavtsev's monologue, he becomes the focus of the story.

Another interesting feature of this translation is that while most past perfective verbs are translated as "-ta" forms, the treatment given to past imperfective verbs varies. We have come to expect imperfective past tense verbs to be translated as "-te iru" forms, emphasizing aspectual meaning. In this translation, however, an almost equal number are translated as "-te ita" form verbs, expressing the past tense. These "-te ita" form verbs appear in the following two cases. When the focus of the narrative is on Yaroslavtsev, to the extent that it becomes a first-person narrative, his recollections are often conveyed using "-te ita" form verbs expressing the past tense. Then, towards the end of the story, when the narrator reasserts his presence, "-te ita" form verbs are used to objectively give an account of the main characters' actions, as shown in the following examples:

1. **Кирилл Иванович** давно уже поднял голову и стал перед койкой на колени, все обнимая ноги Кравцова. Теперь он закинул голову немного назад и с восхищением смотрел в лицо Кравцова, не отрываясь ни на секунду от него. (Gorky 1908: 169)

[**Kirill Ivanovich** had long lifted his head and had knelt by the bed, still embracing Kravtsov's legs. Now he had thrown his head back slightly and was gazing at Kravtsov's face with rapture, not turning away from him even for a second.]

**ヤロスラーフツェフは**疾から面を擧げて、クラフツォフの足を抱いたまゝ、寢臺の前に跪いてゐたが、演説の終る頃には、少し反身になつて、あからめもせず相手の面に視入り、ほとほと感に堪へてゐた。(Futabatei Shimei 1964d: 28)

[**Yaroslavtsev** had long lifted his head up and knelt by the bed, still embracing Kravtsov's legs. Towards the end of the talk he threw his head back slightly and looked at his companion without blushing, and was deeply struck with admiration.]

2. **Трое людей** стояли и смотрели на него тоже с каким-то боязливым любопытством и догадкой. (Gorky 1908: 172-173)

[**Three people** were standing and looking at him, also with a kind of timorous curiosity and conjecture.]

**視廻された方も**其處に衝立つて不審がつた危險さうな面で、矢張相手の面をヂロヂロ視てゐた。(Futabatei Shimei 1964d: 32)

[**The people who were being watched** were also standing there and staring at him timidly and suspiciously.]

These examples clearly show the re-emergence of the narrator towards the end of the *Two Madmen.* Futabatei translates the subjects of sentences faithfully and in combination with the use of "-te ita" form verbs this clearly indicates the presence of the narrator outside the story.

It is thus clear that in *Two Madmen* Futabatei initially continued the general practices found in his earlier translations from Gogol and Gorky. Although some comic element remains, Futabatei's focus in *Two Madmen* was on the psychology of Yaroslavtsev, who is going mad under the influence of another man's insanity. Futabatei partly transforms the third-person narrative of *A Mistake* by converting part of the narrative to Yaroslavtsev's monologues. In this transformation of the narrative, Futabatei appears to be paving the way for his next translation, that of Gogol's *Notes of a Madman,* a first-person narrative devoted entirely to the psychology of a man who is going insane.

## *Kyōjin nikki [A Madman's Diary]* (from Gogol's *Zapiski sumasshedshego [Notes of a Madman]*)

Gogol wrote *Notes of a Madman* during 1833 and 1834. His notes reveal that he initially intended to give his story the title *Zapiski sumasshedshego muzykanta [Notes of a Mad Musician].* Apparently Gogol was fascinated by the stories in Odoevsky's *Dom sumasshedshikh [The Madhouse],* which dealt with the theme of the imaginary or real madness of highly-gifted musicians such as Bach, Piranesi and Beethoven. The central character of *Notes of a Madman* turned out to be not a talented musician, but a low-ranking official. This was due in part to the influence of a preceding, unfinished work of his own, the drama *Vladimir tret'ei stepeni [Vladimir of the Third Degree].* In it Gogol attempted to portray an official whose ambition was to earn a Vladimir medal of the third degree. When he is unable to achieve this goal, he goes mad and imagines that he has become the award he so covets. It has also been observed that Gogol's own experience of serving as an official in the Russian bureaucracy casts a shadow over these works (Gogol 1973b: 697-705).

The most striking feature of *Notes of a Madman* is its first-person narrative style. Although some of Gogol's other stories, such as *Nos [The Nose]*, feature low-ranking officials, *Notes of a Madman* is the only one written as a first-person narrative:

> *Notes of a Madman,* specifically as *notes,* i.e. the protagonist's account of himself, have neither precedent nor analogy in Gogol's work. ... The theme of madness in all the three simultaneous aspects (social, aesthetic, and personal-biographical) which Gogol found in it, could be most naturally developed in the direct speech of the protagonist, ... (Gogol 1973b: 704)

Richard Peace makes a similar observation regarding the title of the story:

> The story is usually translated as the 'diary' of a madman, but more accurately it should be 'notes' (*zapiski*). The fact that it purports to be a written self-revelation is important, since the concept of writing is central to the whole work. (Peace 1981: 125)

When Futabatei selected this story for translation he must have recalled that the very first story he translated for publication was Turgenev's *Rendezvous* from the collection *Zapiski okhotnika [A Sportsman's Sketches].* In the case of Turgenev's work, translating *zapiski* as "sketches" focuses attention on the characters who are described in the work, rather than on the narrator. In the case of Gogol's work, translating *zapiski* as "a diary" focuses attention on the author of the notes. These notes, moreover, ironically reveal the author's inability to write coherently, despite his having to write in the daily course of his duties. The "notes" written by Gogol's protagonist are far less edited and systematic than those of Turgenev's "sportsman". Consequently, whilst *The Rendezvous* is written mostly in the past tense, reflecting the narrator's fixed retrospective point of view, the tense forms in *Notes of a Madman* frequently shift from past to present.

In *Notes of a Madman* the isolated and middle-aged Poprishchin, a low-ranking and incompetent civil servant, is secretly in love with his director's daughter, Sophie. When his love is not reciprocated he goes mad, retreating into the illusion that he is the king of Spain in order to free himself from a feeling of insecurity. The story ends "with a tragic monologue from the main character" (Araya 1967: 64). This tragic ending is, however, capped off with a comic inversion. At the very end of the story Poprishchin despairingly cries out for help in the mental asylum:

> Матушка, спаси твоего бедного сына. Урони слезинку на его больную головушку! посмотри, как мучат они его! прижми ко груди своей бедного сиротку! ему нет места на свете! его гонят!— Матушка, пожалей о своем больном дитятке!... **А знаете ли, что у Алжирского дея под самым носом шишка?** (Gogol 1874b: 272)[3]

> [Mother, save your poor son! Shed a tear on his aching head! See how they are torturing him! Press a poor orphan to your breast! There is no place for him in this world! He is persecuted! — Mother, have pity on your poor sick little child! **... And did you know that the Bey of Algiers has a lump right under his nose?** ][4]

> 阿母(おつか)さん、お前の倅(せがれ)は憂き目を見てゐる、助けて下され、助けて！切(せ)めて哀れを泣いて下され！これ、こんなに憂目を見てるでないか！便りない兒を抱締めて下され！己や此世に身の置處(おきどころ)がない。虐(いぢ)められてるぞい！阿母(おつか)さん、病身の兒を可哀(かはい)さうだと思つて下され！……**ときに、アルジールの王樣の鼻の下に瘤(こぶ)が出來たを御存じかい？** (Futabatei Shimei 1964d: 60)

> [Mother, your son is suffering misery, save me please! Just cry over your pitiable son! See how he is suffering misery! Embrace a poor orphan tightly! There is no place for me in this world. He is persecuted. Have pity on your sick little child. **...By the way, did you know that the King of Algiers has a lump right under his nose?**]

Richard Peace (1981:125) regards this famous ending as the most striking example of the Gogolian formula "laughter through tears". The final sentence is "not 'laughter' which mocks the preceding 'tears', it is rather a sudden tension projected on to the mood of pathos, which heightens and sharpens its impact". *Notes of a Madman* thus creates a tension between tears and laughter, and Futabatei's translation reproduces that tension brilliantly with its familiar colloquial style.

In order better to appreciate Futabatei's translation, let us compare it with two other Japanese translations of the same passage, the first made by Imano Gukō in 1889, and the second made by Yokota Mizuho in 1976:

---

[3] Because of the strict political censorship of the time, Gogol was unable to use the expression "the king of France", which appears in later editions. I have used this early edition as it was apparently the one used by Futabatei in his translation.

[4] Adapted from Constance Garnett's translation (Gogol 1923: 162).

1. 嗚呼母よ、汝の哀れなる子を救へ、汝が子のうな垂れたる熱鐵の頭上に汝が一滴の涙を注げ。見よ、汝の子は今や無實の罪を受けて他人の爲に苦められ虐げらる。希がはくは汝の寄邊なき子を抱き去て只汝の胸に睡らしめよ。汝の子は鞭うたれ踏にじらる。天下廣しと雖も復た汝の子を居くに處なし。嗚呼母よ、只汝の便なき子を不便と思へ……**汝はアルジーヤの總督は鼻下に疣あるを知る乎、（疣は贅肉のみ、而も截べからず、）噫、噫、噫、**（結） (Gogol 2000: 199)

[Mother, save your poor child, shed a tear on the drooping, iron-hot head of your son. Look, your son is now falsely accused and suffering for someone else. It is to be hoped that you will press your lonely son to your breast and let him sleep. Your child is whipped and trampled. There is no place for your child in this wide world. Mother, have mercy on your pitiable child**... Did you know that the governor-general of Algiers has a wart under his nose (a wart is superfluous flesh, yet it cannot be removed). Oh, oh, oh.**]

2. おっ母さん、このあわれな息子を救っておくれ！この痛い頭に、せめて一滴、涙を注いでおくれ！あんたの息子がどんなにひどい目にあわされているか、まあ見ておくれよ！このあわれな孤児を胸に抱きとっておくれよ！広い世の中に身のおきどころがないんだ！みんなが追いかけてくる！—おっ母さん、この病気の息子をあわれんでおくれよ！……**ところでご存じですかね、アルジェリアの総督の鼻の下には瘤があるのを？**

[Mother, save your poor son! Shed a tear on his aching head! See how awfully his is tortured! Press a poor orphan to your breast! There is no place for him in this world! Everyone is persecuting me! — Mother, have pity on your sick son! **...By the way, did you know that the governor-general of Algeria has a lump right under his nose?**]

Yokota's translation is clearly the most literal, while that by Imano Gukō departs most from the original, not only through the free insertion of additional material, but also in its style, which may be characterized as *kanbun kundoku tai,* (a translation style which results from adding Japanese grammatical particles to traditional Chinese text). In Imano's version there is no stylistic difference between Poprishchin's desperate plea for help and the last sentence with its sudden comic inversion and consequent tension. In Futabatei's version, on the other hand, Poprishchin's cries for help are translated in the polite form, while the final incongruous sentence is translated in the plain form and a colloquial style. In this regard, Futabatei's version is not as literal as Yokota's, yet it brilliantly conveys the tension created by the sudden inversion from tragedy to comedy of the original.

In Futabatei's translation the stylistic dynamism, the shift in form from polite to plain (or vice-versa) often produces the effect of revealing Poprishchin's strange character as a minor civil servant, a mixture of subservience and arrogance. The following passages demonstrate how skillfully Futabatei reproduces the complexity of Poprishchin's oppressed character by employing polite "-desu/-masu" forms:

> 1. Правда, у нас за то служба благородная, чистота во всем такая, какой во веки не видеть губернскому правлению, столы из красного дерева, **и все начальники на *вы***. Да, признаюсь, если бы не благородство службы, я бы давно оставил департамент. (Gogol 1874b: 253)
>
> [It is true, on the other hand, our workplace is top class, the cleanliness everywhere is such as you will never see in a provincial office, the desks are mahogany, **and all the heads address us in the polite form *vy***. I must confess, if it were not for the high standards of the workplace, I would have left the department long ago.]
>
> 其代り吾儕(われわれ)の勤向(つとめむき)は高尚なものだて、此様(こんな)な綺麗づくめは縣廳じや一生經(た)つても見られやしない、何しろテーブルはマホガニイと來る、**長官は皆(みんな)君ツて言ひます**。かう上品でなかつたら、己(おれ)は疾(とつ)くに役所を退(ひ)いてる所なんだ。(Futabatei Shimei 1964d: 39)
>
> [On the other hand our workplace is top class, you will never see such a high standard of cleanliness as ours in a provincial office, for instance, our desks are made of mahogany **and all the heads address us in the polite form**. I must confess that if there weren't high standards at work, I would have left the department long ago.]
>
> 2. Письмо писано очень правильно. Пунктуация и даже буква ъ везде на своем месте. **Да этак просто не напишет и наш начальник отделения**, хоть он и толкует, что где-то учился в университете. Посмотрим далее: (Gogol 1874b: 260)
>
> [The letter is written very correctly. The punctuation is correct and even the letter 'ъ' is everywhere in the right place. **Even our head of department could not write like that**, though he tells us that he studied at some university or other. Let us read on: ]
>
> や、文句になつてる。句讀(くとう)の切方も、假名遣(かなづか)ひも、間違つてないやうだ。課長は何處かの大學に居たつて威張るけど、**かうは書けません**。それから、—— (Futabatei Shimei 1964d: 47)
>
> [Well it reads well. It seems that the punctuation and the use of *kana* are all correct. **Even the head of our section cannot write this well**, although he tells us pompously that he studied at some university or other. Let us read on…]

The complexity of Poprishchin's character as a civil servant, his timid humility towards his superiors and bold arrogance towards subordinates or clients, is skillfully reproduced with the use of the polite form. Whenever he speaks of his supervisors, no matter what he says about them, Futabatei has Poprishchin use the polite "-desu" or "-masu" forms. Normally these forms would primarily convey respect for the listener or reader, and Poprishchin's use of them here is inappropriate, revealing his incapability of writing coherently and providing further evidence of his mental instability. In the second passage just cited from Poprishchin's notes, where he reads the letters exchanged between two dogs (one of which is the lapdog belonging to Sophie), he politely criticizes his superior's inability to write properly, closing his eyes to his own lack of ability. The first passage reveals the importance Poprishchin attaches to formal politeness, while the second shows the superficiality of that politeness, when it can just as easily clothe disrespectful comments.

In the latest translation, by Yokota, the same passages are translated in the plain form:

> 上役の連中だってみんなあなた言葉だ。
>
> [**All the senior officials address us using the you word [anata kotoba]**.]
>
> うちの課長なんか、どこかの大学をでたと言っているが、**とてもこんなふうにちゃんと書けやしない**。 (Gogol 1983: 175, 191)
>
> [**The head of our section cannot write as properly as this one**, although he tells us that he graduated at some university.]

In the first example, whereas Yokota translates the polite form "vy [you]" directly as "anata kotoba [you word]", Futabatei uses the standard form for addressing a subordinate "kimi [you]", conveying Poprishchin's superior's politeness with the use of the "-masu" form ("kimi tte īmasu [[They] politely address us with kimi [you]]"). Yokota attempts a foreignizing strategy in his rendition of "vy", but the result is rather ambiguous. Although Futabatei's use of the polite form "-masu" does not directly reflect the grammatical form of the original, it brilliantly conveys Poprishchin's subservience. In successfully conveying the cultural content of the original, Futabatei might be said to be adopting a foreignizing strategy.

The following example of the use of the polite form presents further evidence of Futabatei's loyalty to the cultural values of the original:

> **Хотелось бы заглянуть** туда, на ту половину, где ее пр-во, вот куда **хотелось бы мне!** в будуар, как там стоят все эти **баночки, скляночки**, цветы такие, что и дохнуть на них страшно, как лежит там разбросанное ее платье, больше похожее на воздух, чем на платье. **Хотелось бы заглянуть** в спальню... там-то, я думаю, чудеса, там-то, я думаю, рай! **Посмотреть бы ту скамеечку**, на которую она становит, вставая с постели, свою **ножку**, как надевается на эту **ножку** белый как снег **чулочек**... ай! ай! ай! ничего, ничего ... молчание. (Gogol 1874b: 258)
>
> [**I would like to peep in** there, on that side, where Her Excellency is, that is where **I would like to go!** Into her boudoir, where all those **little jars and phials** are standing, where the flowers are such that one is afraid to breathe on them, where her discarded dress is lying, more like air than like a dress. **I'd like to peep into** her bedroom... I think there must be marvels there, I think it must be heaven there! **I'd like to see the**

> **little bench** on which she rests her **little foot** when she gets up from her bed, how a stocking white as snow is pulled on to that **little foot** ...Oh, dear me! Never mind, never mind... silence.]

> お奥が**覗いて見たいな。一寸覗いて見たい。お居間**が見たい。屹度種々な瓶だの壜だのを列べてあるだらう。花なんぞは息氣をするのも氣遣ひというふのがあるね。衣服なぞが取散らしてあります。此奴も衣服といふよりは寧ろ烟か何ぞのやうに見えようといふものだ。**お寢間**も**覗いて見たいな**……屹度見事だ、極楽みたやうだらう。**お起になると、**可愛らしい**お御足**を**お載けなさる**臺がある筈だ。**それも見たいな！**その**お御足**へ雪のやうに白い靴下をかう**お穿かせ申す**……へっ畜生、何も言ふな……内所々々と。
> (Futabatei Shimei 1964d: 44-45)

> [**I would love to peep in** the back of the house. **I would love to have a look at it**. I want to see her boudoir. There must be many jars and phials standing there. The flowers are such that I must be extra careful breathing on them. Her dress is lying there and others scattered around. Her dress looks more like air. **I would love to peep into** her bedroom... It must be splendid, it must look like heaven, I think. There should be a stand, where she puts her lovely tiny foot when she gets out from the bed. **It is lovely to see it** too. Then I pull her snowy white stocking over her lovely tiny foot like this... Oh, dear me, I shouldn't say anything... better be silent.]

Although Futabatei goes beyond the original in making Poprishchin imagine himself pulling on the stocking, the use of the polite form is striking. "Hana nanzo wa iki o suru no mo kizukai to iu no ga aru ne [The flowers are such that I must be extra careful]" and "kimono nazo ga torichirashite ari masu [her dress is lying there and others scattered around]" reveal Poprishchin's obsequiousness, self-satisfaction and rapture at the images thrown up by his imagination. Yokota translated the same words as follows:

> 一、また息を吹きかけるのも気がとがめるようないろいろな花々が置いてあるだろう、またそこにはあのかたの衣装などもぬぎ捨ててあって、一
> (Gogol 1983: 186)

> [... there stand various flowers, on which you dare not to breathe, and also her dress and others scattered around...]

It is apparent that Poprishchin's character emerges far more strikingly in Futabatei's version than in Yokota's, as a result of the use of the polite form. We can almost hear Poprishchin's self-satisfied mutterings as he pens his notes. Futabatei is also more successful in reproducing the effect created by the characteristically Gogolian repetition of the words "khotelos' by zaglyanut' [I would like to peep]". In translating these words as "nozoite mitai na [I would love to peep into]", Futabatei personalizes Poprishchin's monologue with the use of the particle "na", which emphasizes its colloquial nature.

Referring to the same passage, Hatano Kazuhiro (1994: 75-79) suggests that while Futabatei's translation may not be faithful in a literal sense, it is faithful to the overall content. Gogol employs a number of diminutive forms such as "banochki [little jars]", "stklyanochki [little phials]", "nozhka [little foot]" and "chulochki [little stockings]", to reveal Poprishchin's infatuation for the director's daughter. Although Futabatei does not find an adequate Japanese form for each of these diminutives, he employs numerous honorific forms, not only for nouns but also for verbs. Honorific forms such as "oima [her boudoir]", "onema [her bedroom]", and "omiashi [her feet]", for nouns, and "ohin ni naru to [when she gets up][5] ", "onokke nasaru [she puts]", and "ohaka se mōsu [I pull on [the stocking] for her]", for verbs, are effective in conveying Poprishchin's humble position and his longing for Sophie.

Hatano also notes Futabatei's treatment of proper nouns such as "Gorokhovaya [Street]" or "Meshchanskaya [Street]", which are translated as "mame chō [Peas Town]" and "chōnin machi [Tradesmen's Town]". Futabatei chooses to domesticate these place names rather than adopt the more conventional practice of using *katakana* to give an approximate phonetic equivalent. Even Imano's translation, made eight years prior to Futabatei's, adopts the *katakana* versions "Gorohowaya dōri [Gorokhovaya Street]" and "Meshichansukaya dōri [Meshchanskaya Street]". Hatano suggests that Futabatei chose the domesticated versions not simply to produce a comic effect, but also to make the names more meaningful in the overall context of the story. He suggests that the following passage exemplifies this approach.

> Я терпеть не люблю капусты, запах которой валит из всех мелочных лавок в **Мещанской**; к тому же из-под ворот каждого дома несет такой ад, что я, заткнув нос, бежал во всю прыть. (Gogol 1874b: 259)
>
> [I cannot stand cabbage, the smell of which wafts from all the small shops on **Meshchanskaya Street**; besides which from under the gate of every house there reeks such an infernal stench, that, blocking my nose, I ran as fast as my legs could carry me.]
>
> 己(おれ)はキャベヂが大嫌だが、**町人町**の小店の前を通ると、其臭(にほひ)が紛々(ぷんぷん)するのに、何處の家でも屹度(きツと)門の下からおッそろしい臭氣を放つので己は鼻に蓋(ふた)をして一生懸命に駈け抜けた。(Futabatei Shimei 1964d: 45)
>
> [I hate cabbage with a vengeance, when I pass by the little shops in **Tradesmen's Town** they stink terribly of cabbage, besides which all the houses release such an infernal stench from under their gates that I ran as fast as my legs could carry me, holding my nose.]

Futabatei's use of "chōnin machi [Tradesmen's Town]" helps the reader to appreciate Poprishchin's attitude towards lower-class people in general.

We thus see that there are both domesticating and foreignizing elements in this translation. The use of polite and honorific forms and the translation of proper names according to their

---

[5] This is the particular form used by ladies of the court.

meaning are domesticating strategies. Yet these very strategies contribute to Futabatei's success in conveying the cultural phenomenon behind the story, that of a Russian civil servant in whom obsequiousness and arrogance are incongruously combined.

We should now direct our attention to Futabatei's treatment of verb forms, to see whether in this area he adopted more of a domesticating or foreignizing strategy. In all the passages we have cited thus far, both the original and the translation are written mainly in the present tense. Only in the last passage cited do we find in the original the imperfective past tense verb "bezhal [ran]", which interestingly Futabatei translates in the past tense, using the "-ta" form, as "kakenuketa [[I] ran through]". This sentence is typical of the whole entry in the diary from which it is taken, with its complex mix of tense forms. Donald Fanger (1979: 117) points out that all the other diary entries, with the exception of the one in which Poprishchin reads the correspondence between two dogs, are "conventionally retrospective, summarizing the day's happenings and reflecting on them". In the original most entries begin using past tense verbs of perfective or imperfective aspect. Futabatei generally translates these using the "-ta" forms. The following are typical examples of the openings of diary entries:

1. Сегодняшнего дня случилось необыкновенное приключение. (Gogol 1874b: 252)

[An unusual adventure happened today.]

今日は餘程(よっぽど)變な事があつた。(Futabatei Shimei 1964d: 38)

[Today a peculiar adventure happened.]

2. Сегодня среда, и потому я был у нашего начальника в кабинете. (Gogol 1874b: 255)

[Today is Wednesday, and so I was at the office of our head of department.]

今日は水曜だから、局長の官邸の方へ出勤した。(Futabatei Shimei 1964d: 41)

[Since it is Wednesday today, I went to the office of the head of our department.]

3. Я сегодня все утро читал газеты. (Gogol 1874b: 265)

[Today I read newspapers all morning.]

今朝は新聞ばかり讀んでた。(Futabatei Shimei 1964d: 53)

[This morning I only read the papers.]

4. Я было уже совсем хотел идти в департамент, но разные причины и размышления меня удержали. (Gogol 1874b: 265)

> [I was already quite wanting to go to the department, but various reasons and reflections detained me.]
>
> 餘程役所へ行かうかと思つたが、種々仔細があつて屈託してゐたから止めた。(Futabatei Shimei 1964d: 53)
>
> [I was almost ready to go to the department, but I decided not to go, as I was depressed for various reasons.]

These are the openings of the entries written before Poprishchin completely succumbs to madness. Futabatei translates both imperfective and perfective past tense verbs as "-ta" forms expressing the past tense, reflecting the retrospective viewpoint of the original.

When we examine the use of "-ta" forms in *A Madman's Diary*, we find the following. While the number of "-ta" forms used to translate past perfective verbs, with fifty-five instances, makes it still the dominant use, the number used to translate past imperfective verbs, at twenty-four, is unusually high compared with other translations Futabatei made from Gogol. Of the fifty-five instances where "-ta" forms are used to translate past perfective verbs, nine are of the form "-te shimatta", emphasizing perfective aspect. Of the twenty-four instances where past imperfective verbs are translated, five are of the form "-te ita", emphasizing the meaning of the past tense. Thus, "-ta" forms are used in *A Madman's Diary* to express both past tense and perfective aspect. In particular, "-ta" forms used to translate past perfective verbs appear to carry the meaning both of past tense and of perfective aspect. The following is the diary entry written in a state of complete mental confusion with the heading "Yanvar' togo zhe goda, sluchavshiisya posle fevralya [January of the same year, falling after February]":

> До сих пор не могу понять, что это за земля Испания. Народные обычаи и этикеты двора совершенно необыкновенны. Не понимаю, не понимаю, решительно не понимаю ничего. Сегодня выбрили мне голову, несмотря на то, что я кричал изо всей силы о нежелании быть монахом. Но я уже не могу и вспомнить, что было со мною тогда, когда начали мне на голову капать холодною водою. Такого ада я еще никогда не чувствовал. Я готов был впасть в бешенство, так что едва могли меня удержать. (Gogol 1874b: 271)
>
> [I still cannot understand what sort of country Spain is. The national customs and court etiquette are really most peculiar. I do not understand, I do not understand, I really do not understand at all. Today they shaved my head, even though I shouted at the top of my voice of my unwillingness to become a monk. But I cannot even recall what possessed me when they began to splash cold water on my head. Never before had I gone through such hell. I was prepared to fall into such a fury that they could barely restrain me.]
>
> 今だに未だ西班牙といふ國の本體が分らん。國風も宮中の儀式も皆世間並を外れてゐる。どうも變挺で、不思議で、譯が分らん。今日も己は坊さんになるのは厭だつて一生懸命に喚いたけれども、無理に頭を剃られて了

つた。冷水(ひやみず)を頭から打掛(ぶツか)けられる時には全(まる)で夢中だつた。あんな厭な想(おもひ)を爲(し)たのは生れて初てだ。狂人(きちがひ)のやうになつて騒いだが、大勢に抑へつけられて了つて。(Futabatei Shimei 1964d: 58)

[I still cannot understand what sort of country Spain is. People's customs and court etiquette are really extraordinarily unusual. They are so unusual and peculiar that I cannot understand them at all. A strange thing happened today too. Although I shouted as loud as I could that I did not want to be a monk, they shaved my head by force. When they poured cold water over my head, I lost all my senses. It is the first time I experienced such an unpleasant thing. I shouted in a frenzy, but I was held down by many people.]

As we can see from this passage, Poprishchin's diary is often written with mixed tense forms. Past perfective verbs consequently carry the meanings of both past tense and complete aspect. Hence in *A Madman's Diary* Futabatei emphasized neither the aspectual meaning of completion of past perfective verbs, nor the continuous aspect of past imperfective verbs. All the "-te iru" forms found in this translation are employed to translate present imperfective verbs, and not past imperfective verbs as found in earlier translations. Of the eleven instances of "-te iru" forms in *A Madman's Diary,* ten are used to translate present tense verbs. The only exception is used, unexpectedly, to translate a past perfective verb:

В восемь часов отправился в департамент. Начальник отделения показал такой вид, как будто бы он не заметил моего прихода. Я тоже с своей стороны, как будто бы между нами ничего не было. Пересматривал и сверял бумаги. Вышел в четыре часа. Проходил мимо директорской квартиры, но никого не было видно. После обеда большею частью лежал на кровати. (Gogol 1874b: 258)

[At eight o'clock I set off for the department. The head of the section gave the appearance that he did not notice my arrival. I too, for my part, [pretended] as if there were nothing between us. I examined and checked papers. I left at four o'clock. I walked past the director's apartment, but there was no one to be seen. After dinner I mainly lay on my bed.]

八時に役所へ行つた。己(おれ)が行つても、課長奴知らん顔をしてゐる。己も負けずに澄してゐた。書類を檢(しら)べたり讀合(よみあはせ)をしたりして、四時に退(ひ)いた。局長の官邸の側を通つたが、誰の姿も見えずさ。晩餐後(ばんめしご)は大方寢臺(ねだい)の上でごろごろしてゐた。(Futabatei Shimei 1964d: 44)

[At eight o'clock I set off for the office. The head of the section pretends not to take any notice of my arrival [at the office]. For my part I also pretended to look unconcerned. I checked and read through the documents and left the office at four o'clock. I passed by the directors official residence, but there was no-one to be seen. After dinner, most of the time I was lying on my bed.]

The exceptional attentiveness to the translation of verb tense which is found here has hitherto been observed only in *Four Days*, *The Tryst* and *A Chance Encounter.* Apart from the single exception just noted, all the verbs in this and the preceding passages correspond closely in tense with the verbs in the original. While *Four Days* describes the stream of consciousness of a wounded soldier, using mainly present tense verbs, *Notes of a Madman* depicts the process by which Poprishchin's rational reflection about past events is gradually overtaken by his sick imagination, with increasing use of present tense verbs. The use of present tense verbs reaches a peak in the passage where Poprishchin imagines he is reading letters exchanged by two dogs. The use of the past tense, on the other hand, is an indication that Poprishchin is still in touch with reality, though cognizance of that reality dwindles away, as shown in the above passage. Futabatei's exceptional attentiveness to present and past tense forms in *A Madman's Diary* is necessary in order to accurately reproduce the portrayal of Poprishchin's gradual descent into insanity. The following is the beginning of the diary entry which reveals beyond doubt that Poprishchin has become insane.

> Год 2000 апреля 48 числа
> Сегодняшний день есть день величайшего торжества! В Испании есть король. Он отыскался. Этот король я. Именно только сегодня об этом узнал я. Признаюсь, меня вдруг как будто молнией осветило. (Gogol 1874b: 266)
>
> [The year 2000. 48th April.
> Today is a day of great celebration! Spain has a king. He has been found. I am that king. I only discovered this today. I must confess [the realization] came to me like a bolt of lightning.]
>
> 第二千年四月四十八日
> 今日は非常にお目出度い日だ！西班牙(スペイン)に王様はござる。見付かつた。その王様といふのは斯くいふ拙者だ。今日になつて初て分つた。宛然(まるで)目が偶(ふ)と覺めたやうな氣持がする。(Futabatei Shimei 1964d: 53)
>
> [April 48th 2000.
> Today is a day of great celebration. There is a king in Spain. He has been found. That king is me. Only today I discovered this. I feel as if I have suddenly woken up and realized it.]

Poprishchin's insanity is revealed in the confused date at the head of the diary entry and in Poprishchin's impossible delusions, and this revelation is facilitated by the use of the present tense. Once again Futabatei attempts to reproduce the tense forms of the original, employing the auxiliary verb "-da" and "-(r)u form verbs, and this may be considered to be evidence of a foreignizing strategy in respect of the translation of verbs. Indeed the overall strategy of the translation may be deemed to be a foreignizing one. Even those features which might be considered elements of a domesticating strategy (the use of polite form and honorifics, translation of proper nouns according to their meaning) serve the purpose of describing a foreign cultural phenomenon: the peculiar two-faced mentality fostered by Russia's hierarchical civil service.

Unlike earlier translations from Gogol's third-person narrative stories, Futabatei emphasizes not the aspectual meaning, but the tense of the original verb forms. Futabatei may have realized, when translating the first-person narrative of *Notes of a Madman,* that the use of the present tense was indicative of the mental instability of the narrator-protagonist. He may have noted the striking contrast with the tense forms used in Turgenev's first-person narratives, where the predominant use of the past tense is indicative of the mental stability of the narrator, and guarantees a firm retrospective point of view. When the boundary between the past and the present is clear, the narrator's present state of mind remains generally unaffected by past incidents, and is stable.

Futabatei completed the serialization of *A Madman's Diary* in May 1907, only four months before commencing his third and final original work, *Mediocrity,* which was written as a first-person narrative. How would Futabatei portray the protagonist and his state of mind in *Mediocrity?* Would he use verb forms similar to the ones used in his translations of Turgenev's and Tolstoy's first-person narratives, in which the narrator's retrospective viewpoint is emphasized, or would he use verb forms like those in his translations of first-person narratives by Gogol and Garshin, to portray a stream of consciousness?

## Futabatei's Final Original Work *Heibon [Mediocrity]*

*Mediocrity* consists of five complete episodes. The first episode is about the protagonist's doting grandmother and parents; the second is about his faithful dog Pochi; the third episode (reminiscent of *Floating Clouds*) is about his transitory love for Yukie, the only daughter of an uncle with whom he resides as a house boy; the fourth is about his becoming a writer; and the fifth is about a rather sordid relationship he develops with a chambermaid named Oito, on the pretext of searching for a life as a writer. The whole work is written as a confession (particularly the final three episodes), as a parody of the works of the Japanese naturalists. It is therefore necessary for Futabatei first to establish the narrator's present time in the story:

> 私は今年三十九になる。人生五十が通相場なら、まだ今日明日穴へ入らうとも思はぬが、しかし未來は長いやうでも短いものだ。過去つて了へば實に呆氣ない。（中略）
> いや、しかし私も老込んだ。三十九には老込みやうがチト早過ぎるといふ人も有らうが、氣の持方は年よりも老けた方が好い。それだと無難だ。（中略）
> 老込んだ證據には、近頃は少し暇だと直ぐ過去を憶出す。(Futabatei Shimei 1964d: 100-101)

> [This year I am turning thirty-nine. If the current estimate of a man's life at fifty years be true, I do not expect to go to the grave today or tomorrow, but although it seems far off, the future comes quickly. When it passes by it seems, indeed, to come too quickly....
> Well, indeed I have grown old. Some people may say that it is too hasty to grow old at thirty-nine, but it is better to feel older than one really is. Then one is safe. ...

> As for proof that I have grown old, of late, whenever I have spare time, I fall to thinking of the past.][6]

All five episodes are narrated by a "mediocre" writer named Furuya, who offers us "mediocre" recollections of his past. Furuya, who is made deliberately reminiscent of Futabatei himself, regretfully recalls his past life, sprinkling his recollections with epigrams. As one would expect, Futabatei frequently employs the "-te ita" form when describing the narrator's past actions and states of mind in the form of a confession. The use of "-te ita" forms intensifies when Furuya recalls his first love, Yukie, and when he bitterly remembers his attitude to literature:

> 1. 少し妙のやうだが、なに、妙でも何でもない。私は實は雪江さんに惚れてゐたので。
> 惚れては居たが、夫だから雪江さんを如何しやうといふ氣はなかつた。其時分は私もまだ初心だつたから、正直に女に惚れるのは男兒の恥辱と心得てゐた。女を弄ぶのは何故だか左程の罪惡とも思つて居なかつたが、苟も男兒たる者が女なんぞに惚れて性根を失ふなどゝ、そんな腐つた、そんなやくざな根性で何が出來ると息巻いてゐた。が、口で息巻く程には心で思つてゐなかつたから、自分もいつか其程に擯斥する戀に囚はれて了つたのだが、流石に囚はれたのを恥て、明かに然うと自認し得なかつた氣味がある。から、若其頃誰かゞ面と向つて私に然うと注意したら、私は屹度、失敬な、惚なんぞするものか、と眞紅になつて怒つたに違ひない。が、實は惚れたとも思はぬ中に、いつか自分にも内々で、こツそり、次序なく惚れて了つてゐたのだ。(Futabatei Shimei 1964d: 152)
>
> [...It looks a little strange, but there is nothing strange at all. To tell you the truth, I was in love with Yukie-san.
> Although I was in love with her, I did not have any particular intentions towards her. At that time I was still innocent, and thought it shameful for a man to be honestly in love with a woman. Somehow I did not think it a great crime to trifle with a woman, but I was indignant with a man, if he ever lost his mind by being in love with a woman, and wondered what he could do with such a weary, useless mind. Yet I was not so firm in this belief as I openly expressed it, as I had fallen captive to the love I so much despised; but as one would naturally expect, I was ashamed of myself for being a captive to love, and I apparently did not want to positively acknowledge it. So, if anybody at that time had warned me of it, I would surely have turned red with anger and retorted: "How rude. Do you think I have fallen in love?" But, in fact, before I could realize I was in love, in a blindness that extended to my mind, I had carelessly fallen in love with her.]

[6] In making this translation I have referred to Glenn W. Shaw's translation (Futabatei Shimei 1927: 1,4)

2. あゝしかし、文學を責めるより、友を責めるより、自ら責めた方が當つてゐやう。（中略）詩人と名が附きや、皆普通の人より勝つてるやうに思つてゐた。小説、殊に輸入小説には人生の眞相が活字の面に浮いてゐるやうに思つてゐた。西洋の詩人は皆東洋の詩人に勝るやうに思つてゐた。作の新舊を論じて其價値を定めてゐた。自分は此樣な下らん眞似をしてゐながら、他の額に汗して着實の浮世を渡る人達が偶文壇の事情に通ぜぬと、直ぐ俗物と罵り、俗衆と罵つて、獨り自ら高しとしてゐた。獨り自ら高しとする一方で、想像で姦淫して、一人で堕落してゐた。(Futabatei Shimei 1964d: 171-172)

[Ah, but rather than blame literature, rather than blame my friends, it would be better to blame myself...I thought, if a person was called a poet, he was greater than all ordinary people. I thought that in novels, especially in novels from abroad, the reality of human life floated on the surface of each letter. I thought that western poets were all greater than eastern poets. I valued literary works according to whether they were new or old. While I spent my life in such a foolish way, if others who were living honest lives by the sweat of their brow happened not to know the condition of the literary world, I immediately abused them as worldlings, or as the common herd, and raised myself alone on high. While I raised myself on high, I committed adultery in my imagination and was depraved secretly.]

Once again we should be aware of Futabatei's motivation for writing *Mediocrity.* His intention was to write a satirical response to Tayama Katai's *Futon [The Quilt]*, which is normally regarded as a middle-aged writer's confessions of his sexual feelings towards his young female disciple, disguised in the form of a third-person narrative. The following is the opening passage from *The Quilt,* where the narrator-protagonist, a writer, reflects upon his relationship with the young woman:

數多い感情づくめの手簡——二人の關係は何うしても尋常ではなかつた。妻があり、子があり、世間があり、師弟の關係があればこそ敢て烈しい戀に落ちなかつたが、語り合ふ胸の轟、相見る眼の光、其底には確に凄じい暴風が潜んで居たのである。機會に遭遇しさへすれば、其の底の底の暴風は忽ち勢を得て、妻子も世間も道徳も師弟の關係も一擧にして破れて了うであらうと思はれた。少くとも**男は**さう信じて居た。それであるのに、二三日來の此の出來事、此から考へると、**女は**確かに其感情を僞り賣つたのだ。自分を欺いたのだと**男は**幾度も思つた。けれど文學者だけに、**此男は**自から自分の心理を客観するだけの餘裕を有つて居た。(Tayama Katai 1968: 71)

[All those emotional letters—their relationship was surely something out of the

> ordinary. He had a wife, he had children, he had a reputation to consider, and, moreover, he was her teacher, so they hadn't gone as far as falling madly in love. And yet the beating of their hearts when they talked together, the sparkle in their eyes when they looked at each other—there was definitely something tremendously powerful deep beneath it all. He felt that, if only there was an opportunity, this hidden force would suddenly gain strength and destroy at a stroke that teacher-pupil relationship, that morality, that reputation, that family of his. At least **the man** believed in this. Yet, judging from the incidents which happened in the last couple of days, **the woman** surely deceived herself and betrayed her own feelings. **The man** thought several times that the woman deceived him. However, because he was a man of literature, **this man** had enough composure to see himself objectively.][7]

The "-te ita" form verbs observed in these three passages equally facilitate the confessional mode of the narrative, even though the passage from *The Quilt* is written as a third-person narrative, adding to the story a degree of objectivity. As Oketani Hideaki correctly points out, the protagonist of *The Quilt* and the author himself doubt neither "the tempest in their hearts" nor the significance of confessing it, though nothing happens between the protagonist and his disciple. Even the "incident"—the revelation of the young disciple's love for a divinity student—does not impede his confession. Oketani concludes:

> After all, (for Katai) a confession is simply the way to realize his literary ambition. By contrast, what Futabatei attempted in *Mediocrity* was a confession that focused on a fundamental misgiving about and denial of literature, as if to throw cold water on Katai's faith in art, a faith that, whatever else it doubted, could not doubt literature. (Oketani 1997: 277)

The whole of *The Quilt* consists of such self-complacent confession, and employs "-te ita" form verbs throughout, in order to assure the confessional mode. Futabatei, on the other hand, portrays a writer who confesses his misgivings about literature, and denies the illusion held by some writers, that merely by confessing their sins they had achieved some literary truth. It is rather significant that Futabatei employs "-te ita" form verbs only where these particular confessions are made: of his first love and of his doubts about the value of literature. In most of *Mediocrity,* the protagonists recollections are made with the use of "-(r)u" or "-te iru" forms.

In short, in order to advance his literary ambitions, Katai confessed his own experience in the guise of a third-person narrative, while Futabatei wrote a parody in the guise of a confession, using a first-person narrative. For his confession, Katai needed to employ "-te ita" form verbs in order not to be confronted by his past. In consequence, the narrative of *The Quilt* becomes extremely serious in tone, to an extent that at times becomes laughable, given the triviality of the content. Futabatei, on the other hand, needed to employ "-te ita" form verbs only in scenes where his protagonist makes straightforward confessions, free of literary pretension. Most of *Mediocrity* is more in the nature of a recollection than a confession. Whereas Katai limits his protagonist's actions to the past, where they will not

---

[7] In making this translation I have referred to Kenneth Henshall's translation (Tayama Katai 1981: 35)

confront him, Futabatei keeps his protagonist's memories alive in the present, and allows his protagonist to reflect on them and react to them. This is especially true when describing Furuya's wholehearted love for his dog Pochi. The following is a description of a happy day spent with his dog:

> 私は生來の朝寢坊だから、毎朝二度三度覺されても、中々起きない。優しくしてゐては際限がないので、母が最終には夜着を剥ぐ。これで流石の朝寢坊も不承々々に床を離れるが、しかし大不平だ。額で母を睨めて、津蟹が泡を吐くやうに、沸々言つてゐる。ポチは朝起だから、もう其時分には疾くに朝飯も濟むで、一切り遊んだ所だが、私の聲を聽き付けると、何處に居ても一目散に飛んで來る。
> これで私の機嫌も直る。急に現金に莞爾々々となつて、急いで庭へ降りる所を、ポチが透さず泥足で飛付く。細い人參程の赤ちやけた尻尾を懸命に掉り立つて、嬉しさうに面を膽上る。視下す。目と目と直たりと合ふ。堪まらなくなつて私が横抱に引ン抱く。ポチは抱かれながら、身を藻掻いて大暴れに暴れ、私の手を舐め、胸を舐め、顋を舐め、頰を舐め、舐めても舐めても舐め足らないで、惡くすると、口まで舐める。父が面を顰めて汚い汚いと曰ふ。成程、考へて見れば、汚いやうではあるけれども……しかし、私は嬉しい、止められない。如何して是が止められるもんか！私が何も好い物を持つてゐるぢやなし、ポチも其は承知で爲る事だ。利害の念を離れて居るのだ、唯懷かしいといふ刹那の心になつて居るのだ。(Futabatei Shimei 1964d: 121)

[As I am a lie-abed by nature, I do not get up at once in the morning, even though I am called two or three times. Since if she let things go on gently there will be no end, my mother finally pulls off my bedding. At that, even such a lie-abed as I reluctantly crawl out of bed, but with great discontent. Glaring at her through my forehead, I am grumbling like an estuarial crab blowing bubbles. As Pochi is an early riser, he has finished his breakfast long ago and has been playing for a while, but as soon as he hears my voice, he comes dashing to me, no matter where he is.
This immediately changes my mood. Suddenly smiling all over my face, I jump down to the yard, and Pochi quickly jumps up to me with his feet covered in mud. Pochi looks up into my face in delight while wagging his reddish, carrot-like tail furiously. I look down at him. My eyes meet his eyes squarely. Overwhelmed by emotion, I hold him under my arm. As I hold him, Pochi squirms and twists madly in my arms, and licks my hands, my chest, chin and cheeks; he cannot lick enough, and at his worst, he even licks my mouth. My father frowns and says that it is dirty, dirty. Indeed, when I come to think of it, it does seem dirty... but I am delighted and cannot stop. How can I stop this? I haven't got anything which is worth anything, and Pochi, knowing this, does as he does. He has no thought of gain and loss; he has only the feelings of love of the moment.]

The whole episode begins with the following sentence, which distinctively indicates the protagonist's retrospective viewpoint with a "-ta" form: "wasure mo se nu, sobo no nakunatta yokuyokutoshi no, harusame no shitoshitoto furu usurazamui aru yoru no koto de atta [I can never forget, it was the second year after grandmother died, on a chilly night when the spring rain was falling gently]". Following this opening sentence the narrator's recollections are conveyed mainly with the use of "-(r)u" and "-te iru" forms. Where "-ta" forms are used, they appear to carry the meaning of complete aspect rather than past tense. Some appear in the specific form "-te shimatta", which, as well as emphasizing complete aspectual meaning, conveys various emotional connotations such as the main characters' regret, disappointment or surprise. The "-(r)u" forms, and especially the "-te iru" forms, once again make the description of actions particularly vivid. The "-te iru" forms are applied particularly to the description of Pochi's actions, Pochi being the one observed by the narrator, similarly to the way they were used in Futabatei's translations of Turgenev's first-person narrative stories. We find a similar use of "-te iru" forms in other episodes where the protagonist's observations of other characters are recorded, including observations of his cousin Yukie, the chambermaid Oito, and his father's body.

What distinguishes the Pochi episode from the others, is that the use of "-(r)u" and "-te iru" forms extends to the actions of the protagonist himself, as observed in the above passage. This passage depicts the past habitual, affectionate exchanges between the protagonist and his dog, as if they are unfolding before the reader's eyes. We might say that the protagonist's memories are so clear that he cannot help using "-(r)u" or "-te iru" forms.

Komori Yōichi (1994: 45-51) offers an explanation for the prominence of the Pochi episode. He first acknowledges that the use of "-(r)u" forms enhances the vividness of the description, and transports reader and narrator into the time in which the incident takes place. Then he notes that when describing how Pochi was left as a stray near the protagonist's gate, the subject who is making the observations (the narrator) retreats into the background, and the object of the narrator's observations (Pochi) becomes the subject of his recollections:

> 其時忽ち暗黒から、茸々と毛の生えた、節くれ立つた大きな腕がヌツと出て、正體なく寢入つてゐる所を無手と引掴み、宙に釣す。驚いて目をポツチリ明き、いたいげな聲で悲鳴を揚げながら、四足を張つて藻掻く中に、頭から何かで包まれたやうで、眞暗になる。窮屈で息氣が塞りさうだから、出やうとするが、出られない。久らく藻掻いて居る中に、ふと足掻が自由になる。と、領元を撮まれて、高い高い處からドサリと落された。うろうろとして其處らを視廻すけれど、何だか變な淋しい眞闇な處で、誰も居ない。茫然としてゐると、雨に打れて見る間に濡しよぼたれ、怕ろしく寒くなる。身慄ひ一つして、クンクンと親を呼んで見るが、何處からも出て來ない。(Futabatei Shimei 1964d: 117)

[Then all at once from out of the darkness a big, hairy, knotty arm suddenly appears, and seizing him firmly as he lies fast asleep, swings him up into space. Widely

> opening his eyes in surprise and crying aloud with his poor little voice, he struggles with his four legs spread wide. Then everything goes black, as if I have been covered with something from the head down. As I am so uncomfortable and I am nearly suffocating, I try hard to get out, but I cannot. While I am struggling, suddenly my paws become free. I am picked up by the scruff of the neck, and [the next thing I know] I have been dropped roughly from a very high place. I look around in confusion, but I am in some strange, lonely, pitch dark place, and there is nobody around. I am bewildered; then pounded by the rain, I am rapidly drenched and become terribly cold. I shiver once and try calling my mother by sniffling, but she does not come.]

Examining the verbs employed in this passage, Komori suggests that they all portray the abandoned dog's movements from the dog's point of view. The observed becomes the observer. It may be said that the protagonist's memory is so clear and insightful in recalling the Pochi episode, and Pochi is visualized with such affection, that the boundary between the observer and the observed is eliminated.

The Pochi episode has been widely praised and frequently appears in school textbooks as a model of fine descriptive writing. It clearly stands out from other episodes in its graphic use of "-(r)u" and "-te iru" forms. So involved in his memory is the protagonist, that not only the boundary between observer and observed, but also the boundary between the narrator's past and present disappears.

In other episodes, and especially in the episode which relates how the narrator became an author, "-ta" and "-te ita" form verbs predominate, establishing a firm retrospective point of view. In the description of the protagonist's visit to an old master from a literary circle, which is reminiscent of Futabatei's visit to his mentor, Tsubouchi Shōyō, only one "-te iru" form is observed. The dominant "-te ita" form verbs set the confessional mode of the narrative, and there is almost no sense of the present time flowing through the episode. In the other three episodes, describing Furuya's parents and grandmother, his first love for his cousin Yukie and his experimental love with his chambermaid Oito, Futabatei employs "-te iru" forms to describe the actions of the characters observed by the narrator-protagonist, and "-te ita" form verbs for the actions of the narrator himself. The stream of time flowing in the episode described, and the present time of the narrator himself are thus both acknowledged, though these two streams never meet as they do in the Pochi episode.

It is notable that the episode which is dominated by the confessional mode is the one least highly regarded by critics. Hasegawa Tenkei, Futabatei's contemporary, and a member of the naturalist school, was critical of the second half of *Mediocrity,* especially the account of how Furuya becomes a writer, since he considered Futabatei made a mockery of his protagonist (Futabatei Shimei 1964d: 426). Written satirically, it has lost currency with the decline of its target, the naturalist school of writing. The Pochi episode, on the other hand, in which no trace of the confessional mode is present, is the most highly regarded part of the book and has enjoyed the greatest longevity. This graphic narrative style, employing mostly "-(r)u" and "-te iru" form verbs, which we observe in four of the five episodes of *Mediocrity,* is the very style Futabatei developed in the course of his translation work during the second and third periods of his literary activity. More precisely, it corresponds to a narrative style developed during the translation of Turgenev's and Tolstoy's first-person narrative stories, in which two streams of time flow side by side. The recollections found in *Mediocrity* are highly edited and organized, unlike those found in Garshin's *Four Days* or the notes found in

Gogol's *Notes of a Madman*, in which present tense verbs convey a stream of consciousness and reveal a drift into insanity. In the translations of these two stories Futabatei employed "-(r)u" or "-te iru" forms as direct translations of the present tense verbs of the original, and therefore did not create two streams of time in the story.

We are now in a position to see the cyclical nature of the interaction between Futabatei and the writers of the naturalist school. Futabatei's early translation of Turgenev's *The Rendezvous,* published under the title *The Tryst,* made a strong impression on writers of the naturalist school, including Katai, a hitherto unsuccessful writer, who rose to prominence with *The Quilt,* at the same time establishing naturalism as a dominant trend in Japanese literature. In *The Quilt* a firm retrospective narrative point of view is set with the use of "-ta" and "-te ita" form verbs, showing the direct influence of the first version of *The Tryst.* Katai attempted to disguise the confessional nature of *The Quilt* by writing it as a third-person narrative. Futabatei responded to it by writing *Mediocrity* as a parody of *The Quilt* and other stories of the naturalist school. Futabatei employed a first-person narrative in order to expose the essential nature of their works. Yet he did not employ "-ta" and "-te ita" as the predominant verb forms, as this could have concealed the protagonist's present and created a confessional mode. Instead, in *Mediocrity* the protagonist's recollections are presented mainly with the use of "-(r)u" and "-te iru" forms. With the exception of the account of Furuya's induction as a writer, Futabatei rejects a firm retrospective narrative point of view in favour of a more vivid narrative which blends two streams of time, as found in several translations of Turgenev's first-person narrative stories. The two streams of time—the narrator's present time and the time flowing in his narrative—merge completely for a moment in the moving account of Pochi, just as they did in *One-sided Love,* Futabatei's translation of Turgenev's *Asya.* Interestingly, this style was developed to overcome the perceived defects of the early versions of *The Tryst* and *A Chance Encounter,* the repetitive use of "-ta" forms used to create a firm retrospective narrative point of view. *Mediocrity* is thus not a direct parody of the style of the naturalist school, but rather of its essence. Futabatei presented the narrator-protagonist's recollections in his own style, which was influenced by his translation style.

## Natsume Sōseki's *Kōfu [The Miner]* and Shimazaki Tōson's *Haru [Spring]*

To conclude this chapter, we shall briefly examine the style of *The Miner*, by Natsume Sōseki, who famously voiced his criticism of the writers of the naturalist school. We shall also look at the style of Shimazaki Tōson's *Spring*. These two novels were serialized successively in the *Tokyo Asahi shinbun*, immediately following the publication of Futabatei's Mediocrity. Having firmly established his reputation as a writer with his debut novel *Wagahai wa neko de aru [I am a Cat]* (1905-1906), in April 1907 Sōseki began to write professionally for the same newspaper that employed Futabatei. Sōseki resigned from his teaching posts, which included a prestigious position as lecturer in English literature at the Tokyo Imperial University, and signed an exclusive contract to write for the *Tokyo Asahi shinbun*. Sōseki and Futabatei were invited to serialize their novels in turn. In 1907 Sōseki's *Gubijinsō [The Poppy]* was followed by Futabatei's *Mediocrity*. These works were to have been followed by Shimazaki Tōson's *Haru [The Spring]*, but Tōson was unable to meet his deadline. Instead, in December 1907, while Futabatei was busy preparing for his departure to Russia, Sōseki began to write an experimental novel entitled *Kōfu [The Miner]*.

The material on which *The Miner* was based came from a young man named Arai, who visited Sōseki and offered to sell him the story of his own experience as a miner. Initially Sōseki suggested the young man write his own story, but Arai had no aptitude for this task. When Sōseki was requested to fill the gap left by Tōson, he sought Arai's permission to use his story of working in a copper mine as the basis for a novel.

Like *Mediocrity*, *The Miner* is written in the form of a first-person narrative, and the narrator's viewpoint is retrospective. The narrator-protagonist, who refers to himself simply as "jibun [I]", looks back over his past and describes how he became a miner, in "tough, telegraphic, colloquial prose" (Rubin 1988: 166). In spite of the retrospective viewpoint, the narrative often employs "-(r)u" or "-te iru" forms. The following extract is from the opening scene, in which the narrator is spotted by a procurer of cheap labour, who is scouting on behalf of a mine. The narrator has just completed a long walk through a changeless landscape of pine trees, and has stopped outside a cheap tea house:

> 掛茶屋がある。葭簀の影から見ると粘土のへつゝいに、錆た茶釜が掛かつて居る。床几が二尺許り往來へ食み出した上から、二三足草履がぶら下がつて、袢天だか、どてらだか分らない着物を着た男が背中を此方に向けて腰を掛けてゐる。
> 休まうかな、癈さうかなと、通り掛りに横目で覗き込んで見たら、例の袢天とどてらの中を行く男が突然此方を向いた。煙草の脂で黒くなつた齒を、厚い唇の間から出して笑つてゐる。是はとすこし氣味が惡くなり掛ける途端に、向ふの顔は急に眞面目になつた。（中略）男は眞面目になつた顔を眞面目な場所に据ゐた儘、白眼の運動が氣に掛かる程の勢ひで自分の口から鼻、鼻から額とぢりぢり頭の上へ登つて行く。鳥打帽の廂を跨いで、脳天迄届いたと思ふ頃又白眼がぢりぢり下へ降つて來た。今度は顔を素通りにして胸から臍のあたり迄來ると一寸留まつた。臍の所には蟇口がある。三十二錢這入つてゐる。(Natsume Sōseki 1956: 5-6)

> [Here is a tea stand. Through the reed blind I see a rusty kettle hanging over a clay stove. A bench out front is sticking a couple of feet into the road. A few straw sandals are hanging over it, and a man in a kimono—a *hanten* or *dotera*[8] or something—is sitting there with his back facing this way.
> I am moving past and peering from the corner of my eye and wondering whether I should stop and rest or forget it, when [I notice] this fellow somewhere halfway between a *hanten* or a *dotera* has turned his face towards me. He is smiling with his black teeth, stained with tobacco, sticking from his fat lips. I start feeling weird, but then [notice] his face has turned serious...

[8] As noted by Rubin (1988, 3), the *hanten* and *dotera* are two kinds of thickly padded cloaks worn in cold weather. The *hanten* is a short jacket, the *dotera* a full length *kimono* normally used like a dressing gown.

> ... While he keeps his serious face in a serious position, the whites of his eyes start creeping up my face with noticeable force—mouth to nose, nose to forehead and up to [the crown of] my head. When they have crept up to my visor and reached the crown of my head they have started to creep down again. This time they go past my face to my chest, to my navel, and there they have stopped. There is my wallet near the navel. There are thirty two *sen* inside it.][9]

In this passage the predominant verb form is "-(r)u" (seven out of eleven verbs). Of the seven "-(r)u" forms, four are "-te iru" and one is in the "-te iku" form, both of these being defined as aspectual forms by Teramura (1984: 123). Komori Yōichi has also commented on these "-te iru" forms in the opening scene of *The Miner*. He suggests that what they express is not the present tense, but the continuation of a certain state or action for a certain period of time. Komori (1996: 25-29; 224-229) also suggests that the "-ta" forms in this passage are expressions not of the past tense, but of the perceived completion of the action.

In aligning the "-(r)u" and "-ta" forms with the continuous and complete aspects, Komori suggests that Sōseki has intentionally shifted the narrator's viewpoint from retrospective to introspective in most scenes of *The Miner*. In particular, the frequent use of "-te iru" forms strengthens the introspective viewpoint of the narrator. These "-te iru" forms evoke such graphic images that the reader begins to let slip the present time of the narrator, from which he recalls his past experiences.

As a matter of fact, when we analyze Sōseki's use of verbs in *The Miner*, we find that the number of "-ta" forms slightly exceeds that of "-(r)u" forms. However, when we compare aspectual forms, we find that "-te iru" is used nearly twice as often as "-te ita". These "-te iru" forms are used mainly to express the continuous actions of characters and states of being. Only in a few instances are they used to express repeated or habitual actions. The most striking feature of Sōseki's use of "-te iru" forms in *The Miner* is that they are used to describe the continuous actions of characters other than the narrator-protagonist. In the passage cited above, "(koshi) o kakete iru [is sitting]" and "waratte iru [is smiling]" refer to the actions of the procurer, as observed by the narrator.

The continuous actions of the narrator-protagonist, on the other hand, are often described using "-te ita" forms:

> 1. 手を出さうかなと思ふ矢先へもつて來て、急に黒い斑點(はんてん)が、晴夜(せいや)の星宿(せいしゆく)の如く、縱横に行列するんだから、少し辟易(へきえき)して仕舞つて、ぼんやり皿を見下(みおろ)して居た。 (Natsume Sōseki 1956: 15)
>
> [I was on the verge of reaching for a *manjū* [rice cake with bean filling] when the spots suddenly arranged themselves into a network of lines, like the constellations on a starry night, I held back, and was staring down at the plate.]

---

[9] In making this translation I have consulted Jay Rubin's translation (Natsume Sōseki 1988: 3-4).

2. **自分が**直接に長蔵さんと應對してゐる間は、人格も何も忘れてゐるんだが、自分が赤毛布(あかげつと)になつて、君儲(まう)かるんだぜと説得されてゐる體裁(ていさい)を、**自分が**傍(わき)へ立つて見た日には方(かた)なしである。**自分は**果してこんなものかと、少しく興を醒まして赤毛布(あかげつと)を、つらつら観察してゐた。 (Natsume Sōseki 1956: 51)

[As long as **I** was directly dealing with Chōzō, I could forget about my 'individuality', but how hard for **me** to stand aside and observe myself, as the red blanket, being promised by Chōzō that I would make "lots of money". **I** was looking hard at the red blanket with the bitter thought that this was the real me.]

Most "-te ita" forms are used to convey the narrator's reflections on his past experiences, using forms such as "omotte ita, kangaete ita [thought]", "shinjite ita [believed]" and "omoitsumete ita [was obsessed with]". The number of "-te ita" forms expressing the continuous actions of the narrator is relatively small, but they are significant in strengthening the retrospective viewpoint of the narrator, and are in striking contrast to the "-te iru" forms used to describe the continuous actions of characters other than the narrator. In this way Sōseki makes a clear distinction between the observer and the observed, and creates a double stream of time: the present time of the narrator and the time which flows in his narrative.

Incidentally, this is very similar to the practice which Futabatei began in his translations of first-person narratives, and applied in *Mediocrity*. Moreover, whereas in *Mediocrity* this approach seems to have been a more or less unconscious application of his translation style, in *The Miner* Sōseki appears to have used the same method consciously and with greater rigour.

In *The Miner* Sōseki demonstrates mastery of a style that Futabatei had applied, though rather less consistently, in *Mediocrity*, a style in which vivid images are conveyed to the reader through the use of "-te iru" forms, while the perfective aspect is expressed through "-ta" forms. At the same time Sōseki prudently offered coherent explanations of the narrator's actions, using "-te ita" forms. *The Miner* is thus not only an internal monologue, in which an attempt is made to "observe minutely the stream of consciousness of the hero" (Nakamura Shinichirō 1973: 255), but also an attempt to create vivid images within the framework of a retrospective first-person narrative.

Both Futabatei and Sōseki were deeply impressed the Tōson's first novel *Hakai [The Broken Commandment]* (1905), and commended his work to the *Tokyo Asahi shinbun*. Tōson's second novel, *Spring*, was serialized in that newspaper from April 1908, immediately after *The Miner*. Nakamura observes that "In *Spring* Tōson deliberately avoided elaborating a fictitious plot, something he had struggled with while writing *The Broken Commandment* (Nakamura Mitsuo, cited in Shimazaki Tōson 1970: 311). In *Spring* Tōson portrays his close friends, a group of writers associated with the journal *Bungakkai [The World of Literature]*, as realistically as possible. Consequently, all the main characters are modelled on real writers. The first half of the novel recounts the life of Aoki, who is modelled on Kitamura Tōkoku, an idealistic poet who committed suicide. The second half is autobiographical, as the character of Kishimoto is modelled on Tōson himself.

Unlike *Mediocrity* and *The Miner*, *Spring* is written in the form of a third-person narrative. As is the case with many works of the naturalist school, however, the third-person narrative structure is employed to disguise the confessional mode of the novel. As in Katai's *The Quilt*, which was written only months earlier, the number of "-ta" forms by far exceeds the number of "-(r)u" forms. The following passage describes a meeting between the protagonist Kishimoto and a former student, Katsuko:

勝子は今岸本の前に居る。もし來たら彼樣言はうかしらん、斯樣言はうかしらん、と種々聞いて見たいことや話したいことなぞを考へて置いたが、さて逢つて見ると、岸本は思ふやうに話すことも出來なかつた。斯うして長く居ることは事情が許さないといふ風で、何となく勝子は沈着かないやうに見える。それに一度師弟の關係があつたといふことは、自由な談話を妨げた。斯のあわただしい邂逅の間にも二人は禮儀を失ふまいとした。
よく自堕落な教師の話なぞが出ると、眉を顰める方の岸本であるから、餘計に勝子の前では嚴格になる。第一師弟の關係が岸本には深い苦痛の種である。**彼は**八戸の酒屋の名を認めたものを勝子に渡したりなぞして、復機会があつたら、と再會を約したが、心には許婚のある人に逢つて話をするといふことの是が最初でも有り又最終でも有るかのやうな氣がした。
勝子は別離を告げて出た。
入口のところには車夫が待つて居た。格子戸を出て、勝子は名殘惜しさうに岸本の方を見た。二人は無言の思を交換した。其時ばかりは、師弟の禮儀を守つたとも言へなかつたのである。
（中略）
其日から**彼の**胸は餘計に苦しくなつて來た。**彼は**反つて勝子に逢はない方が可かつたと思つた。旅に出た頃は唯其人の面影にあこがれるといふ風で、僅かに岡見の妹を通して意中を傳へたに過ぎなかつたが、それだけで**彼は**滿足して居た。さあ、斯うして逢つて話をして見ると、猶々聲が聞きたくなる。**彼は**最早面影ばかりに滿足することが出來なくなつた。有體に言へば、勝子といふ人が欲しくなつて來た。(Shimazaki Tōson 1972: 69-70)

[Katsuko is now sitting in front of Kishimoto. Kishimoto had thought long and hard about the questions he wanted to ask her and the things he wanted talk about, when Katsuko would come. Once they met, Kishimoto somehow couldn't speak as he wished. Katsuko appears to be nervous as the circumstances do not permit her to stay long. The fact that they had once had a teacher-student relationship prevented them from talking openly. They tried to observe proper decorum during this fleeting rendezvous. Kishimoto is a man of propriety, who knits his brows when he hears about debauched teachers. He becomes even stricter in front of Katsuko. The teacher-student relationship causes Kishimoto to agonize. **He** gave Katsuko a piece of paper on which the name of a *sake* shop in Hachinohe was written, and promised to meet

her again at some other time. Deep in his mind, however, he felt as if this would be the first and the last chance to see her, as she had a fiancé. Katsuko went out after giving him some parting words.
At the entrance a rickshaw driver was waiting for her. When she stepped out the lattice door, Katsuko looked at Kishimoto with the sorrow of parting. The two persons exchanged the silent greetings. At that moment they couldn't observe the propriety due between teachers and students…
From that day on **his** heart started suffering more agony. **He** thought it would have been less painful if he had not seen Katsuko at all. When he roamed around, he only longed for her image. **He** was utterly happy when he expressed his feelings through Okami's sister. Once he has met her and talked with her, he wants to hear her voice more often. **He** couldn't be satisfied with her image any longer. To put it plainly, he wanted to possess her.]

The protagonist agonizing over his relationship with a female student is clearly reminiscent of Katai's *The Quilt*, as is the frequent use of the third-person pronoun "kare" to refer to the protagonist Kishimoto, and the frequent use of "-ta" form verbs. In the passage just cited fourteen out of nineteen verbs are "-ta" forms. Of the fourteen "-ta" forms, "-te ita" and "-te kita" appear twice each. These are the past tense of the aspectual forms "-te iru" and "-te kuru" (Teramura 1984: 123) and appear to strengthen the past tense meaning of the passage.

When we analyze Tōson's use of verbs in *Spring* we find that "-ta" forms are employed a little more than twice as often as "-(r)u" forms. When we compare aspectual forms, as we did in the case of Sōseki's *The Miner*, we find a similar result: the number of "-te iru" forms exceeds the number of "-te ita" forms (in the ratio 1.5:1). However, the "-te iru" forms in *Spring* do not evoke the same graphic images as are created in *The Miner* by Sōseki, as Tōson uses them mainly to describe states of being. Hardly any continuous or habitual actions are described by these "-te iru" forms. The "-te ita" forms, while less numerous, are frequently employed to describe the continuous or habitual actions of the two protagonists, Kishimoto and Aoki. The following passage illustrates the typical use of "-te iru" and "-te ita" forms in *Spring*:

汚れた疊の上に寢轉び乍ら、三人は岸本の來るのを待つて居た。
『最早見えさうなものだなあ。』
と言つて青木は身を起した。
青木は瘦ぎすな方で、新しい紺飛白の單衣を着て、兵児帶を無造作に巻き付けて居る。寛げた懐からは白い夏シャツがあらはれて居て、その紐釦の外れたところに、すこし胸の肌が見える。この男の物を視る眼付、迫つた眉、蒼ざめた頰、それから雄々しい傲慢な額なぞの表情は、傷つけ破らざれば休まずとでも言つたやうな、非常に過敏な神經質を示して居た。
(Shimazaki Tōson 1972: 53)

[Three persons, lying on a dirty *tatami* mat, were waiting for Kishimoto.
"He should have come by now", said Aoki, raising himself up.

> Aoki is rather scrawny. He wears an unlined *kimono* of dark-blue cloth with white splash patterns, casually tied around with a drawing belt. A white summer undershirt is revealed under the loose *kimono*, and from an unhooked button his skin shows slightly. The expression in his eyes, close eyebrows, pale cheeks and his gallant and arrogant forehead—all these things showed his extremely sensitive nerves, and seemed to say that he wouldn't stop fighting till the very end.]

The first instance of an aspectual form, "matte ita" [were waiting] describes the past continuous action of the characters, one of whom is Aoki. Then "makitsukete iru [ties around]", a "-te iru" form describing a state of being, is used to describe Aoki's clothing. The most peculiar use of an aspectual form in this passage is "hijōni kabinna shinkeishitsu o shimeshite ita [showed his extremely sensitive nerves]". When the narrator describes Aoki's features the verb form becomes "-te ita", which clearly indicates the past tense. In this way Tōson's use of "-te ita" forms in *Spring* sets the narrator's viewpoint outside the story. The rather subjective and obscure portrayal of Aoki and Kishimoto is often made retrospectively by this externally positioned narrator.

The style of *Spring* offers a striking contrast to that of *The Miner*. The "-te iru" forms employed in Sōseki's first-person narrative convey vivid and graphic images to the reader by describing the continuous actions of characters other than the protagonist, as well as states of being. Moreover, while "-te ita" forms in *The Miner* offer coherent and objective explanations of the narrator-protagonist's actions, in *Spring* such forms provide rather subjective and obscure information about the two protagonists. Tōson relates his own confessional story under the guise of a third-person narrative, but the most striking difference between *Spring* and *The Miner* is the use of "-ta" forms. In *Spring* such forms are used primarily to indicate the past tense, while in *The Miner* they are used principally to indicate complete aspect. It is significant that the aspectual form "-te shimatta" is hardly used in *Spring*, while Sōseki uses them quite frequently in *The Miner*.

Karatani Kōjin suggests that many of Sōseki's early works were written with a conscious intent to avoid "-ta" forms expressing the past tense, as these eliminate or neutralize the narrator's role (Karatani 1992: 242-250). Indeed, in Sōseki's debut masterpiece *Wagahai neko de aru [I am a Cat]* (1906), the narrator, a cat, is crucial to the novel, and the predominant verb form is "-(r)u". In *The Miner* a similarly prominent narrator-protagonist makes graphic use of "-(r)u" and "-te iru" forms. It would appear that Sōseki and Futabatei both attempted to create dramatized narrators in their works, but that these narrators were not imitated by subsequent writers. The narrative models provided by writers of the naturalist school, such as Katai and Tōson, in which "-ta" forms generally express the past tense, set the tone for the next hundred years. That style, developed by Futabatei in his very first published translation, became the dominant style in Japanese literature. In it, the narrator, the implied author, and even the protagonist, appear as one, united by the use of "-ta" to create a firm retrospective point of view.

# Conclusion — Re-evaluating Futabatei's Translations and their Significance for Contemporary Literature

Futabatei's numerous translations, greater in extent than his original works, have been for the most part undeservedly neglected. Only the first versions of *The Tryst* and *A Chance Encounter,* and then later *Floating Weed* and *An Account of Bloodied Laughter,* were widely acknowledged at the time of publication. His first two translations, particularly *The Tryst*, enjoyed immense popularity among the young writers of the naturalist school such as Tayama Katai, Kunikida Doppo and Shimazaki Tōson. *Floating Weed* and *An Account of Bloodied Laughter* were regarded as Futabatei's most important translation works, and were critically acclaimed when published in 1908, after Futabatei's departure for Russia. From a stylistic point of view, however, it is *The Tryst* which has been most influential. It is generally considered that its innovative style made even more of an impact on Japanese literature than his first novel *Floating Clouds* (Yoshida Sei'ichi 1965).

The style of Futabatei's first two translations differs from that of all the translations that followed, including the revised second versions. What differentiates their style from that of the later translations is the treatment of "-ta" forms. In the early version of *The Tryst* and in *A Chance Encounter* "-ta" forms are used to translate all the past tense verbs of the Russian original, regardless of their aspect. The "-ta" ending is used exclusively as a tense marker. (In employing "-ta" endings to render every past tense verb, Futabatei brought to fruition Kawashima Chūnosuke's endeavours to pioneer faithful translation.) In later translations "-ta" forms are employed mostly to translate past perfective verbs and the "-ta" ending serves principally as a marker of complete aspect.

Although in both the earlier and later translations of *The Rendezvous* and *Three Encounters* Futabatei attempts to translate verb forms faithfully, the later versions were almost entirely neglected by Futabatei's contemporaries. Nearly half a century after their publication, the influential critic Nakamura Mitsuo (1958: 214) summarized the general attitude to the later versions suggesting that "in the revised versions published in 1896 Futabatei consciously negates the achievement of the first versions, as though negating his own youth". Nakamura considers the style of the second versions to be a compromising return to an existing, old-fashioned Japanese style, and a turning away from earlier innovation. Mizuno Kiyoshi (1958) suggests that there is a stylistic resemblance between the revised versions and the works of members of the Ken'yūsha group such as Ozaki Kōyō and Hirotsu Ryūrō. He considers this to be due to the stylistic influence of these works on Futabatei, and he, too, considers the revisions to have been retrogressive.

Japanese critics with specialist knowledge of Russian literature, including other translators from Russian literature, also appear to regard Futabatei's translations highly, though they, too, focus mainly on his translations from Turgenev. The master translator from Russian Jinzai Kiyoshi praises the early versions of *The Tryst* and *A Chance Encounter* enthusiastically for their extreme loyalty to the originals. The following comments from Jinzai characterize Futabatei as a foremost translator of works by Turgenev:

> Indeed, for Futabatei, Turgenev was the most congenial Russian writer. From a stylistic point of view, Turgenev was the writer whose style was most suited to Futabatei's own,

> at least during the first and second periods of his literary activity, and the translation of Turgenev's works must have been Futabatei's favourite field of work. (Futabatei Shimei 1965e: 176)

Futabatei did indeed make more translations from Turgenev's works than from any other writer, with seven being concentrated in his first two periods of literary activity, and Jinzai's comments appear justified. Yet, if Turgenev's style suited Futabatei the best, why did he feel the need to make such substantial revisions of the earlier, "most faithful" versions of *The Tryst* and *A Chance Encounter*? Why did he turn away from a style which had made such an impression on the writers of the naturalist school? Why, in particular, did he eliminate a significant number of "-ta" forms from the earlier versions?

Five of the seven translations from Turgenev which Futabatei made during the first two periods of his literary activity are first-person narratives, whereas Futabatei's first translation of a third-person narrative was not of a story by Turgenev, but of Gogol's *The Portrait.*[1] This is significant, given that *Floating Clouds* is also a third-person narrative. In *Floating Clouds* Futabatei makes use of a pre-modern narrator, who appears to physically exist in the novel, and who addresses the reader directly. The narrative of Part One of *Floating Clouds* is written employing mainly "-(r)u" and "-te iru" forms, which indicate the presence of the pre-modern narrator as an on-the-scene commentator. The sudden increase in "-ta" forms in Part Two, which is supposed to be attributable to the direct influence of Futabatei's work on *The Tryst* and *A Chance Encounter,* tentatively disguises the presence of the pre-modern narrator. Yet these "-ta" forms, which carry the meaning of the past tense, are unable to change the whole structure of the novel, and the narrator returns in Part Three, which Futabatei left unfinished.

While the first versions of *The Tryst* and *A Chance Encounter* only pointed the way to a tentative disguising of the narrator through the use of "-ta" forms, Part One of *The Portrait* introduces a quite different narrative style, and one that Futabatei might have adopted successfully in *Floating Clouds.* The narrative of *The Portrait* is one that Futabatei arrived at by thoroughly applying the practices he developed in the second version of *The Tryst* and in *A Fortuitous Encounter.* As we observe in these, and in many subsequent translations, Futabatei employs "-ta" forms to translate past perfective verbs, and "-(r)u" and "-te iru" forms to translate past imperfective verbs. Consequently most "-ta" forms describe complete or successive actions, while "-(r)u" and "-te iru" forms are used to describe states of being and continuous, repeated or habitual actions. Hence all the verbs in Part One of *The Portrait* tend to be more heavily laden with aspectual meaning than with tense meaning.

Another significant feature of the use of verb forms in *The Portrait* is that the use of "-te iru" forms is initiated by the use of present imperfective verbs in the original. In the opening passages of *The Portrait* Gogol uses both past and present imperfective verbs to describe the shop where the portrait of the moneylender is purchased. Initially, when past imperfective verbs are used, the description is rather neutral. Once Gogol shifts to the present tense

---

[1] Futabatei made a further two translations during his third period. One (*Keburi [Smoke],* a translation of *Dym [Smoke]*) was never completed. The other, *Wakarazuya [The Blockhead]* (a translation of *Zavtrak u predvoditelya [Breakfast with the Marshall of the Nobility]*) is an obvious adaptation.

the narrative becomes more personal. Together with expressions such as "I suppose" and "without doubt", the present imperfective verbs explicitly show the narrator's presence. Futabatei translates the opening of *The Portrait* in a unique fashion, using a dramatized narrator within the story, employing "-(r)u" and "-te iru" forms along with the abundant use of words rooted in Japanese culture. The result is a style very similar to that used in the early passages of *Floating Clouds*. One is tempted to suggest that this style is one indeed suited to Futabatei, even more than that found in Turgenev's works.

Moreover, during the climax of the story, when the protagonist's repeated hallucinations lead to the discovery of money concealed in the portrait's frame, the point of view of the dramatized narrator merges with that of the protagonist. This transition in *The Portrait* is successfully navigated through the use of "-(r)u" and "-te iru" forms, and through omission of third-person pronouns. This suggests a narrative device Futabatei might have used to successfully complete *Floating Clouds*. In my view, the inner thoughts and "hallucination" of Bunzō might have been described without creating a conflict between Bunzō's monologue and the narrative of the pre-modern narrator, if Futabatei had adopted the same devices he contrived in his translation of *The Portrait*.

While in Part One of *The Portrait* "-ta" forms carry the meaning of complete aspect, and the whole narrative is made from the point of view of a dramatized narrator, in *Floating Weed* (the translation of Turgenev's third-person narrative *Rudin*) "-ta" forms carry the meanings of both complete aspect and past tense. The revival of "-ta" forms carrying the sense of the past tense is due to the omniscient narrative point of view of Turgenev's narrator in *Rudin*. However, Futabatei continued to experiment with the innovative narrative style demonstrated in *The Portrait*, using a dramatized narrator in many subsequent translations. These included his translations of *Petushkov* (Turgenev's most 'Gogolian' work), of Gorky's *Heartache,* and of Gogol's *Old-fashioned Landowners.* Then Futabatei wrote his second original work: *In His Image.*

Amongst these 'Gogolian' translations there was one which, like *The Tryst, A Chance Encounter, Floating Weed* and *An Account of Bloodied Laughter,* received considerable attention from critics, and that was *The Depression Bug,* Futabatei's translation of Gorky's *Heartache.* However, the response to this work was overwhelmingly negative, with much criticism directed at Futabatei's excessive use of dialect, which domesticates the whole text. In fact Futabatei domesticated the original not so much through the use of dialect, as through the conversion of the original narrative to a 'Gogolian' one, told by a dramatized narrator. For this reason many scenes in *The Depression Bug* are reminiscent of scenes in *Floating Clouds,* with a garrulous narrator (such as we also find in *The Portrait*) often mocking the main characters. The introduction of a dramatized narrator within the story makes *The Depression Bug* one of Futabatei's most creative translations, yet this very creativity became the target of many critics and translators of Russian literature, Yonekawa Masao (1963) amongst them. This translation needs to be reevaluated, with credit being given to the successful demonstration of its innovative narrative style.

In *In His Image,* written immediately after the translation of Gogol's *Old-fashioned Landowners,* we may clearly discern a battle between a 'Gogolian' narrative, told by a dramatized narrator, and a 'Turgenevan' narrative, told from an omniscient point of view. The apparent resemblance between the opening of *In His Image* and that of *Floating Clouds* suggests that Futabatei initially adopted 'Gogolian' narrative devices, with the narrator mocking the main characters and creating a humorous narrative with some pathos. However, the similarity of the plot with that of *Floating Weed* led Futabatei to shift to a narrative more in the style of Turgenev, with an omniscient narrator positioned outside the story. The increase in the number of "-ta" forms carrying past tense meaning in the denouement of *In His Image* is clear evidence of this shift in narrative style.

We thus see that in both of Futabatei's original third-person narratives, *Floating Clouds* and *In His Image,* there is a conflict between the style of narrative which shows the influence of translating Turgenev's stories, and that which was adopted initially in *Floating Clouds,* and subsequently reinforced through the translation of stories by Gogol.

As pointed out by Araya Keizaburō (1967), the first version of *The Tryst* impressed young writers of the naturalist school not so much with its central content (the chance witnessing of an encounter between a peasant girl and an arrogant servant), as with more secondary elements: the subtle description of the forest, the clear indication of the subject with the first-person pronoun "jibun", and the use of "-ta" forms to indicate the past tense. In the second version of *The Tryst* and in *A Fortuitous Encounter,* Futabatei aimed to focus attention on the central episode of the story, to animate the young couple's encounter, by eliminating the repetitive use of "-ta" forms which so emphasized the past tense. However, the revised versions were poorly received, as by then the retrospective confessional mode created by the use of "-ta" forms was in vogue with the young writers of the naturalist school.

*The Tryst* is translated from Turgenev's first-person narrative *The Rendezvous,* and the use of "-ta" forms in the first version was very effective in reproducing the clear indication of the subject and the reflective, retrospective point of view. It is perhaps not surprising that the revisions of the second version were not welcomed, and that Futabatei's attempts to produce a more animated version were regarded as a failure. He was more successful in creating an animated narrative in *The Portrait.* The style he adopted in that translation, with its use of "-ta" forms for past perfective verbs, was most suitable for Gogol's third-person narrative story. Araya has questioned whether the Russian writer whose style Futabatei was closest to was indeed Turgenev, suggesting that Gogol's narrative style was closer to Futabatei's. It does seem that Futabatei's translations of Gogolian third-person narratives show the way he might have taken when writing *Floating Clouds* and *In His Image.*

Futabatei was also creative in his translations of first-person narratives. Despite the relative failure of the second version of *The Tryst* and *A Fortuitous Encounter,* Futabatei went on to develop another innovative narrative style in subsequent translations of Turgenev's first-person narratives, where he developed two coexisting streams of time through his treatment of past imperfective verbs. The present time of the narrator-protagonist is implied by the use of retrospective "-te ita" forms, while the time flowing in the story is indicated by "-te iru" forms. Both "-te ita" and "-te iru" forms are renditions of past imperfective verbs from the original. In his final original work *Mediocrity* we can see the influence of these translations of Turgenev's first-person narratives.

Yet it is in the third-person narratives that Futabatei most clearly demonstrated his originality. Third-person narratives, told by a narrator whose presence within the story is implied, in which "-(r)u" and "-te iru" are the dominant verb forms, with limited use of "-ta" forms carrying the meaning of complete aspect, display the most characteristic style developed by Futabatei. This style has its origins in *Floating Clouds,* and is developed and revitalized in his translations of third-person narratives by Gogol and Gorky.

Araya (1967: 46) comments: "We could have made the definitive statement that all writers of the Meiji period came from Futabatei's works, just as Dostoevsky alleged that all Russian writers came from Gogol's [*Overcoat*]". Unfortunately Futabatei's influence on the following generation of writers flowed from only a limited number of his works, and principally from the first version of *The Tryst,* which does not yet show the full flowering of his originality. The influence of his original novels *Floating Clouds* and *In His Image,* and of his translations of Gogol's and Gorky's third-person narratives, which show his original style most clearly, is minor by comparison. Indeed some of these works were subjected to strong criticism by readers, writers and critics, due to their superficial stylistic resemblance to works of the Ken'yūsha group.

Only Sōseki can be seen to have developed stylistic devices similar to those developed by Futabatei in his translations of Gogolian narratives, purposefully employing fewer "-ta" forms in the narratives of his early works. It is regrettable that more writers did not adopt some of Futabatei's later innovations. The translation style developed in Futabatei's translations from Gogol and Gorky (in which "-ta" forms carry the meaning of complete aspect, and "-te iru" forms are used to translate past tense verbs of imperfective aspect) offer a striking alternative to the style which has dominated Japanese translations for the past century (in which "-ta" forms are used to translate all the past tense verbs of the original). This dominant translation style has been consistently criticized by Yanabu Akira (1983: 99-101), whose suggested usage of "-te iru" and "-ta" forms is remarkably similar to the usage adopted by Futabatei. Yanabu defines "-te iru" and "-ta" endings not as present and past tense markers, but as something more akin to aspectual markers. In his view "-ta" forms objectify and confirm the actions taking place before the reader's eyes, while "-te iru" forms indicate that the speaker participates and witnesses the actions, but has not yet confirmed them. If we adopt Yanabu's definition, the dramatized narrator can be the speaker, and "-te iru" and "-ta" from verbs may be employed not as tense markers, but as markers which distinguish between facts confirmed and unconfirmed. We thus see that "-te iru" and "-ta" forms have been used most effectively as the "spoken language" of the dramatized narrator in Futabatei's translations of Gogolian stories. This dramatized narrator addresses the reader, not so directly as in *Floating Clouds,* with more sophistication, but still in a spoken style which emphasizes the aspectual meanings of the verbs.

Another significant feature of Futabatei's style, when translating stories by Gogol and Gorky, is the omission of third-person pronouns. Here again Futabatei demonstrates an alternative to the common practice amongst Japanese translators of literally translating third-person (and other personal) pronouns. Although Futabatei did make frequent use of third-person pronouns in *The Hard Life of a Jew,* in other translations of third-person narratives, and particularly in *The Portrait* and *Two madmen,* he strictly limited their use. In *The Portrait* the absence of third-person pronouns facilitates the merging of the dramatized narrator's point of view with that of the protagonist. In *Two Madmen* it assists the introduction of the protagonist's monologue into the third-person narrative, effectively converting it for a time to a first-person narrative.

It is curious that such strategies as these have not been taken up more by contemporary translators. One translator who has acknowledged the elimination of "-ta" forms from the second version of *The Tryst,* and the zero-rendition of third-person pronouns in both versions of that work, is Yanase Naoki (2000: 12-52). He advocates avoiding the use of pronouns in translation, and follows this principle in his own translations from English.

In conclusion, this study has shown that while Futabatei has been very influential, there are still lessons to be learnt from Futabatei's work, and particularly from the various creative methods he devised in the course of his many translations. Contemporary translators would do well to re-examine Futabatei's legacy.

# Appendix — A List of Futabatei Shimei's Translations and Original Works

(original works are underlined)

### 1st period of literary activity

| | | |
|---|---|---|
| 1886 | Feb (?) | Translation of an unidentified work by Gogol. This translation was of a short story of some 30 pages, made in the colloquial *genbun itchi* style. Although no longer extant, it is recorded as having been shown to Futabatei's mentor Tsubouchi Shōyō |
| 1886 | Mar | "Kyomutō katagi [The Characteristics of Nihilists]". This was an extract from Turgenev's *Otsy i deti [Fathers and Sons],* shown to Tsubouchi Shōyō and intended for publication. Its publication did not eventuate and it is no longer extant |
| 1887 | Jun | *Ukigumo [Floating Clouds],* Part One |
| 1888 | Feb | *Ukigumo,* Part Two |
| | Jul-Aug | *Aibiki [The Tryst]* (the first version of Turgenev's *Svidanie [The Rendezvous]*) |
| | | *Oitachi [Childhood]* (a short extract from Goncharov's *Oblomov,* discovered and published in 1913) |
| 1888/9 | Oct-Jan | *Meguriai [A Chance Encounter]* (the first version of Turgenev's *Tri vstrechi [Three Encounters]*) |
| 1889 | Jul-Aug | *Ukigumo,* Part Three (unfinished) |

### 2nd period of literary activity

| | | |
|---|---|---|
| 1896 | Nov | *Aibiki* (the second version of Turgenev's *Svidanie*) |
| | | *Kigū [A Fortuitous Encounter]* (the second version of Turgenev's *Tri vstrechi*) |
| | | *Katakoi [One-sided Love]* (Turgenev's *Asya*) |
| 1897 | Jan-Mar | *Shōzōga [The Portrait]* (Gogol's *Portret [The Portrait]*) |
| | Apr | *Yumekatari [Dream Talk]* (Turgenev's *Son [The Dream]*) |
| | Apr-Oct | *Ukikusa [Floating Weed]* (Turgenev's *Rudin*) |
| 1898 | Jan | *Yudaya-jin [The Jew]* (Turgenev's *Zhid [The Jew]*) |
| | Jul | *Oyakokoro [Parent's Heart]* (original source not yet identified) |
| | Nov | *Kusare-en [The Mismatch]* (Turgenev's *Petushkov*) |
| 1899 | Jan | *Sakabukuro [Drunkards]* (original source not yet identified) |

### 3rd period of literary activity

| | | |
|---|---|---|
| 1903 | Dec | *Keburi [Smoke]* (Turgenev's *Dym [Smoke]*) (unfinished, and unpublished, but the manuscript is extant) |
| 1904 | Jan | *Kokuryūkōhan no yūfu [A Courageous Woman of the Amur River* |

*Region]* (Elets' *Amurskaya geroinya: Pri osade Blagoveshchenska Kitaitsami [A Heroine of the Amur River: During the Siege of Blagoveshchensk by the Chinese]*)

1904 Feb *Yonin kyōsan-dan [Four Person Communist Group]* (Potapenko's *Istoriya odnoi kommuny: Iz vospominanii starogo studenta [The History of a Commune: From the Recollections of an Old Student]*)

Jul *Tsutsu o makura [A Rifle for a Pillow]* (Tolstoy's *Rubka lesa [The Woodfelling]*)

Jul *Yokka-kan [Four Days]* (Garshin's *Chetyre dnya [Four Days]*)

1905 Jan *Wakarazuya [The Blockhead]* (an adaptation of Turgenev's *Zavtrak u predvoditelya [Breakfast with the Marshall of the Nobility]*)

Jan *Rosuke no tsuma [The Wife of a Russian]* (an adaptation of Shcheglov's *Nevozmozhnyi kharakter [An Insufferable Character]*)

Feb-Mar *Jū no ukiyo [The Hard Life of a Jew]* (Gorky's *Kain i Artem [Kain and Artem]*)

1906 Jan-Mar *Fusagi no mushi [The Depression Bug]* (Gorky's *Toska [Melancholy]*)

Feb *Nenashi-gusa [Rootless Grass]* (Garshin's *To, chego ne bylo [That Which Was Not]*) - translated in a pseudo-classical style

Apr *Hai iro bito [Person in Grey]* (Gorky's *O serom [About the Colour Grey]*) - translated in a pseudo-classical style

May *Mukashi no hito [Olden Day People]* (Gogol's *Starosvetskie pomeshchiki [Old-fashioned Landowners]*)

Oct-Dec *Sono omokage [In His Image]*

1907 Feb-Aug *Shishi no matsugo [The Last Moments of a Revolutionary]* (Polivanov's *Konchilsya [He Is Dead]*)

Mar *Ni kyōjin [Two Madmen]* (Gorky's *Oshibka [A Mistake]*)

Mar-May *Kyōjin nikki [A Madman's Diary]* (Gogol's *Zapiski sumasshedshego [Notes of a Madman]*)

Jul *Kojiki [The Beggars]* (Gorky's *Ded Arkhip i Len'ka [Grandpa Arkhip and Lenka]*)

Oct-Dec *Heibon [Mediocrity]*

1908 Jan *Kesshōki [An Account of Bloodied Laughter]* (Andreyev's *Krasnyi smekh [Red laughter]*)

(This list is derived from Futabatei Shimei 1971b, 1985a & 1985b; Nakamura Mitsuo 1958.)

# References


Anonymous (1906) "Fusagi no mushi' no hankyō [A Response to 'Fusagi no mushi']', Waseda bungaku [Waseda Literature] (April), cited in Futabatei Shimei (1964c: 385-391).

Anonymous (1908) "Ukikusa' no hankyō [A Response to 'Ukikusa']', in Teikoku Bungaku [Imperial Literature] (November), cited in Futabatei Shimei (1964b: 376).

Anonymous (1907) "Sono omokage' no hankyō [Responses to 'Sono omokage'], in Teikoku Bungaku [Imperial Literature] (October), cited in Futabatei Shimei (1964c: 394-399).

Araya Keizaburō (1967) 'Futabatei yaku 'Aibiki' no mondai [A Problem Concerning Futabatei's Translation 'Aibiki']', Waseda Daigaku Hikaku bungaku nenshi [Waseda University Annual Journal of Comparative Literature] (July): 46-68.

Aston, W.G. (1899) A History of Japanese Literature. 2nd ed., rpt. Tokyo: Tuttle, 1972.

Booth, Wayne C (1961) The Rhetoric of Fiction, Chicago and London: The University of Chicago Press.

Bulwer-Lytton, Edward (1839) Ernest Maltravers, London: Belin & Co.

Cockerill, Hiroko (2003) 'Style and Narrative in the Translations and Novels of Futabatei Shimei', doctoral dissertation, University of Queensland.

Comrie, Bernard (1976) Aspect: An Introduction to the Study of Verbal Aspect and Related Problems, Cambridge: Cambridge University Press.

Cuddon, J.A. (1992) The Penguin Dictionary of Literary Terms and Literary Theory, Third Edition, New York: Penguin Books.

Fanger, Donald (1979) The Creation of Nikolai Gogol, Cambridge Massachusetts: Harvard University Press.

Fukuda Kiyoto (1992) Ken'yūsha no bungaku undō [Ken'yūsha's Literary Activities], Tokyo: Nihon Tosho Sentā.

Futabatei Shimei (1919) An Adopted Husband, translated by Buhachirō Mitsui and Gregg M. Sinclair, New York: Knopf. Reprinted by Greenwood Press, 1969.

----- (1927) Mediocrity, translated by Glenn W. Shaw, Tokyo: Hokusei dō Press.

----- (1964a), Futabatei Shimei zenshū [Complete Works], Vol. 1. Sōsaku, hon'yaku 1 [Original Works and Translations 1], Tokyo: Iwanami Shoten.

----- (1964b) Futabatei Shimei zenshū [Complete Works], Vol. 2. Sōsaku, hon'yaku 2 [Original Works and Translations 2], Tokyo: Iwanami Shoten.

----- (1964c) Futabatei Shimei zenshū [Complete Works], Vol. 3. Sōsaku, hon'yaku 3 [Original Works and Translations 3], Tokyo: Iwanami Shoten.

----- (1964d) Futabatei Shimei zenshū [Complete Works], Vol. 4. Sōsaku, hon'yaku 4 [Original Works and Translations 4], Tokyo: Iwanami Shoten.

----- (1965a) Futabatei Shimei zenshū [Complete Works], Vol. 5. Hyōron, kansō, sono ta [Critical Essays, Reflections, Other], Tokyo: Iwanami Shoten.

----- (1965b) Futabatei Shimei zenshū [Complete Works], Vol. 6. Nikki, techō 1 [Diaries and Memoirs 1], Tokyo: Iwanami Shoten.

----- (1965c) Futabatei Shimei zenshū [Complete Works], Vol. 7. Nikki, techō 2, shokan [Diaries and Memoirs 2, Letters], Tokyo: Iwanami Shoten.

----- (1965d) Futabatei Shimei zenshū [Complete Works], Vol. 8. Sōkō, zassan 1 [Manuscripts, Other 1], Tokyo: Iwanami Shoten.

----- (1965e) Futabatei Shimei zenshū [Complete Works], Vol. 9. Sōkō, zassan 2 [Manuscripts, Other 2], Tokyo: Iwanami Shoten.

----- (1971a) Nihon kindai bungaku taikei [Selected Works from Modern Japanese Literature]

Vol. 4, Futabatei Shimei shū [Selected Works], Tokyo: Kadokawa Shoten. (Annotated by Hata Yūzō and Yasui Ryōhei)

----- (1971b) Meiji bungaku zenshūō [Complete Works of Meiji Literature] Vol. 17, Futabatei Shimei, Saganoya Omuro shū [Selected Works], Tokyo: Chikuma Shobō.

----- (1971c) Gendai nihon bungaku taikei [Selected Works from Modern Japanese Literature] Vol. 1, Seiji shōsetsu [Political Novels], Tsubouchi Shōyō, Futabatei Shimei shū [Selected Works], Tokyo: Chikuma Shobō.

----- (1984) Futabatei Shimei zenshū [Complete Works], Vol. 1, Tokyo: Chikuma Shobō. (Annotated by Togawa Shinsuke and Yasui Ryōhei)

----- (1985a) Futabatei Shimei zenshū [Complete Works], Vol. 2, Tokyo: Chikuma Shobō. (Annotated by Togawa Shinsuke and Yasui Ryōhei)

----- (1985b) Futabatei Shimei zenshū [Complete Works], Vol. 3, Tokyo: Chikuma Shobō. (Annotated by Togawa Shinsuke and Yasui Ryōhei)

----- (1993) Futabatei Shimei zenshū [Complete Works], Bekkan [Supplement], Tokyo: Chikuma Shobō. (Annotated by Togawa Shinsuke and Yasui Ryōhei)

Garshin, Vsevolod (1897) Pervaya knizhka rasskazov [A First Book of Stories], St. Petersburg: M. M. Stasyulevich.

----- (1988) From the Reminiscences of Private Ivanov and Other Stories, translated by Peter Henry, Liv Tudge, Donald Rayfield and Philip Taylor, London: Angel Books.

Genette, Gerard (1980) Narrative Discourse: An Essay in Method, translated by Jane E. Lewin, New York: Cornell University Press.

Gogol, N.V. (1874a) 'Starosvetskie pomeshchiki [Old-fashioned Landowners]' in Russkaya biblioteka [Russian Library] III: Nikolai Vasil'evich Gogol', St. Petersburg: Stasyulevich.

----- (1874b) Polnoe sobranie sochinenii N.V. Gogolya [Complete Works of N.V. Gogol] Vol. 4, Moscow: A.I. Mamontov & Co.

----- (1923) The Overcoat and Other Stories, translated by Constance Garnett, London: Chatto and Windus.

----- (1973a) Polnoe sobranie sochinenii, tom vtoroi, Mirgorod [Complete Works, Vol. 2, Mirgorod], Nendeln/Liechtenstein: Kraus Reprint. (From 1937 Akademiya Nauk edition)

----- (1973b) Polnoe sobranie sochinenii, tom tretii, Povesti [Complete Works, Vol. 3, Novellas], Nendeln/Liechtenstein: Kraus Reprint. (From 1938 Akademiya Nauk edition)

----- (Gōgori) (1983) Kyōjin nikki, ta nihen [A Madman's Diary and Two Other Stories], translated by Yokota Mizuho, Tokyo: Iwanami Shoten (paperback).

----- (Gōgori) (2000) 'Fūshi shōsetsu Kyōjin nikki [A Satirical Novel: A Madman's Diary]', translated by Imano Gukō, in Kawato Michiaki, Sakakibara Takanori (eds) Meiji hon'yaku bungaku zenshū [Complete Meiji Translation Literature] Shinbun zasshi hen [Newspaper and Journal Publications] Vol. 37, Gōgori shū [Selected Works], Tokyo: Ōzorasha,175-199.

Gorky, M. (1908) Rasskazy [Stories], Vol. 1, 10th edition, St. Petersburg: Znanie.

----- (1939) A Book of Short Stories by Maxim Gorky, translated by Avrahm Yarmolinsky and Baroness Moura Budberg, London: Jonathan Cape.

----- (1960a) Sobranie sochinenii, tom pervyi, Proizvedeniya 1892-1896 gg. [Collected Works, Vol. 1, 1892-1896], Moscow: Khudozhestvennaya literatura.

----- (1960b) Sobranie sochinenii, tom vtoroi, Proizvedeniya 1896-1899 gg. [Collected Works, Vol. 2, 1896-1899], Moscow: Khudozhestvennaya literatura.

----- (1968) Polnoe sobranie sochinenii, tom pervyi, Rasskazy, Ocherki, Nabroski, Stikhi, 1885-1894 [Complete Works, Vol. 1, Stories, Sketches, Drafts, Poetry, 1885-1894], Moscow: Nauka.

----- (1969a) Polnoe sobranie sochinenii, tom vtoroi, Rasskazy, Ocherki, Nabroski, Stikhi, 1894-1896 [Complete Works, Vol. 2, Stories, Sketches, Drafts, Poetry, 1894-1896], Moscow: Nauka.

----- (1969b) Polnoe sobranie sochinenii [Complete Works] Vol. 4, Moscow: Nauka.

----- (1970) Polnoe sobranie sochinenii, tom sed'moi, varianty [Complete Works, Vol. 7, Variants], Moscow: Nauka.

Hatano Kazuhiro (1982) 'Futabatei to Gōgori: 'Ukigumo' no buntai o megutte [Futabatei and Gogol: Concerning the Style of 'Ukigumo']', Waseda Daigaku Hikaku bungaku nenshi [Waseda University Annual Journal of Comparative Literature] (March): 64-80.

----- (1994) 'Gōgori no Futabatei yaku o megutte [On the Translation of Gogol's Works by Futabatei]', Roshiago Roshia bungaku kenkyū [Studies in Russian Language and Literature] 26(October): 69-81.

Henry, Peter (1983) A Hamlet of His Time: Vsevolod Garshin: The Man, His Works and His Milieu, Oxford: Willem A. Meeuws.

Hirotsu Ryūrō (1965) Meiji bungaku zenshū [Complete Works of Meiji Literature], Vol. 19, Hirotsu Ryūrō shū [Selected Works], Tokyo: Chikuma Shobō.

Ikari Akira (1961) Ken'yūsha no bungaku [Ken'yūsha's Literature], Tokyo: Hanawa Shobō.

Isahaya Yūichi (1982) 'Futabatei to Roshia bungaku: Gōgori o chūshin ni [Futabatei and Russian Literature: Mainly on Gogol]', Shinshū Daigaku Jinbun kagaku ronshū [Shinshū University Collection of Articles in the Humanities] 16(March): 51-61.

Itō Sei (1973) 'Ozaki Kōyō', in Itō Sei zenshū [Complete Works], Tokyo: Shinchōsha, 8-22.

Jinzai Kiyoshi (1954) 'Futabatei no hon'yaku taido: Toku ni Tsurugēnefu no bāi ni tsuite [Futabatei's Attitude Towards His Translations: Especially About His Translations of Turgenev's Stories]', in Futabatei Shimei (1965e: 171-189).

Karatani Kōjin (1988) Nihon kindai bungaku no kigen [Origins of Modern Japanese Literature], Tokyo: Kōdansha (bungei paperback).

----- (1992) Sōseki ron shūsei [A Collection of Articles about Sōseki], Tokyo: Daisanbunmeisha.

Karlina R. G. (Kārurina, Eru) (1962) 'Hasegawa Futabatei to Roshia bungaku no sōsaku jō no tsunagari [The Connection between Futabatei Shimei and Russian Literature as Expressed in His Own Work] Nihon bungaku [Japanese Literature] 11(July): 27-40.

Kataoka Ryōichi (1965) 'Ozaki Kōyō: Sakka to shite no shōgai no rinkaku [Ozaki Kōyō: An Outline of His Life as a Writer]', in Meiji bungaku zenshū [Complete Works of Meiji Literature], Vol. 18, Ozaki Kōyō shū [Selected Works], Tokyo: Chikuma shobō, 375-399.

Kaun, Alexander (1968) Maxim Gorky and His Russia, New York: Benjamin Blom, Inc.

Kazama, Rikizō (1976) 'Dōsatai no seikaku to sono Hyōgen keitai [Characteristics of Verb Forms and their Descriptive Forms], cited in Kindaichi (1976: 29).

Keene, Donald (1978) World within Walls: Japanese Literature of the Pre-Modern Era 1600-1867, Tokyo: Charles E. Tuttle.

----- (1984) Dawn to the West: Japanese Literature of the Modern Era, Vol. 1, New York: Holt, Rinehart and Winston.

Kimura Shōichi (1956) 'Futabatei no Tsurugēnefu mono no hon'yaku ni tsuite [On Futabatei's Translations of Turgenev's Works]', Bungaku [Literature] (May): 41-49.

Kimura Takashi (1997) 'Futabatei ga mochi'ita Tsurugēnefu sakuhin shū [Turgenev's Selected Works Used by Futabatei]', Bungaku (Spring): 120-128.

Kindaichi Haruhiko (1950) 'Kokugo dōshi no ichi-bunrui [A Classification of Japanese Verbs]', Gengo kenkyū [Language Studies] 15: 48-63.

----- (ed) (1976) Nihongo dōshi no asupekuto [Aspect of Japanese Verbs], Tokyo: Mugi Shobō.
----- (1988) Nihongo [The Japanese Language] Vol. 2, Tokyo: Iwanami Shoten.
Kindaichi Masumi (1994) Roshiago jisei ron; Rekishiteki genzai to sono shūhen [The Russian Language Tense System: Historic Present and Other Peripheral Rhetorics], Tokyo: Sanseidō.
Kitaoka Seiji (1965) "Shōsetsu sōron' zaigen kō: Futabatei to Berinsukī [Identifying Materials Used in Writing 'A General Discussion of the Novel': Futabatei and Belinsky]', Kokugo to kokubungaku [National Language and Literature], (July): 12-30.
----- (1967) 'Futabatei to Roshia bungaku: Shōsetsukan o chūshin ni' [Futabatei and Russian Literature: Mainly on His Idea of the Novel], in Shimizu Shigeru ed., Kindai bungaku kanshō kōza [Series on the Appreciation of Modern Literature], Vol. 1, Futabatei Shimei, Tokyo: Kadokawa Shoten, 292-307.
Knowles, A.V. (1988) Ivan Turgenev, Boston: Twayne Publishers.
Komatsu Katsusuke (1971) 'Futabatei Shimei ni okeru Gōrikī [What Gorky Meant for Futabatei Shimei]', Kōbe Gaidai ronsō [Kōbe University of Foreign Studies Collection], 22(1-2) (July):19-35.
Komori Yōichi (1985) 'Hon'yaku buntai ni okeru 'ta' to 'ru' ['Ta' and 'Ru' Forms in Translation Style]', in Futabatei Shimei zenshū [Futabatei Shimei Complete Works], Vol. 3, Monthly Bulletin 3, Tokyo: Chikuma Shobō, 3-5.
----- (1988) Kōzō to shite no katari [Narrative as Structure], Tokyo: Shin'yōsha.
----- (1994) 'Futabatei Shimei 'Heibon': Kōtsū suru shukyaku [Futabatei Shimei's 'Heibon': Interchanging Subjects and Objects]', Kokubungaku kaishaku to kyōzai no kenkyū [Reading National Literature and Studies of Teaching Materials], (June): 45-51.
----- (1996) Dekigoto to shite no yomukoto [Reading as an Event], Tokyo: Tokyo Daigaku Shuppan Kai.
Kondō Masaomi and Wakabayashi Judy (1998) 'Japanese Tradition' in Mona Baker (ed) Routledge Encyclopedia of Translation Studies, London & New York: Routledge, 485-494.
Kubo Yumi (1984) 'Kindai bungaku ni okeru jojutsu no sōchi: Meiji shoki sakka tachi no 'rikkyakuten' o megutte [Narrative Devices in Modern Literature: On the 'Standpoint' of Early Meiji Writers], Bungaku [Literature] 52(April): 98-111.
Kunikida Doppo (1974) Meiji bungaku zenshū [Complete Works of Meiji Literature], Vol. 66, Kunikida Doppo shū [Selected Works], Tokyo: Chikuma Shobō.
Maruoka Akira (1967) 'Kōyō no bungakuteki isan [Kōyō's Literary Legacy]', in Fukuda Kiyoto (ed) Kindai bungaku kanshō kōza [Series on the Appreciation of Modern Literature], Vol. 2 Kōda Rohan, Ozaki Kōyō, Tokyo: Kadokawa Shoten, 299-308.
Masamune Hakuchō (1926) 'Ozaki Kōyō', in Gendai nihon bungaku zenshū [Complete Works of Modern Japanese Literature], Vol. 2, Ozaki Kōyō, Yamada Bimyō, Hirotsu Ryūrō, Kawakami Bizan shū [Selected Works], Tokyo: Chikuma Shobō, 1954, 383-389.
----- (1928) 'Futabatei ni tsuite [About Futabatei]', Kaizō [Change] 10(10), cited in Satō Seirō (1995: 448).
Minamoto Takashi (1989a) 'Futabatei Shimei yaku 'Kesshōki' ni tsuite [About Futabatei Shimei's Translation 'Kesshōki']', Waseda Daigaku Yōroppa bungaku kenkyū [Waseda University Studies in European Literature], 36: 69-83.
----- (1989b) "Kesshōki' kara 'Heibon' e [From 'Kesshōki' to 'Heibon']', Roshiago Roshia bungaku kenkyū [Studies in Russian Language and Literature] 21(October): 1-12.
----- (1989c) 'Futabatei no kichō ni tsuite: Kōki Futabatei ron no zentei to shite[On Futabatei's Return to Japan: As a Prelude to His Later Literary Activity], Waseda daigaku daigakuin bun-

gaku kenkyūka kiyō [Bulletin of Literary Studies, Waseda University Postgraduate Studies], Supplement No. 16, Bungaku geijutsu hen [Literature and Art Section]: 103-114.
----- (1997) 'Shinkei suijaku no bungaku: Tanizaki Jun'ichirō to Roshia bungaku [The Literature of Neurasthenics: Tanizaki Jun'ichirō and Russian Literature]', in Waseda daigaku daigakuin bungaku kenkyūka kiyō [Bulletin of Literary Studies, Waseda University Postgraduate Studies], No. 43, Daini bunsatsu, Eibungaku, Furansu bungaku, Doitsu bungaku, Roshia bungaku, Chūgoku bungaku [Second Supplement: English Literature, French Literature, German Literature, Russian Literature, Chinese Literature]: 83-92.
Mizuno Kiyoshi (1958) "'Ukigumo', 'Aibiki',' Meguriai': Ji no bun ni okeru bunmatsugo ni tsuite ['Ukigumo', 'Aibiki', 'Meguriai': Concerning the Sentence Endings of their Narratives]', Gengo seikatsu [Language Life], (May): 62-64.
Momiuchi Yūko (1999) 'Futabatei Shimei yaku 'Aibiki' ni okeru 'onchō' to 'bunchō' ni tsuite ['Tone' and 'Style' in Futabatei Shimei's Translation 'Aibiki']', Roshiago Roshia bungaku kenkyū [Studies in Russian Language and Literature], 31: 98-108.
Munakata Kazushige (1994) 'Ozaki Kōyō 'Tajō takon': Shōzōga to shashin [Ozaki Kōyō's 'Tajō takon: Portraits and Pictures]', Kokubungaku kaishaku to kyōzai no kenkyū [Reading National Literature and Studies of Teaching Materials], 39(7) (June): 24-30.
----- (1995) 'Genbun itchi undō [The Genbun itchi Movement]' in Ōya Yukiyo, Kanda Yumiko, Matsumura Tomomi (eds) (1995) Sutairu no bungakushi [A History of Literary Style], Tokyo: Tōkyōdō Shuppan, 36-41.
Nakamura Mitsuo (1958) Futabatei Shimei den [Futabatei Shimei: A Life], Tokyo: Kōdansha.
----- (1968) Modern Japanese Fiction (1868-1912), Revised Edition, Tokyo: Kokusai Bunka Shinkō Kai.
----- (1970) 'Kaisetsu [Expository Commentary]' in Shimazaki Tōson, Haru [Spring], Tokyo: Iwanami Shoten, 309-315.
Nakamura Nobuaki (2002) "Shinsetsu Hachijū nichi kan sekai isshū' no ichi [The place of the novel 'Shinsetsu Hachijū nichi kan sekai isshū ']", in Shin nihon koten bungaku taikei [A New Series of Classic Japanese Literature], Meiji hen Vol. 15, Tokyo: Iwanami Shoten.
Nakamura Shin'ichirō (1973) 'Sakuhin Ron', in Natsume Sōseki (1973) Kōfu, Tokyo: Kadokawa Shoten, cited in Keene (1984: 322).
Nakayama Shōzaburō (1937) 'Futabatei to Roshia bungaku [Futabatei and Russian Literature]', Bungaku [Literature] 5(9): 56-80.
Natsume Sōseki (1956) Sōseki zenshū [Sōseki's Complete Works] Vol. 6 Kōfu [The Miner], Tokyo: Iwanami Shoten.
----- (1988) The Miner, Translated by Jay Rubin, Stanford: Stanford University Press.
Nekrasov, N.A. (1898) Niva [The Meadow] Ezhemesyachnye literaturnye prilozheniya [Monthly Literary Supplement] (2):344, cited in Tolstoy (1972: 309-310).
Nihon Daijiten Kankō Kai (ed) (1972-6) Nihon kokugo daijiten [Great Japanese Dictionary] 20 vols., Tokyo: Shōgakukan.
Nogami Toyoichirō (1938) Hon'yaku ron [Translation Theory], Tokyo: Iwanami Shoten.
Noguchi Takehiko (1980) 'Shōsetsu no nihongo [The Japanese Language in Novels]', in Ōno Susumu (ed), Nihongo no sekai [The World of Japanese Language], Vol. 13, Tokyo: Chūōkōronsha.
----- (1994) San'ninshō no hakken made [To the Discovery of the Third-person Narrative], Tokyo: Chikuma Shobō.
Odagiri Hideo (1970) Futabatei Shimei: Nihon kindai bungaku no seiritsu [Futabatei Shimei: The Establishment of Modern Japanese Literature], Tokyo: Iwanami Shoten.

Oketani Hideaki (1997) Futabatei Shimei to Meiji Nihon [Futabatei Shimei and Meiji Japan], Tokyo: Ozawa Shoten.

Okumura Tsuneya (1954) 'Daimeishi 'kare', 'kanojo','karera' no kōsatsu: Sono seiritsu to bungo kōgo [An examination of the Pronouns 'He', 'She', 'They': Their Formation and Use in Written and Colloquial Language], Kokugo kokubun [National Language and Literature], 23(11): 63-78.

Ōta Hiroko (1997) Futabatei Shimei 'Aibiki' no hyōki kenkyū to honbun: sakuin [Research into the Scripts of Futabatei Shimei's 'Aibiki' and the Original Text: With Index], Ōsaka: Izumi Shoin.

Ozaki Kōyō (1954) Gendai nihon bungaku zenshū [Complete Works of Modern Japanese Literature] Vol. 2, Ozaki Kōyō, Hirotsu Ryūrō, Yamada Bimyō, Kawakami Bizan shū [Selected Works], Tokyo: Chikuma Shobō.

----- (1965a) Meiji bungaku zenshū [Complete Works of Meiji Literature], Vol. 18, Ozaki Kōyō shū [Selected Works], Tokyo: Chikuma Shobō.

----- (1965b) Gendai bungaku taikei, Vol. 2, Ozaki Kōyō, Izumi Kyōka shū [Selected Works], Tokyo: Chikuma Shobō.

----- (1993) Kōyō zenshū [Complete Works], Vol. 3, Tokyo: Iwanami Shoten.

Ozaki Satoakira (1967) Kindai bunshō no reimei [The Dawn of Modern Composition], Tokyo: Ōfūsha.

Peace, Richard (1981) The Enigma of Gogol: An Examination of the Writings of N.V. Gogol and their Place in the Russian Literary Tradition, Cambridge: Cambridge University Press.

Rimer, J. Thomas (ed) (1995) A Hidden Fire: Russian and Japanese Cultural Encounters, 1868-1926, Stanford: Stanford University Press.

Rubin, Jay (1988) 'Afterword' in Natsume Sōseki (1988) The Miner, translated by Jay Rubin, Stanford: Stanford University Press, 165-181.

Ryan, Marleigh Grayer (1967) Japan's First Modern Novel: Ukigumo of Futabatei Shimei, New York: Columbia University Press.

Saitō Ryoku'u (1990) 'Shōsetsu hasshū [Eight Schools of the Modern Novel]' in Saitō Ryoku'u zenshū [Complete Works], Vol. 1, Tokyo: Chikuma Shobō.

Satō Seirō (1995) Futabatei Shimei kenkyū [Futabatei Shimei: A Study], Tokyo: Yūseidō.

Seeley, Frank Freideberg (1991) Turgenev: A Reading of His Fiction, Cambridge: Cambridge University Press.

Seki Ryōichi (1967) "Ukigumo' no seiritsu [Ukigumo's Genesis]', in Shimizu Shigeru (1967: 308-317).

Shifman A.I. (1960) 'Primechaniya [Notes]' in Tolstoy, L.N. Sobranie sochinenii [Collected Works] Vol. 2 Povesti i rasskazy [Novellas and Stories] 1852-1856, Moscow: Khudozhestvennaya literatura.

Shimazaki Tōson (1970) Haru [Spring], Tokyo: Iwanami Shoten (paperback).

----- (1972) Meiji bungaku zenshū [Complete Works of Meiji Literature] Vol. 69. Shimazaki Tōson shū [Selected Works], Tokyo: Chikuma Shobō.

Shimizu Shigeru (1958) 'Kōki no Futabatei [Futabatei in His Late Period]', Nihon bungaku [Japanese Literature] Vol. 3/4/7, reprinted in Nihon Bungaku Kenkyū Shiryō Kankō Kai (ed) (1979) Nihon bungaku kenkyū shiryō sōsho: Tsubouchi Shōyō, Futabatei Shimei [Collection of Research Materials on Japanese Literature: Tsubouchi Shōyō, Futabatei Shimei], Tokyo: Yūseidō, 264-294.

----- (1960) 'Shikitei Sanba to Futabatei Shimei: Ketsuron no nai nōto [Shikitei Sanba and Futabatei Shimei: Notes with No Conclusion]', Nihon Bungaku (4), reprinted in Nihon Bungaku

Kenkyū Shiryō Kankō Kai (ed) (1979) Nihon bungaku kenkyū shiryō sōsho: Tsubouchi Shōyō, Futabatei Shimei [Collection of Research Materials on Japanese Literature: Tsubouchi Shōyō, Futabatei Shimei], Tokyo: Yūseidō, 180-195.

----- (ed) (1967) Kindai bungaku kanshō kōza [Modern Literary Appreciation Series], Vol. 1, Futabatei Shimei, Tokyo: Kadokawa Shoten.

----- (1983) 'Futabatei 'Shinpen Ukigumo' no bōtō oyobi Gōgori, Dosutoefusukī to no kanren ni tsuite [The Beginning of Futabatei's 'Shinpen Ukigumo' and its Relationship to Gogol's and Dostoevsky's Works]' Waseda Daigaku Hikaku bungaku nenshi [Waseda University Annual Journal of Comparative Literature] 23: 34-51.

Suge Satoko (2000) 'Kōyō bungaku ni okeru 'riaru' no henshitsu: Mō hitotsu no 'fūzoku' no kōyō [The Shift of Reality in Kōyō's Works: Another Effect of 'Customs']', Bungaku [Literature] 1-2: 109-118.

Sugiyama Yasuhiko (1968) 'Hasegawa Futabatei ni okeru genbun itchi [Genbun itchi Written by Hasegawa Futabatei]', Bungaku [Literature] 36(September): 34-51.

Takahashi Tarō (1976) 'Sugata to mokuromi [Aspect and Intention]', in Kindaichi (1976) Nihongo dōshi no asupekuto [Aspect of Japanese Verbs] Tokyo: Mugi Shobō, 117-153.

Tanaka Kunio (1998) 'Futabatei Shimei 'Ukigumo' no seiritsu [The Formation of Futabatei Shimei's 'Ukigumo']', Ōsaka Keizai Daigaku kenkyū sōsho [Ōsaka University of Economic Studies Collection of Research Papers], Vol. 32, Tokyo: Sōbunsha Shuppan.

Tayama Katai (1909) 'Futabatei Shimei kun [Mr. Futabatei Shimei]', in Tsubouchi Shōyō, Uchida Roan (eds) Futabatei Shimei: Kakuhōmen yori mitaru Hasegawa Tatsunosuke kun oyobi sono tsuikai [Futabatei Shimei: Hasegawa Tatsunosuke from Various Points of View and Recollections about Him], Tokyo: Ifūsha.

----- (1923) 'Kindai no shōsetsu [Modern Novels]', cited in Hasegawa Izumi and Isogai Hideo (eds) (1979) Shiryō ni yoru kindai nihon bungaku [Commentaries on Modern Japanese Literature], Tokyo: Meiji Shoin, 18.

----- (1968) Meiji bungaku zenshū [Complete Works of Meiji Literature], Vol. 67, Tayama Katai shū [Selected Works], Tokyo: Chikuma Shobō.

----- (1981) The Quilt and Other Stories, translated and with an introduction by Kenneth G. Henshall, Tokyo: University of Tokyo Press.

Teramura Hideo (1984) Nihongo no shintakusu to imi [The Syntax and Semantics of Japanese], Vol. 2, Tokyo: Kuroshio Shuppan.

Togawa Shinsuke (1971) Futabatei Shimei ron [Futabatei Shimei Studies], Tokyo: Chikuma Shobō.

Tolstoy, L.N. (1873) Sochineniya grafa L.N. Tolstogo, Chast' tret'ya [Works of Count L.N. Tolstoy, Part 3], Moscow: Katkov & Co.

----- (1960) Sobranie sochinenii, Vol. 2, Povesti i rasskazy 1852-1856 [Collected Works Vol. 2, Novellas and Stories 1852-1856], Moscow: Izdatel'stvo khudozhestvennoi literatury.

----- (1972) Polnoe sobranie sochinenii [Complete Works] Vol. 3, Nendeln/Liechtenstein: Kraus Reprint. (from 1932 Moscow edition)

----- (1993) How Much Land Does a Man Need and Other Stories, translated by Ronald Wilks, Harmondsworth: Penguin.

Turgenev, I.S. (1865) Sochineniya [Works] (1844-1864), Volumes 1 & 2, Karlsrue: Brothers Salaev.

----- (1894) Rudin, translated by Constance Garnett, London: Heinemann.

----- (1895) A Sportsman's Sketches, translated by Constance Garnett, London: William Heinemann.

----- (1897) Dream Tales and Prose Poems by Ivan Turgenev, translated by Constance Garnett, London: William Heinemann.

----- (1898) A Lear of the Steppes and Other Stories by Ivan Turgenev, translated by Constance Garnett, London: William Heinemann.

----- (1899a) The Jew and Other Stories by Ivan Turgenev, translated by Constance Garnett, London: William Heinemann.

----- (1899b) A Desperate Character and Other Stories by Ivan Turgenev, translated by Constance Garnett, London: William Heinemann.

----- (Tsurugēnefu) (1952) Katakoi, Fausuto [One-sided Love, Faust] translated by Yonekawa Masao, Tokyo: Shinchōsha (paperback).

----- (1963a) Sochineniya [Works], Vol. 4, Zapiski okhotnika [A Sportsman's Sketches], 1847-1874, Moscow-Leningrad: Akademiya nauk SSSR.

----- (1963b) Sochineniya [Works], Vol. 5, Povesti i rasskazy, Stat'i i retsenzii [Novellas and Stories, Articles and Reviews], 1844-1854, Moscow-Leningrad: Akademiya nauk SSSR.

----- (1963c) Sochineniya [Works], Vol. 6, Povesti i rasskazy, 'Rudin', Stat'i i vospominaniya [Novellas and Stories, 'Rudin', Articles and Memoirs], 1853-1856, Moscow-Leningrad: Akademiya nauk SSSR.

----- (1964) Sochineniya [Works], Vol. 7, Povesti i rasskazy, 'Dvoryanskoe gnezdo', [Novellas and Stories, 'A Nest of Gentlefolk]', 1856-1858, Moscow-Leningrad: Akademiya nauk SSSR.

----- (1966) Sochineniya [Works], Vol. 11, Povesti i rasskazy [Novellas and Stories], 1871-1877, Moscow-Leningrad: Akademiya nauk SSSR.

----- (1974) Ivan Turgenev's Selected Stories, translated by Constance Garnett, London: Heinemann.

Turney, Alan (1985) Sōseki's Development as a Novelist until 1907: With Special Reference to the Genesis, Nature and Position in his Work of 'Kusa Makura', Tokyo: The Tōyō Bunko.

Twine, Nanette (1975) 'The Genbunitchi Movement: Its Origin, Development and Conclusion', doctoral dissertation, University of Queensland.

----- (1991) Language and the Modern State: The Reform of Written Japanese, London: Routledge.

Uchida Roan (1925) 'Omoidasu hitobito [The People I Remember]', in Usui Yoshimi (ed) (1980) Meiji bungaku zenshū [Complete Works of Meiji Literature], Vol. 98, Meiji bungaku kaikoroku shū [A Collection of Memoirs on Meiji Literature], Tokyo: Chikuma Shobō, 308-358.

Uspensky, B.A. (1970) Poetika kompozitsii: Struktura khudozhestvennogo teksta i tipologiya kompozitsionnoi formy [The Poetics of Composition: The Structure of Fictional Texts and a Typology of Compositional Forms], Moskva: Izdatel'stvo 'Iskusstvo'.

Venuti Lawrence (1998) 'Strategies of Translation' in Mona Baker (ed) Routledge Encyclopedia of Translation Studies, London & New York: Routledge, 240-244.

Verne, Jules (1977) Le Tour du Monde en 80 Jours, Le Rayon-Vert [Around the World in 80 Days, Green Ray], Paris: Hachette.

----- (1991) Around the World in Eighty Days, translated by Jacqueline Rogers, New York: Signet.

----- [Verunu, Jūru] (2002) Shinsetsu: Hachijū nichi kan sekai isshū [Eighty Days Around the World], translated by Kawashima Chūnosuke, in Shin nihon koten bungaku taikei [New Series of Classic Japanese Literature], Meiji hen Vol.15, Hon'yaku shōsetsu shū [Selected Works of Translation Literature] Vol. 2, Tokyo: Iwanami Shoten.

Wade, Terence (1992) A Comprehensive Russian Grammar, Oxford: Blackwell.

Walker, Janet (1995) 'The Russian Role in the Creation of the First Japanese Novel, Futabatei

Shimei's 'Ukigumo", in J. Thomas Rimer (ed.) (1995) A Hidden Fire: Russian and Japanese Cultural Encounters 1868-1926, Stanford: Stanford University Press, 22-37.

Washburn, Dennis C. (1995) The Dilemma of the Modern in Japanese Fiction, New Haven: Yale University Press.

Woodward, James B. (1969) Leonid Andreyev: A Study, Oxford: Clarendon Press.

Yamamoto Masahide (1965) Kindai buntai hassei no shiteki kenkyū [Historical Research into the Genesis of the Modern Style], Tokyo: Iwanami Shoten.

----- (1971) Genbun itchi no rekishi ronkō [A Historical Study of Genbun itchi], Tokyo: Ōfūsha.

Yanabu Akira (1983) Hon'yaku gakumon hihan: Nihongo no kōzō, hon'yaku no sekinin [Criticizing Translation Studies: The Structure of the Japanese Language and the Responsibilities of Translation], Tokyo: Nihon Hon'yakuka Yōsei Sentā.

Yanagi Tomiko (1971) 'Tsurugēnefu to Futabatei Shimei [Turgenev and Futabatei Shimei]', in Nihon kindai bungaku no hikaku bungakuteki kenkyū [Comparative Studies of Modern Japanese Literature], Tokyo: Shimizu Kōbundō Shobō, 43-71.

----- (1973) 'Futabatei no shoki no yakugyō: Hon'yaku sanbun ron [Futabatei's Early Translations: Studies in Prose Translation]', in Haga Tōru, Hirakawa Sukehiro (eds.) Kōza Hikaku bungaku [Series in Comparative Literature], Vol. 2, Nihon bungaku ni okeru kindai [Modernity in Japanese Literature], Tokyo: Tokyo Daigaku Shuppan Kai, 83-117.

Yanagida Izumi (1935) Meiji shoki no hon'yaku bungaku [Literary Translations Made During the Early Meiji Period], Tokyo: Shōhakukan Shoten.

Yanase Naoki (2000) Hon'yaku wa ikani su beki ka [How Translations Should Be Made], Tokyo: Iwanami Shoten (shinsho).

Yasuda Yasuo (1976) 'Tsurugēnefu [Turgenev]', in Fukuda Mitsuharu, Kenmochi Takehiko (eds.) Ōbeisaka to Nihon kindai bungaku [European Writers and Modern Japanese Literature], Vol. 5, Roshia, Hokuō, Nan'ō hen [Russia, Northern Europe and Southern Europe], Tokyo: Kyōiku shuppan sentā, 46-83.

Yonekawa Masao (1963) 'Futabatei no hon'yaku [Futabatei's Translations]', Kokubungaku kaishaku to kanshō [National Literature Reading and Appreciation], (May): 88-96.

Yoshida Sei'ichi (1954) 'Kaisetsu [Expository Commentary]', in Gendai nihon bungaku zenshū [Complete Works of Modern Japanese Literature], Vol. 2, Ozaki Kōyō,Yamada Bimyō, Hirotsu Ryūrō, Kawakami Bizan shū [Selected Works], Tokyo: Chikuma Shobō, 410-417.

----- (1965) 'Futabatei no eikyō [Futabatei's Influence]', in Futabatei Shimei (1965e: 125-147).

# Index